FORD COUNTRY

By David L. Lewis

Published by Amos Press, Inc.,
911 Vandemark Road, Sidney, Ohio 45365

Amos Press, Inc.

First Edition Copyright 1987

Second Edition Copyright 1999

Introduction

"Ford Country" first was discussed in the spring of 1974 in the Sesser, Ill. office of *Cars & Parts* Editor/Publisher George Slankard. George and I had grown up in Sesser, and I was home for a visit.

I had started writing articles for *Cars & Parts* the previous year, and suggested to George that I might prepare a monthly column based on Ford history. George liked the idea, adding that we could also include Ford club news. We didn't talk pay; never did talk pay with George. Now and then he'd forward a check for the column, various articles, and travel expenses, and that was that.

The column was introduced in June, 1974, with a simple statement: " 'Ford Country,' a new *Cars & Parts* column, will keep readers posted on activities of Ford-related clubs and recent developments associated with Ford history." The column caught on, mostly among Ford enthusiasts, but others, too. Over time a few readers - probably Chevy owners - complained to the editor that they were sick and tired of reading about Henry Ford's every sneeze and the Model T's every rattle. I sympathized with them, but "Ford Country" loyalists invariably rushed to the rescue, even counterattacked. A friend accused me of planting occasional barbs to flush out a few compliments. I didn't do it, and nobody can prove that I did.

Some readers said I wasn't hard enough on Henry. Others said I was too hard on him (items about his anti-Semitism, antiunionism, cruelness toward his son, and possible paternity of John Dahlinger being cases in point). Truth is, the column's generally been sympathetic toward things Fordian, only now and then tracking a muddy footprint. Mistakes? I've made them, of course, each being called to my attention thrice over. Every comeuppance reminded me of Henry Ford's remark, "Through criticism I get my education."

"Ford Country" has been fun to write, a labor of love, although I'm also paid for it - a lovely combination. Editor Slankard's successors also drove the pony with a light rein; and *Cars & Parts* staff members have been highly supportive ever since Amos Press acquired *Cars & Parts* in 1978.

The column, like Henry Ford and Model T, has been enduringly consistent. It emphasizes, as it always has, days of yore and stories and updates on people, places, and products tied to Ford history, plus a potpourri defying description. In deference to some readers' interests in matters modern - and as I have joined the Seventies, if not the Eighties - the column increasingly runs contemporary Fordiana. Club news, which tends to be repetitive, has been phased out.

"Ford Country" seems to write itself. Ideas for items fill my library and permeate my study. Other items are sparked by articles I've run across, or had forwarded to me by readers, ex-students, and friends. Still other items are based on readers' reminiscences and views, always a delight to pass along, and often containing data of genuine historical import.

A fringe benefit of writing the column has been exchanging letters with hundreds of readers, some of them very regular correspondents. I respond to all letters, usually enclosing Ford-related articles that my pen pals may not otherwise see. Thus, "Ford Country," like riding on a crowded Chinese train, enables one to make lots of new friends.

The column may be unique. At least I know of no other column devoted to a family and its business and venerable products. The column also transcends the entertainment value it may have in that it frequently presents unpublished historical material, most of it furnished by readers. Future Ford biographers and historians will be well-advised to consult it.

In preparing this manuscript, I set aside hundreds of items and heavily edited hundreds of others, then organized and shipped the remainder to *Cars & Parts*. The text of this book represents about a fourth of the material that originally appeared in the 150-plus editions of the column. It is truly the BEST of "Ford Country."

I hope to keep the column going for a long time to come. Being only 60, and with the kind of luck I'm accustomed to, "Ford Country" could be a staple of *Cars & Parts* well into the 21st century. If so, I like to think that it will improve with age.

— David L. Lewis

Postscript, 1999: This reprint of "Ford Country" contains 451 stories and 209 photographs, and is identical to the first edition except for one photograph, that of Edsel Ford II on page 61. That photo depicts a decidedly boyish-looking, longhaired Edsel at age 25, shortly after joining the Ford Motor Company as a product planning analyst in 1974. Two years after *Ford Country's* publication in 1987, Edsel informed me that he had enjoyed reading the volume, while complaining that he was being razzed unmercifully by associates about the photo in question. He requested that this picture be replaced, if the book went to a second printing. Accordingly, the original photo has been replaced by another depicting Edsel at age 30.

Contents

Introduction II

Part I – THE FORD FAMILY 1

Part II – THE COMPANY . . 68

Part III – THE PRODUCTS . . 124

Part IV – OTHER PEOPLE, PLACES, AND THINGS 172

Index 218

I

THE FORD FAMILY

The Ford family, now in its fifth generation, is one of America's best known business dynasties, in a class with the Rockefellers, du Ponts, and a handful of others. Founder Henry Ford towers over the family, just as the present patriarch, Henry Ford II, eclipses all save his grandfather.

The first Henry Ford was extraordinarily influential. His Model T, mass production methods, and wage-price theories revolutionized American industry. He was both rich and popular, an unusual combination, and was respected because he had made a product that met a public need instead of manipulating money. He also was admired for having retained the common touch, for being "just like me except that he's got a billion dollars."

Ford was a late bloomer; for him life began at 40. Born in 1863, he made two false starts as an auto manufacturer before founding the Ford Motor Company in 1903. Within a decade he had become the industry's dominant figure, and gained a measure of national prominence. In 1914 he became an international celebrity by more than doubling the wages of most of his workers. Ford's prime extended into his late 60s, and perhaps would have lasted longer had it not been for the Great Depression of the 1930s. Even so, he remained vigorous and continued to guide and personify his company even in his 80s.

The founder had several outstanding qualities: native intelligence and common sense, even though the latter occasionally failed him; an intuitive mind which leaped beyond the present, and a special engineering talent that combined creativity with practicality, a remarkable memory, a missionary's zeal, and a lifelong capacity for hard work, especially thinking. He also had, or made, his share of good luck. His entry into automaking and the introduction of his Model T were perfectly timed. He was teamed, by accident, with James Couzens, who contributed as much as Ford the Ford Company's early success.

Ford also was fortunate in marrying a woman who understood and complemented him. Three years younger than her husband, she was convinced from the time they were married in 1888 that her husband would accomplish something notable. Ford called her "The Believer." Henry's sweetheart in springtime, his nurse during the autumnal years, his companion in all seasons, Clara encouraged and stood by her husband for 59 years.

The Fords' only son, Edsel, born in 1893, grew up with the Ford Company. He was named president of the firm in 1918, but remained in his father's shadow. Competent and respected, he gradually gained responsibility for styling, sales and advertising (but never for labor relations, engineering, or manufacturing). In the 1930s the company would have benefited greatly had Edsel been allowed to assume his aging father's mantle. Edsel and his wife, Eleanor Clay, born in 1896 into a socially prominent Detroit family, had four children between 1917 and 1925 - Henry II, Benson, Josephine, and William Clay.

Henry II could have been a Horace E. Dodge, Jr., a playboy purely and simply, or a Walter P. Chrysler, Jr., an art collector purely and simply. But at age 26 in 1943, following his 49-year-old father's death and 80-year-old grandfather's resumption of Ford's presidency, he rejoined the family firm, learned the ropes, became president at age 28, cleaned house, hired a mentor, Ernest R. Breech, and got his company back on track. He worked hard, always putting the business first. But he was no drudge, tempering work with play, and developing a balance between the two which others might envy.

A natural leader, he led. He was a generalist, not a specialist. But he had an abiding interest in overseas operations, long neglected by fellow executives preoccupied with a big home market and a preference for digging their spurs into Dearborn desks. He channeled some of the company's best brains abroad, promoted stateside those who produced, and saw to it that international operations were encouraged and adequately funded. For all that he did for Ford overseas, the company owes as much to HFII as its founder. Henry II also was a good judge of managerial personnel. He bet on some men who wouldn't do - foremost among them Bunkie Knudsen and Lee Iacocca. But he picked scores of winners, bequeathing a rich legacy of talent upon retirement in 1979.

HFII is candid and honest. He never suffered fools lightly, nor those who didn't do their homework or tried to hoodwink him. But he was no tyrant; on the contrary, he valued and rewarded professionalism whenever he found it. He mended fences with Jews, who had been maltreated by his grandfather; he built bridges for blacks, who had been mistreated by almost everybody. He earned the respect of his employees. They now cheer him when he appears at a plant. He already has an honored place in auto history, and his reputation will grow through the years.

Henry II's eldest brother, Benson, died in 1978, following an honorable, if undistinguished, career with the company, culminating in the chairmanship of the Dealer Policy Board. Sister Josephine, who married a man named Ford, lives quietly in Grosse Pointe Farms, Mich. Youngest brother William Clay, after reviving the Continental and heading the styling function for many years, is vice-chairman of the company. His primary interest, however, is his ownership of the Detroit Lions football team.

Four fourth-generation Fords are employed by the company — Henry II's son, Edsel II; William Clay's son, William Clay, Jr.; the late Benson's son, Benson, Jr.; and Josephine's son, Walter Buhl III. As of this writing, Edsel, 38, is general sales manager of Lincoln-Mercury Division, Bill, 30, director of commercial vehicle marketing for Ford of Europe, Ben, 37, a sales analyst with Parts & Service Division, and Buhl, 43, a sales coordinator for Lincoln-Mercury Division. One of Detroit's burning questions focuses on Edsel II and Bill: which, if either, eventually will head Ford Motor Company? The sole honest answer: time will tell.

Among the nine other fourth-generation Fords, the most publicized are Henry Ford II's daughter, Charlotte, 46 and Josephine's son, Alfred Brush, 37. Charlotte has repeatedly demonstrated a bent for business, and it's often been said that she'd be a successful Ford executive had she been born male or 20 years later. Today she is one of America's leading arbitrators of manners and etiquette. Alfie, a gentle soul, has generated headlines as a Hare Krishna devotee. Two fourth-generation Fords, Benson's daughter, Lynn Alandt, 36, and William Clay's second eldest daughter, Sheila Hamp, 37, serve quietly on the Henry Ford Museum/Greenfield Village Board of Trustees; Lynn's husband is executive director of the Edsel and Eleanor Ford House. The other fourth-generation family members and their spouses have no direct affiliation with the company or related enterprises.

Fifth-generation Fords have proliferated since Buhl's daughter, Briget, was born in 1964 and Elena Niarchos, Charlotte's daughter by Stavros Niarchos, arrived in 1966. Edsel II alone has fathered three sons, the oldest, Henry III, being born in

Australia in 1980. Suffice it to say that an ample supply of Fords should be available for company service well into mid-21st century. We had intended to list the names of fifth-generation Fords. But some family members, concerned about the children's security, prefer that it not be done, and we respect their feelings.

The Ford family controls less than 10 percent of the company's total stock, but 40 percent of its voting (Class B) stock, as it has since the firm went public in 1956. The family can keep company control for as long as its members retain 30 to 40 percent of the voting stock. That may be increasingly difficult to manage, given family growth, occasional costly divorces, and the inevitability of death and taxes. The negative portent notwithstanding, it's still sweet to be a Ford - and it should be a long time before any Ford exchanges frock coats for shirt-sleeves.

Ford Family Portrait

In 1953, to mark the 50th anniversary of the Ford Motor Co.'s founding, members of the Ford family gathered at the Grosse Pointe Shores, Mich. home of the matriarch, Mrs. Edsel Ford, for this group photo, their first. Separate photos of the Ford men and the Ford women subsequently were published in *Life*. Here's the whole family. Standing, left to right, are Walter Buhl Ford II, of the wealthy Wyandotte chemical family, who married Edsel's daughter, Josephine; Benson Ford; William Clay Ford; and Sheila, 1, being held by her mother, Mrs. William Clay Ford, nee Firestone. The second tier, left to right, shows Josephine, who is holding her son, Alfred, 2; Walter Buhl Ford III, 9; Mrs. Edsel (Eleanor) Ford; Edsel Ford II, 4 (standing between his grandmother and his father); Henry Ford II, with Benson Ford, Jr., 3, seated just below Edsel II. Seated or kneeling on the floor, left to right, are Josephine's daughter, Josephine, 3; Mrs. Benson Ford and her daughter, Lynn, 1; Josephine's daughter, Eleanor, 6; Henry Ford II's daughter, Anne, 10; William Clay's daughter, Martha, 4; Mrs. Henry Ford II, and her daughter, Charlotte, 11.

Ford Women

Four generations of Fords pose on Mother's Day, 1949. From right to left are Henry Ford's wife, Clara, her daughter-in-law, Edsel's widow, Eleanor, her granddaughter, Josephine Ford (married to a non-auto Ford), and great-granddaughter, Eleanor (now Mrs. Frederic A. Bourke, Jr.). The picture was taken on Josephine Ford's estate. Clara lived until 1950, Eleanor until 1976.

Ford Family Stock Sale

The Ford family will sell another 120,000 shares of its special Ford Motor Co. Class B stock to meet expenses connected with the estate of Edsel Ford's widow, Eleanor. The shares, which can be owned only by Ford family members, will be converted to common stock; they are worth about $4 million at today's prices.

The Class B shares were created to assure Ford family control of the company. Each share carries more than four votes compared to one for a share of common stock. Thus the family has 12 percent of the equity in the company, but 40 percent of the vote.

The number of Class B shares has been slowly declining as family members convert their shares and sell them to raise money for estate taxes and other expenses. The number of outstanding Class B shares is currently thought to be just under 14 million.

Over the next 25 to 50 years, according to the Ford family lawyer, Pierre V. Heftler, the family will lose control of the firm.

Mrs. Ford, who died in 1976, left an estate worth more than $80 million. Of that amount, $15 million was put into an endowment fund for the maintenance of her Grosse Pointe Shores, Mich. estate.

Residential "Ford Country"

"Ford Country" - Provencal Road in Grosse Pointe Farms, Mich. - lies beyond these gates, for five Ford families, including Henry Ford II and his wife, Kathy, live on the thoroughfare. Here the ever-present guard salutes a resident who is driving in, while another person proceeds on foot. The road's guardhouse is on the left; signs which state, "Private No Trespassing Residents and Guests Only," are posted on both sides of the entrance. The road is seven-tenths of a mile long, and has 35 mansions. In addition to the family patriarch, other families on "Ford Row" include: HFII's son, Edsel Bryant Ford II; sister, Josephine; a nephew, Walter Buhl Ford III, and a niece, Lynn Ford Alandt.

Grosse Pointe's "Ford Row"

Provencal Road in Grosse Pointe Farms, Mich. is not much of a street. It's just two blocks long, measuring about seven-tenths of a mile. But it's the heart of Grosse Pointe's "Ford Country"; five Ford families live on this street.

Henry Ford II's sister, Josephine, who married Walter Buhl Ford II (no relation), has lived on Provencal for many years. Their son, Walter Buhl Ford III and his wife, Charlene, live nearby. But the younger Fords may move soon; their house is too large for their needs, and is up for sale.

Newer arrivals on Provencal are Henry Ford II and his wife, Kathy; HFII's son, Edsel II and his family; and HFII's niece, Lynn Ford Alandt, daughter of the late Benson Ford, and her husband, Paul. Edsel lives in the same house in which his father and mother, Anne, lived in the early 1940s.

Can you joyride along the road? No. An entrance sign says "Private, No Trespassing, Residents and Guests Only," and an ever-present guard will read the sign to you if you can't. Thus Henry II now has the privacy that he was denied when living on nearby Lake Shore Road, which is traveled by thousands of cars daily.

If you can't Fordwatch on Provencal, you might try running across HFII jogging in the early morning. "He's always wearing a black jumpsuit and fur cap," reports Jeanne Bocci, a physical education instructor at Grosse Pointe North High School, while another early riser says Ford has been spotted in an otter-skin flightsuit, carrying a walking stick. Regardless of his dress, seeing The Deuce on the run should be a sight worth seeing.

Richest of the Rich

Henry Ford II's wealth is estimated at $250 million; that of William Clay Ford, HFII's youngest brother, at $360 million; and that of their sister, Josephine Clay Ford, at $205 million in *Forbes* latest listing of America's 400 wealthiest people.

Two of Henry II's closest friends and ofttimes business associates, real estate developer A. Alfred Taubman and financier Max Fisher, are estimated to be worth $800 million and $225 million, respectively.

Explaining Henry

Through the years many of Henry Ford's associates have tried to "explain" Henry Ford. Few, if any, have totally succeeded. One of those who came closest - and admitted that he couldn't truly fathom the auto king - was thoughtful W.C. Cowling, the company's general traffic manager from 1920-21, its sales manager from 1931-37.

"I think," said Cowling in his oral reminiscences, taped by the Ford Archives in 1951, "Henry Ford's personality was almost ethereal. You might not see him for months, but the spirit of Henry Ford was in that organization always. His personality dominated people whether he said anything or only sat there. He dominated a group because of his personality, not his money, but his personality I can't describe. I think he would have been the same if he'd only had 20 cents."

"I've read everything that people have written that I could get my hands on about Henry Ford and I've never agreed with any of them in toto. I don't know of anybody that really captured him. I don't feel that I'm smart enough, able enough in any way to give a true portrait of the character of Henry Ford. A lot of people claim they knew him, but I don't think so. They were honest enough in thinking that they knew him.

"I sat around that luncheon table (with Ford) year after year, and now I look at it in retrospect and I find that I was simply an observer, although I thought at the time that I knew something as far as Henry Ford was concerned. But I was just an observer. He had a deep philosophy of life. He must have had a deep spiritual insight, religiously spiritual or a deep subconscious mind. I don't think Mr. Ford cared what anybody thought about him, if he first made up his mind he was right ...

"Conversations on these (luncheon) occasions didn't settle on Henry Ford at all, but you couldn't get him away from your own thoughts. Here was a man sitting at a table, almost worshiped by every man around the table. We believed in him. I still believe in him. You thought he was a wonderful man regardless of what he said to you or did to you. Today, he's a god among a lot of workmen. You can't tear that mythical mantle away from him. I don't know what quality led to that. It goes right back to the fact that the man's whole face, his eyes and everything, were just different. Henry Ford was a great man, regardless of any weaknesses he might have had."

Cowling was harassed out of the company by Harry Bennett, Ford's hatchet man, in late 1937.

The Ford Family

Henry Ford (1863-1947)
married Clara Jane Bryant (1866-1950)
Edsel Bryant Ford (1893-1943)
married Eleanor Clay (1896-1976)

Henry Ford II (1917-)
married Anne McDonnell
married Cristina V. Austin
married Kathleen DuRoss

Benson Ford (1919-78)
married Edith McNaughton (1920-80)

Josephine C. Ford (1923-)
married Walter Buhl Ford II

William Clay Ford (1925-)
married Martha Firestone

Charlotte Ford (1941-)
(Mrs. Edward R. Downe)

Anne Ford (1943-)
(Mrs. Chuck Scarborough)

Edsel Bryant Ford II (1948-)
married Cynthia Neskow

Benson Ford Jr. (1949-)
married Lisa Adams

Lynn Ford (1951-)
(Mrs. Paul D. Alandt)

Walter Buhl Ford III (1943-)
married Barbara Possellius
married Charlene Decraene

Eleanor C. Ford (1946-)
(Mrs. Frederic A. Bourke Jr.)

Josephine C. Ford (1948-)
(Mrs. John W. Ingle Jr.)

Alfred Brush Ford (1950-)
married Sharmilla Bhattacharya

Martha P. Ford (1948-)
(Mrs. Peter C. Morse)

Sheila Ford (1951-)
(Mrs. Steven Hamp)

William Clay Ford Jr. (1957-)
married Lisa Vanderzee

Elizabeth Ford (1961-)
(Mrs. Charles Kontulis)

Ford's Heroes

Henry Ford, according to Fred L. Black, a close associate of the auto king from 1919-42, had three heroes; Abraham Lincoln, William Holmes McGuffey, and Thomas A. Edison. Ford admired Lincoln, said Black in his reminiscences on file at the Ford Archives, because the Illinoisan was "a man who came from very humble beginnings, as did Henry Ford; was a man who, through his own efforts, made a place for himself in history; and was a simple man who had a strong feeling of responsibility toward his own institution and the general public - all of which I am sure Mr. Ford had."

The magnate, observed Black, credited McGuffey and his readers with having educated him. "He felt that McGuffey had a great impact on education ... he would like to have his readers used in schools today. He believed in them thoroughly."

As for Edison, Ford, as did millions of others, admired the inventor as a national hero; and especially was grateful for the inspiration which the older man gave the struggling young engineer in 1895 at a power convention in Manhattan Beach, N.Y. Told that Ford was working on an internal combustion engine for a horseless buggy, Edison advised the Detroiter, "You keep right after that, you keep right on working. You're on the right track. You'll have a power plant that won't be dependent on batteries." Ford, according to Black, "always said that this was one of the great moments of his life ... and made him even more determined to continue with his work on gasoline engines."

Aside from these three men, Ford also was very fond of a number of other persons including Rabbi Leo Franklin, John Burroughs, Luther Burbank, Harvey Firestone, Sr., Charles A. Lindbergh, George Washington Carver, and Will Rogers.

Family Coat Hook

Three generations of Fords - Henry, Edsel and Henry Ford II, Benson and William Clay - have used coat hook No. 43 at the venerable Detroit Club.

"The first Henry Ford," recently recalled doorman Cary Radcliffe, "would shake your hand the minute he grabbed the front door. He was a very pleasant person."

Ford's Will

Ever wonder about Henry Ford's will - to whom he left all those millions? If so, you may be interested in the following excerpts from the document, which was made out on February 3, 1936, and witnessed by two of Ford's secretaries, Frank Campsall and Rex Waddell:

"I have heretofore provided generously for my wife, Clara J. Ford, and am satisfied that she is now in a position of complete financial independence. I wish my wife to have, however, and I hereby bequeath to her, all of my personal effects in and about our home 'Fairlane,' at Dearborn, Michigan, including all household furniture, automobiles, and everything used in connection with our home; and, further, any other article or articles of a personal nature which she may wish to retain because of the sentimental value."

To the Ford Foundation, Ford left "all of my shares of stock in the Ford Motor Company, which are non-voting shares known as Class 'A' stock, save such as it may be necessary to sell to pay the obligations of my estate ... All of my real estate other than such real estate as may be a part of our home, 'Fairlane,' I give and devise to The Ford Foundation, save such as it may be necessary to sell to pay the obligations of my estate."

The will continued, "I wish to divide all of my voting stock, known as Class 'B' stock, in the Ford Motor Company, into five equal parts to be disposed of in the following manner: I bequeath one of such five parts to my son, Edsel B. Ford

... The other four parts I bequeath for the benefit of my four grandchildren, Henry Ford II, Benson Ford, Josephine Clay Ford, and William Clay Ford ... I give, devise, and bequeath all the rest and remainder of my estate to my son, Edsel B. Ford, and his heirs." Edsel was also named executor of the estate.

Since Edsel died before his father, the senior Ford on June 1, 1943, added a codicil to his will which made his wife the executor of his estate. The codicil was witnessed by Campsall and manufacturing executive Charles E. Sorensen.

In plainer English, Ford left his voting stock in the Ford Company to his daughter-in-law and four grandchildren, his nonvoting stock to the Ford Foundation. The family thus retained control of the firm; and to this day maintains control. Estimates of Ford's estate (which some have equated with the worth of the Ford Company) ranged to $700,000,000. But the government valued the firm at $466,141,500 at the time of Ford's death, and the magnate's estate was reckoned at $80,319,445. The estate included a $26,500,000 personal bank account and $20.00 "due from the sale of hay" from a Ford farm.

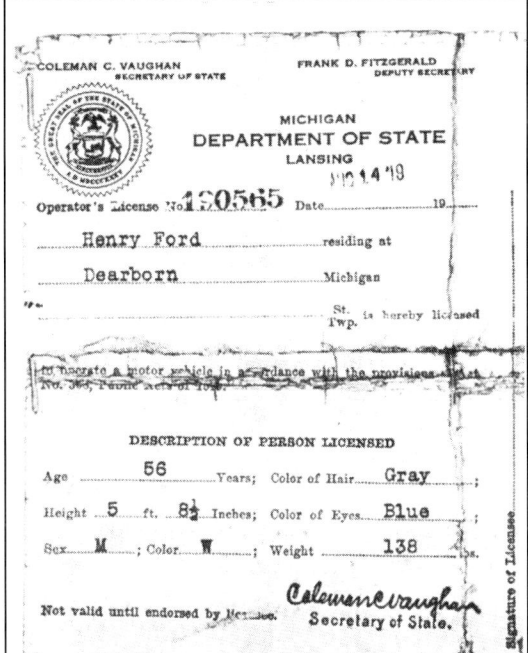

Vital Statistics

Henry Ford often gave the impression of being taller - perhaps because he was so slender - than he actually was. Ford, in reality, was five feet eight inches tall, and weighed 138 pounds. At least that's what his driver's license above, said in 1919, when the automaker was 56 years of age. The license also notes that Ford's hair was gray, his eyes blue. A few other documents list Ford's height at five feet nine inches, but none cite him as being taller. His weight also was fairly constant throughout his life. (Courtesy Ford Archives, Dearborn, Michigan)

Breaking the Camera

Every highly-publicized figure has had a "dingbat" photograph taken of himself, and Henry Ford was no exception. This shot was made of the auto magnate in July, 1938, after he entered his car following a meeting at the White House with President Franklin D. Roosevelt. I don't think this picture has been published since 1938.

FORD COUNTRY

Presidential Visits

"When President Reagan visited Ford's Kansas City Assembly Plant in April, was it the first time a President had visited a Ford factory?" asks Wiley Williams, of Kansas City.

No. Ex-President William Howard Taft in 1915 inspected Ford's Highland Park, Mich., plant and described it as "wonderful, wonderful." President Woodrow Wilson, after a July 10, 1916, Detroit speech, also visited Highland Park, where 30,000 Ford workers were permitted to leave their machines to greet him with "earsplitting cheers" and huge banners reading, "Hats Off to Woodrow Wilson, the President who Kept Us Out of War." President Herbert Hoover participated in Greenfield Village's dedication ceremony in 1929. President Franklin D. Roosevelt toured Ford's Willow Run Bomber Plant on Sept. 18, 1942. Since that time, insofar as I can recall, no President has visited a Ford facility. But it wouldn't be a surprise if one or another of the Presidents did so, either while campaigning for office, or while in power.

The Kansas City Plant was selected for Reagan's visit, according to White House spokesman Larry Speakes, because it offered "an opportunity to meet with workers, labor and management officials, and to highlight

Ex-President William Howard Taft, center, sits in Henry Ford's chair during a visit to Ford's Highland Park factory in 1915. Ford is at right; a Detroit banker at left. Thomas A. Edison's picture is on the wall. Ford's desk probably had been spruced up for Taft's visit, and the candlestick phone arranged just so. But the automaker's desk usually was uncluttered, if only because he spent little time at it. (Photo courtesy Greenfield Village, The Edison Institute)

President Herbert Hoover starts a "perpetual fire" in a courthouse in which Abraham Lincoln practiced law on the day of the Edison Institute's dedication, Oct. 21, 1929. Henry Ford stands at Hoover's side. The fire died out a long time ago. (Photo courtesy Greenfield Village, The Edison Institute)

President Franklin D. Roosevelt, left, with Henry Ford seated between him and Eleanor Roosevelt, unseen in this photo, ride through Ford's Willow Run Bomber Plant on Sept. 21, 1942. Traveling in the Presidential limousine, Roosevelt received a "deafening" welcome from employees. Ford, for one of the few times in his life at the edge of the spotlight, bitterly resented the cheers, according to manufacturing executive Charles E. Sorensen, seated in front of the President. Never, said Sorensen in his memoirs, had he seen the auto king as "gloomy or mean" as during his tour of Willow Run with Roosevelt, whom he heartily disliked anyway. (Photo courtesy Greenfield Village, The Edison Institute)

one of the blue-ribbon examples of economic recovery." The plant recently added 800 new employees to a second shift.

Reagan addressed a large gathering of employees, then ate lunch with Ford Chairman Philip Caldwell and workers in the plant cafeteria.

President Ronald Reagan steps to the podium at Ford's Kansas City Assembly Plant in April. Ford Chairman Philip Caldwell is second from left. The President addressed employees, then, with Caldwell and others, dined in the plant cafeteria.

FORD COUNTRY **11**

Rare Photo of Ford

Photos of Henry Ford wearing glasses are almost scarce as hen's teeth, and not without reason. Ford prided himself on his eyesight and was reluctant to let anyone see him wearing his specs. But he couldn't help himself when called upon to read a speech at the dedication of Dearborn's Ford Field in 1936. Henry never looked up when reading the speech; too afraid he'd lose his place.

Henry's Way

Henry Ford, according to a recent *Reader's Digest* article, once hired an efficiency expert to evaluate his company. After a few weeks, the expert made his report, which was highly favorable except for one thing.

"It's that man down the hall," said the expert. "Every time I go by his office he's just sitting there with his feet on his desk. He's wasting your money."

"That man," replied Mr. Ford, "once had an idea that saved us millions of dollars. At the time, I believe his feet were planted right where they are now."

That story reminds one of another yarn concerning William J. Cameron, Ford's ghostwriter and spokesman. Cameron, constantly ignored an edict requiring office employees to start work at 8:30 a.m., and, in fact, often delayed his arrival at the office until early afternoon. In response to complaints by other employees, Ford merely remarked, "Well he's all here when he gets here."

Closest to Ford

Readers have inquired about an article I wrote for another magazine on the 10 most important people in Henry Ford's life, and have asked me to list the names of these persons. They are, in the order in which Ford became acquainted with them, his wife, Clara; his son, Edsel; his closest friend, Thomas A. Edison; a brilliant engineering aide, C. Harold Wills; his company's early business manager, James Couzens; his manufacturing boss, Charles E. Sorensen; his personal secretary, Ernest G. Liebold; his friend and aide (and probably the mother of a son by him), Evangeline Côté Dahlinger; his hatchet man, Harry Bennett; and spokesman, William J. Cameron.

Among others who played important roles in Ford's life - and might well have been listed among the 10 most important people in this category - were Alexander Malcomson, Ford's chief backer in the formation of the Ford Motor Company; P. E. Martin, who, with Sorensen, was the company's top manufacturing boss for several decades; Ray and John Dahlinger, husband and son of Evangeline; Samuel Crowther, Ford's chief literary collaborator during the automaker's lifetime; and Albert Kahn, Ford's architect and builder.

Still others who played an important part in Ford's life included such friends as tire manufacturer Harvey Firestone, Sr., naturalist John Burroughs, Hearst editor Arthur Brisbane, and Detroit banker William Livingstone, and such business associates as racing driver Barney Oldfield, John F. and Horace Dodge, production executives Charles Hartner, Clarence W. Avery, and William S. Knudsen, personal secretary Frank Campsall (after Liebold's decline), branch managers/friends Gaston Plantiff and Duttee Flint, Ford of England managing director Sir Percival Perry, peace advocate Rosika Schwimmer, spiritual adviser Samuel S. Marquis, dancing master Benjamin Lovett, publicist Fred L. Black, grandson Henry Ford II, his mother who died when Henry was thirteen, and his father.

Oh, to be Young Again!

Henry Ford aged gracefully until the death of his son Edsel in 1943, when the magnate was 80 years of age. He frequently predicted that he would live to be 100 years old and said that anyone would "live to be 125 or 150 if he would keep the carbon out of his system." His prescription for longevity included exercise, and his photograph often appeared in the newspaper as he jogged along on foot or pedaled a bicycle. He challenged scores of people, particularly reporters, to foot races, and only the most fleet-footed could stay with him over 100 yards. And he was still racing when he was 80 years old.

But on at least one occasion Ford revealed a desire to be chronologically young again. "One day," recalled Wallace J. Newton, interior decorator to many of Detroit's royal families, "I was delivering some drapery samples to Fair Lane (the Ford's home) and Mr. Henry Ford was sitting by a window. I was as nervous as a cat on a hot tin roof. I didn't know what to say, just stood there. Finally, I told him I didn't know how one human being could accomplish what he had done in one generation. Mr. Ford answered, 'Young man, I would give all I have and much more for your youth.' "

Ford and Alcoholism

Henry Ford Hospital's new $3-million alcoholism treatment center, Maplegrove, recently was dedicated by Betty Ford, wife of former President Gerald R. Ford. Also attending the dedication ceremony was Ford Vice Chairman William Clay Ford, Henry Ford's youngest grandson.

Establishment of the treatment center would have pleased Old Henry, who had strong views on alcoholism. An ardent prohibitionist, in 1928 he declared that the army and navy should enforce the Prohibition Amendment. In 1929, he announced that "if booze ever comes back to the United States, I am through with manufacturing." The statement was vigorously debated throughout the country with most of the nation's press criticizing Ford's attitude. The *Asbury Park* (N.J.) *Press* simply remarked, "The Detroit oracle accomplished his purpose. The story made the front page."

Ford refused to serve alcoholic beverages at company functions until the press preview of his 1934 cars. The gesture, so incompatible with the industrialist's "notorious and violent objection to alcohol," created a sensation and received more attention in some news stories than the new models themselves. Ford's ploy received additional attention when a controversy developed over whether the motor magnate actually did serve beer to the 200 newsmen in attendance.

Business Week, which did not have a representative at the preview and based its story on a report from one of the guests, declared that "the (beer) yarn was utterly untrue." The newsmen who had sipped beer and smoked in Ford's presence (while asking the Dearbornite if he recalled his earlier tirades against alcohol and tobacco), held to their original reports.

Ford frowned on most employees who drank, but was tolerant of certain valued employees who imbibed excessively. Commenting on the occasional toots of his spokesman, William J. Cameron, he observed, "This is due to sickness. We're going to cure him. We'll never give up." And he never did; Cameron stayed with the company past Ford's retirement.

Ford's preachings on alcohol generated considerable resentment among brewers and distillers, some of whom boycotted his products during the pre-World War II era.

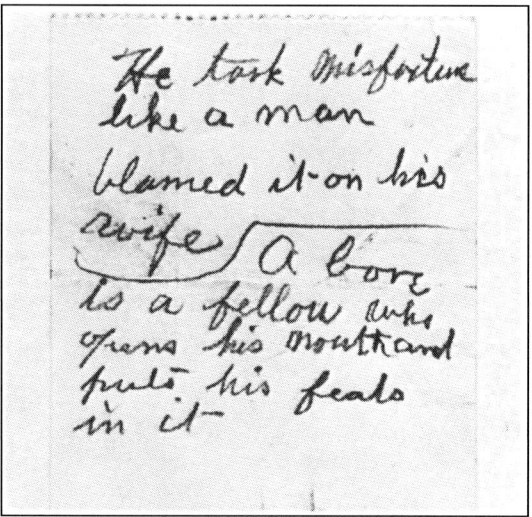

A Billionaire Anyway

Henry Ford was a notoriously poor speller, and was as little concerned with punctuation and grammar, as evidenced again and again in the thoughts he continually jotted down. "Sails," he wrote, "begins on the drawing board." "He took misfortune like a man blamed it on his wife," he penned on another occasion, then added, "A bore is a fellow who opens his mouth and puts his feats in it." (Photo courtesy Ford Archives and Research Library, Edison Institute, Dearborn, Mich.)

So Who's Perfect

Advertising executive/journalist Bruce Barton, who in 1925 authored a bestseller about Jesus Christ, The Man Nobody Knows, once wrote Henry Ford, asking if he might interview the automaker in connection with a series of magazine articles entitled, "The Greatest Mistake That I Ever Made."

Barton also corresponded with Alfred P. Sloan, Jr. and Charles Kettering of General Motors and Paul Hoffman of Studebaker, according to Matt Joseph, director of the Wisconsin Society of Automotive Historians, writing in the Society's fine publication, The Spark.

Ford, noted Joseph, who is working with the Barton papers in the Wisconsin State Historical Society, did not reply to Barton's letter. Instead, one of Ford's secretaries responded, suggesting that Barton could as well leave Ford out of the series because "Mr. Ford simply doesn't make mistakes."

But, of course, Ford made mistakes; lots of them, including some whoppers. A few years ago, while discussing the 12 greatest blunders in U.S. auto history at an Automotive News World Congress, I spoke of two of them: Ford's alienation of Jews and his abandonment of the Model T without a successor car in sight. The automaker's anti-Jewish crusades cost his company tens of millions of dollars and left a legacy which continues to be harmful to the firm's interests. His abrupt discontinuation of the Tin Lizzie led to a two-year loss of industry leadership and losses exceeding $100 million.

Ford-Related Markers

Eleven of Dearborn's 31 "more significant" historical markers deal with the life of Henry Ford and Ford Motor Co. history, reports Winfield H. Arneson, editor of the *Dearborn Historian*, in the publication's Summer, 1984 issue.

The markers subject headings and their locations include: Harry Brooks [Henry Ford's favorite test pilot, killed in line of duty], Henry Ford Museum premises; Henry Ford's Home, Michigan Avenue, west of Southfield Road underpass; Ford Tri-Motor-Ford Airport, entrance of Dearborn Inn, Oakwood Boulevard; Edison Institute, Henry Ford Museum premises; Henry Ford Birthsite, Ford Road, east of

Greenfield Road; Ford Rouge Plant, Rouge Plant Gate No. 4, Miller Road, and two other nearby locations; Fair Lane Mansion—Henry & Clara Ford's Home, University of Michigan-Dearborn; Henry Ford, Henry Ford Centennial Library; and Dearborn Inn, Oakwood Boulevard.

Ford Psychology

Henry Ford knew that praise, as opposed to criticism, often carried the day. Consider the following incident, as related in the Nov. 10, 1911 issue of the *Detroit News*:

"Mr. Ford was walking through the great machine shop (of the Highland Park Plant), where the parts of automobiles ... are made, and he happened to espy a bill drill that glistened like a lieutenant's sword when a visit from the colonel is expected.

"Mr. Ford thought the machine must be a new one which had never been operated. He took a second glance and found that it was even then running, the man in charge of it being industriously at work. According to one of the department heads who saw the incident, Mr. Ford went over to the workman, and said, as he slapped him on the back:

" 'Young man, I would hate to see you leave here, but if they ever should let you go, don't worry about another job, because any man that keeps his machine in the fine condition that yours is, is sure to come out on top. That is the best looking machine I ever saw in a bag machine room.'

"A few days later Mr. Ford passed through the same department and the glistening steel fairly blinded him. Every machine in the department was polished until it shone like a diamond. The slap on the back had spread."

Grandfather Ford

"I loved him," William Clay Ford, 57, recently said of his grandfather, Henry Ford. "I looked forward to times when we'd [Bill and his brothers, Henry II and Benson] go out and spend the weekend with him. He'd take us out hiking. We'd spend the whole night in the woods. It was neat."

"To me," Bill recently told the *Detroit News*, "he was super. I was very, very close to him, as a grandchild to a grandfather. He took me under his wing. Much to my parents' consternation, he taught me how to shoot guns. Now gun collecting is one of my hobbies. At the age of 10, we'd plunk away at tin cans with a .22. We'd also ride bikes around. Obviously, he was a controversial person. There were a lot of detractors who say he was ruthless. I never saw this ogre side people write about now.

The man whom Henry Ford's youngest grandson, William Clay Ford, describes as "neat." The auto king, shown here in 1926 beside Sudbury Pond, near Wayside Inn, South Sudbury, Mass., is putting on the skates which he told reporters and photographers he had made seven years earlier from a Model T axle. True or not, the majority of the nation's newspapers carried stories and photographs of the "flivver skates" and their owner.

"In his private life he just always liked to fool around with things, to try

FORD COUNTRY **15**

different things. I remember once I walked into his bathroom. I saw this glass. It looked like it was water, except it was the foulest looking water I ever saw. He was putting his razor blades in the water. He had a theory that the iron from the blades would rust in the water, and he mixed in some kind of natural oil, I don't know if it was olive oil. Whatever it was, he thought the combination would make a perfect hair tonic."

"I also remember going over one day and finding his whole estate and front lawn plowed up with soybeans growing all over the place. We ate whole meals practically of soybeans. By the same token he made fenders for cars out of soybeans. There's that wonderful picture of him with an ax in his hand and whacking his soybean fender. It was the forerunner of plastics and all that."

Bill Ford, after graduation from Yale, joined the Ford Motor Co. in 1949, and became a vice-president in 1953. Designer of the Continental Mark II, he had charge of the firm's product design programs after 1956. He was named to the company's Office of Chief Executive in 1978, and has been vice-chairman since 1980.

The company's largest single shareholder, Ford owns 2.2 million Class B shares, held only by family members. This stock traded at 51 7/8 in 1978; at 18 in 1982; thus Bill has absorbed a paper loss of $70 million. His present worth is estimated in excess of $100 million.

Fordwatchers

Detroit has had thousands of "Fordwatchers" since the first Henry came to prominence in 1914, and two of the most avid of them are shown in this photo. At left is George McCall, a tour guide at Ford's estate at Fair Lane; at right Eleanor Breitmeyer, staff writer of the Detroit News. Both attend most of the public events at which the Fords turn out, plus many other gatherings identified with the family. At center, is McCall's girlfriend, Nancy Bershback, who, in the best tradition of girlfriends and wives of old-car enthusiasts, has become a Fordwatcher herself.

Echoes of the Past

Henry Ford's anti-Semitic book, *The International Jew*, recently was reprinted in the English language by the Kingdom of Saudi Arabia. The Anti-Defamation League of B'nai B'rith has asked the Saudi government to condemn the publication.

The International Jew, a compilation of anti-Semitic articles in Ford's national newspaper, the *Dearborn Independent*, was first published by the industrialist in 1922. It quickly was translated into most European languages by foreign anti-Semites, and undoubtedly influenced many readers, all the more because it carried the imprint, not of a crackpot publisher in an alleyway, but of one of the most famous and successful men in the world.

Ford, in apologizing to Jews in 1927, agreed to withdraw *The International Jew* from the book market. But copies with Ford's name on the title page or with his photograph inside turned up in large numbers throughout Europe and South America in the 1930s. By late 1933 the Germans alone had published 29 editions of the book, each carrying Ford's name on the title page and lauding the auto king in the preface for the 'great service' that he had done America and the world by attacking Jews. The book also was widely distributed in America by anti-Semitic groups.

In 1947, Henry Ford II found it necessary to declare publicly that *The International Jew* was "entirely without the sanction, authorization or approval of Mr. Henry Ford, the Ford Motor Company or (myself)." Taking note of the disavowal, the *Canadian Jewish Review* observed, "He was doing something which he probably will be called on to do at intervals during his whole life because his grandfather unloosed an evil which will not be cleaned up in the grandson's time." It is a fact that the book still circulates, although on a much lesser scale, both in the U.S. and abroad.

Nazis Rate Ford Highly

The most important man in the world in 1932? Maybe Henry Ford, maybe Adolf Hitler, according to a Nazi election poster recently published in Anthony Rhodes's *Propaganda - the Art of Persuasion: World War II*.

The faces of Ford and Hitler are easily recognizable on the poster, whose headline screams out "Wer ist der Wichtigste Mann der Welt?" So are the faces of Benito Mussolini, German president Paul von Hindenberg, scientist Albert Einstein, and Max Schmeling, then the world's heavyweight boxing champion. Others on the poster appear to be German politician Franz von Papen; Leon Trotsky, the Russian exile; Ramsay MacDonald, prime minister of Great Britain; and one or another of the premiers of France in 1932.

Ford thus is the only American and businessman pictures on the poster. Hitler, who undoubtedly decided whose faces should appear in the grouping, was a great admirer of the auto king, who is the only American mentioned in the dictator's autobiography, *Mein Kampf*. Most surprising, given Hitler's hatred of Jews, is Einstein's inclusion on the poster.

Anti-Semitic Legacy Lives On

Ford's history, specifically the Arab League's boycott of its products, appeared to have been an issue of considerable concern to Toyota as the Japanese company unsuccessfully negotiated a proposed joint manufacturing venture with the Dearborn firm. The boycott, in turn, was brought on by Ford's cooperation with Israel, a reaction to Old Henry Ford's anti-Semitism.

Ford launched America's first full-fledged anti-Jewish campaign in 1920 and he was justly criticized for his anti-Semitism during the following two decades. After his retirement in 1945, his company, led by his grandson, Henry Ford II, began placating Jews in America and Israel in atonement for the founder's sins. In 1966, after Ford licensed a dealer to assemble knocked-down vehicles in Israel, the 13-member Arab League boycotted the company's products. Toyota, which annually sells 200,000 vehicles in the Arab market, had to consider whether the Arabs might also boycott its products if it does business with Ford.

Before the Arabs banned Fords, the Dearborn-based firm sold more vehicles in the Middle East than any other automaker; its market share stood at 18 percent. The market itself has grown from 14,000 vehicles in 1965 to 760,000 in 1980. Of that number, GM sold 110,712 units last year. The Israeli market is tiny, Ford's share amounting to only a few thousand vehicles per year.

The boycott issue is not the only one which soured Toyota-Ford negotiations; and may not be the most important one (the two couldn't agree on which vehicle to build jointly). But it reared its head, as the legacy of Henry Ford's anti-Semitism has so often in the past.

Henry Ford II Chair

A Henry Ford II Chair in Transportation will be established at the Technion, the Israel Institute of Technology, in

FORD COUNTRY **17**

Haifa, Israel, according to Evelyn de Rothschild, international chairman of the Technion board of governors. The chair is the first to be named for a non-Jew by the University.

Ford is being honored, says de Rothschild, "in recognition of his many years of interest in the Technion, his opposition to the Arab boycott, and his support of Israel." The chair will be financed by a $300,000 endowment.

Ford's 114th Birthday

Along with 114 other Ford zealots, your commentator recently commemorated Henry Ford's 114th birthday at Ford's Dearborn estate Fair Lane. The parties are organized by two Dearbornites, Iris Becker and Helene Pierce, the former a retired teacher who knew Ford well, the latter a daughter of Ford's barber, who in 1943 had the foresight to sweep up and preserve six light brownish hair swatches from Ford's 80-year-old head.

Among those in attendance was a Ford nephew, Edward Bryant, a number of the motor magnate's former associates and friends, and others with an interest in Ford's life. The parties consist of a reception, a dinner in "The Pool," a new restaurant opened in Ford's former swimming pool by Fair Lane's owner, the University of Michigan-Dearborn, and the serving of Henry's "birthday cake," plus reminiscing by those present.

The celebrations grew out of committee efforts to observe the centennial of Ford's birth in 1863. Pleasant to attend, the parties would be even more so if the postdinner programs were better organized and shortened. Among guests with whom I enjoyed talking were Gus Munchow, who served for many years as Greenfield Village's director of gardens and buildings, who told me that he frequently visits Ford's grave; John Carroll, Fairview Park, Ohio, a painter of fine watercolors associated with Ford's life; and veteran ex-Fordman Al Newman, the electrician who kept Fair Lane bright; Roy Schumann, one of Ford's ace troubleshooters; and "man about the Rouge," Glen L. Simpkins.

Nephew Bryant showed guests the sunroom toward the rear of the house which looks out on the Rouge River. "This is where Uncle Henry used to do his reading," he said. "We spent a lot of time together here." Someone asked if the view of the river and woods might be the same as when Henry Ford was living. Bryant exploded. "No, no. Uncle Henry wouldn't have allowed dead wood like you see now." Bryant then thought for a moment, and added, "You know, one thing hasn't changed — the Rouge River was just as muddy then as it is now."

Favorite Ford Books

A reader recently asked, "If you were banished, like Napoleon, to a faraway isle, and could take only three Ford books with you, which three would they be?" If I can take only three Ford books, I won't go. I want to take eight; and here they are:

The Allan Nevins/Frank Ernest Hill trilogy, *Ford: The Times, The Man, The Company*; *Ford: Expansion and Challenge, 1915-1932*; and *Ford: Decline and Rebirth, 1933-1962*; my own *The Public Image of Henry Ford: An American Folk Hero and His Company*; Samuel S. Marquis' *Henry Ford: An Interpretation*; William C. Richards' *The Last Billionaire*; William Greenleaf's *From These Beginnings: The Early Philanthropies of Henry and Edsel Ford, 1911-1936*; and Henry Ford's (with the collaboration of Samuel Crowther) *My Life and Work*.

This list omits a number of highly entertaining books (e.g., Harry Bennett's *We Never Called Him Henry*) and some excellent picture books. But if you are going to be on a desert isle, with no one around to turn pages for you, you'll want weighty volumes, not frothy books which can be leafed through quickly and don't leave much food for thought.

Hawaiian Quintette

Henry Ford loved music, all kinds. In 1915, after hearing a group of Hawaiian musicians play at the San Francisco's Panama-Pacific Exposition, he took the group to Detroit, where they performed under the auto king's auspices for many years. Ford's Hawaiian Quintette, as the group was called despite its seven members, was comprised of Henry Kailimai, Sr., seated, and his five sons, plus another musician. The elder Kailimai remained in Ford's employ until the post-World War II era.

"Vagabonds On Tour"

Old-timers continue to recall the memorable 1918 motor tour of Appalachia by Henry Ford, Thomas A. Edison, Harvey S. Firestone, Sr., Harvey S. Firestone, Jr., and naturalist John Burroughs, who styled themselves as "Vagabonds."

The late Stanley McMann and Herbert Wickline, as small boys, carried water for the party in Gap Mills, W.Va., remembers Mrs. McMann. Each lad was given a dime by Edison. Herbert soon spent his dime, but Stanley proudly showed his coin to others until it wore a hole in his pocket and was lost.

Another Gap Mills youth, according to Mrs. Glenna McMann Cruise, excitedly told his teacher that Henry Ford was in town. "Please do not tell me these stories which you know are not true," the schoolmarm admonished the boy, "as you know Henry Ford is not in Gap Mills."

At Lindside, W.Va., the party visited the Ford dealer, Arthur W. Boon. "My father was very pleased and flattered with the visit," recalls Eunice Boon Smith, now of Union, W.Va. "While at the dealership a motorist stopped for gasoline, but to his dismay could not find a supply. However, he did not leave empty-handed as the Edison caravan furnished him gas from their supply."

The 16-member party, including chauffeurs and a chef, traveled in "two high-powered cars, two Fords, and two 80-horsepower trucks." Edison was the expedition's host, and rode in a $14,000 car, which, chuckled the *Monroe* (Union, W.Va.) *Watchman*, spared Ford from riding in a Model T.

Our thanks to reader Leonard Fleshman, Columbus, Ohio, for forwarding a July 28, 1983 *Watchman* article which recalls the "Vagabonds" tour.

Ford's Legacy To Dancing

Henry Ford's legacy to square dancing is recorded in an article, "The Happiest Way to Health and Tranquility," in a recent issue of *Prevention* magazine.

"Strange as it may seem," notes the article, "Henry Ford — the Henry Ford - deserves much of the credit for the popularity of square dancing in the United States today. Although modern square dancing traces its roots back to the quadrilles and cotillions of the royal courts of England and France, it was slowly heading for extinction until 1923, when Ford happened to take lodgings at the Wayside Inn in Sudbury, Massachusetts.

"There Ford met Benjamin Lovett, a dance instructor under contract to lead the Wayside Inn's guests in various gavottes, mazurkas, reels and minuets, along with square dancing. Ford became so enthusiastic about Lovett and his dances, the story goes, that he purchased the inn and Lovett's contract in one grand gesture, and spirited

Lovett back to Dearborn, Michigan.

"Ford began at once to introduce square dancing to the American public as zealously as he had introduced the Model T. He invited 200 dance instructors from Ohio and Michigan to study under Lovett. He sponsored a weekly radio show on square dancing, financed square dancing programs in public schools and universities, and even commissioned Thomas Edison to make recordings of square dance music. Ford also bought Stradivarius violins and an Irish dulcimer to be used for those records and, in 1926, he published a book on early American square dancing entitled *Good Morning*.

Ford, it may be added, continued to dance until past his eightieth birthday.

Ford, T Rate Highly

The Associated Press recently asked a nationwide sample of newspaper editors and radio-TV news directors to name the top 20 stories of the past 200 years in America. They rated as tenth "Henry Ford, his Model T and the rise of the automobile"; and the only stories ranked higher were the American Revolution, drafting of the Constitution, Civil War, American moon landings, development of the atomic bomb, 1929 stock market crash and ensuing Great Depression, Watergate scandal and the resignation of President Nixon, and World War I.

20   FORD COUNTRY

A Violinist He Was Not

To look at this photograph, you'd think that Henry Ford, center, was playing the violin with his old-fashioned dance orchestra. But Ford, according to the Henry Ford Museum's curator of musical instruments, played only the Jew's harp, an instrument placed between the teeth, and whanged by a protruding metal prong. (Photo courtesy Henry Ford Museum, Dearborn, Michigan)

Ford, the flivver, and the auto outpolled the assassinations of Presidents Lincoln and Kennedy, the development of television and the electrification of the nation, the Vietnam War, New Deal, changing role of women, growth of aviation, Louisiana Purchase, and the 1945 Supreme Court decision outlawing segregation, all of which were rated among the top 20 stories.

Among Most Admired

The selection of President Carter by Gallup poll respondents as the person Americans most admired in 1978, brings to mind the fact that Henry Ford is one of the few businessmen ever named among the top 20 in this poll.

In 1946, Ford, then in the last year of his life, was ranked as the 18th most admired person living in any part of the world. If the poll (started in 1946) had been taken between 1914 and 1943, Ford very likely would have been included among the 10 most admired figures every year, and probably would have topped the list a few times.

Even as late as November, 1945, a cross section of the *Woman's Home Companion* readership, when asked, "What five American men and women now living do you admire most?" rated only Generals Eisenhower and MacArthur, President Truman, and Eleanor Roosevelt ahead of Ford. In December, 1945, representative voters, invited by the Gallup poll to select the nonpolitical figure best qualified for the Presidency, gave only MacArthur, Eisenhower, and industrialist Henry J. Kaiser, more support than the automaker. Ironically, Ford at the time was senile.

Changing Times

In 1928, 682 children in Belleville, N.J. schools were asked who they'd like to be, if they were not themselves. Their choices, in order of selection, were Charles A. Lindbergh, Calvin Coolidge, Henry Ford, Benito Mussolini (then a heroic figure to everyone), and my Dad.

In 1981, 2,000 U.S. eighth-graders were asked by *World Almanac & Book of Facts* whom they would most like to emulate when they grew up. Their choices, in order of selection, were actors Burt Reynolds, Richard Pryor, Alan Alda, Brooke Shields, John Ritter, Scott Baio, Bo Derek, George Burns, boxer Sugar Ray Leonard, and comedian Steve Martin.

No world leader, scientist, politician, or businessman was among the top 30 persons named. All were actors, entertainers, or sports figures.

I leave it to you to appraise the values of schoolchildren in 1928 and 1981.

Ford's Individualism Noted

Henry Ford is among 271 intrepid Americans, past and present, who exemplify the principles of the Giraffe Society, a new creation of *Quest/80* magazine to "honor and recognize the people in our society who are out of the ordinary, who buck the odds, who get things done, and who don't believe the humdrum and the negative and the norm." In other words, they stuck their necks out.

Among those honored with Ford are Susan B. Anthony, Amelia Earhart, Albert Einstein, Thomas A. Edison, Ralph Waldo Emerson, George Washington, Mae West, and Alvin T. York.

"The Henry Ford Of" ...

If one mark of greatness is having one's name represented as the ultimate yardstick for achievement in various fields, then Henry Ford must be a great man. During the past three decades, dozens of leaders have been referred to as "the Henry Ford of" their nation or sphere or activity — Britain, France, shipbuilding, aviation, Japan's appliance industry, etc.

Most of those compared with Ford

are automotive pioneers, exponents of mass production, or wealthy men. The founder of Morris Motors, William R. Morris (Lord Nuffield), for example, has often been described as "the Henry Ford of Britain." Louis Renault, the founder of the French company which bears his name, has frequently been identified as "the Henry Ford of France." Karl Benz, who designed and built the world's first workable motor car driven by an internal combustion engine, has been called "Mannheim's Henry Ford."

Henry J. Kaiser was being identified as "the Henry Ford of shipbuilding" as early as 1943. William T. Piper, the builder of the Piper Cub, was frequently referred to between 1945 and his death in 1970 as "the Henry Ford of" the light plane industry, the air age, or aviation. Detroit's department store king, Joseph L. Hudson, was called "Merchandising's Ford." Milton Hershey has been described as "the Henry Ford of the confectionery field"; Theodore Presser was called the "Henry Ford of music." Konosuke Matsushita has been described as "the Henry Ford of Japan's appliance industry." Matsushita's "hero" is, who else, Henry Ford. Automaker Yen Tjing-ling is called "Free China's Henry Ford."

Others who have been compared with Ford have a wide range of activities. Frank Gallo, one of the nation's top contemporary artists, who often mass-produces his art, has been called "the Henry Ford of the Art World"; Jack Simplot, the richest man in Idaho, has been referred to as "the Henry Ford of potatoes." Michiganian Fred Bear, world's leading manufacturer of bows and arrows, has been described as "the Henry Ford of archery"; and the clown's clown, Paul Jung, has been cited as "the Henry Ford of the clown prop industry."

Ford is even being compared with entrepreneurs yet to make their marks. "We are going to have a Henry Ford in space," predicts Tom Jones, president of Northrup Corporation. "I'm sure of it."

Folk Hero

Let there be no doubt that Henry Ford is an authentic folk hero, for his name is among those of 25 "famous Americans' used to complete a puzzle on a contemporary Kellogg's corn flakes box.

Ford is described as a "famous automobile maker." Others whose names are cited are Daniel Boone, Davy Crockett, Abraham Lincoln, Charles A. Lindbergh, Thomas Edison, Thomas Jefferson, Walt Disney, Alexander Graham Bill, Eli Whitney, Martin Luther King, Jr., Paul Revere, Pearl Buck, John F. Kennedy, Franklin D. Roosevelt, Douglas MacArthur, Mark Twain, Nathan Hale, J. Edgar Hoover, Henry Wadsworth Longfellow, Robert Fulton, Lyndon Baines Johnson, John Adams, Louis Armstrong, and Dwight David Eisenhower.

Will The Real Henry ...

The Micro Age's answer to Henry Ford? We may not know for some time, but at least three computer moguls have been compared to the Model T's creator, according to *PC* (Personal Computer) Magazine.

Radio Shack has drawn a parallel between its head man, Lewis Kornfeld, and the auto king in its advertising. Osborne Computer Corp. similarly likened founder Adam Osborne to the auto king, concluding its TV commercials with the line, "You can have your computer in any color you want, as long as it's blue." Osborne recently declared bankruptcy. Apple Corp. also has measured its cofounder, Steven Jobs, for Old Henry's shoes, says *PC*.

If your commentator may venture an opinion, none of these men is to computers what Ford was to autos, and none will be.

Ford's Railcar Restored

Henry Ford's former railroad car, *Fair Lane*, has been renovated and returned to Michigan by Detroit investor Richard Kughn, also owner of the Lionel toy train company.

Kughn bought the 82-foot railcar four years ago from the Cherokee Indian Nation, which used it for office space at its Tahlequah, Okla. headquarters. He had the vehicle trucked 19 miles to the nearest tracks, then transported to Rail Passenger Service Co., a Tucson, Ariz. restoration firm.

"It was probably the most complete rebuilding of a private railway car ever done anywhere," Bob Stout, vice-president of Rail Passenger, told the *Detroit News*. "We stripped off just about everything down to the walls and wheels ... only the priceless original maple paneling was left. We replaced it all with new fixtures and materials, although much of that was made to duplicate those of the 1920s." The renovation cost exceeded $1.2 million.

Ford had the *Fair Lane* built for his wife, Clara, in 1921, at a cost of $153,000. Mrs. Ford and her friends often took the car to New York for shopping expeditions, and she and her husband rode it to and from their winter/summer homes in Florida, Georgia, and Northern Michigan. They also used it to entertain such luminaries as Presidents Harding and Coolidge, Thomas Edison, and Luther Burbank. In 1942, because of its advanced age and World War II travel restrictions, the *Fair Lane* was sold to the St. Louis Southwestern Railway, whose executives used it for business trips until 1972. The car then was donated to the Cherokees.

Kughn plans for the *Fair Lane* — which at 100 tons is one of the heaviest private cars ever built — to be the main attraction in a transportation museum which he plans to build in Allen Park, Mich., a community adjacent to Dearborn.

Owner of a private collection of antique cars and a classic car restoration company, Kughn and his wife, Linda, were aboard the car when it was moved in midsummer from Arizona to Michigan. The trip was made without incident except for the brief failure of the air-conditioning system. The vehicle sleeps eight, and also has quarters for a chef and steward.

The Fair Lane in 1942, just before its sale to the St. Louis Southwestern Railway. The compartment of Henry and Clara Ford was located just over the letters "Fair Lane." The car is parked behind the Henry Ford Museum. (Photo from the Collections of the Henry Ford Museum and Greenfield Village)

Sought Farm Facts

Henry Ford, like his friend, Thomas A. Edison, was a "cut-and-try" innovator; in fact, Ford declared that he avoided books because they "muss up my mind."

But Ford's early office correspondence reveals that he left few stones unturned to add to his scientific knowledge of agriculture, as revealed in a recent *Dearborn Historian* article by Ford R. Bryan.

In 1910, says Bryan, Ford wrote to the federal and every state department of agriculture, plus major universities, requesting that his name be added to their mailing lists for all their published literature. In 1911, he corresponded with food chemists concerning the best method of producing dry milk powder from whole milk. A letter that same year to George Westinghouse evinced Ford's interest in using ultraviolet radiation for the sterilization of milk and water.

"So," concludes Bryan, "Mr. Ford, that 'crazy farmer,' was not an ignorant farmer."

Ford Tomato Juice

Its contents long gone, a bottle once filled with Ford tomato juice awaits a purchaser at Hershey's 1982 swap meet. The label, featuring Ford script, informs prospective buyers that the juice, "rich in vitamins A, B, and C, was made from selected tomatoes grown on the Ford Farms, Dearborn, Michigan," and also would be "good in tomato cocktails, cream of tomato soup, meat dressing, etc." In addition to being bottled by Ford, the juice was sold in one of Ford's commissaries.

Ford Cemetery

A recent visit to the Ford Cemetery, on Joy Road just west of Greenfield Road, in Detroit, found the old burying ground excellently maintained. The cemetery is located on the front lawn of St. Martha's Episcopal Church, which was planned and financed by Ford's widow, Clara, who died in 1950, three years after her husband.

Mrs. Ford provided for a ninety acre Ford holding in the area to be given to religious institutions, and today the parcel encloses the Islamic Center of Detroit, Saint Vartan Armenian Roman Catholic Church and Lutheran High School, plus an Episcopal-sponsored child society and home for boys. Rosary High School recently was taken over by Wayne County Community College for its Greenfield campus. Another religious group, after obtaining a parcel of land, sold it to a supermarket chain. In addition to the store built by the chain, apartment buildings and more than a dozen small business establishments have sprung up across from the cemetery on Joy Road. These businesses range from a nursing home and drugstore to a car wash, beer and wine distributor, and service station, the night lights of which illuminate the cemetery's tombstones.

Ford's grave is visited by only a

handful of people inasmuch as few persons know its location. The graves initially were guarded around the clock to prevent desecration. To eliminate the need for a guard and guardhouse and to provide for permanent protection against vandalism, the Fords' bodies were exhumed, then reburied in a concrete vault to which a metal grille rising 18 inches above the ground was anchored. The grille is unlocked only for grass cutting, as well as on the anniversary of Ford's death when flowers are placed on the Fords' graves

Resting in Peace

Greenfield Village schoolchildren place wreaths on the graves of Henry and Clara Ford in 1964.

Firestone-Ford Saga

"We all know that Henry Ford and Harvey Firestone were lifelong friends," writes William O. Paulson, Sacramento, Calif. "but how did they meet?"

The pair first met in Detroit in 1896, when Firestone, then selling carriages in Detroit, sold Ford a set of rubber carriage tires. But their long business relationship and friendship dates from 1906, when Firestone traveled from Akron to Detroit to sell Ford his new pneumatic tires.

Convinced that Firestone's product was superior, Ford ordered 2,000 sets of Firestones, the largest single order placed by an auto manufacturer up to that time. This order was quickly followed by orders for 4,000 then 2,000 more sets. Thanks to these orders, Firestone, previously a minor producer, became an industry leader.

On various occasions there were rumors - none factual - that Ford wished to buy out Firestone. Firestone often supplied as much as 65 percent of the tires for Ford's new cars. And the dynasties were united in marriage when Martha Firestone, Harvey's granddaughter, wed William Clay Ford, Henry's grandson.

Ford's Idol

Henry Ford's idol, Thomas A. Edison, also was one of his best friends. Edison was partially deaf, so Ford had to shout into the inventor's ear to make himself heard. The picture shows the pair in a characteristic pose in 1925. (Photo from the Collections of the Henry Ford Museum and Greenfield Village.)

Two Folk Heroes

Charles Lindbergh's recent death brings to mind the warm and enduring friendship of the Lone Eagle and Henry Ford.

The industrialist, Lindbergh once observed, had been a living legend to him since childhood, for he had driven a Model T car at age 11. Ford's first flight

FORD COUNTRY   **25**

was with Lindbergh in The *Spirit of St. Louis* on August 11, 1927. Since the plane had been designed for a single occupant, Ford, Lindbergh later recalled, "had to sit bent over, on the arm of my pilot seat. But he seemed to enjoy the flight very much."

In 1928, Lindbergh, as one of a group establishing an airline from New York to Los Angeles, selected the Ford Trimotor as the best commercial plane, and the new company ordered ten of them.

Lindbergh and his wife, Anne Morrow Lindbergh, repeatedly visited Ford's estate, Fair Lane. Ford and Lindbergh were allied as isolationists from 1939-41; and Lindy served as a consultant and test pilot at Ford's Willow Run Bomber Plant in 1942-43.

Wanted Carver's Secret

Henry Ford named Dearborn's George Washington Carver Laboratory for the black scientist in hopes that Carver would part with his supposed knowledge of how to make rubber from plants, according to Bob Smith, who worked in the laboratory in the 1930s and 1940s.

Ford assigned Smith and another employee to pry the secret out of Carver when the scientist worked in the laboratory for a couple of weeks. But they were never able to do so "because there was no such secret." Smith added that Carver was a good speaker and publicist, but that he "never did much except talk about what he did or was going to do."

The Carver laboratory, still standing, originally was Dearborn's waterworks. After being taken over by Ford, a powerhouse and greenhouse were added. A six-foot high tunnel runs from the basement under the Rouge River to Ford's estate, Fair Lane. Carver's name once was on the door leading to the tunnel; it no longer is. The area around the lab is raised because tanks for water storage were located underneath. When Henry Ford had the building, the tanks held apple cider. The lab now belongs to Greenfield Village, and is used for storage and flower plantings.

Ford and Lindbergh

Charles A. Lindbergh chats with Henry Ford on the first day of his Ford Motor Co. employment, April 3, 1942. At the time, Lindbergh was in poor repute because of his pre-World War II isolationist stand, and had been all but blackballed from government service and other war-related employment by the Roosevelt Administration. Ford, who didn't care what Roosevelt or anybody else thought, figured Lindy could be of service to Ford's Willow Run Bomber Plant, and was proved right.

Strikes Out With Wilson

Henry Ford liked to spin jokes about the Model T, and told one to President Woodrow Wilson on a visit to the President's office in 1915. At the time Ford was trying to win Wilson's support for the Peace Ship he had chartered in a vainglorious effort to put an end to World War I. Wilson refused his support, but responded to Ford's joke with this limerick he had written two years earlier:

26 FORD COUNTRY

"I sat next to the duchess at tea; it was just as I feared it would be. Her rumblings abdominal were truly phenomenal, and everyone thought it was me."

There's no record of what Ford thought of Wilson's limerick. But the auto king was disgusted with the President's stand on his peace effort. "He's a small man," Ford told aides upon leaving the Oval Office.

Historic Marker

Henry and Clara Ford's "Honeymoon House" was dedicated as a Michigan Historic Site on the auto king's birthday, July 30, 1982.

The house was built near the intersection of Dearborn's Ford and Southfield roads. It was moved to its present site, 29835 Beechwood, Garden City, in 1952 by Bob Smith, to whom the Fords took a fancy because of his physical resemblance to Henry Ford.

Text of the marker reads as follows: "In 1891 the Fords left this house for Detroit where Ford's career as an automaker began. They kept the house as a summer cottage until 1937. Ford then gave it to a friend, Robert Smith, now known for his soybean research. After the Fords died, the land on which the house stood was acquired by the Ford Land Development Corporation. Smith was told to move the house or tear it down. He moved it here on the anniversary of Ford's birthday, July 30, 1952. It was listed in the National Register of Historical Places in 1980."

Henry and Prince "Louie"

Glenn L. Simpkins, Milan, Mich., recently informed me that he worked closely with Crown Prince Louis Ferdinand, the grandson of Germany's Kaiser Wilhelm II, when the nobleman was employed by the Ford Company during the pre-World War II era.

"Louie," as he was affectionately called, and another German aristocrat, Erhardt Junkers, liked to drink beer during their off hours. The more they drank, said Simpkins, the more pronounced their German accents, and the more they liked to talk about their dueling scars, of which both were inordinately proud.

Henry Ford was fond of Louie, even to the point of becoming a godfather of one of his children. Louie's friendship with Ford usually stood him in a good stead wherever he went in America. But it was no asset when in 1933 he visited beer baron Adolphus Busch, Jr., in St. Louis. Resentful of Ford's support of Prohibition, Busch greeted Louis with the words, "As a grandson of dear Kaiser Wilhelm you are welcome to me and my family. But please don't mention the name Ford in my presence."

Ford-Carver Friendship

Dr. George Washington Carver and Henry Ford share a tidbit. Photo courtesy of Tuskegee University Archives, Tuskegee, Ala.

"When and how did Henry Ford and George Washington Carver first meet, and what was the basis of their relationship?" asks reader Wilson Schmidt, Charlotte, N.C.

They met in 1936 at the second Dearborn conference of the National Farm Chemurgic Council, hosted by Ford, according to an article by Ford R. Bryan in the Summer, 1983 issue of the *Dearborn Historian*. Ford at the time visited with Carver in his Dearborn Inn suite.

Impressed with Carver's research at Tuskegee Institute on the commercial and nutritive uses of weeds and crop by-products, Ford, when Carver returned to Dearborn in May, 1937, invited the black scientist to attend chapel services in Greenfield Village, and chat with students. In March, 1938, Ford repaid Carver's visit, making his first trip to Tuskegee, to which he had contributed funds as early as 1910. Ford and Carver discussed the needs of both the institute and Ford's Richmond Hill, Ga. plantation.

Correspondence between Ford and Carver increased in 1939, according to Bryan's detailed article, with Carver doing most of the writing. The scientist praised Ford's educational philosophy, as exemplified in the Edison Institute, and his exercise and eating habits. Both men agreed that plants represented the best solution to world problems, and that "it wasn't necessary to have cows."

As the pair's friendship ripened, Tuskegee students were hired at Ford's Rouge Plant, and Carver's chief assistant, Austin W. Curtis, Jr., spent a summer working with Robert Boyer, head of Ford's Chemical Plant. Boyer's research reports routinely were forwarded to Carver. In response to one of them, Carver in July, 1941 referred to "Sida spinosa," a plant of the milkwood family, saying, "I am very certain that it contains rubber as nearly all the milkweeds do."

Ford in March, 1941 again visited Tuskegee, where he and his wife, Clara dedicated the Carver Museum. The Fords also donated soybeans and a variety of soybean plastic car parts for deposit in the museum's cornerstone, then inscribed their names in cement. During the visit, Ford donated an elevator to the campus inn to assist Carver in getting to his second floor apartment.

"America's Sweetheart"

The appearance of 84-year-old Mary Pickford on the 1976 Academy Awards show recalls her friendship with Henry Ford. Here's "America's Sweetheart" in middle life, chatting with the auto king in Dearborn. Ford liked movie stars and welcomed Charlie Chaplin, Will Rogers, Spencer Tracy, Mickey Rooney, and many other entertainers to Dearborn, usually showing them around the Henry Ford Museum and Greenfield Village. (Photo courtesy Ford Archives, Henry Ford Museum, Dearborn, Mich.)

Will and Henry

Will Rogers, left, and Henry Ford were great friends, and the warmth of their friendship shows in this previously unpublished photograph taken in Greenfield Village in the mid-1930s, not long before Rogers' death in a plane crash. Rogers frequently mentioned Ford in his nationally-syndicated column. Ford valued Rogers' values, as well as his sense of humor, and found the folksy comedian comfortable to be around. The photo was furnished by Florence Diamond, Ann Arbor, Michigan whose father, A. Roy Barbier, was a Ford advertising executive from the early 1920s until the 1940s.

"The Little Tramp"

Henry Ford, as one of the world's best-known figures and as the "Detroiter" whom every Motor City visitor most wanted to meet, inevitably played host to many of the leading personalities of his day. They ranged from Presidents Taft through Roosevelt through sports stars Ty Cobb and Dizzy Dean to entertainers such as Will Rogers and Charlie Chaplin.

Chaplin's recent death - and the subsequent theft of his coffin - recalls the "Little Tramp's" 1923 visit to Ford's Highland Park Plant, where he posed with Henry and Edsel Ford. Ford admired Chaplin for his film portrayals; Chaplin admired Ford for his money.

Chaplin Visits Fords

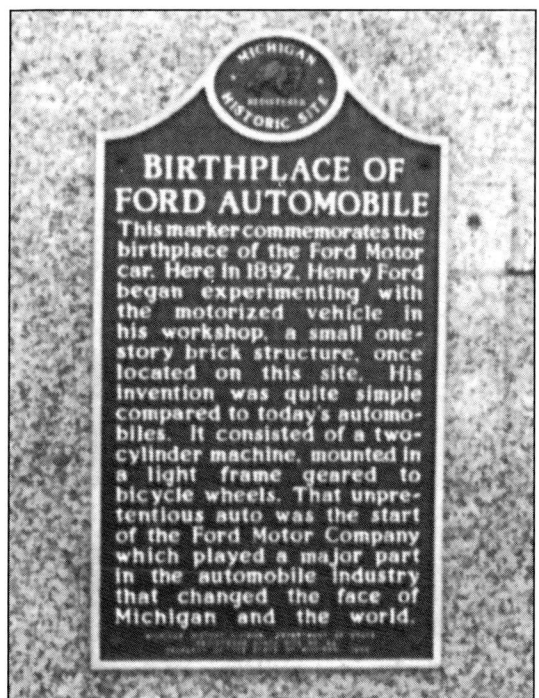

First Ford Car Marker

A State of Michigan historical marker entitled, "Birthplace of Ford Automobile," recently was placed near the doorway of the Michigan Building, 220 Bagley Avenue, Detroit, the address of which was 58 Bagley when Henry and Clara Ford

Edsel Ford, left, Charlie Chaplin, center and Henry Ford chat in the Henry Ford Museum in 1923. Photo from the Collections of the Henry Ford Museum and Greenfield Village.

FORD COUNTRY 29

occupied a small house on the premises. The marker, a replacement for a brass plaque stolen in 1977 reads as follows:

"This marker commemorates the birthplace of the Ford Motor car. Here in 1892, Henry Ford began experimenting with the motorized vehicle in his workshop, a small one-story brick structure, once located on this site. His invention was quite simple compared to today's automobiles. It consisted of a two-cylinder machine, mounted in a light frame geared to bicycle wheels. That unpretentious auto was the start of the Ford Motor Company which played a major part in the automobile industry that changed the face of Michigan and the world."

Ford's first car, which he called a quadricycle, was completed in the workshop in 1896.

Home Sweet Home

It doesn't look like much, but Henry and Clara Ford called this sagging duplex home in 1891-92. The Fords' living room was beneath the Money Orders sign; their bedroom upstairs. Location is 4420 John R Street, a few blocks south of the Detroit Institute of Arts. The building has been vacant since about 1970; its last tenant was a barbershop.

Harper Home Razed

I was cruising through Detroit's inner city, checking out sites and structures related to Henry Ford's life. Daydreaming along Harper Avenue, I passed by the 400 block without seeing a familiar building in which Henry and his wife Clara, occupied a flat between 1905-08.

After wheeling past Ford Co.'s nearby Piquette and Beaubien plant—built in 1904 and the second and oldest of Ford's surviving factories—I drove along Harper again. Arriving at the 400 block (Brush Street), I found a fenced-in parking lot where the Ford dwelling once had stood. Neighbors told the story: the adjacent Oakland Avenue Baptist Church, owner of the property, razed the building in May to provide parking space for parishioners. Scratch one of the five remaining Detroit-area

homes in which Henry and Clara once lived.

When I first photographed the Ford's Harper home in 1972, the owner rushed out and asked, "Why are you taking pictures of my building?" I replied, "Because Henry Ford lived in that flat on the right." "Is that so," he mused. "I'm going to raise the rent."

30   FORD COUNTRY

Edison Avenue Home

The home at 140 Edison Avenue, Detroit, in which Henry and Clara Ford lived from 1908-15, as it looked last fall when visited by the volunteer staff of Dearborn's Henry Ford Estate. The exterior of the house has changed little over the years, but the interior has been considerably altered. The new owners, Mr. and Mrs. Jerry Mitchell, plan to restore the interior to its original state. Ford held old-fashioned dances on the top floor (see windows jutting out of the roof). The house is located in America's largest national residential historic district, comprised of approximately 930 single family dwellings built between 1904-30.

Fordophiles Mike Skinner, left, and Jerry Mitchell, stand in front of the Detroit home in which Henry and Clara Ford lived from 1908-15. Skinner arranged a tour of the Ford home for the volunteer staff of Dearborn's Henry Ford Estate, where the Fords lived from 1915 until the end of their lives. The Detroit residence is now owned by Mr. and Mrs. Jerry Mitchell.

The arbor which Henry Ford's wife, Clara, had built eight decades ago at her 140 Edison Avenue, Detroit, home. Here's the way it looked before leaf raking last fall.

Henry Ford's garage at 140 Edison Avenue, Detroit, from 1909-15. Upstairs, Henry fitted a workshop for his son, Edsel. The shop had several power tools including a woodworking shaper on which the youth took off the top of a middle finger. The tools are now displayed at Greenfield Village. The garage is connected by tunnel to the house, to the left of the garage.

FORD COUNTRY **31**

Famed architect Frank Lloyd Wright hoped to design Fair Lane, the home of Henry and Clara Ford. But a Wright associate, after having had the inside track, lost out to a Pittsburgh architect. The unattractive mansion could have used the Wrightonian touch, although, considering the strong wills of Henry Ford and Wright, it seems most unlikely the two could ever have successfully collaborated on designing the Fords' home.

Although Wright never drew a line for Ford, he may have hoped to return to the project and blamed von Holst for losing it. As for Fair Lane, there are faint traces of early Frank Lloyd Wright and of English Gothic in the building; but in general it is simply a rather plain, oblong structure, broken by a few abortive irregularities. The most attractive part of the mansion is the rear, which overlooks the Rouge River.

Not Wright For Ford

Reader William S. Frazier, Long Beach, Calif., asks whether famed architect Frank Lloyd Wright had a hand in designing Henry Ford's home, Fair Lane.

Yes and No.

To begin with, the Fords' son, Edsel, when scarcely out of his teens, sought to persuade his parents to commission Wright to design the Ford residence. Negotiations were begun with the avant-garde architect and one of his associates, Herman V. von Holst, later of the Chicago architectural firm, Von Holst & Fyfe, as retained by Ford during the summer of 1913. Next year, however, the auto magnate, disenchanted with Von Holst & Fyfe, engaged W.H. Van Tine, of Pittsburgh, who took over both construction and landscape gardening.

Ford Forest

Fair Lane, the Dearborn, Mich. estate on which Henry Ford and his wife Clara, lived the last three decades of their lives, originally was perceived by the Fords to be a nature preserve, nothing more. But the couple, their privacy threatened by fame accompanying Henry's announcement of the five-dollar day in

1914, moved from their streetside Detroit home to the well-insulated estate in 1915.

Most of the estate has been converted into the University of Michigan-Dearborn campus, or otherwise developed. But 43 acres have been preserved by the university as an Environmental Study Area. This area, bordered on the west by sweeping curves of the Rouge River and on the east by fencing which separates it from the university campus, has been permitted (partially as a cost-cutting measure) to grow wild; and it's surprising how rapidly nature reclaims her own.

Tramping the area at twilight, one is rewarded by a succession of stunning visual images: a clump of dogtooth violets closing their yellow trumpets against the night; a warbler at rest on the low branch of a willow; a magnificent shagbark hickory standing solitary, weathered and majestic; a group of violets glowing against the grass. There also are foxes and raccoons, opossums and owls, muskrats and moles, and, down by the long man-made lake, toads trilling for mates and mallards paddling along the bank.

Old Henry, were he to come back for a day, likely would feel more at home in his forest primeval than anywhere else in Dearborn.

Macon Home for Sale

Henry Ford's ex-home in Macon, Mich. — 50 miles southeast of Detroit — is up for sale. Built in 1830 and restored by Ford in 1932, the Greek Revival-styled home is listed in the Michigan Register of Historical Sites.

The auto king often stayed in the house overnight in the 1930s and 1940s after tramping through his soybean fields and inspecting his hydropowered "village industries" around Macon. Ford executives sometimes were summoned there, and cajoled into playing softball on the spacious front lawn. Occasionally they were joined by Henry Ford II and Benson Ford, the magnate's teenage grandsons. Determined to preserve the old-fashionedness of his rural home headquarters, Ford ordered that electric switch plates be hidden in the walls and camouflaged with wallpaper. His telephone was hidden in the closet. The basement floor was re-laid with bricks on top of flagstone; today either would be an extravagance. The Macon home also has a tunnel — a hallmark of Ford construction — leading from the basement to the summer kitchen in the farmyard. The house was sold by the Ford Company after its founder's death in 1947, and passed through several hands before acquired by the current owners, John and Lucille Banks. Asking price for the 100-acre property, a member of the family informed me, is in the neighborhood of $250,000.

Fort Myers Home

One of Henry Ford's least-known residences is this house, still standing in Fort Myers, Florida. Ford bought the home so he and his wife could winter next door to the auto king's greatest friend, Thomas A. Edison. After Edison's death in 1931, the Fords seldom visited Fort Myers; instead wintered at their plantation near Richmond Hill, Ga. The Ford's Fort Myers house was sold in 1945. Now a private residence, it is not opened to the public, but can be seen from the street.

Ford Summer Cottage

Henry Ford's former summer cottage in Pequaming, Mich., overlooking Lake Superior's southern shoreline, is for sale. Asking price is $85,000, but the owners, Richard and Sharon Christison, 2032 James Avenue, St. Paul, Minn. 55105, are "open to offers." The house was built in 1914 by Charles Hebard, who also erected the lumbering town of Pequaming. Ford took over the place, called "The Bungalow," when he bought the village, lock, stock, and barrel, in 1922. The residence has eight bedrooms, six baths, a meeting room, and large living and dining rooms, and a kitchen with assorted pantries. Some of the furnishings are original, having been made by industrial education students in Ford-operated Pequaming schools.

Henry Ford's Richmond Hill, Ga. Plantation mansion (above) as it looked when the auto magnate and his wife, Clara, were in residence. Shown below is the front entrance of the abandoned house in 1972, when visited by the author. The mansion now is being converted into the headquarters of Interdec, a company controlled by Saudi Arabian financier Ghaith Pharon.

Plantation Plans

Henry Ford's former Richmond Hill, Ga. plantation will be converted into the headquarters of Interdec, the corporation controlling the business interests of Saudi Arabian financier Ghaith Pharon.

The 1,875-acre tract, to be renamed the "Cherry Hill Plantation," will be converted into an international enclave containing residential, recreational, and commercial facilities, according to a spokesman for owner Pharon. Plans call for the construction of 200 single-family dwellings to be sold to Pharon's friends and business associates, with each residence carrying a $1 million price tag.

The interior of the plantation's mansion, a restaurant in recent years, will be "totally redone." An asphalt parking lot which served restaurant patrons will be removed. Ford's old rice mill is to be made into Interdec offices, and a new "carriage house" has been built to provide staff living quarters and a six-car garage.

The name "Cherry Hill" was taken from the long lane leading from a paved road back to the mansion. The name was borrowed by the Fords from one of Dearborn's more attractive residential thoroughfares.

An important consideration in Pharon's selection of the plantation as the site for his headquarters is its proximity to Savannah's airport, which can handle his private jet.

Our thanks to reader Edward A. Abercrombie, Statesboro, Ga., for providing the above information.

Fair Lane Grant Axed

A proposed $50,000 state grant for the preservation of Henry and Clara Ford's Dearborn home, Fair Lane, was stricken from Michigan's fiscal 1986-87 budget by Governor James J. Blanchard.

But Fordophiles shouldn't take it personally. The governor also vetoed proposals to spend $30,000 to restore President Gerald R. Ford's boyhood home in Grand Rapids and $8,000 for a national trout memorial.

From the Heart

Henry Ford's gifts came from his heart as well as his pocketbook, says ex-Ford employee Dick Hagelthorn.

"A number of years ago," recalls Hagelthorn, "my neighbor's home was near Henry Ford's woods. Her sisters, ages 10 and three, were picking raspberries by the Cyclone fence that enclosed the Ford property. Mr. Ford was out walking, saw the children, and came over an engaged them in conversation on a level they understood, and shook fingers with them through the fence. The next day a book, *Mary Had a Little Lamb*, signed by Mr. Ford, was delivered to the 10-year-old, a Shirley Temple doll to the three-year-old."

Chicken Double Take

One of my favorite stories about Henry Ford is told by Bob Smith, who worked in Ford's soybean laboratory in the 1930s and 1940s. The yarn goes like this:

A servant at Fair Lane, the Ford estate, brought a live chicken to Mrs. Ford, who, declaring that the fowl was too scrawny for the meal she had in mind, ordered the man to exchange it for a larger one. On his way out of the mansion, the servant ran into Henry Ford, who asked why he was taking a chicken away. The servant explained. "Don't take it back," said Henry, "just wait a while and take the same chicken back to her." The servant did as he was told, and Clara, upon examining the bird, told him, "That's much better. This one will do fine."

If every man knew his woman that well, there'd be a lot less fuss 'n feathers.

Favorite Librarian Dies

Rachel MacDonald, 83, Henry Ford's favorite reference librarian, died recently in Flagler Beach, Fla.

Mrs. MacDonald, a tiny woman with sparkling blue eyes, delighted friends with stories about her association with Ford. Typically, she'd say, Ford would phone her, urgently requesting information on the correct size for the hole in a wren house. She would promptly relay the answer (7/8th of an inch), and later learn that on the basis of the information Ford would have had recut the holes in dozens of wren houses on his estate, Fair Lane.

Mrs. MacDonald also recalled visits to her library by Ford's grandsons, Henry II and Benson, when they were young. The floors being slick, the boys would slide around on them as though they were on a skating rink.

A native of Brockton, Mass., Mrs. MacDonald joined Ford in 1927 at the big Highland Park Plant, then moved to Dearborn, where she cataloged objects which Ford was acquiring for Henry Ford Museum/Greenfield Village. Among the acquisitions, she laughingly told friends, was a complete set of the "Little Orphan Annie" comic strip, a Ford favorite.

Psychology at Work

Nothing pleased Henry Ford more than helping people help themselves. An anecdote published recently in "Our Daily Bread," a syndicated newspaper column by the Rev. A. Purnell Bailey, proves the point.

"Henry Ford," recalls the Rev. Bailey, "once visited the Berry School at Mt. Berry, Ga. As he was leaving, Miss Martha Berry asked him to give her a dime. Ford smiled and said, 'Is that all you want? I am usually asked for gifts larger than a dime.'

" 'A dime is all I want, Mr. Ford, but I do want to show you what I can do with a dime,' replied Miss Berry.

"When Ford asked her what she would do with a dime, Miss Berry responded, 'I want to buy 10 cents worth of peanuts to plant.'

"Several years later, Mr. Ford visited her again and she showed him the return in money which could directly be traced to those peanuts. He was so pleased that he gave her a new building, and two years later gave her school a whole quadrangle of beautiful Gothic stone buildings."

Thanks to Gary Custer, of Harrisonburg, Va., for forwarding the Rev. Bailey's column.

Martha Berry, left, founder of Berry School (later College), Mt. Berry, Ga., Henry Ford, Henry Ford's wife, Clara, and youths attending the self-help institution. The Fords first visited the school between 1922-24 during one of their winter trips to Florida. They revisited it every year for almost 25 years, and starting in 1926 began making generous contributions to it. Both accepted honorary degrees from Berry shortly before the auto king's death in 1947. (Photo from the Collections of the Henry Ford Museum and Greenfield Village.)

The Ford Quadrangle at Berry College, Mt. Berry, Ga. The Gothic stone buildings include two dormitories, Mary Ford Hall and Clara Ford Hall; a recreation hall and gymnasium; a dining hall and kitchen; offices and classrooms; and the Henry Ford Chapel. The buildings cost about $3.2 million. (Photo from the Collections of Henry Ford Museum and Greenfield Village.)

Ford's Way

Henry Ford looked after his hometown, recalled the late Joseph Karman, one of the Dearborn area's leading political figures during the 1920s and 1930s. Karman's reminiscences are on file at the Dearborn Historical Museum.

During hard times, recalls Karman, Springwells — later renamed Fordson, which in turn became part of Dearborn — was about to pay script to municipal employees rather than cash. Karman asked Henry Ford "whether he could find room to employ the people that lived in Springwells due to the fact that his plants were there."

" 'Well, no, Joe,' Ford replied, 'we make cars and sell them all over. We can't just hire people from Springwells because the Springwells people couldn't buy enough cars to keep us going. I'll tell you what to do. Tell your city assessor to put another million dollars valuation on the Ford industry.' That took us out of the red," added Karman, "and we didn't have to use the script. That increased valuation was never taken off."

Tales of Henry and Edsel

"Each day after work," writes 82-year-old Detroiter Frances R. Reeves, "Henry Ford patronized a bar near his small shop at Bagley and Second Sts. for one five-cent beer, and that was it." Ford lived on Bagley from 1893-97, and built his first car there in 1896.

Does this sound like the Henry Ford we know? Hardly, because the Henry we know was agin beer, and had little truck with them that wasn't. Still, anything is possible.

"Also," Mrs. Reeves continues, "my sister told me that Edsel drove a yellow convertible Stutz Bearcat in 1916 or 1917. He used to park it on Woodward at the Highland Park Plant, and his fiancée waited for him in it."

Could be. Edsel liked to drive stylish non-Fords (and not least in an era when all Fords were Model Ts), and it would have been in character for him to be driving a Stutz. Moreover, 1916 would have been just right for his girl, Eleanor, to be joyriding with him; the two were married on Nov. 1 of that year.

Remembering Ford

"I remember Henry Ford as being quick of movement, alert, immaculate, smartly dressed," remembers Frank Caddy, former president of the Edison Institute (Greenfield Village and Henry Ford Museum).

"He drove with abandon and impulsiveness," added Caddy. "He'd drive up to a group of visitors, be quickly surrounded, then be off again. He also was very energetic. He liked to challenge to a footrace the person he was with, and to chin himself on the branch of a tree as he walked by. He was very much at ease in the presence of children."

Romney Recalls Ford

George Romney, on whose memoirs I am working, recalls Henry Ford with affection.

Romney, ex-president of American Motors, former head of the Automobile Manufacturers Assn., and governor of Michigan from 1963-69, organized the Automotive Golden Jubilee celebration in 1946.

"We had a big parade down Woodward Avenue," remembers Romney, "and I was in the lead car. Henry Ford and his family were sitting in the big window in J.L. Hudson's Department Store. It looked up Woodward. As I went by, Ford looked right at me and rotated his fists like a prizefighter."

"Meaning what?" I asked Romney.

"I don't know what he meant," he replied. "But I guess he thought I was a pretty good fighter, a pretty good battler. Maybe he meant, 'More power to you.' "

Romney also heard the auto king

speak at the dedication of an expressway leading to Ford's Willow Run Bomber Plant in 1943. After each of three speakers had talked for half an hour, the master of ceremonies, recalled Romney, said, "We have an unexpected visitor. I am sure we'd all like to hear from him. Our unexpected visitor is Mr. Henry Ford." Old man Ford [then 79] toddled up to the microphone and said "I can't talk, but I'll do all I can."

The speech, observed Romney, was brief, but apropos. "That's what people wanted to be sure of, that somebody was going to do all he could."

Romney also prepared, at the invitation of the Ford Co., the list of auto industry dignitaries who were permitted to attend Henry Ford's funeral.

Brother-in-Law Dies

Edgar Leroy (Roy) Bryant, 90, Henry Ford's last surviving brother-in-law, died on May 1. Bryant, youngest brother of Ford's wife, Clara, had been a Ford dealer in Dearborn for half a century.

Left out of the will of his sister, who died in 1950, Bryant waged a four-year battle to gain control of her $27,000,000 estate. He settled his claim, according to Detroit newspapers, in 1955 for $15,000. Old friends of the Ford family say this figure is ridiculous; it wouldn't even have paid for Bryant's legal fees. Other estimates of Bryant's settlement - for services he claimed were rendered the Fords during their declining years - range up to $18,000,000. In any event, Bryant who lived in a Ford-built home across the Rouge River from the Fords' estate, lived very comfortably until life's end.

By a coincidence, a few weeks before Bryant's death, I was leafing through a foot-high stack of papers in the Wayne County (Detroit) Building in an effort to learn more about Clara Ford's estate. Sure enough, Clara's will left her kid brother out in the cold (and also left pitifully small sums to longtime servants).

Nephew-in-Law Honored

The late Harry Wismer, one of Henry Ford's nephews-in-law, a sports broadcaster, and cofounder of the American Football League, recently was named to the Port Huron (Mich.) Sports Hall of Fame. Wismer married Mary Elizabeth Bryant, a niece of Ford's wife, in 1940.

The auto magnate, wishing to help the newlyweds, handed Harry, an advertising neophyte, the lucrative Lincoln advertising account. Wismer's "main contribution to the business," recalled Ford Advertising Manager A.R. Barbier years later, "was to come out to Dearborn now and then and ask 'How are our men coming along?' "

Wismer later served as "key contact man" on the Mercury account and on the truck, by-products, and service, parts, and accessories accounts which he successfully solicited for his ad agency, Maxon, Inc., in the last half of 1941.

The Wismers were divorced in 1959, and Mrs. Wismer married ex-U.S. Senator Charles E. Potter in 1960. The Potters now live in Maryland.

While with Ford, Wismer was friendly with Henry Ford's top aide, Harry Bennett. For both it was a marriage of convenience. Of Wismer, Bennett said during my 1973 interview with him: "He was a cocky, lazy, big mouth playboy who went to work for us during World War II to escape the draft. He'd sometimes introduce himself through his wife who was a sweet little thing."

Brother Bill

While forwarding a 1937 Life photo of William Ford, David G. Currie, Euclid, Ohio, suggests that an item on Henry's younger brother might be of interest.

William, born in 1871 and eight years younger than Henry, was a farmer and operated a threshing rig as a young man. He later was a partner in Ford-Allen, a farm implement business in Highland Park, Mich., but his firm went bankrupt in 1934.

Meantime, William had acquired a farm near Brighton, Mich., 45 miles northwest of Detroit, where he demonstrated his equipment. He was living in retirement on his farm at the time of his death in 1959, a niece, Catherine Ruddiman, daughter of his sister, Margaret, recently informed me.

Margaret, the last survivor of Henry Ford's immediate family, died in February 1960 at age 92. Another brother, John, born in 1865, passed away in 1927; a sister, Jane, born in 1869, died in 1906. Two other brothers died in infancy, in 1861 and 1876, the latter along with the Fords' mother, Mary. Another brother, Robert, lived only from 1873 to 1877.

Ford Relative Finds Niche

A relative of Henry Ford, Ford R. Bryan, 69, of Dearborn, is a valued volunteer at the Edison Institute (Greenfield Village/Henry Ford Museum).

One of Bryan's grandmothers was Ford's cousin. "She was seven years older," recalls Bryan, "and lived on a neighboring farm." Bryan specializes, not surprisingly, in answering questions about his family's genealogy.

A retired scientific researcher for Ford Motor Co., Bryan also prepares subject guides for the Ford Archives, sells stamps at the Village's post office and lectures on the postal building, and writes for the *Dearborn Historian* and *The Herald*, published by the Dearborn Historical Commission and the Institute, respectively.

While working for the Ford Co., Bryan used to look out his window toward the Henry Ford Museum and think, "Maybe I'll volunteer there when I retire." After his wife's death two years ago, he "made a lunge for Greenfield Village. My work here," he says, "is now my main occupation."

Logging 826 hours during 1981, his first year as a volunteer, Bryan was named the Institute's Volunteer of the Year. "He is a low-key individual who enjoys contact with people," Douglas Bakken, director of the Institute's Archives and Research Library, recently told the *Detroit Free Press*. "He's an invaluable person to have working here; in fact, he is one of a kind!"

Edward L. Bryant

Henry Ford's nephew-in-law, Edward L. Bryant, at left in the picture, taken at Henry Ford's 1977 birthday party, died recently in Detroit at age 87. With Bryant are ex-Ford engineer Roy Schumann, center, and John Carroll, of Fairview Park, Ohio.

In 1977 your commentator spent a full day with Bryant visiting the former homes of Detroit's auto greats. Eddie seemed to know where everyone had lived, and up-and-down the streets we went, looking at and photographing the houses in which Barney

FORD COUNTRY

Oldfield, James Couzens, the Dodge boys, etc., had resided, and also at buildings where obscure makes of cars had been built. Occasionally Bryant would get mixed up, and we'd go down a blind alley. After all, it'd been half a century and more since he'd visited some of the places.

Eddie delighted in asking me obscure questions to which only he could have the answers. When I'd reply, "I don't know," he'd pounce on me, saying, "see, you don't know anything." I never disputed the matter; just drove on. Besides, given Eddie's cantankerousness and the cane he always carried, one couldn't be too careful.

We had lunch at a Belle Isle yacht club, of which Bryant was a member. My car, a 1968 Ford Galaxie 500, had embarrassingly limped into the posh club midst a cloud of oil fumes emanating from under the hood. I thought the old Green Dream Machine was done for, and was prepared to call a towing service, send Eddie home in a taxi, and take a bus back to Ann Arbor. But Eddie sized up the car, fulminated a few minutes, then commanded me to get into the car and drive him home. I think he also caned the vehicle a time or two. I didn't believe the car had another mile in it, but it ran thereafter sans fumes, and continued to run for another three years until put out of commission in an auto accident. After that episode, I had new respect for Eddie.

The last time I saw Bryant was a couple of years ago at the entrance to the Detroit Public Library, where he was people watching. We exchanged greetings, and reminisced about the day we had spent together, and how he had miraculously cured my car of fuming. I told him I thought he was a magician. He didn't deny it.

Rumored Purchases

A recent *Time* article on the Eiffel Tower states that Henry Ford once tried to buy the famed Parisian monument. A couple of readers have inquired whether this was so, and, if so, what Ford intended to do with it. Insofar as I am aware, Ford never considered buying the tower. If he had bought it, what would he have done with it? The only possibility that comes to mind is its relocation in Greenfield Village. But the tower would have been totally out of character with the rest of the Village. Moreover, the Village is adjacent to the old Ford Airport, since the mid-thirties a company test track, but prior to that time Detroit's air terminus.

Ford was rumored to be interested in purchasing for the Village King Henry VIII's love nest, Longfellow's famous smithy, Frederick the Great's flute, the Chinese imperial treasures, and an historic London church. It also was erroneously rumored that he would sell cars for $100 on the day that Virginia went dry; that he was taking instructions from a Catholic prelate; and that he would give a free car to any woman bearing eleven or more children.

Ford for Penny Rumor

The recent sale for $10,000 of a copper cent, which, according to Mint records, does not exist, revived anew the 1943 rumor that Henry Ford would give a new car to anyone finding a '43 copper.

Officially, all one-cent pieces minted in 1943 were made of zinc-coated steel in order to conserve copper for the war effort. However, the existence of a small number of cents struck in copper (or more accurately in bronze) has long been rumored in numismatic circles. As the rumors have it, 20 to 30 bronze cents were struck in error at the Philadelphia Mint, and released to circulation in 1943.

The story that Ford would give a new car in exchange for a '43 copper sparked a nationwide search for the coin, and over the years people have flooded the Mint with hundreds of supposedly genuine '43 coppers. All, however, have proved spurious. To this date, the Mint maintains that it has never seen a genuine 1943 copper cent.

Fords' Chauffeur

Henry and Clara Fords' private chauffeur, Robert Rankin, was the best in the business, a not unbiased judge, Rankin's daughter, Mrs. Roberta Mallast, of Dearborn, recently informed me. Rankin, who served the Fords from 1937-50, was so skilled a driver, says his daughter, that he could motor the dozen or so miles from Dearborn across Detroit to Edsel Ford's home in Grosse Pointe Shores without missing a traffic light. At the same time, in the fashion of the very best of chauffeurs, he'd acquaint the Fords with the latest news and happenings around town.

Rankin was recommended to the Fords by Edsel, after the death of the chauffeur's Grosse Pointe employer, Charlie Hodges. Although Rankin was not the only man who drove the Fords —company drivers also occasionally drove them — he was the chauffeur, and thus occupied one of the servants' cottages on the estate (still standing and used for offices by Fair Lane's present owner, University of Michigan-Dearborn). Mrs. Mallast, having been reared at Fair Lane, often saw Ford riding his bike or walking past her family's cottage.

Ford Servant Dies

Rosa Buhler, longtime personal servant of Henry and Clara Ford, died Oct. 17, 1983 in Detroit. She was 86.

The word which best describes Miss Buhler, said her biographer, Dick Folsom, is "dedication." She worked six days a week for 15 years doing "whatever was needed."

Rosa's loyalty manifested itself anew five years ago while recovering from a heart attack. Concerned that her Ford years diary would fall into the wrong hands, she burned it, according to Folsom.

But Miss Buhler commented on Clara's frugality to her nephew, Harold Schauer, saying that Henry Ford once ordered her to buy him 12 pairs of socks without informing her mistress, who believed in hanging on to everything, including socks with holes in them.

Miss Buhler, along with Clara, was present at Henry Ford's deathbed in 1947. After Clara died in 1950, Rosa lived on in Fair Lane for a year. She was a nurse's aide in Dearborn and Detroit until her retirement in 1962.

Any Mail From Henry?

A typewritten, signed letter by Henry Ford is worth $150 to $300, and a handwritten letter by Ford commands from $400 to $1,500, according to autograph dealer Charles Hamilton, of New York. "Henry Ford was as tight with his signature as he was with his money," says Hamilton, who is considered the country's leading dealer in signatures and letters of famous persons and the most astute appraiser of their value. He recently sold at auction a letter from Declaration of Independence signer Button Gwinnett for $100,000, the highest price ever paid for a signed letter.

An Edsel Ford autograph will bring only $10 or so, declares Hamilton, who adds that there is little interest in the signature of Henry Ford II or Alfred P. Sloan, Jr., who headed General Motors from the 1920s until the mid-1950s. But autographs of David Buick and Walter P. Chrysler will bring $50 and up.

Although Hamilton says that Henry Ford II's signature commands little interest, an Oct. 26, 1979 auction conducted by the Friends of the Detroit Public Library belies his opinion. At that sale, three books signed by HFII last Oct. 1, the day of his retirement as Ford Motor Co.'s chief executive officer, fetched from $80 to $180. The books were my own *The Public Image of*

FORD COUNTRY **41**

Henry Ford: An American Folk Hero and His Company; Lorin Sorensen's *The Ford Road: 75th Anniversary, Ford Motor Company, 1903-1978*; and Beverly Rae Kimes' *The Cars That Henry Ford Built: A 75th Anniversary Tribute to America's Most Remembered Automobiles.*

Each of these books retails at far less than the auction's selling price; thus the difference between the retail and auction prices had to be HFII's signature, which made these particular copies special.

Distinctive Bathroom

Perhaps the only bathroom in the country adorned with a signed photograph of Henry Ford can be found in Henry Ford's former country home in Macon, Mich., now owned by Jack and Virginia Frazier. The industrialist's "official" Ford Motor Co. photograph, taken in 1933 and signed "Henry Ford," hangs above the stool. The photo is displayed against a backdrop of wallpaper featuring Model Ts and other nostalgic automotive scenes. Taken together, the setting is rather blissful, especially to a Fordophile.

Six of the 11 stamps honoring Henry Ford and Ford cars are shown here. They include Yemeni stamps, at left, issued in 1972, one showing Ford's 1898 "quadricycle" another, a 1970 Ford sedan; and two Monegasque stamps, upper center and right, featuring a picture of the industrialist with a 1903 Model A and a 1908 Model S. It can be plausibly questioned whether the portrait actually is one of Ford. At lower center is a Hungarian stamp, depicting a "1906 Model T," which ignores the fact that the Tin Lizzie was not produced before 1908; and America's 12-cent stamp, lower right, issued in 1968.

Eleven Ford Stamps

More stamps — 11 issued by seven countries — honor Henry Ford and Ford cars than any other American industrialist or product. All of the Ford stamps have been issued within the last 14 years. Three of them were issued by Umm al Quwain, two by Monaco, two by Yemen, and one each by the United States, Hungary, Sharjah, and Bhutan. Another stamp not labeled "Ford," but obviously showing a 1914 Model T, is one of a series issued by New Zealand for the 13th International Vintage Car Rally.

The first Ford stamp, valued at 20 francs, was issued in Monaco as part of a 1960-62 series honoring 14 pioneer automobiles. The stamp features an illustration of a 1908 Model S. The second of the Monaco stamps, which commemorates the 100th anniversary of Henry Ford's birth, was issued in 1963. The 20-franc stamp pictures Ford in the upper left corner and a 1903 Model A in the foreground. The balding figure purported to be Henry Ford resembles the auto king, but it is not he. The Monegasques made a mistake.

The American stamp honoring Ford is the current 12-center, part of the "Prominent American" stamp series. Issued in 1968, the stamp features a portrait of the industrialist superimposed on the silhouette of a 1909 T touring.

The 1969 Umm al Quwain trio features Henry Ford's 1896 quadricycle, a 1903 Model A, and a 1909 Model T. Sharjah's 1970 issues depict a 1908 and a 1970 Ford. Yeman's issues show the 1896 quadricycle and a 1970 Ford. A 1972 Hungarian stamp, oblivious to the fact that the first Tin Lizzie was not produced until 1908, honors the "1906" Model T. The Bhutan stamp features a T coupe of late vintage.

Ford cars have three stamp firsts: they appear on more stamps than any other auto; they are on the stamps of more countries than any other car; and the T is the only auto identified by make to appear on an American postage stamp.

This statue of Henry Ford was unveiled in front of Dearborn's Henry Ford Centennial Library. At the lectern is sculptor Marshall Fredericks. The tableaux on the monument portray American transportation scenes. On the back of the monument are three of Henry Ford's quotations.

Dearborn Statue Unveiled

There are now two life-sized statues of Henry Ford — one erected in front of Ford of Britain's Dagenham factory in 1948, the other unveiled in front of Dearborn's Henry Ford Centennial Library, 16301 Michigan Avenue, in June.

Dearbornites first decided in 1948 to build a statue to their foremost citizen. But it took more than a quarter-century to see the monument erected. Meantime, fund-raising campaigns came and went. Finally, between 1968-70, sustained drives pushed the statue fund over the targeted $50,000 mark.

The statue's base is made of a green marble that matches the outside decor of the library. Ford's effigy is cast in green bronze.

"I studied hundreds of photographs of Ford," said Fredericks, "talked to people who had known him, and I met him twice myself. But I couldn't see him doing anything active. This pose — the thoughtful look — represents him in the best way. I like to see him thinking."

Edsel Ford II, Henry Ford II's son, now a Ford executive, represented the

FORD COUNTRY **43**

Ford family at the ceremony.

A commemorative medallion showing Ford's effigy on one side, Ford-Dearborn landmarks on the other, was presented to those attending the dedication ceremony.

Life-Size Statue

The statue of Henry Ford which stands next to Dearborn's Henry Ford Centennial Library seems undersized when seen from Michigan Avenue out front. But it's life-size, as attested to by this recent photograph of the author standing alongside. The statue, financed by $50,000 in admirers' gifts, was erected in 1976. It is one of two life-size Ford statues, the other being in front of Ford of England's headquarters at Dagenham, England.

Ford Memorialized

Henry Ford is one of 12 figures memorialized in the nave clerestory windows of San Francisco's Grace Cathedral.

The windows, as noted in a brochure distributed by the Episcopal cathedral, "are devoted to Human Endeavor, which is made possible by the creative and sustaining action of God's grace." The figures on the south clerestory are John Glenn - Exploration, Henry Ford - Industry, Thurgood Marshall - Law, Jane Addams - Social Work, William Welch - Medicine, Frank Lloyd Wright - Fine Arts ... north clerestory ... Robert Frost - Letters, Franklin D. Roosevelt - Government, John Dewey - Education, Luther Burbank - Agriculture, John L. Lewis - Labor, and Albert Einstein - Natural Science."

The cathedral, completed in 1966, occupies a city block near the summit of historic Nob Hill.

Henry Ford, as memorialized in a nave clerestory window of San Francisco's Grace Cathedral.

Wax Effigy

Would you trust this man to check under your hood? Of course you would, were he really Henry Ford. But what we have here is a wax figure of the auto king, checking out a 1912 flivver in Washington's National Wax Museum. An effigy of Ford's closest friend, Thomas A. Edison, not shown in this photo, stands next to the T.

Father of Briquets

Henry Ford is credited with having invented the first charcoal briquets, according to a recent article in the *Bangor* (Me.) *Daily News*.

Before 1920, the *News* reports, most charcoal was made in lumps. "It was not uniform in size or in heat output, and was used primarily as an industrial fuel or for home cooking in wood-burning stoves. It was not very efficient. Ford's idea was to chip the wood into small pieces, and then, after the wood was turned into charcoal, grind it into a powder, add a binder, and compress the mix into the now familiar pillow shape of the charcoal briquet.

Ford enlisted his friend, Thomas A. Edison, to design a briquet plant in Kingsford, Mich. By early 1921 the factory was in operation, using wood scraps from Ford's nearby sawmill. Power was supplied by a Ford built-and-owned dam and hydroelectric facility. The by-products drawn off during the charring process were run through a condenser to make ketones for paint for Ford's cars and methanol for antifreeze. The briquets first were sold directly to industry, later through dealerships to the public.

The article adds that Ford, an avid camper, designed the station wagon to carry his camping equipment and the charcoal briquet for easier handling and steadier heat while camping.

The Kingsford plant was sold and renamed the Kingsford Chemical Co. Its successor, the Kingsford Co., today is a subsidiary of the Clorox Co.

Thanks to Leo C. Mathews, of Bangor, for forwarding the article.

Ford's Pioneering Cited

Henry Ford's promotion of ethanol - ethyl alcohol - is discussed in a lengthy treatise on ethanol in a recent issue of the *New Yorker*.

The magazine states that "the carburetors in some of (Ford's) early cars could be adjusted to use either gasoline or ethanol." It also recalls Ford's manufacture of auto parts from farm products and his 1935-36 sponsorship of national conferences on "chemurgy" - a term invented to describe the conversion of farm products into industrial materials.

Ford had a lifelong interest in developing fuels from nonpetroleum

A globe for a Ford Benzol pump, one of many fuel pump globes on sale at a recent Hershey meet.

FORD COUNTRY   **45**

sources. In the teens he produced Ford Benzol, a light oil which was a by-product of his coke ovens. Mixed with gasoline, Ford Benzol was sold at service stations in the Detroit area - 2.5 million gallons - by 1921. Production ceased in the late 1930s or early 1940s.

Benzol helped eliminate engine knock before the word "octane" came into general use. Ford also claimed that Benzol provided better engine performance by cleaning spark plugs and other parts. Motorists often used it every third tankful.

Why no Benzol today? Because Benzene, the main ingredient in Benzol, is suspected of causing leukemia. Also, because modern auto engines would have to be extensively redesigned to make use of the by-product.

Henry's 20-20 Vision

As soybean curd, which the Japanese call tofu, gains in popularity with Americans, Henry Ford's vision is looking better than ever.

Tofu, once found only in health stores and Oriental restaurants, is sold today in major supermarket chains, served in schools and hospitals, and added to cakes, quiches and casseroles available at urban delicatessens.

Many nutritionists regard tofu as an ideal diet food since it is low in fat and calories, contains no cholesterol, and is high in protein, vitamins B, iron, potassium, and phosphorous. In addition, tofu's mild flavor and soft texture permits it to be incorporated into a wide range of dishes, as well as served to babies, the elderly, or those with digestive problems. And it costs only 55 to 85 cents per pound.

But Henry Ford had all this figured out in the late 1930s, and ate many meals consisting of only soybean derivatives. On at least three occasions between 1934 and 1943, Ford, seeking to publicize his soybean experimentation, summoned reporters to soybean luncheons. Every course was partially or wholly composed of the legume. The chief items were tomato juice with soybean sauce, celery stuffed with soybeans, soybean bread and butter, apple pie with soybean sauce, soybean coffee, soybean milk, soybean ice cream, and soybean cookies and candy.

"Nothing we newsmen ate that day," a guest wrote years later, "led us to foresee that soybeans were destined to become an ingredient in many popular food products." Yet soybean-derived foods are expected within a few years to be as popular as yogurt, itself little known until recent years.

Ford's Soybean Lab

It's off the beaten track and thus not all visitors to Greenfield Village are aware of it, but this building - the laboratory in which Henry Ford conducted numerous experiments exploring the potential of soybeans and other agricultural products into industrial materials - is one of the most historically significant in the Village compound. Built in 1929, it now serves as the Village's shipping and receiving office.

A Piker Compared to Al

Life does have moments of disillusionment. All along I had thought that Henry Ford had - during his financial heyday in the early and mid-1920s - a greater annual income than any other private citizen in world history. But the 1974 edition of the authoritative *Guinness Book of World Records* notes that "the highest

46   FORD COUNTRY

gross income ever achieved in a single year by a private citizen is an estimated $105,000,000 in 1927 by the Chicago gangster Alphonse (Scarface Al) Capone." Henry Ford, according to *Guinness* was runner-up in the income derby, earning "about $70,000,000 per annum at his peak."

A Lonely Widow

A revealing glance at Henry Ford's widow, Clara, who outlived her husband by three and a half years, is provided by the Ford's chauffeur, Robert Rankin, in a brochure published by Fair Lane Estate in commemoration of the auto magnate's 121st birthday in 1984.

Clara, recalled Rankin, sometimes became very quiet as they were driving along. On such occasions, he added, "I would pull over to the curb and I wouldn't say a thing to her. After about five or ten minutes she would say, 'All right, Rankin. I'm all right now. Go ahead.'

"I'd say to her, 'It's a natural thing that you should do that, Mrs. Ford.' She would answer, 'But it makes me so embarrassed.'

"Then I'd argue, 'Well, what do you care? You've got your feelings like anybody else. Crying doesn't do anybody any harm at any time.' "

First Plastic Car

Lowell Overly is seated in the world's first plastic car, which he designed, built and introduced to the public on August 13, 1941, at the climax of Dearborn's annual community festival. The vehicle, completed under Henry Ford's close supervision, was a forerunner of vehicles to come, being small, lightweight, and fuel-efficient.

"You have to project yourself back to what we knew about plastic 40 years ago to realize how advanced this idea was," Overly recently recalled. *The car was not mass-produced, however, because of problems associated with the plastic, including its smell. It was molded from several common crops including soybeans, wheat, hemp, flax, and ramie.*

Overly, who retired as a process engineer in Ford's Metal Stamping Division in 1967, always felt that the car was on the right track. "And from what I hear about today's new uses of plastics in cars, I guess I was right," *he adds. The initial plastic car generated tremendous publicity, and represents one of the outstanding achievements of Henry Ford's later years. In 1941, there were numerous jokes about the vegetable content in the vehicle. My favorite is this one:*

Mother (to recalcitrant small son): "Now eat your succotash, Freddy, like a good boy."

Freddy: "I say it's a flivver, and I say to hell with it!"

"The Believer"

Henry Ford called his wife, Clara, "The Believer," because she believed in him when many others thought he was wasting his time trying to build an internal combustion engine and an automobile. The couple sat for this photo in their home, Fair Lane, in 1930, when Ford was 73, Clara 70. Of his mate, Ford once said, "If I were to die and come back to another life, I would want the same wife." (Photo from the Collections of Henry Ford Museum and Greenfield Village.)

Edsel's Greatest Mistake?

The famous Diego Rivera mural commissioned by Edsel Ford for the Detroit Institute of Arts is suffering the ill effects of air pollution. Lower portions of the huge mural, unveiled in 1933, also were recently covered by plastic to prevent museum visitors from touching it.

At the time of the unveiling, many Detroiters were displeased with the mural - which purports to depict industrial Detroit - saying that it failed to capture the Motor City's spirit, and too strongly reflected Rivera's Mexican heritage and communistic beliefs. The *Detroit News* said the mural should be whitewashed and forgotten. But Edsel Ford, in the name of artistic freedom, allowed the $25,000 "work of art" to remain. And there it is to this day, as overpowering, ugly, and depressing as ever.

Rivera later gleefully observed how he had taken the money of capitalists, and then skewered them with the Detroit work. All things considered, one can make a case for this mural, both commissioning and retention of it, as one of Edsel's greatest mistakes. The Institute's mural may indeed be a work of art, but, if so, it belongs in Moscow, not Detroit.

Debonair Edsel

We recently were asked about our favorite picture of Henry Ford II. That set us to thinking about our favorite photo of Edsel Ford. How about this one? Here we see Edsel as handsome, debonair, and dashing as a movie star of the 1930s, when this photo was taken. The print was furnished by Florence Diamond, daughter of A.R. Barbier, who, as the company's advertising chief, was close to Edsel for many years.

Edselites Pay Tribute

The "President's Letter" in a recent issue of the *Edseletter*, publication of the International Edsel Club, pays tribute to Edsel Ford.

"As we recognize the Edsel as a design years ahead of its time," noted President David R. Babb, "we should also remember that Edsel Ford himself was a man ahead of his time. Few peers in the turbulent prewar years appreciated his foresight and his modern and liberal viewpoint. Few leaders recognized Edsel Ford as the prologue of an entirely new economic era. Edsel passed away quietly and prematurely. The man is forgotten. The Edsel car is immortalized. The historical study of mankind might be better served if their positions were reversed."

Edsel Was Straight

Your commentator is accustomed to being asked "far-out" questions about the Ford family and the company that bears its name. But his composure was shaken when his one-seventh of a secretary and her friends, after having seen the film, *The Betsy*, asked whether Edsel Ford was gay.

One of the characters of this movie, based on the trashy book of the same name, is an auto pioneer's son who is homosexual and kills himself. Some misguided souls are of the opinion that author Harold Robbins modeled the tycoon after Henry Ford, and the tycoon's son therefore is Edsel. Robbins denies having based his book's character on the Ford dynasty. Even without his denial, this fact is obvious to any reader or filmgoer familiar with the Fords. Robbins simply mixed passion with gasoline, and in the manner of all his best sellers came up with a sex-laden yarn that makes it clear that the great American automotive novel has yet to be written. And for the record, Edsel Ford was straight.

Cows Absolved

Although Edsel Ford died of stomach cancer, he also suffered from undulant fever at the time of his death. It's always been assumed that he contracted the fever from unpasteurized milk produced by his father's herd of Ayrshire cows. But Bob Smith, who lived only 500 yards from those same cows and drank the same milk that Edsel did, insists that Edsel didn't get the fever from the bovines. Smith, a Ford chemist, and his family were living in Henry and Clara Fords' "Honeymoon House" at the time of Edsel's death in 1943. The milkhouse for Ford's cows was only 100 feet from their home.

The milk, according to Smith, was tested for bacteria and butterfat content, but not for undulant fever. Smith and his wife drank milk from this herd, and so did their daughter, born in 1940, and son, born in 1943, as soon as they were old enough to do so. The Smiths continued to drink the milk until 1945, and if they didn't get undulant fever from this milk, Smith recently told me, Edsel could not have done so either. He's got a point.

Has to Pay $2

Mrs. Edsel B. Ford, who has contributed millions of dollars to the Detroit Institute of Arts, recently made an unexpected payment to the museum. Wishing to view a special Russian exhibit, for which there was a charge of $2, she fished around in her purse for the Art Institute Founders Society membership card which would have provided free admission. Unable to find the card, she was made to cough up two bucks by the young girl at the gate. Mrs. Ford's husband died in 1943; she has been a Motor City civic leader since her marriage to Edsel in 1916.

Edsel/Eleanor Ford Mansion

The Edsel and Eleanor Ford home, located in Grosse Pointe Shores, Mich., is a State of Michigan historic site, as indicated by the marker in the accompanying photo. Text of the marker reads as follows:

"Edsel Ford, president of the Ford Motor Company for many years, and his wife, Eleanor Clay, completed this 87-acre estate in 1927. Architect Albert Kahn derived the design from precedents in Cotswold, England, and many of the building materials, including the staircase, paneling, and fireplaces, were brought from old English homes. Noted landscape architect Jens Jensen developed the grounds. The Fords were collectors of art and antiques, and benefactors of local and national institutions. Edsel was instrumental in the creation of the Ford Foundation in 1936. He died here on May 26, 1943. His wife, who lived here until her death on October 19, 1976, endowed the property and directed it be maintained for public use."

Eleanor Ford Dies

Eleanor Ford, long a patron of the arts and Motor City civic leader, died on October 19, 1976 at age 80. Her death was attributed to circulatory problems.

Your commentator attended Mrs. Ford's funeral at Christ Episcopal Church, Grosse Pointe Farms. In attendance were all of her children and grandchildren, plus several great-grandchildren. Henry Ford II, 59, now the eldest member of the family, led the family procession, accompanied by his second oldest daughter, Anne, 33. Also on hand were leading executives of Ford and other auto companies and political and civic leaders of the Detroit area. Mrs. Ford's body was removed in a Cadillac hearse to Woodlawn Cemetery, Detroit. Her casket was initially placed in the big Hudson mausoleum (Mrs. Ford was a niece of Detroit department store magnate Joseph L. Hudson, for whom the Hudson car was named) until the tomb in which her husband had been buried could be opened by a Toledo firm. Nearby are the graves of a veritable Who Was Who in the Auto Industry — John and Horace Dodge, James Couzens, C. Harold Wills, Roy D. Chapin, Sr., George Holley, Robert C. Hupp, Bill Metzger, and Harry Jewett to name a few. The Fords' tomb, of black Swedish granite, expresses the couple's preference for simplicity. Although they had more money than any of the other wealthy folk buried in Woodlawn, their marker is more modest than many others.

The day of Mrs. Ford's funeral was cold and windy throughout, sunny at the morning church services, gray in midafternoon when I visited the cemetery. The sun broke through again in late afternoon, when to break through the gloom, I drove around the River Rouge Plant, then visited the little arboretum which the Ford Company has developed on the grounds of its World Headquarters. All around the Detroit area Ford flags were flying at half-mast — at the old Highland Park Plant, over the old Administration Building in which Edsel's offices were located, and at the World Headquarters itself. Ford Country won't be the same without Eleanor Ford, who, like her husband, Edsel, was at the top of Detroiters' list of most admired persons.

No Place Like Home

"Be it ever so humble," as Henry Ford II kiddingly told visitors, *"there's no place like home"*; and this is the home which Edsel Ford built for his family in 1926-27. The mansion and its 87-acre grounds, in Grosse Pointe Shores and St. Clair Shores, was given by Edsel's widow, Eleanor, in 1976 to a charitable foundation with the request that it be operated as a historical and cultural center. An endowment of $15 million was set up for maintenance and operation.

Favorite Ford Photo

"Show us your favorite photo of Henry Ford II," writes James Winchester, of Atlanta. I don't know that I have a favorite, any more than I can name one of my four kids as a favorite. But I've always liked the above photo a lot. It shows The Deuce laughing with "Der Alt," German Chancellor Konrad Adenauer. What, one must ask himself, can be so funny?"

FORD COUNTRY

Fords in Maine

The Seal Harbor (Me.) summer home of Walter B. and Josephine "Dodie" Ford, Henry Ford II's sister, is featured in the April issue of *Architectural Digest*. The Fords' home, the Anchorage, was built in 1947 for Nelson Rockefeller, whose widow sold the estate to the Fords five years ago.

Josephine's mother, Mrs. Edsel (Eleanor) Ford, started visiting Seal Harbor as a two-year-old in the 1890s. Her family, prominent Detroiters, came by train and steamer, and stayed at a summer hotel. Edsel and Eleanor eventually built a large home on a hill with a sweeping view of the sea and the mountains, and summered there with their four children.

Just opposite the Edsel Fords, on another high hill, lived Mr. and Mrs. John D. Rockefeller, Jr., with their five boys, including Nelson. The Fords often rode horseback through the sunlit woods of the 51 miles of carriage roads the Rockefellers built on their vast property.

In 1980 I asked Henry Ford II how he felt about his boyhood summers at Seal Harbor. His reply:

"I liked it up there until I was about 14 or 15. Then I felt that I would have liked to have been doing something [else] in the summertime. A couple of summers we had a tutor, and that idea wasn't exactly to my liking because I didn't like to be constrained or to study in the summertime. We rode a lot of horseback up there. I didn't keep it up. But I did a lot of it when I was 12, 13, 14."

Neither Henry II nor his brother, William Clay, now summer in Maine. Their grandparents, Henry and Clara Ford, never did, preferring their Michigan "cottages" in Harbor Beach on Lake Huron and in the sawmill community of Pequaming and in the posh Huron Mountain Club, both on Lake Superior. (Thanks to Mike Skinner, Detroit, Mich., for forwarding *Architectural Digest*'s article.)

King Henry II

A recent *Detroit Free Press* photo feature on Detroit's celebrities correctly mirrors the stature of Henry Ford II vis-à-vis the Motor City's other leaders.

A picture of the celebrities shows Ford, crown on head, scepter in hand, as ruler of the realm, and towering over such lesser lights as GM President Thomas Murphy, UAW President Douglas Fraser, Mayor Coleman Young, automaker John Z. De Lorean, etc. The article offers the following comment:

"In contemplating the nature of celebrity in Detroit, we inevitably find ourselves staring into the shadow of Henry Ford II. There is no other magnifico of comparable radiance in the vicinity ... An Iacocca is nothing without a product to peddle ... Fraser, however enticing his personality during contract negotiations, however flavorful his description of corporate chieftains as 'horses asses,' tends to his labors during the intervals and evokes little interest among the connoisseurs of glamour.

"Murphy's corporation is even larger and more powerful than Henry's, but stripped of his title, he is a mere cipher. It could be argued that he is not much more than that in full regalia, General Motors executives being as interchangeable as the spare parts of their cars.

"But the Fords are our Medici ... (and) Henry Ford serves as a Caesar for our times. Instead of a national state, he has enjoyed the leadership of his own multinational corporation. Finally, in the fullness of his years, he has renounced his powers and padded off into retirement. Diocletian himself, who once ruled over the dominions of Rome and then quit the job, would have envied the ease of Henry's abdication."

Garbageman Awe-Struck

Henry Ford II is so newsworthy in the Detroit area that even his garbageman receives attention in the daily press. The *Detroit Free Press* recently ran a half-page story on Norm Champine, Henry Ford II's garbageman. "Every once in a while," says Norm, "he (Ford) will say, 'Hi, how're you doing?' You feel sort of uncomfortable, but you also feel great."

HFII Lends a Hand

"During the final year of World War II," an Inkster, Mich. woman recently wrote a *Detroit News* columnist, "we lived in the country, were without a car, and couldn't get one for love or money. My husband walked four miles to get to his job at Ford Motor Co. The children walked long distances to get to school.

"Henry Ford II had taken over the company by then. He sent employees bulletins, telling them of his plans, asking for their cooperation and suggestions. We were desperate. I wrote, telling him our problem.

"Months passed. The war ended. Cars were being made again, but there was such a backlog dealers refused to even take orders.

"One day my husband was called into an office at Ford and asked about my letter. They arranged for us to buy one of the very first cars."

HFII: 'I Am Out'

Henry Ford II finds it necessary to continually deny that he'll ever return to active management of the company bearing his name.

"You couldn't pay me enough money, or give me enough things to get me back," he recently told reporters. "I am out." Of the firm's present management, Ford said, "I think they are doing an excellent job, much better than I would if I were still there."

HFII stays active, however. He recently participated in groundbreaking ceremonies for Fairlane Woods, a luxury condominium being built on his grandfather Ford's estate, Fair Lane, by the company's land development subsidiary. He also recently accepted appointment as one of five directors of the new Detroit-Wayne County Port Authority.

"Prince Charming"

Henry Ford II is one of the world's 10 top candidates for title "Prince Charming," according to the December issue of *Harper's Bazaar*. Others are ballet king Mikhail Baryshnikov, screen star Warren Beatty, international jeweler Gianni Bulgari, Prince Charles of Great Britain, tennis champ Jimmy Connors, baseball star Reggie Jackson, movie idol John Travolta, Canadian Prime Minister Pierre Trudeau, and Iranian ambassador Ardeshir Zahedi.

Rapped By Gallagher

HFII recently was described by *Gallagher Presidents' Report* as one of the 10 worst chief executives for his "lack of achievement" in 1978. The *Report*, a confidential letter to chief executives which is sent to about 5,000 major corporations around the country, criticized Ford for his one-man rule and for negative publicity generated by the Ford Company's massive recalls during 1978.

Three Cheers For HFII

Henry Ford II has been acclaimed and criticized for his contributions to Ford Motor Co. over the past 35 years. But without question he has been underpraised for his contribution to his company's overseas operations, which at present are sustaining the firm financially.

Ernest R. Breech, the brilliant executive who helped young Henry reorganize and turn around Ford in the immediate post-World War II era, took little interest in the firm's overseas domain. It thus was left to HFII to provide inspiration, guidance and tangible assistance to foreign subsidiaries.

Ford's leadership has been such that the company's overseas profits more than balanced its North American losses in 1979. Ford of Britain alone posted profits of $572.7 million, and where would the parent firm be today without this kind of a performance from its foreign affiliates?

Consistent Contributor

Henry Ford II has contributed $100,000 annually to the United Jewish Appeal since 1967, according to his close friend, Max Fisher, America's leading Jewish philanthropist.

Ford, who has accompanied Fisher to Israel twice, has consistently championed Israeli and American Jewish interests in the Arab World. Ford products have been boycotted by the Arab League since 1966.

Fisher and Ford maintain homes side by side in Palm Beach, Fla.

Some Enchanted Evening

Can you believe that Henry Ford II's wife, Kathy, didn't recognize her future husband upon first meeting him at a party at Ford's home? 'Tis so, according to a new book, *Marrying Up*, by Joanna T. Steichen, widow of the famed photographer.

The book, aimed at those who wish to marry a rich mate, quotes Kathy as saying, "When I walked in, I noticed this very attractive man and wondered who he was. Later I found out it was my host."

I've always believed that fairy tales can come true, it can happen to you, if you're young at heart. Now I also believe in enchanted evenings and what can happen if you see a stranger across a crowded room.

"I Just Don't Like You"

A great deal has been written about Henry Ford II's recent firing of Ford President Lee Iacocca, and it remains only to be said that Henry's reason for firing Lee - "I just don't like you" - is one of the most honest and refreshing statements since Henry Ford's firing of William S. Knudsen for getting "too big for his britches." The fact is, Iacocca, above left with Henry Ford II, while possessed of great drive and ability, was not the world's most likable guy whether one worked over or under him.

Here's how Henry Ford's wife, Kathy (left), looked across a crowded room in December 1982. Standing with Mrs. Ford is a friend and skilled photographer, who a few seconds later took a picture of Kathy and your commentator.

Death Valley Scotty

One of those who preceded Henry Ford II in saying "never complain, never explain," was Death Valley Scotty. The epitaph over Scotty's grave ends with "Don't complain. Don't explain." Scotty is buried on a hill above his Death Valley castle.

Everybody Said It

The comment, "never complain, never explain," made by Henry Ford II after having been detained for drunken driving in 1975, perhaps was borrowed from the 1939 film, *Ninotchka*, this column dutifully reported in December 1982.

Another possible source of the phrase, according to Frank Robinson, Bellevue, Wash., was former British Prime Minister Benjamin Disraeli. Still another source, says Dr. Iden Hill, Glen Ellyn, Ill., was "Death Valley Scotty," longtime denizen of California's hottest desert. Seems to me that English author Rudyard Kipling also may have used the phrase, and likely others as well. In any event, the comment is handy for anyone caught a dollar short and a day late, to coin another phrase.

Greets Chinese Official

It isn't often that Henry Ford II greets someone who rolls up in a rival company's car. But such a great leap backward occurred when Chinese Vice Premier Teng Hsiao-ping motored up to Ford's assembly plant outside Atlanta in a bulletproof, government-owned Chrysler Imperial. Nonetheless, HFII and President Philip Caldwell graciously greeted America's No. 1 tourist of 1979, then gave him a tour, via golf cart, of the plant.

Bench Cosell

Ford's ex-chairman once asked ABC to bench Howard Cosell, according to Leonard Goldenson, the network's chairman. His request was made after the 1970 launch of "Monday Night Football," cosponsored by the Ford Company. "Leonard," The Deuce is quoted as saying, "take that fella Cosell off the air. It's impossible to watch the game." Goldenson said he put Cosell on probation, but four weeks later heard again from Ford, who had called back to say he had changed his mind about dumping Cosell.

No Frills

In any contest having to do with the simplest business card, Henry Ford II likely would emerge the winner. His card simply says, "Henry Ford II."

Henry II and his wife, Kathy recently bought a home in Palm Beach, and HFII swapped his Michigan driver's license for a Sunshine State license.

Still Tells It As It Is

Although Henry Ford II now seldom speaks in public, he has lost none of the occasional irreverence that once characterized his leadership of the Ford Co.

Recently, after addressing the Executive Dinner Forum of the University of Pennsylvania's Wharton Entrepreneurial Center, he was asked about changes in the way cars are marketed.

"Let me tell you," he replied, "that I don't think that, speaking for Ford Motor Co., that we've made any progress in the sales and marketing end of our business in the last 50 years. We haven't done anything really new. It's the same old monkey business. Now that's got nothing to do with the dealer. Now there has been some progress with the dealer. The dealers are better, much better. But I'm talking about internally, in the company. Now they'll all bite me when they hear this, if they ever do, when I get back. But I'm not getting back too quickly."

Ford added that he stands clear of day-to-day operations of the company, and refused to accept credit for the firm's comeback from losses of $3.3 billion in 1980-82 to a record profit of almost $3 billion in 1984. The magnate, 67, is a company director and chairman of the finance committee.

Asked whether he had read Lee A. Iacocca's book, Ford said, "no," then, after a moment's hesitation, remarked, "I read *Newsweek* (which excerpted portions of the book including some highly critical comments of Iacocca's ex-boss)." Pressed for comment on Iacocca's criticism, Ford observed, "I've never made any response, and I'm not going to start now."

Henry Ford II, sporting a plant cap, shakes hands with employees of Ford's Livonia (Mich.) Transmission Plant. Seated at right is Plant Manager Marvin Craig.

That Old Ford Magic

That old Ford magic cast its spell when Henry Ford II recently visited his company's Livonia (Mich.) Transmission Plant. The visit was HFII's first to a Ford North American factory since his retirement.

Ford caught some employees speechless as he casually strolled into offices, shook hands, and signed autographs. While taking a 2 1/2-mile production line tour in a golf cart-type vehicle, he repeatedly was applauded by workers, many of whom reached out to shake his hand and ask for his signature.

"The adrenaline was flowing," said 19-year-old bullard job setter Robert McCallum. "Word of Mr. Ford's visit spread throughout the plant within minutes, and excitement mounted." McCallum's words were echoed by John Henry Clark. "All of us were extremely excited," he grinned almost disbelievingly. "There was electricity in the air, especially for some of us 'old-timers.' "

Ford's "response was enthusiastic and sincere," said pipe fitter Pat Patterson, vice-president of UAW Local 182. "He smiled and talked and laughed with us. It was absolutely great!"

Plant Manager Marvin Craig perhaps best summed up the 3 1/2-hour visit: "Mr. Ford is, first and foremost, a major image in our company as well as a legend to employees ... The visit was a

56   FORD COUNTRY

unanimous success and deeply appreciated by all of us."

The sense of anticipation, excitement, and awe are reminiscent of Old Henry Ford's plant visits, recollections of which today are voiced in reverential tones by those who merely saw the founder, much less had a word or a handshake with him.

A half-century from now Livonia retirees will similarly savor the day HFII came calling.

Henry II's Homes

This column has reported from time to time on Henry Ford's former homes - in Dearborn, Harbor Beach, Big Bay, and Macon, Mich., Fort Myers, Fla., and Richmond Hill, Ga. But it has not yet commented on Henry Ford II's homes, past and present, and in response to a request will do so now.

HFII and his wife, Cristina, before their separation, maintained a home in Grosse Pointe Farms, Mich., a residence in the English countryside, a townhouse in London, a penthouse at the Carlyle Hotel in New York, a condominium in the Bahamas, and a lodge at a shooting marsh in Canada.

With the exception of the Canadian and Bahama haunts, the residences were, according to court records of the couple's pending divorce case, "sumptuously appointed with museum-piece furniture, exquisite porcelain, and one of the most extensive private collections of Impressionist paintings in the world."

In 1976, Henry sold the marsh property for $2 million, and in the spring of 1977 he also parted with the Carlyle apartment for $330,000. He also sold more than $2 million worth of furnishings from the Grosse Pointe home. HFII now lives a nomadic existence, sometimes sleeping at a cottage behind the Dearborn Inn, in a penthouse at the 800-room Dearborn Hyatt Regency Hotel across from Ford headquarters, or in a suite just off his office. When Cristina is away from Grosse Pointe, he is said to live there too.

Divorce, Ford Style

Detroit's most spectacular divorce case ever - that's the way the Motor City billed the Henry Ford II - Cristina trial - was settled out of court even before it truly got underway in late February. Nobody knows how much money flowed from ex-husband to ex-wife, but estimates range between $5 million and $15 million.

Italian-born Cristina, 49 or so, fought back tears during a televised postsettlement interview, thereby eliciting the sympathy of every female viewer. She continued to profess her love for HFII, while saying that if she knew 15 years ago what she knows now she'd have avoided marriage to the magnate.

Henry, when interviewed, managed that wan smile that he has patented for occasions when, if things aren't good, they aren't altogether bad. He expressed relief that it was all over, and, in line with his philosophy, "you win some, you lose some, and some are rained out," he neither complained nor explained.

One has the feeling that Henry would still receive a standing ovation if introduced to a large gathering of males, as was the case several years ago at a Detroit banquet following his arrest on a drunk driving charge in the company of a beauteous companion.

The man does have charisma, he's a man's man, and in some ways he's like a lot of us except that he's worth umpteen million, less 5 to 15 truly big ones. What do we care if a visible fly or two had landed on him? We like him anyway.

Henry II's House

Detroit area visitors who wish to see how a multimillionaire lives - in this instance, Henry Ford II - can do so merely by driving by the Ford chairman's residence on Lake Shore Drive, Grosse Pointe Farms, which follows the Lake St. Clair shoreline. Henry's home, sans protective fence, wall, or shrubbery, may be photographed from the street, just as this photo was last February 17. Both Henry II's father, Edsel, and grandfather, Old Henry, lived on heavily guarded estates far removed from the public eye.

Hoppin' Mad

Henry Ford II's former Grosse Pointe Farms, Mich. mansion recently was razed to make way for the construction of 18 houses to be sold for $300,000 each.

Shortly before the mansion was demolished, HFII threatened to prosecute a souvenir hunter for pilfering three brass window-heater covers and some marble. "I'm fed up with the way people have taken whatever they want from the mansion," said Henry II. "It's supposed to be all locked up, and if someone breaks in and takes something, that's against the law as far as I'm concerned."

The thief, a 42-year-old General Motors engineer, apologized, saying he had been told that the mansion soon would be torn down and that other people also were taking items. "I don't believe him," The Deuce snapped. "And even if that's true, he still doesn't have the right to go into a private home and steal."

A few days later Ford dropped the charges, without saying why.

The main staircase, above, and dismantled living room, below, of Henry Ford II's Grosse Pointe Farms, Mich. home, shortly before it was razed.

Benson Ford Dies

Editor's note: The item below was written before Benson Ford's death from a heart attack while aboard his yacht on Lake Michigan, near Cheboygan, Mich., on July 27. He suffered his first heart attack in 1957, another in 1969, and was hospitalized in 1974 for treatment of angina.

Occasionally one is asked about Benson Ford - Henry Ford's second grandson and the much-more publicized Henry Ford II's next-eldest brother - specifically, what does he do, what is he like, and how's his health? Benson, 59, is a vice-president of the Ford Company and chairman of its Dealer Policy Board. After attending Princeton for two years, he worked in Ford's experimental garage and purchasing department prior to World War II. He enlisted as a private in the Army in 1942, and rose to a captaincy before being mustered out in 1946. Assigned to Lincoln-Mercury Division, then the Planning Division, he was elected a vice-president of the company in early 1948, and general manager in late 1948. He was named Group Director-Mercury and Special Product Divisions in 1955, and appointed to his present position in 1956. A member of the company's executive, finance, product planning, and design committees, he has been president of the Ford Motor Company Fund - the firm's giving arm - since 1961. He also is chairman of Henry Ford Hospital and a board member of Edison Institute (Henry Ford Museum and Greenfield Village).

If an unkind word has been written or said about Benson, your commentator has yet to read or hear it. Everyone likes him. His career has, of course, been overshadowed by that of his older brother, but he has taken this circumstance in stride and without the slightest evidence of rancor. Benson's health has not been as robust as he might have wished, and has contributed importantly to his lessened pace within the company. Your commentator last saw him at a 75th anniversary celebration in June, at which time he gave a good talk and thoroughly enjoyed mixing with those present. On this occasion, I informed his wife of 38 years, Edith, that the last time I had seen her - except at the funeral of Benson's mother, Eleanor, in October, 1976 - was at the rededication of Fair Lane's famed rose garden in June, 1953. We both recalled that the day was hot and humid; and she asked me how the rose garden looks today. Regretfully, I had to inform her that it is now roseless, although the pavilion remains and the grounds are kept fairly neat by the present owners, the University of Michigan-Dearborn.

Ford Grandson

Benson Ford conferring with an aide in his office.

HFII Ties The Knot

Henry Ford II is news across the length and breadth of this land, so few readers will learn here that he recently took his third bride. She's Kathleen DuRoss; and the couple was wed in a short, civil ceremony in Carson City, Nev.

After saying their "I do's," the 63-year-old Ford and his 40-year-old bride, a widow for 20 years, left for a honeymoon in Europe, where Ford also had business commitments.

Justice of the Peace Thomas Davis, who married the couple, said he had no idea he was to officiate at the Fords' wedding until he recognized the magnate from pictures he had seen of him, and confirmed his impression when he looked at the marriage license.

FORD COUNTRY

"I mentioned that I had a Ford four-wheel-drive pickup," said Davis. "Mr. Ford smiled and said, 'How does it run?' I said I had no complaints, I've had Fords all my life."

The Fords are living in Grosse Pointe Farms, Mich.

Diamonds From Henry

Henry Ford II's wife, Kathleen, had a ready answer to a question asked of her at a posh benefit sponsored by Sotheby's, the world's leading auction house, for New York's Metropolitan Museum of Art.

Did the rubies and diamonds at her neck and ears and on her wrists and fingers come from Sotheby's, as did the jewels of some of the other guests? "No," she replied with a smile, "from Henry."

William C. Ford Elevated

A month after Philip Caldwell replaced Henry Ford II as chairman of Ford Motor Co., HFII's youngest brother, William Clay, 55, was elected vice-chairman of the firm. He likely will occupy this post until a fourth-generation member of the family can work his way to a top position within the company.

William Clay was named a director in 1948 and assigned to the Sales Division in 1949. He headed the Continental Division in the mid-1950s, after which he assumed responsibility for corporate product planning and design. He was elected chairman of the Executive Committee in 1978. In recent years he has devoted much of his time to the Detroit Lions, the Motor City's professional football team.

Memories of Bill

How long has Henry Ford II's brother, William Clay, been with the Ford Company?" asks Jack Martin, Indianapolis, Ind.

Thirty-six years. In the accompanying photo the vice-chairman, right, is being presented the traditional anniversary clock on the occasion of his 35th anniversary with the firm. Making the presentation is Philip Caldwell, who recently retired as company chairman.

William Clay was named as director of the company in 1948, a year before becoming an employee. I first saw Bill - only I didn't call him Bill - in the fall of 1952, when I joined Ford's News Department in Dearborn. Our department was housed in a barrackslike structure in the middle of a cornfield a quarter-mile or so north of the present World Headquarters Building. At the other end of the building, newly vacated by the Henry Ford Trade School, was Special Products Operations, whose engineers and designers, headed by William Clay, were planning the Continental Mark II. An older associate, in pointing out Bill, winked and said, "Now there's a young man who's going to go places in this company!" He was very perceptive: Bill was elected a vice-president the following spring.

But even a Ford vice-president, and one with his name on the building, wasn't immune to Detroit's heat and traffic jams of those years. One sweltering August day in the mid-Fifties, as traffic inched along Detroit's Warren Avenue near Grand River

60 FORD COUNTRY

Avenue, I glanced at the guy in the Ford next to mine. It was Bill, sweating like any other mortal in days of yore. Somehow, the sight of a suffering multimillionaire had a soothing, if not refreshing, effect. Misery does, indeed, love company.

Edsel II Disliked Name

Edsel Bryant Ford II, when younger, hated his first name. "Each night," he said at a recent student press conference, "I wished it were George, Larry or Ralph. I was 16 when I fully accepted it and the pressures that came with being born a Ford."

Asked if he had much support from his father, Henry Ford II, the 32-year-old Ford scion replied, "None. He just said, 'Go get it and don't depend on me.' I tried to work hard to get where I am through my own accomplishments."

Edsel said he and his wife, Cynthia, shop in many stores, including Kmart. He noted that he was a disc jockey during his spare time while a student at Babson College. "I was the only one that gave away a lot of stuff, like Ford Motor key chains. I played a lot of Fifties tunes and reviewed movies."

The only question Edsel ducked related to golf, his favorite sport. He refused to divulge his scores.

Ford in Ford's Future

Edsel Bryant Ford II, Henry Ford II's only son, has launched his career as a product planning analyst in the Ford Company's overseas operations. At this time he's primarily concerned with the company's Australian product mix. The 25-year-old Ford scion says he has but one ambition - to succeed his father as the firm's chairman.

Edsel II Moving Up

In Henry Ford's day, nobody, but nobody knew where he stood within the Ford organization - and that's the way Henry wanted it. Today, the company has 27 grade levels, and almost everyone knows where everyone else stands.

Chairman Henry Ford II's son, Edsel II, 28, who started out at grade five in 1974, attained grade 11-13 on the strength of his last promotion to an assistant manageship in the Boston district sales office of Lincoln-Mercury Division. At grade 11-13, Edsel is entitled to a business card, a telephone with a hold button, the traditional "rug and jug," executive dining room privileges, an assigned parking space, a salary between $32,988 and $46,188 a year, and a personal Christmas card from his father the chairman.

When Edsel gets his next promotion, he'll qualify for window drapes, pictures for his wall (selected form the company catalog), a squawk box for interoffice communications - and a second telephone line to go along with his hold button.

A Not So Instant Replay

Edsel Ford II, top, recently swung an ax on the new Sable car's "light bar" to demonstrate the toughness of polycarbonate plastic. The demonstration emulated a publicity stunt of his great-grandfather, Henry Ford, shown swinging on the plastic trunk lid of a 1940 V-8. Edsel II's swing appears a trifle tentative. It could be that his great-grandfather, a woodcutter in his youth, was more comfortable with an ax in hand.

W.C. Ford, Jr. Aboard

William Clay Ford, Jr., great-grandson of Henry Ford and only son of William Clay Ford, chairman of Ford Motor Co.'s executive committee, recently joined the family firm. He's beginning his career as a product planning analyst in the Advanced Vehicles Development Department.

This position presumably is the first in a series of assignments, already tentatively programmed, which will help prepare the youth for a top executive position within the company.

Ford Forever

Asked recently if he'd ever considered working for a company other than Ford, Edsel Ford II replied, "The problem is the blue oval tattoo on my leg. With that I couldn't very well go to work for Chrysler or anyone else."

Henry Ford II's son, 34, also said that his family comes first with him, then jokingly added that motor racing is next most important, followed by the company. "If there's a race on, I'll find it, and probably nine times out of 10 go to it."

Edsel's current chief interest is the new Thunderbird. "Its style is the wave of the future," said Ford, who is marketing product plans manager for Ford Division.

Edsel II Promoted

Edsel Ford II has been promoted to general marketing manager of the Ford Co.'s Lincoln-Mercury Division. He had been advertising manager of the larger Ford Division.

Edsel's career has been strongly identified with staff functions, as opposed to operations.

Charlotte Praises Father

Ford Motor Company's recent annual meeting lasted a record four hours and fifteen minutes, and featured a bevy of "celebrity" speakers including two antagonistic toward Henry Ford II (Senator Joseph McCarthy's old sidekick, attorney Roy Cohn, and HFII's nephew, Benson Ford, Jr.) and one highly sympathetic to the chairman (eldest daughter, Charlotte

Ford). Charlotte's speech was in the best tradition of the loving daughter, and ran as follows:

"Mr. Chairman, I'm Charlotte Ford. We all know today is your last stockholder meeting as the Chief Executive Officer. I want to say on behalf of the family - and especially our generation - how grateful we are to you for what you have done for the family, the Ford Motor Company, its stockholders, its employees, the city of Detroit and the world in the past 38 years. You are a great human being, generous, loyal, and above all honest. You have understood so many social and political problems and have been in the forefront of so many social changes in our society and our times. We are proud of you and will always be forever grateful for your outstanding contribution."

Father Ford's reply: "Thank you very much, Charlotte, I appreciate that from the bottom of my heart. I love you."

Practical Ford

Charlotte Ford is miffed over New York landlords' rejection of Richard Nixon and Gloria Vanderbilt as tenants. She would have welcomed both had they applied to her Sutton Place (Manhattan) residential building.

Nixon's presence would be "terrific," the practical Charlotte observed, because "there would be a guard in the lobby 24 hours a day. Think of the security."

The heiress, author of the best-selling Charlotte Ford's Book of Modern manners, says she has a solid, old-fashioned Midwestern approach to life. "I clean the house all the time," she maintains. "After the cleaning woman leaves, I clean on my hands and knees, the floors."

Ford Women Write Book

Charlotte and Anne Ford, daughters of Henry Ford II, have written a book for women car buyers, their first assignment from the auto company that bears their name.

The book, according to the company, is part of marketing tactics aimed at women, who buy 39 percent of all new cars. Entitled How to Love the Car in Your Life, the 60-page book is being distributed by dealers. It offers "fresh, new, contemporary views of the world of motoring, including tips on driving." Charlotte is 39; Anne 37.

William Clay Ford, Jr.

"Do you want to run the company?" William Clay Ford, Jr., 29, recently was asked by *Metropolitan Detroit*. "Well, sure," he replied.

"What about Cousin Edsel?"

"We get along fine," he said of Uncle Henry's son. "I think people like to see rivalry there, but it doesn't exist. He's older (37). He seems to like sales and marketing, while I'm production and finance oriented. The company's certainly big enough for both of us. And since it's a publicly held company - hell, neither of us may get it."

Bill recently was named director of commercial vehicle marketing for Ford of Europe, headquartered in England. Holder of a bachelor's degree in history

FORD COUNTRY   **63**

from Princeton and a master's degree in management from MIT, Bill has been with the family firm since 1979, and now is in his ninth position.

He says he didn't decide to join Ford until halfway through Princeton. "Growing up, I really didn't give joining Ford a lot of thought. There was no family pressure." Asked why he studied history, he replied, "I have friends who say, 'What good is a history degree?' But I think there's a danger in specializing too early. Having a broad educational background is imperative." As for the auto business, he declares. "First, I like it. If I didn't, I wouldn't stay here. I like cars, and I like business. I'd hate to be working for a company where you couldn't get excited about the product."

Bill, according to *Metropolitan Detroit*, is highly enthusiastic - a take-charge, straight-ahead guy not prone to agonizing over past decisions or previous mistakes. "I don't look back much," he cheerfully admits. "I'm not reflective. I suppose I should be a little more."

Yet Bill remembers vividly when the first Escort came down the line at the Wayne (Mich.) Assembly Plant, where he was working at the time. When he saw the car, it had yet to be painted, the Ford name yet to be affixed. But the company had a lot riding on the Escort/Lynx. "Let's just say," says the Ford scion, "the significance of that car line was not lost on me."

Before moving to Europe, Bill was a car product development manager. His job took him to Japan for talks with Ford's partner, Mazda. He describes that work as "fun" and "new" because there was no manual to refer to, often no one to turn to for guidance. Bill has taken a few Japanese language classes, and plans to take more. He speaks Spanish. "We're facing both increased foreign competition and cooperation with foreign companies," he observes. "Car companies are becoming more and more international every year."

Anne and Charlotte

Henry Ford's daughters, Anne, second from left, and Charlotte, third from left, confer with Ford Marketing Staff employees while researching their book, How to Love the Car in Your Life.

Distaff Ford

Charlotte Ford spends about three months a year in Southampton, N.Y., while living in Manhattan, according to a recent *Detroit News* article. Among her Long Island neighbors are the likes of Alan Alda, Woody Allen, Howard Cosell, Dustin Hoffman, Mick Jagger, and Cheryl Tiegs.

Charlotte grew up in Grosse Pointe, Mich., but always spent time in Southampton, in an oceanside family compound which once belonged to her mother's parents, the James McDonnells.

A fashion designer, Charlotte recently introduced the Charlotte Ford for Jondel Collection, consisting of 35 "separates" which permit, for example, a jacket and skirt to team as a suit, a jacket to pop over pants for a weekend outfit, or a skirt to accompany a sweater to lunch. In keeping with great-grandfather Henry's auto pricing, Charlottes's collection is sensibly priced - from $32 to $80.

Charlotte says she remains "very close" to her sister, Anne, married to New York TV anchorman Chuck Scarborough, and is "as close as I can be to my brother, Edsel II." She sighs, "he works so hard," and worries, as older sisters often do.

Charlotte has a good head for

business, and it's been said for years - and she's said it too - she'd have a top spot within the Ford hierarchy had she been born a male.

Black Sheep Returns

Benson Ford, Jr., 34, after almost 15 years in California, has returned to Detroit - a city he once renounced - to start his life over.

"He moved to California for the girls and the sunshine," reported the *Detroit Free Press*, "and allied himself with a business partner his family detested. He called his late father a drunk, sued his mother in an attempt to overturn his father's will, and charged his uncles William Clay Ford and Henry Ford II with mismanaging his assets."

"I know what I did," the Ford scion told the *Free Press*. "I took on my family, I took on the whole Ford Motor Co. It was stupid. The worst thing I ever did."

His hair flecked with gray, Benson now walks stiffly, aided by a cane. An auto accident in California more than a year ago left him with a steel plate in his hip and a four-foot scar down his leg. The mustache and the boastful demeanor he once affected are gone.

Benson recently bought his cousin Edsel II's home in Grosse Pointe Farms, Mich., and announced plans to marry Lisa Adams, 30, his girlfriend of five years. Until he can move into his new home this summer, he is living with his sister, Lynn Alandt, in a mansion once owned by his parents. He says he wants to talk with his uncle, Ford Vice-Chairman William Clay Ford, about a job.

"It's going to take some time for the family to accept me," says Benson, "And I understand that I have to prove myself. I have to show them all something. I can't just walk back in here and expect them to forgive me.

Benson Ford, Jr., at lectern, blasting his Uncle Henry and Ford Motor Co. at the firm's 1979 annual meeting in Detroit.

And I don't want them to. I want to show them I'm sincere."

Meantime, Benson is suing his former psychotherapist and business partner, Louis Fuentes, alleging that Fuentes during a 13-year association gained control of more than $10 million worth of his Ford stock and other assets while doling out to him an allowance of

$350 to $500 a week.

"We don't know how much money is gone," says Pierre Heftler, a longtime attorney for the Ford family now representing Benson, Jr. "That's what we're trying to find out."

Benson began to question his relationship with Fuentes last year after crashing his Lincoln Continental into a concrete ditch when returning home from a party. His sister, with whom he had not spoken in a long time, visited him in the hospital. "That was very thoughtful of her," he said. "That was when my mind started changing. I finally decided I'd had it (with Fuentes)."

Benson, Jr. Joins Ford

Benson Ford, Jr., 36, a great-grandson of Henry Ford and nephew of Henry Ford II, has joined the Ford Motor Co. as an owner relations analyst, in the Parts and Service Division in Dearborn.

Benson's father died in 1978, after which the Ford scion fought a court battle against his mother and other family members in an effort to overturn his father's will and gain access to a $7.5 million trust fund established in the will. He also tried unsuccessfully to win a seat on Ford's board of directors.

Two years ago, Benson began to reconcile himself with family members, and since that time has filed suit against his former therapist and mentor, Californian Louis Fuentes. Benson alleges that Fuentes misled him into pouring millions of dollars into bad business deals.

Krishna's Patron

"The Medici of the Krishnas" is the way Swami Visnupada describes Henry Ford's great-grandson, Alfred Brush Ford, who has provided most of the money for a $2.8 million Hare Krishna culture center on Detroit's east side.

Ford has abandoned the shaved head and robes worn by most members of the sect. Asked why, the Ford scion replied that Krishna devotees are not obligated to dress in traditional costume, and added, "I have to look after my fortune."

Henry Ford III

Henry Ford III - the first of Henry Ford II's grandsons to receive the famous name - was born on June 4 in Melbourne, Australia. The baby's father, Edsel Ford II, son of HFII, is assistant managing director of Ford of Australia.

We don't know if the infant has a middle name. But it doesn't matter. He has all the name he needs.

Hare Krishna Cultist

Some of Henry Ford's money now is indirectly supporting the "Hare Krishna" religious cult. Alfred B. Ford, 25, Ford's great-grandson by granddaughter, Josephine Ford, who married a Ford, is a member of the Hare Krishna Consciousness Temple on Detroit's east side.

Ford, now called Ambarish Das, handles the temple's business affairs; before that he was chanting prayers on the streets of downtown Honolulu. Another member of the temple is Walter Reuther's daughter, Elizabeth, 28.

A Ford Prefers A BMW

Nothing personal, Alfred Brush Ford, recently told the press in Melbourne, Australia, but he prefers to drive a BMW.

"I should drive a Ford I suppose," said Ford, a member of the Hare Krishna movement, "but I like the BMWs because they're a good car."

Asked how much he was worth, Ford replied, "It's millions ... a few." Ford, who sometimes dresses in conventional suits, in Australia was attired in Indian garb, complete with a flower garland and the head markings of his sect.

Henry Ford II's nephew has contributed large sums to Hare Krishna, especially toward the renovation of its Detroit temple, the former mansion of Lawrence P. Fisher of the body-builder family.

Dullest Americans

Alfred Brush Ford, great-grandson of Henry Ford, has been named one of the "10 Dullest Americans" by International Dull Folks Unlimited, of Rochester, N.Y.

Of Ford, the tongue-in-cheek organization said. "Alfred, the Ford Motor Co. heir married a fellow Hare Krishna devotee Sharmilla Bhattacharya, and the two mutually pledge to have sex only once a month," and for procreation purposes only.

Topping the list of dull Americans is comedian Rodney Dangerfield. Also included are popcorn king Orville Redenbacher, TV interviewer Barbara Walters, and the Rev. Jerry Falwell.

II

FORD MOTOR COMPANY

Ford Motor Company was just another auto firm in 1903, being one of 15 Michigan enterprises and one of 88 American firms introducing a car that year. But Ford was not to remain commonplace for long. From the outset it could be distinguished from most of the auto class of 1903 - and indeed from many of the established companies in the industry - in that it made money. By 1911 Ford was the world's largest automaker, and its Model T bobbed over the roads of every civilized country on earth.

As cars rolled out and money rolled in, Ford in the teens and Twenties became America's most prestigious business institution. The firm's acclaim did not stem entirely from its size, its wealth, its importance on the economic scene, or even its product, for in 1926 three corporations employed more people than Ford, four showed bigger net profits, seven had higher market valuations, and nine listed greater assets. Of far more importance to Ford's reputation than bricks and mortar and balance sheets were the ideas for which the company stood or with which it was associated. The average citizen was far less likely to think of the Ford Company as a huge profitmaking machine than he was to think of the efficient mass production techniques, enlightened labor policies, and price reductions which had become the firm's hallmarks. Ford's breathtaking Highland Park and River Rouge plants, Ford straddling the globe, Ford in railroading, aviation, and agriculture, Ford on the Great Lakes and the seven seas, Ford in a dozen other pathbreaking spheres - all further convinced people that Henry Ford's company was the prime exemplar of American ingenuity and industry.

During the Great Depression, Ford fell upon hard times, its founder's pace slowed, and the company in some respects became just another troubled industrial giant. The firm's well-publicized World War II performance restored lost luster, and the "New Ford Company," under the guidance of Henry Ford II, rebounded smartly during the postwar era. The company prospered for a solid generation, as the American Dream approached fulfillment and domestic manufacturers held sway with big, powerful cars. But sustained success bred overconfidence, even smugness. The industry, as Henry Ford II later confessed, "took its eye off the ball," and paid a massive price for doing so. Government-mandated vehicle safety, emissions, and fuel economy standards, oil crises, sticker shock, Japan's redefinition of quality, a flood of imports - all took their toll - and contributed to record industrywide losses. Chrysler got the publicity and government bailout, but it was Ford which in 1980-82 lost more money than any company had ever lost before, and survived.

Henry Ford II retired in late 1979, and a new management team headed by Philip Caldwell, Donald E. Petersen, and Harold "Red" Poling spearheaded a comeback unparalleled in U.S. business history. Record profits were reported in 1984, and again in 1986, when the company outearned General Motors for the first time since 1924.

"We'll build this (company) as well as we know how," Henry Ford once told Edsel, "and if we don't use it, somebody will. Anything that is good enough will be used." Henry and Edsel, and Henry II too, built well. Today Ford, in addition to being the world's most profitable automaker, is the second largest auto firm, and the biggest outside its home market. Known to anyone who knew anything in Henry Ford's day, the company is equally well-known today, its brand name and trademark vying with Coca-Cola's as the world's most recognizable.

Today Ford is on a roll, and at a time when GM is not. Moreover, Ford's prospects for future success in the increasingly globalized auto market are most promising. The company strikes many observers as being highly receptive to change, dynamic, exciting. For the first time in decades, there's talk of Ford Division outselling Chevrolet Division, of Ford trucks outselling GM's combined Chevy/GMC truck lines, of Ford being in a position to diminish GM's leadership role. Verily, just thinking about such things is enough to make one positively dizzy, put one in a perfect tizzy, and inspire one to haul out Old Lizzie, although not necessarily in that order. The spin in Lizzie must come first.

Industrial Milestone

The founding of Ford Motor Co. in 1903 is cited as one of the 18 most significant events in U.S. 20th century industrial history in the newly published The *Smithsonian Book of Invention*. The company's first factory, as pictured in the June, 1903 issue of *Cycle and Automobile Trade Journal*, is shown above.

Other industrial events cited in the book's "Invention Time Chart" include the organization of U.S. Steel (1901), the first regularly scheduled U.S. radio broadcast (1920), the first commercial television broadcast (1941), the first flight of a U.S. jet (1942), the introduction of Marki, the first true computer (1944), the first U.S. atomic plant for electrical power (1957), and the opening of the Alaskan pipeline (1977).

Other portions of the time chart relate to significant technological and scientific, as opposed to industrial, advances of the 20th century. To my surprise, the chart makes no reference to the moving assembly line or mass production, much less Ford's identification with the process.

Historic Ford Dates

In the overall scheme of world history, the founding of the Ford Motor Company was quite important, if we may take *The World Almanac and Books of Facts'* word for it. In its section on "Memorable Dates" in world history, from 300 B.C. to the present, the *Almanac* lists only five items under the year 1903. One of them states: "Henry Ford, having withdrawn from the Detroit Automobile Co. in 1901, organized Ford Motor Co." Other items mentioned under 1903 refer to the first auto trip across the U.S., the Wright brothers' first successful flight, the secession of Panama from Colombia, which paved the way for the digging of the Panama Canal, and the

FORD COUNTRY **69**

Chicago Iroquois Theater fire in which 602 people died.

One other Ford-related milestone is mentioned in the *Almanac* - the introduction of the $5.00 day in 1914. Only two other events unrelated to World War I are mentioned under the year 1914; passage of the first ship through the Panama Canal and the meeting of the Second (Communist) International in Brussels. Ford is one of only a handful of business enterprises mentioned in the "Memorable Dates" section, and the only company cited twice.

Report Extolls Heritage

Ford Motor Company's newly released 1977 Annual Report, whose theme is "A 75-Year Perspective," expertly blends Ford history with an accounting of the company's 1977 activities and performance. If this handsome and imaginative report isn't judged to be the best annual report for 1977 - and become a collector's item in the old-car fraternity as well - your commentator will be surprised.

The report's front and back covers show the company's first product, a 1903 Model A, and Henry Ford's first vehicle, the 1896 Quadricycle, plus a Ford Fairmont Futura and Mercury Zephyr Z-7. The first inside page features a statement by Henry Ford II superimposed on a striking picture of a brass Model T. Inside, the report contains pictures and/or sketches of Henry Ford, his first car and first plant, Barney Oldfield and the 999 racing car, the Model T, Fordson tractor, Model A, Ford Trimotor, B-24 bomber, Edsel Ford, 1941 Lincoln Continental, etc., plus reproductions of the company's Articles of Association (Incorporation) and a front page announcing the five-dollar day, as well as pictures of other products, plants, and historical scenes. The text also skillfully ties together history and the contemporary.

Quite apart from its treatment of Ford history, the report provides a detailed and interesting account of Ford's performance during 1977, itself good reading inasmuch as the company had record dollar sales, earnings, and employment this past year.

No company has a more magnificent history than Ford, and it's good to see the firm extol its heritage in its report to shareholders.

Advertising Taboos

Henry Ford had strong beliefs - and taboos - with respect to advertising. During the early V-8 era, he insisted that his company's advertising, irrespective of any claims advanced by rival automakers, not be too "competitive." "Don't exaggerate," the magnate admonished his admen, "the truth is big enough."

Ford would not permit his advertising agency, N.W. Ayer & Son, to describe his cars as the best, the most economical, or the lowest price car (although it could be referred to as the best automobile that the Ford Company had ever made). Other taboos prohibited the agency from making number-of-miles-per-gallon claims for Ford cars; using pictures with people smoking - or even describing the cigarette light as anything more than a "lighter"; or showing white sidewall tires in illustrations of the standard V-8.

Whether because of or despite old Henry's conservatism and taboos, his ad agency consistently won awards for its campaigns.

Brewers Unwelcome

In 1947 Ford and Gillette were permitted to sponsor the first telecasts of baseball's World Series solely because Commissioner A.B. "Happy" Chandler refused to permit a brewer to serve as the sponsor.

Liebmann Breweries, Inc., of Brooklyn, offered organized baseball $100,000 for the series' telecasting rights, $40,000 more than Ford and Gillette combined. But Chandler, moving to high ground, rejected the Liebmann offer with the assertion that "it would not be good public relations for baseball to have the series sponsored by the producer of an alcoholic beverage." The telecasting rights thereupon were sold for $65,000 to "respectable sponsors," Ford and Gillette.

In subsequent years, baseball and other sports' bigwigs have been more than willing to sell time to brewers and every other advertiser not specifically barred by government edict; and never mind the public relations.

Ford Vehicles On Film

Ever notice that more Ford products are cruising, racing, chasing, and being chased in movies and on TV than the motor vehicles of any other auto company?

Ford has, in fact, been supplying cars and trucks to moviemakers for almost 40 years, and today is the only major automotive manufacturing company that makes cars available to producers on a continuing basis.

"Ford gets a bundle of free advertising by supplying cars to studios and producers," says Jack Ellis, manager of Ford's Los Angeles Studio-TV Car Office, "and filmmakers are pleased to have use of our cars because they recognize our leadership in designing distinctively different cars." At present more than 270 current-model Ford cars and trucks are available to studios.

Blimp Advertising

Ford was the first industrial firm to advertise by blimp - in 1946. One side of the dirigible featured the slogan, "There's a Ford in Your Future," the other side the message, "Ford's Out Front." The surplus Navy blimp, shown here at its home base, Dearborn's Ford Airport, hovered over cities and athletic contest for two years. The expenditure for the service - $496,000 - probably was the company's soundest advertising investment during the immediate post-World War II period. (Photo courtesy of the Ford Archives, Henry Ford Museum, Dearborn, Mich.)

Is Loving Ford Enough?

Mary Wells, head of the advertising agency, Wells, Rich and Greene, which recently landed Ford's corporate, Ford Motor Credit Company, Ford Motor Land Development Corporation, and Glass Division accounts, was reported to have clinched the deal by convincing Ford executives that "I can make everyone love Ford, and if they love Ford, they'll buy them." Really?

The fact is, through the 1930s and 1940s, the general public loved Henry Ford and Ford Motor Company, but preferred General Motors products. A Ford-sponsored 1944 survey by pollster Elmo Roper, for example, showed that both Henry Ford and his company had

FORD COUNTRY **71**

a "large reservoir of goodwill. The Ford Motor Company is still, in the minds of most Americans, our No. 1 corporation, the standard of comparison by which other corporations are judged."

Roper also found that Americans thought that Ford had done more to advance industrial progress, had contributed more to the war effort, and had treated its employees better than any other motor car manufacturer. But these findings were outweighed by others, which indicated that "a substantially large number of people would buy an $800 [postwar] car produced by General Motors rather than one produced by Ford." Why? Because, concluded Roper, they valued GM's superior styling and quickness to adopt mechanical improvements.

All this brings to mind one of the first things I heard upon joining General Motors in 1959, after having spent five years with Ford. Then, as in 1944, opinion polls were showing that the public loved Ford more than GM. But sales charts made it very clear that this same public was buying GM cars in greater numbers than Ford products. Looking over the survey results one day, my boss smiled and said, "Let them love Ford all they want - as long as they buy our products." Mary Wells and Ford's management might well ponder this point of view.

Ford In Future Slogan

This typical late 1944 "Ford in Your Future" ad shows a family gathered around a 1946 Ford, and proclaims that new cars "are rolling off the production line in limited numbers." The numbers were limited indeed - only 34,439 Fords in all of 1945. (Photo from the Collections of the Henry Ford Museum and Greenfield Village.)

Ford's 1940's advertising slogan, "There's a Ford in Your Future," is among the "10 All-Time Best Ad Slogans" selected by John O'Toole, ex-chairman of a leading ad agency, Foote, Cone & Belding. The list was published in *Good Housekeeping*'s July edition.

One other auto slogan made the list, "Wouldn't You Really Rather Have a Buick?" Surprisingly, Packard's "Ask the Man Who Owns One" wasn't included.

Also on O'Toole's list: "The Pause That Refreshes" (Coca-Cola); "Does She or Doesn't She?" (Clairol); "Good to the Last Drop" (Maxwell House); "Breakfast of Champions" (Wheaties); "99.44 Percent Pure - It Floats" (Ivory Soap); "When You Care Enough to Send the Very Best" (Hallmark); "We're No. 2 and

The article and illustration which inspired one of Ford's most famous slogans, "There's a Ford in Your Future." The article appeared in the July, 1944 issue of the Ford Times. *(Photo from the Collections of the Henry Ford Museum and Greenfield Village.)*

We Try Harder" (Avis); and "When It Rains, It Pours" (Morton Salt).

During the past three decades the "Future" slogan has given rise to countless variations on its theme, especially when Gerald R. Ford was active in politics. After Ford became vice-president, for example, the *Detroit Free Press* declared that "it is splendid to have another Ford in our Future"; while a *Detroit News* cartoon showed a palm reader telling her client, an elephant labeled GOP, that there's "a Ford in your future." After Ford became President, the *New York Daily News* pictured the Chief Executive looking into a crystal ball under the caption "The Future in Our Ford."

The Ford Company dusted off the slogan for the introductory ad campaign of its 1978 Fairmont model.

75th Anniversary Ideas

The Ford Motor Company will observe its seventy-fifth anniversary in 1978, and, for what it's worth, here are a few gratuitous ideas as to how it might approach this milestone from a public relations standpoint. (I venture to offer these suggestions since I wrote most of the historical news releases for the company's fiftieth anniversary in 1953. These releases also were used for the centennial observance of Ford's birth in 1963).

First of all, in conducting its seventy-fifth anniversary campaign, the company should cloak itself with Henry Ford's identity. It should identify the company with the man just as Bicentennial planners have tied in events with Washington and other founding fathers, as Democrats perennially do with Jefferson, Republicans with Lincoln, and blacks with Martin Luther King, Jr. It's a perfectly respectable propaganda technique; and, among the world's auto companies, only Ford can make it work. Thus the company's promotional effort, especially overseas, might well be keyed to Henry Ford's Company," or "Mr. Ford's Company," rather than the Ford Motor Company.

The seventy-fifth anniversary effort also might be keyed to Henry Ford's vision, for the auto magnate was one of the most visionary men who ever lived - an easily documented fact. The company might also look to some of its old advertising campaigns for ideas, especially the "Famous Ford 'Firsts' " campaign which ran during 1944-45, and was personally directed by Henry Ford. This campaign was institutional inasmuch as the firm had no cars to sell at the time it ran. But today, if revamped, it could serve both institutional and product needs. For the seventy-fifth anniversary, the company might also consider reviving that great old slogan, "Watch the Fords Go By," one of the two most famous in automotive history. Another memorable slogan that might have some application during the anniversary year is "There's a Ford in Your Future."

The company should also get behind the election of Henry Ford to the Hall of Fame for Great Americans at New York University and the Aviation Hall of

FORD COUNTRY **73**

Fame at Dayton, Ohio. Moreover, it should take a financial interest in preserving certain places associated with Henry Ford's memory, especially his Dearborn mansion, Fair Lane, and the Garden City, Mich., "Honeymoon House," which Mrs. Ford designed and for which Henry cut the timber and helped build.

Anniversary Fan Mail

Ford's 75th anniversary has prompted a flood of "fan mail" expressing affection for and interest in the company and its products. Thousands of cards and letters have arrived at Ford World Headquarters from as far away as Russia, Norway, Poland, India, and Central America - and from as near as Detroit.

Typical of the letters was one from a South Carolina woman, who wrote that a news story she had seen on the anniversary reminded her of her father's first car, a Model T. "Oh, how we enjoyed that car," she said. "It was an open car with two seats and a top. We stopped and put up the curtains if it rained. My father chained the car to a sapling at night. You should see that tree now. It's massive."

In sending his congratulations, a Tennessean recalled his days on Ford assembly lines and in Ford dealerships: "I believe the records will show I sold the last Model T (a 1927 four-door sedan) in stock at George Cole Motor Company. This was prior to the introduction of the Model A - and my customer didn't want one of those newfangled Fords."

Ford Innovations

In 1983 Ford Motor Co. observed its 80th anniversary with a modest amount of hoopla. Its monthly employee publication, *Ford World*, ran a brief article on the subject, which highlighted "a steady stream of innovations that demonstrate not only Ford's technological leadership, but also a sense of responsibility." These innovations are cited as follows:

"Introduction of the Model T; announcement of the $5 daily wage; first use of safety glass as standard equipment; first mass-produced V-8 engine; establishment of the Supplemental Unemployment Benefit for hourly employees, and introduction of the 'World Cars,' Escort and Lynx."

Okay. But how about the introduction of the moving assembly line and mass production to the auto industry; building the world's largest auto factories, Highland Park and River Rouge; creation of the industry's first vertically-integrated company; tying of the five-dollar day to price cuts which in turn fostered mass consumption; building of the Model A and V-8; and construction of the world's first plastic car?

Back to the Mines

It's back to the mines, the coal mines, that is, for Ford. The firm has joined with three other companies in developing a huge shaft mine near Pikeville, Ky. When at peak operation in 1977 the mine will supply about 15 percent of Ford's annual coal needs.

Henry Ford owned and operated coal mines in Kentucky and West Virginia from 1920 until the 1940s. During these years the company sold one-quarter of its output to the public, while offering coal and coke to employees at low prices.

Highland Rose Cold Cream

"After my mother died, I went through her belongings and found a small glass jar labeled 'Highland Rose cold cream for the complexion, Ford Motor Co., Detroit, Mich.,' " a Detroiter recently wrote the *Detroit News*. "Can you find out about this jar? I am interested in selling it."

The newspaper went to the fount of Fordiana, the Ford Archives, and Reference Archivist David R. Crippen furnished a plausible answer.

The Ford Motor Co., noted Crippen, operated commissaries for its workers. The first of the stores, opened at the Highland Park Plant in 1919, sold only such items as sugar, flour, and canned goods. Meat was added later, followed by clothing, hardware, shoes, drugs, sundries, and fertilizers. Crippen speculates that Highland Rose cold cream likely was a house brand packaged for Ford by a supplier. Other house brands included coffee, tea, flour, butter, and charcoal.

In addition to its Highland Park commissary, Ford established stores at its River Rouge Plant and 10 additional company locations in Northern Michigan, Kentucky, and West Virginia. The establishments were tolerated by local merchants until they opened their doors to non-Ford employees in 1926. Sharp protests led the company to confine sales to its workers starting in 1927. The stores were phased out by the late 1930s.

Oldest Ford Dealerships

A recent article in the *Stoughton* (Mass.) *Enterprise* reports that Dentch's Stoughton Ford Center claims to be the "oldest Ford dealership in the world." Reader John Sharland, Bridgewater, Mass., who forwarded the article, asks if Dentch's claim is correct.

No. The oldest Ford dealership is Tenvoorde Motor Co., St. Cloud, Minn., appointed in March, 1903. Tenvoorde not only is the oldest Ford dealer, but also the oldest Ford agency with continuous family ownership. Dentch's was founded in 1904, and its ownership changed hands in 1960, when it acquired its present name.

Ford's oldest dealerships with continuous family ownership are located in towns and small cities without exception. They are as follows:

Manley Motor Sales Co., Belvidere, Ill., August, 1906; Harris & Sergeant, Inc., Albion, Pa., October, 1907; Diehl Ford, Bellingham, Wash., November, 1908; Swanson Ford, Ceresco, Neb., April, 1909; Park Motor Co., Fairmont, Minn., April, 1909; Spaulding Automobile Co., Aberdeen, S.D., October, 1909; Jim McKain Ford, Inc., Wexford, Pa., March, 1910; Dils Motor Co., Parkersburg, W.Va., April, 1910; Tiffany Motor Co., Hollister, Calif., April, 1910; Sames Motor Co., Laredo, Tex., June 1910; and Egglefield Bros., Inc., Elizabethtown, N.Y., August, 1910.

Five old Ford dealerships with continuous family ownership have been sold to nonfamily interests or fallen by the wayside during the past eight years, according to Robert J. Bierman, public affairs manager of Ford Motor Co.'s Ford Division, who furnished the above data. They are Curt Sjoberg Ford, Waseca, Minn., July, 1906; Housenick Motor Co., Bloomsburg, Pa., founded in August, 1906; N.B. Wall Motor Co., Sedan, Kan., January, 1907; Langellier Motor Co., Lincoln, Ill., 1907; and Kleeber Motor Sales, Inc., Reedsburg, Wis., May, 1910.

Dealer Antedates Company

A sharp-eyed reader, Jim Petrick, of Madeira, Ohio, observed that this column recently reported that the oldest Ford dealership, Tenvoorde Motor Company, St. Cloud, Minn. was appointed in March, 1903 - three months before the Ford Motor Company was launched. "Did we have a misprint," Petrick asks, "or did Old Hank actually appoint dealers before the company was in operation?"

The answer is in the affirmative. The Ford & Malcomson Company, Ltd., organized in November, 1902, and the predecessor to the Ford Motor Company appointed dealers for the "Fordmobile" prior to the formation of the present-day firm.

Room For All

Shambaugh's Garage, Lafayette, Ind., shown in the accompanying photo as it looked about 1935, is probably the only Ford agency in the country, which has also served as an animal shelter. Shambaugh's was its community's Ford dealer from approximately 1914-27. It sold Buicks from 1916-32, and at the time this photo was taken it was selling Packards and DuPont Paints.

"Shambaugh's was the original Lafayette humane society," writes automotive historian Dave Chambers, of West Lafayette. "During the 1920s a Ford field representative complained to dealer Charles E. Shambaugh about the presence of stray animals within the same area where new Ford Model T cars and TT trucks were being sold and serviced. As a result, some very sharp words were exchanged, as the Shambaughs were noted animal humanitarians. The representative also criticized Shambaugh for wearing greasy coveralls instead of assuming an executive dealer image in a business suit. The field man was escorted to the building exit!

"Note the personal door directly beside the big doors to the service area of the garage," continues Chambers, who supplied this photo. "I am sure that you can envision that Ford field rep rapidly exiting the building with a greasy finger mark on the back of his white collar, and also on the coattail of his suit, as Shambaugh speeded up his departure. You should have heard Charlie's sister, Ethel (the bookkeeper) tell that story as I have so many times."

Dealer Since 1914

A Ford dealer since 1914, North McArthur, of Salina, Kan., recently marked his 80th birthday doing what he has done for more than six decades - selling a car. McArthur joined his father in McArthur and Son, Green, Kan., and has been in Salina since 1936. His son now runs his dealership, and his grandson also is with the firm, making four generations in the business.

Although surveys have shown that seed houses and funeral parlors, symbolic of life and death, are the oldest family-owned enterprises in the country, auto dealerships, off to a late start, seem likely to achieve similar distinction.

Factory Visit Highlight

A visit to the Ford factory in Dearborn once was a highlight of Ford dealers' careers. A 1926 letter from the company's Memphis, Tenn., district sales office to dealers recalls what was on tap for them:

"We will leave from here in a Special Train which will convey us to and from Detroit. All meals en route will be served on special diner. The train will be routed via Chicago ... The program arranged will consist of a trip through the Highland Park and River Rouge plants, lunch at Dearborn, Michigan. This is the home of Mr. Ford, the *Dearborn Independent* (Ford's national weekly newspaper), Ford Broadcasting station, Aeroplane Factory, and new experimental building (Dearborn Engineering Laboratory). Dinner will be served at a hotel at night with appropriate program. Talks will be given by prominent executives of the company and it is possible that Mr. Ford will have a word to say to all of us during our visit."

Henry Ford, as it happened, gave fewer than a score of speeches during his lifetime; so he wouldn't be giving a talk to a group of Memphis dealers. But he might well have mingled with them, inspiring them to renew their efforts to sell the faltering Model T - which at the time was steadily losing ground to the Chevrolet and other low-price cars.

New-Car Black Market

"I've heard that some Ford dealers sold cars in the black market right after World War II," writes Chris Brown, Nashville, Tenn. "Is this true?"

Some did, selling cars for much more than the list price, and without regard to the order in which deposits had been made. The Ford Company between January, 1946 and December, 1948 disfranchised 24 dealers because of what it called "gray market" transactions.

The problem persisted through the launch of Ford's first postwar-styled cars, the '49s, in June, 1948. Within days of the vehicle's introduction, models appeared on used car lots at premiums averaging more than $1,100. By the fall of 1948 new-car buyers could take immediate delivery. The black market evaporated.

Yarns From Yesteryear

"Geo. Holzbaugh Ford on Fort Street and W. Grand Boulevard in Detroit was the world's largest Ford dealer saleswise all through the Thirties," recalls reader Bob Thatcher, Export, Pa., whose father also was a prewar Ford dealer. "Holzbaugh's facility was not on a par with its sales, however; in fact was below a bowling alley.

"Ford's Dearborn sales manager at that time was Harry Mack (a confidant of Harry Bennett, Henry Ford's chief aide)," continues Thatcher. "Mack wanted the world's largest dealership in his territory so he tried to send all Rouge Plant employees looking for new cars out to Holzbaugh's.

"In those days the sales tax on new cars was not paid on each title application," adds Thatcher. "It was paid once or twice a year. Once in a while the state would send in a tax man to go over the books and make sure the tax was paid on each deal. Mr. Holzbaugh was a little remiss in paying the said taxes, and the tax men got him to the tune of $90,000. That was like a million today. He declared bankruptcy, and that was the end of the world's largest Ford dealer in 1940.

"The first '39 Mercury cars' hubcaps were labeled 'Ford-Mercury,' " Thatcher also recalls. "When Old Henry first saw the car, he said, 'That's not a Ford-Mercury. It's a Mercury. I don't want those hubcaps on there.' A big supplier of parts, Lyon's, Inc., of Detroit, was stuck with all those caps that said Ford-Mercury on them."

Ford Brass

"I read recently that since 1979 Ford has reduced the number of officers at the vice-president level and above from 54 to 45," writes Ray Costa, of Los Angeles. "How many officers did the company have in Henry Ford's day?"

In point of fact, Ford Chairman Philip Caldwell said in 1984 that the company had "seven fewer vice-president-or-above level employees than five years ago," without specifying the numbers for either 1979 or 1984.

The number of present-day officers differs greatly from yesteryear, if only because Henry Ford frowned on titles and specific designations of authority. He preferred to indicate certain duties for each of his lieutenants, and to let them develop their own spheres of activity in competition with each other. Consequently, the Ford Co. for years had only a president, vice-president, treasurer, and secretary.

In 1903, the year of the company's founding, John S. Gray was president, Henry Ford, vice-president, Alexander Malcomson, treasurer, and James Couzens, secretary. In 1906, when Malcomson sold his interest in the company, Couzens became treasurer as well as secretary. That same year, when Gray died, Ford became president, John Dodge vice-president. Dodge resigned his vice-presidency in 1913, Couzens taking his place. Couzens resigned as vice-president and treasurer in 1915.

Edsel Ford replaced his father as president in 1918, remaining in that post until his death in 1943. In 1924 the company named two vice-presidents - P.E. "Ed" Martin, first vice-president, who retained the title until his death in 1941, and Edsel's brother-in-law, Ernest C. Kanzler, second vice-president until he left the firm in 1926. The two titles are unique in Ford history.

In 1943, when Henry Ford resumed the presidency, two vice-presidents were elected - Charles E. Sorensen and B.J. Craig, the latter also serving as treasurer. Herman L. Moekle, secretary and assistant treasurer, rounded out the list of officers.

Henry Ford II became vice-president in December, 1943; executive vice-president (the first to hold that title) in April, 1944; and president in September, 1945. After Ernest R. Breech was named executive vice-president in 1946, and began reshaping the company in General Motors' image, Ford began to resemble other firms with respect to the number of its vice-presidents.

Ford Exodus

No auto company, perhaps no company, has furnished more top executives to other firms than Ford.

Ford's leading alumnus today is Lee A. Iacocca, Chrysler's chairman. Other leading alumnus include Gerald Greenwald, Chrysler president; John Naughton, Chrysler vice-president for sales and marketing; John J. Nevin, Firestone chairman; Donald Frey, Bell & Howell chairman; D.R. Beall, Rockwell International president; W. Paul Tippett, AMC chairman; Bennett E. Bidwell, Hertz president; William O. Bourke, Reynolds Metals executive vice-president; and Marvin T. Runyon, Nissan U.S.A. president.

Until recently, ex-Ford men Semon E. "Bunkie" Knudsen, Archie R. McCardell, and J. Paul Bergmoser served as White Motors chairman, International Harvester chairman, and Chrysler president, respectively.

During the 1960s, Ernest R. Breech retired as chairman and subsequently helped rebuild TWA; Robert S. McNamara resigned the presidency to become Secretary of Defense, and later head of the World Bank; and Arjay Miller stepped down as vice-chairman to become dean of Stanford's business school. McNamara and Miller were members of Ford's famed "Whiz Kids," hired by Henry Ford II after World War II. Other Whiz Kids who left the company and filled top jobs elsewhere were Charles B. "Tex" Thornton, chairman of Litton Industries; James O. Wright, president of Federal Mogul; Wilbur Andreson, president of Bekins; and Francis C. Reith, head of Avco's Crosley Division.

Couzen's Legacy

Henry Ford's principal partner, James Couzens, was as hard-boiled as they come.

When Couzens smiled his annual smile, the ice, it was said, broke up on the Great Lakes. Once, when a Detroit newspaper published one of the Ford jokes that was sweeping the country, Couzens canceled advertising in the paper, insisted that the offending reporter be fired, and wrote the editor, "Sir: I hereby forbid you ever again to mention the name of the Ford Motor Company in your publication."

Yet Couzens was a great philanthropist, and in 1929 topped a long series of gifts with a donation of $10 million to establish the Children's Fund of Michigan. Characteristically, he arranged that all of the money should be put to work at once rather than holding back funds to perpetuate the organization. All in all, Couzens gave more than $30 million to charitable works.

Although there is no Couzens Foundation, as there are Ford, Rockefeller, and Carnegie foundations, one of the industrialist's philanthropic entities survives to this day - Oakland Housing, Inc., set up in 1935 to provide good housing for people of moderate incomes.

This foundation was established with a grant of $500,000 from Couzens and $300,000 from the Federal Emergency Relief Commission. The organization's original development was Westacres, a community of 150 small concrete block homes on one-acre lots in now-posh West Bloomfield Township, north of Detroit.

After 45 years, Westacres is regarded as an outstanding success in community planning. The large lots create a parklike atmosphere. The houses, which originally sold for $4,400, now sell for more than $100,000.

Oakland Housing is overseen by a blue-ribbon board of directors, chaired by Couzen's grandson, Frank Couzens, Jr., executive vice-president of Manufacturers National Bank of Detroit. The foundation recently authorized the construction of 20 additional houses, which will sell for $63,000 to $65,000 and be financed at interest rates ranging from 3 to 7 percent. James Couzens, who could squeeze a dollar as hard as any man, would like those rates.

Old Dealership Office

Keith Ashley, ex-president of Ford & Mercury Restorers Club, is well on his way toward decorating his study as an old Ford dealership's office, as this photo attests. In addition to the roll-top desk, candlestick phone, ringer box (top of desk), and pictures of Henry Ford and woodies, Keith, a self-avowed "woodie nut," plans to add to his office a Ford script wall clock, a glass front bookcase for display of a complete collection of chassis and body catalogs and service bulletins, and either a glass showcase or wall shelves on which accessories and brochures can be stored. Keith's object is "merely to have visible the items which I enjoy looking at," not to restore his study as an authentic dealership office. The roll-top desk once belonged to the Lansing, Mich., postmaster. When disassembling it for minor repairs, Keith half expected to find "some of the letters Uncle Sam is accused of not delivering." But he found only one blank empty envelope.

Wills Marker

A commemorative marker on C.H. Wills & Co., founded by C. Harold Wills, one of Henry Ford's key assistants, was dedicated in Marysville, Mich. on August, 19, 1984. The marker, erected by the State of Michigan, Michigan History Division, reads as follows:

C.H. Wills & Company

"C. Harold Wills (1878-1940) began working as a draftsman for Henry Ford in 1902. When the Ford Motor Company was organized in 1903, Wills was its chief engineer and metallurgist. He designed every Ford car until he resigned in 1919. Deciding to manufacture his own car, Wills selected Marysville, a hamlet of 200 on the banks of the St. Clair River, as the site for C.H. Wills & Company. In 1921 the first overhead-cam V-8 Wills-Sainte Claire was produced. Remembered for its Flying Gray Goose radiator emblem, it utilized strong, lightweight

C. Harold Wills as a young executive. (From the Collections of the Henry Ford Museum and Greenfield Village)

An aerial view of C.H. Wills & Co. Marysville, Mich. plant (dark building in foreground), now part of a much larger Chrysler factory. Lake Huron appears at upper left.

molybdenum steel and was the first car to have back-up lights. Hydraulic brakes, balloon tires and a six-cylinder engine were added before the factory closed in 1926 having produced 14,000 cars. The property was purchased by the Chrysler Corporation in 1935."

Chrysler continues to operate the former Wills plant, which, along with Wills' former Detroit residence, was the subject of a photo feature in *Cars & Parts*' May, 1974 issue.

Wills, as the marker's text states, was an important figure in Ford history. The *Ford Times* in 1908 gave him equal credit with Henry Ford for having designed and built the famed 999 racing car, while noting that he "directs the entire working of the manufacturing department." Three years later the magazine placed Ford's and Wills's photographs side by side, over the caption, "Mr. Henry Ford and Mr. C.H. Wills, the two men who have developed the Ford car."

Wills left the Ford Co. in the spring of 1919 to build his own vehicle. "It is my fault," Henry Ford said of Wills's departure and that of John R. Lee, who joined Wills in his new venture. "They are very able men, and you have got to keep something in sight ahead of men of that type. I wasn't able to do it, and they can't be blamed for going into it (the automotive business) for themselves." In his final settlement with Ford Motor, Wills, who from the outset had received a part of Henry Ford's dividends, pocketed $1,592,128.39.

Gift to Library

Mrs. Charles E. Sorensen, widow of Henry Ford's ex-manufacturing boss, has given a jewel cabinet with an appraised value of $20,000 to the Detroit Public Library's National Automotive History Collection. Once owned by a 19th century Russian czar, the cabinet was presented to Sorensen by Joseph Stalin in recognition of his assistance in setting up an auto factory in the Soviet Union.

Clarence W. Avery as he appeared about 1944.

Clarence W. Avery

Among the 29 nominees for election this year to the Automotive Hall of Fame in Midland, Mich. is a man whose name should catch the eye of many a judge - Clarence W. Avery, who may have been more responsible for developing the moving assembly line than anyone else. Whether Avery will be one of the five persons inducted into the prestigious hall in October, remains to be seen. But if he isn't named in 1985, he should be next year, or the next.

A number of the Ford Co.'s Highland Park, Mich. plant executives helped develop the moving assembly line, including, in addition to Avery, Henry Ford, Charles E. Sorensen, P.E. "Ed" Martin, and William C. Klann. But of the group, Avery had the broadest grasp of the subject and showed the most intelligent initiative. Quiet and thoughtful, he had studied at the University of Michigan before becoming first teacher and then supervisor of manual training at the Detroit University School. One of his pupils was Ford's son, Edsel, who admired Avery's grasp of mechanical theory and vision, and introduced him to his father early in 1912. The 30-year-old Avery joined the Ford Co., where he gained a rapid knowledge of machine tools and technological processes. He also read widely, knew the latest European and American advances in engineering, and kept in touch with the ideas of men like Frederick W. Taylor.

In Avery's 15 years with Ford he was to rise to be foreman, superintendent, and chief development engineer. "Among us all," wrote one of the experimental staff, "he was known as pushing the assembly line."

Avery stayed with Ford until 1927, when he joined the Murray Corp., a leading auto industry bodybuilder, as chief engineering and manufacturing manager. A year later he was named Murray's president, in 1930 its chairman, which post he retained until his death in 1949.

Avery was one of the few important figures of Henry Ford's day who left the company with the warm friendship and admiration of the "old man." "I want you to stay," Ford reportedly told Avery, "but you have made up your mind to find self expression elsewhere, and I do not blame you a bit. I will help you in any way I can. I will never feel that you have definitely left me, but always that you are coming back." Years later, when Ford gave a dinner to veteran employees, the only invitee not on the payroll was Avery. Avery's firm, for as long as Ford lived, received large orders from the automaker.

Avery also was widely respected for his enlightened approach to labor-management relations. Thanks to him, Murray was one of the first large firms to address employee grievances in a formal manner. In his day most industrial firms, including Ford, prohibited smoking on the job. Avery permitted it. Not having to sneak cigarettes, workers, it was reported, smoked less, and productivity climbed.

As the above indicates, I'm one Automotive Hall of Fame judge who voted for Avery's election.

Massive Mausoleum

"I've heard that Henry Ford's business manager, James Couzens, was a tightwad, yet has one of the biggest tombs in Detroit," writes James Buckman, of Akron, Ohio. "True or false?"

Couzens' mausoleum, above, is the third largest in the Detroit area. It is located in Woodlawn Cemetery, on Woodward Ave. below Eight Mile Rd. across from the state fairgrounds. It also has the best view in Woodlawn, for whatever that's worth.

Harry Bennett

Manly Motowner

Detroit always has been, and remains, a man's town, according to a recent *Detroit News* article, which cites Henry Ford's chief aide, Harry Bennett as one of Motown's three "most manly men of the past" (others being city founder Antoine de la Mothe Cadillac and ex-Teamster boss Jimmy Hoffa).

Bennett, the article states, "was discharged from the Navy for brawling. He went on to become Henry Ford's pistol-packing right-hand henchman and guard. He was introduced to Ford by New York columnist Arthur Brisbane. 'Can you shoot?' was reportedly the first preemployment question. Of course he could. "Bennett," the article adds, "rose to head the security guard contingent for Ford's Rouge Plant, and was the leader of the infamous gang of union busting thugs who beat union organizers in the famous Battle of the Overpass in 1937. Quite a Man." (Photo from the Collections of Henry Ford Museum and Greenfield Village.)

Bennett Castle Sold

The Ann Arbor, Mich. castle built by Henry Ford and his chief aide, Harry Bennett, for Bennett's occupancy, recently exchanged hands.

Seller was the estate of the late Mrs. Harold Stark, Sr., who, with her husband, bought the property from Bennett in 1948. Mrs. Stark's son, Harold, Jr., and his family leased the castle the last dozen years. Buyer is Terrence Liddy, a suburban Chicagoan who recently moved to Ann Arbor to work for KMS Industries, a high-tech engineering firm.

Henry Ford phoned the castle at 7:30 almost every weekday morning during the 1930s and early 1940s to instruct Bennett as to when and where the two would rendezvous that day.

Bennett sold the castle following his move to Desert Hot Springs, Calif. He died in San Jose, Calif. in 1979. In time his former home gained a reputation as one of the most bizarre houses in Michigan, if not the country. Dr. Frankenstein would have loved it. Alfred Hitchcock could have filmed in it with few alterations.

The castle was first written up by a journalist - your commentator - in 1972. Complete with towers, tunnels, spiral staircases, "switch" steps, secret doors and panels, hidden rooms, a "Roman bath," a lion and tiger den, and all of the electronic and mechanical security equipment that could be dreamed up a half-century ago, the castle mirrored its first occupant, one of the more dramatic, picaresque, and ingenious characters in American history.

Daddy's Dilemma

Harry Bennett, usually had little trouble handling the dirty and other work assigned him by his boss. But Bennett was no different than many another father when it came to his four daughters, one of whom, Gertrude, eloped to her father's consternation.

An old, undated clipping, passed on to this column by Bennett researcher Tom DeWald, tells of Trudy, 17, running away to Auburn, Ind., to marry a 21-year-old amateur drummer and clog dancer, Russell Hughes.

Tough guy Bennett broke down when told of his daughter's marriage. "Leave me alone for a little while," he begged reporters. "Trudy is only a baby. If she had told us, she would have saved us a lot of worry and the authorities a lot of trouble." Bennett had refused to believe that his daughter could have eloped. He thought she had been kidnapped and put Ford detectives, G-men and Michigan state police on the trail.

"Trudy always did what she wanted and told me to go to hell," he acknowledged, "but she never kept anything from me." Friends of the girl revealed, however, that Trudy had been seeing Hughes for some months without her family's knowledge. An enterprising reporter uncovered the marriage license.

After regaining his composure, Bennett quipped, "I hope the guy has a job and can support her. They're on their own now."

Arjay Miller in 1967, when Ford's president.

Last Of The "Whiz Kids"

Ford's "whiz kid" era recently drew to a close with the retirement from Ford's board of directors of Arjay Miller, one of 10 Army Air Corps officers who joined the company en masse in early 1946. Six of the officers became Ford vice-presidents, two presidents. Three went on to chief executive officerships at other firms.

Miller, 70 served as Ford's president from 1963-68, then briefly as vice-chairman. Dean of Stanford University's Graduate School of Business from 1969-70, he built that institution into one of the leading schools of its kind. Upon resigning, he observed that "a man ought to be repotted every 10 years." He continues to live near the Stanford campus.

During the "whiz kids" probationary period, they asked innumerable questions, earning the name "quiz kids," later changed to "whiz kids." Their leader was Charles B. "Tex" Thornton, later head of Litton

Industries. Their best-known member was Robert S. McNamara, who, shortly after being named Ford's president in 1960, became President Kennedy's Secretary of Defense, and later president of the World Bank.

Ernest R. Breech Honored

The late Ernest R. Breech, the man generally and correctly credited with having "turned around" Ford Motor Co. in the immediate post-World War II era, is one of two 1980 inductees into the Automotive Organization Team's Automotive Hall of Fame in Midland, Mich.

Breech, a General Motors executive, joined Ford in August 1946. He quickly hired several key GM executives and reorganized Ford in the image of his ex-employer.

Serving first as executive vice-president of Ford, Breech was promoted to the chairmanship in 1955. He retired in 1960, feeling that his work at Ford was done and that he needed a change. After leaving Ford, he helped to reorganize and revive ailing Trans World Airlines.

Your commentator, as a member of Ford's News Department in the early and mid-1950s, did some writing for Breech. The executive was a taskmaster, and, in the mold of Iacocca, a trifle vain (at one point in his career he even retained a public relations firm to publicize his talents). But by anybody's reckoning, he must be ranked as one of the most capable business administrators in U.S. history.

Breech in 1960 financed the construction of the Breech School of Business Administration at his alma mater, Drury College, Springfield, Mo. He died at the age of 81 in 1978.

Myth Perpetuated

The statement, "The car (VW's Beetle) is not worth a damn," attributed to Ford Executive Vice-President Ernest R. Breech, rapidly is taking its place alongside the myth that all Model Ts were painted black.

The attribution appears anew in a book, *David Frost's Book of the World's Worst Decisions*, by the television commentator and his coauthor, Michael Deakin. Breech, according to the book, sized up the Beetle in 1948, believed that it would fail, and so advised Henry Ford II.

Breech categorically denied the statement in his 1968 biography, *Ernie Breech: The Story of His Remarkable Career at General Motors, Ford, and TWA*, by J. Mel Hickerson. He acknowledged that Ford considered buying VW in 1948, but added that ownership of the German firm was in such dispute that no American company could have acquired it at that time.

Ernest R. Breech, left, and Henry Ford II in the late 1950s pose at Ford Motor Co.'s World Headquarters Building in Dearborn. Breech insists that he didn't predict failure for Volkswagen's Beetle. The picture, aside from showing the company's two top men, also reveals a trait of every company executive photo: the Boss is out front. Although Breech was Ford's chairman between 1955-60, Henry II was chief executive officer, as well as president.

Iacocca Most Admired

Lee Iacocca, recently was named the most respected business executive in America in a Gallup poll conducted on behalf of the *Wall Street Journal*.

Twenty-seven percent of those surveyed named Iacocca as the executive they most admired. More than half of the respondents didn't cite anybody as being worthy of admiration. Iacocca was selected because he helped rescue Chrysler and his exposure on television commercials. Frank Carey, chairman of IBM, placed second in the balloting.

"Misery loves company," said Iacocca upon being notified of the honor. "If you had taken this sample when I was at Ford making a million and a half a year and I was a fat cat, do you think they'd admire and respect me? Admiration goes up directly proportional to the adversity and the ability to deal with it."

The Man Who Never Was

"What does the man who fired him at Ford think of Lee Iacocca's amazing success in turning around Chrysler, which just earned him *Advertising Age*'s Adman of the Year honors and the *Hammond* (Ind.) *Times*' endorsement for President of the U.S.?" asks *Detroit Free Press* columnist Bob Talbert.

Henry Ford II reads a statement at a Ford press conference as his right-hand man, Lee Iacocca, holding cigar, listens. HFII later would say he didn't like Iacocca, without spelling out the reasons. "Maybe," said one wag, upon being shown this picture, "he didn't like Lee's cigar."

The answer, according to Talbert: "He has just ignored it all for the past five years, never mentioning Iacocca's name in public or private, and avoiding all same time appearances professionally or socially. 'He even refused to read any article, pro or con, about Iacocca,' says an intimate. 'It's as if Iacocca no longer existed.'"

It's untrue that Henry Ford II hasn't mentioned Iacocca's name in public the past five years. He certainly did so when interviewed by TV's Barbara Walters in 1980, repeating what he had said at the time of Iacocca's dismissal - that he didn't think Iacocca was the right man to succeed him as company chairman, while refusing to say why.

Iacocca on HFII

Lee Iacocca's forthcoming autobiography will devote a "fair amount of space to Henry Ford II and the way he fired Iacocca from Ford Motor Co.'s presidency in 1978," according to Bill Novak, of Boston, who's collaborating with the Chrysler chairman on the book.

"That's something that Lee has never spoken much about," adds Novak. "He's been very discreet, but he figures it's now time to tell the story." The book, tentatively entitled *Iacocca*, is scheduled for November publication by Bantam Books.

Lee isn't waiting for his

FORD COUNTRY 85

autobiography to appear to blast HFII, however. In a January 29 "NBC Reports" documentary, "Iacocca: An American Profile," he declared of his firing by HFII, "That's something I won't forgive the bastard for."

Raging on, Iacocca said, "I told my kids, 'Don't get mad. Get even' ... I did it in the marketplace. I wounded him badly. It took five years, I could have spilled my guts, and maybe felt good inside if I'd done it in five minutes, but then what have I proved?"

Earlier in the program, Iacocca, the son of Italian immigrants, expressed bitterness toward the Ford family and its wealth.

"I knew how to make money for the company," he said ... [but] "the Ford family practiced the divine right of kings. They were a cut above even WASPS. I mean they wouldn't even socialize with you. You could produce money for 'em, but you weren't about to hobnob with 'em. It never bothered me that much, but I knew I had to scratch for what I got. Nobody was gonna say, 'There's a nice Italian boy, I'd like to take care of him.' "

NBC's profile, hosted by Tom Brokaw, was presented opposite CBS' popular "60 Minutes." The program was well-watched in Detroit, but finished dead last in Nielsen's TV ratings nationwide.

Lee's Billboards

A half-dozen huge billboards have been inviting Michigan motorists to buy Lee A. Iacocca's best-selling book, *Iacocca: An Autobiography*.

"Michigan is a motor state, and this is a book about a motor magnate," said Stuart Applebaum, vice-president of the book's publisher, Bantam Books. "So what more appropriate (advertising) vehicle than one that's seen by motorists on the freeway?"

Three of the billboards are located in Lansing, two in Jackson, and one near Detroit's Metro Airport. The signs were designed by Bantam, and financed by Southern Michigan News Co., a Lansing-based book and magazine wholesale agency.

Getting Even With HFII

Lee Iacocca was given $4 million worth of Chrysler stock to "get even" with Henry Ford II, according to Douglas A. Fraser, ex-UAW president and a former Chrysler director.

In the February issue of *American Heritage*, Fraser is quoted as follows:

"At one of the last Chrysler board meetings I attended, they fixed up this deal for Lee Iacocca. They gave him 150,000 shares at that day's price - I figure it was a cool four million dollars or so. Now he's not in the room when

86 FORD COUNTRY

Lee A. Iacocca, left, and Douglas A. Fraser.

this is discussed. So I get into an argument with these guys on the board about the values in society. That money is I don't know how many times more than I made in 50 years of work, and he makes it in five minutes. In addition to the money, I said, it's the perception of what the workers feel out there, and the general public.

"When I walked out of the board meeting, the first guy I run into is Lee. I told him what I said, and he sort of brushed it off and says, 'Well, I'm not going to get any of it anyway, the kids'll get it.' When I sat down to lunch, I was still mad, and another board member came up to me and said, 'Don't be upset, Doug. Wouldn't you like to see the look on Henry Ford's face when he reads about this tomorrow?' And lightning strikes. This has nothing to do with money - it's let's get even, show Ford that I'm going to be the richest S.O.B. in the auto industry."

Rumor Mill

Rumors about Henry Ford II, as well as his grandfather, have long abounded in Detroit. Latest rumor about HFII to surface in the Motor City also concerns Philip Caldwell, the Ford Co.'s chairman.

Caldwell, so the story goes, expressed an interest in having an oil painting of himself done up for the 12th floor (executive suite) lobby of the firm's headquarters building. To this point only portraits of the Ford family grace the lobby's walls.

Caldwell's proposal, it's said, was vetoed by Henry II at which time The Deuce reportedly said, "I don't like the idea," much as he is said to have told Lee Iacocca, "I don't like you."

The rumor is denied by Walter Hayes, Ford's executive vice-president for public affairs, who probably is closer to HFII than any other Ford executive. "People have been calling me about this," said Hayes, "and it's absolute nonsense; one of those rumors that starts in a pub on Friday and turns up as fact the next Monday morning. There is no oil painting of Caldwell that I know of. But I did have a blown-up picture of him in my office for a while. Maybe that's how this rumor got going."

Nance At Ford

"Is it true that Ford Motor Co. wasn't very happy with Packard's last president, James J. Nance, who bossed the Mercury, Edsel, and Lincoln Division in the late fifties?" inquires William Koerts, St. Louis.

It's true. Nance was fired. In addition to being a disappointment to management, he was looked upon as a tyrant to those who worked for him.

By happenstance, I telephoned a friend at M-E-L Division on the day in 1959 when Nance was dismissed. My friend, still a Ford public relations executive, and his associates obviously were celebrating. I asked what was going on. He replied, "Jim Nance has just been canned. We've declared a holiday, broken out the champagne, and are having a party."

After leaving Ford, Nance joined Central National Bank of Cleveland. He died in July, 1984 at his summer home in Bellaire, Mich.

Ford Chiefs

Ford President Philip Caldwell, left, and Henry Ford II at the company's annual meeting in 1979. Caldwell served as company chairman from 1980-85.

Historic Structures

Eight of Ford Motor Company's Michigan plants and buildings are cited in an inventory of historic engineering and industrial sites newly published by the National Park Service's Office of Archeology and Historic Preservation. The structures (with years built in parenthesis) are:

Ford Engineering Laboratory, Oakwood Boulevard, Dearborn (1924); Highland Park Plant, 15050 Woodward Avenue, Highland Park, (1909-14); Highland Park Sales and Service Building, 15050 Woodward Avenue, Highland Park (1920); Piquette Plant, 411 Piquette Street at Beaubien, Detroit (1904); River Rouge Plant, Dearborn (1917); River Rouge Press Shop (1938); River Rouge Glass Plant (1925); River Rouge Tire Plant (1938).

The inventory also lists the reinforced concrete arches built in 1926-27 by Henry Ford to electrify his Detroit, Toledo & Ironton Railroad between Dearborn and Taylor, as well as a bridge-dam structure built for the railroad by the auto king at Flat Rock in 1928. More Ford landmarks are cited in the survey than those of any other manufacturing company.

New Use For Guest Center

Ford's former Guest Center, above, departure point for Rouge Plant tours from the time it was opened in 1974 until discontinuance of the tours in 1980, is being converted into a service training center. The company halted the tours because of financial reverses, implying at the time that visits would be resumed upon a return to profitability. But conversion of the center into a training facility seems to signal a death knell for the tours.

Triple E Building

One of the least known but most historically significant of the Ford Company's present-day structures is the Triple E (Engine and Electrical Engineering) Building, located behind the Henry Ford Museum. This 51-year-old building was the principal center for the design of the Model A and subsequent Ford vehicles. On the plaza in front of the building, on May 26, 1927, Henry and Edsel Ford drove and posed with Henry's first car, the 1896 "quadricycle," and the fifteen millionth Model T. Both of these cars now are in the Henry Ford Room of the Henry Ford Museum. The Triple E Building is not open to visitors, but tourists may drive onto the plaza and around the structure. Carved into the front of the building are the names of Ford's friends, Thomas Edison, botanist Luther Burbank, naturalist John Burroughs, and other inventors and scientists whom Ford admired.

Founding Site

A State of Michigan historical marker has been installed in downtown Detroit on the site where the Ford Motor Co. was founded in 1903. The marker was to have been installed as part of the company's 75th anniversary observance in 1978, but placement was delayed until the Hart Plaza, which now encompasses the site, was fully landscaped. The plaza fronts the Detroit River just west of the Renaissance Center, the huge hotel/office/shopping complex inspired by Henry Ford II. The marker's text reads as follows:

"Ford Motor Company was incorporated as an automobile manufacturer on June 16, 1903. The articles of incorporation were drawn up and signed in the office of Alexander Y. Malcomson, who operated a coal yard once located on this site. Henry Ford gave the company its name and designed the first product, the 1903 Model A. The purpose of the company was to manufacture and sell motor cars and related parts. In addition to Ford and Malcomson, the original stockholders included other figures important in the history of Detroit: John S. Gray, John F. Dodge, Horace E. Dodge, Albert Strelow, Vernon C. Fry, Charles H. Bennett, Horace H. Rackham, John W. Anderson, James Couzens and Charles J. Woodall. Over

FORD COUNTRY 89

the past seventy-five years the Ford Motor Company has become one of the leading auto producers of the world."

Ford Old-Timers Club

Former Ford employees, many of them ex-executives, remain in touch with each other through an organization called the Ford Old Timers Club. The club, which has 1,335 members, holds annual meetings in Dearborn and Fort Lauderdale, Fla. To be eligible for membership one must have been a Ford employee prior to 1959.

The club's oldest members, in terms of hire dates, are Richard Kroll, Royal Oak, Mich., 1905; Orlie W. Dawson, New Port Richey, Fla. and James F. Miller, Saginaw, Mich., 1908; George Russell, Garden City, Mich. and Fred C. Young, Harper Woods, Mich. 1909; and Fred Easterby, Detroit and Allen E. Hawke, Clarkston, Mich., 1911.

Your commentator, who was employed as editor of employee publications at Ford's St. Louis Lincoln-Mercury Plant in 1950, thus has some catching up to do.

Grime Is Good

Ford's oldest retiree now appears to be 100-year-old Nazar Malkasian, who worked in the Rouge Foundry from 1922-51.

Runner-up in the longevity sweepstakes, according to *Ford World*, a company publication, is Louis V. Plant, 99, who retired as a Rouge crane operator in 1952.

Who says the Rouge's grimy air isn't good for one's health?

Edsel His Helper

Ford Motor Co.'s first "50-year-man," Ernie Grimshaw, Greenville, Mich., began working for the firm at age 17 in 1906, and his helper was none other than Henry Ford's son, Edsel.

Grimshaw was a 17-year-old messenger and one of his duties was sorting the mail. "It was interesting work," he recalls, "and I had a young helper. Thirteen-year-old Edsel Ford would come over and help me. He used to get quite a kick out of it. To think he started with Ford at a younger age than I."

After working at Ford's Piquette, Highland Park, and Rouge plants, and teaching at Henry Ford Trade School, Grimshaw became the first 50-year-man to retire from Ford. Now in his 90s, he paints watercolors.

Debunking Genius

Story-gets-better-every-time department: Bob Grant, 96, of Lapeer, Mich., recently told a newspaper reporter that Henry Ford's employees, not Ford, deserve credit for innovations attributed to the auto king.

Grant claims to have worked in the Ford Company's experimental room between 1901-07. "Worlds and worlds of people today think that Henry Ford is some kind of little God or something," he says. "Well, he's not."

Grant maintains that, while at Ford, he developed the first one-piece camshaft made in the U.S. "Once or twice Henry Ford asked me to do something for him," continues Grant, "but I always told him I wouldn't do anything for you." Still, according to Grant, Ford did not fire him. "He knew I was just too valuable. As for him, he was just a miserable old skunk" (in 1905 Ford was 42, Grant 25). Grant says that he voluntarily left Ford. "As a matter of fact," he adds, "I quit six times before I ever got away." Afterwards, Grant worked at various places in the auto industry, retiring from Lapeer Metal Products in 1945.

One of the good things about being 96, it occurs to your commentator, is that one has almost outlived everybody who can contradict his claims. My own World War II stories get better every year, and by the time I'm 96, I'll be claiming that Admirals Halsey and Nimitz issued orders only after checking with me.

As for Grant, Fact No. 1 is that he never went to work for Henry Ford and the Ford Motor Company in 1901; there was no Ford Company until 1903. Fact No. 2 is that nobody, but nobody, sassed Henry Ford and got away with it. Those who got too big for their britches, and there were some truly big men who outgrew them, were fired. Fact No. 3, however, is that Henry Ford did take credit for innovations developed by others; but, and this is a big but, for years all of the experimental work at Ford was done under the boss's close supervision.

Remembering Jimmy

"I have a photograph which someone found at a yard sale," writes reader Dwight Fackender, of Rockwood, Mich. "It is of a 1939 Ford and a man and woman are standing in front of it. It has tags on it from nine states, and they all read 27,000,000. The picture is hand signed - "To Jimmy Rooney, with best wishes. Sincerely yours, Marilyn Meseke, 'Miss America.' "Do you know who he was and was she really Miss America?"

Jimmy Rooney? I remember him well, having worked with him in Ford's Rotunda Building, the company's "gateway to the Rouge," while a member of Ford's Public Relations Staff in the 1950s. Rooney had joined Ford in 1921, and previously was a vaudeville performer and a baseball player with the Toledo Mudhens.

In 1939, Jimmy drove Ford number 27,000,000 (made in February at the company's Richmond, Calif. plant) from the Golden Gate Exposition in San Francisco to the New York World's Fair, then back to San Francisco. Along the way the car was "inspected" by 400 mayors, 25 governors, and hundreds of other notables including stage and screen stars, President Roosevelt, and Vice-President Garner. It's easy to believe that Miss America was among those photographed with the car, and that Marilyn was Miss America in 1939.

In 1940, Rooney chauffeured Ford number 28,000,000 from the New York Fair to Mexico City, San Francisco, and back through Canada to New York - a 68-day, 13,000-mile tour.

Rooney spent considerable time around Henry and Edsel Ford and other

FORD COUNTRY **91**

Ford officials, and he spun innumerable stories about them. He originated the phrase, "Is everybody happy?" and invariably greeted everyone with the question. Rooney's friend, bandleader Ted Lewis, who borrowed the phrase, made it a national byword.

Rooney served Ford in a variety of public relations capacities. When I worked with him in the early 1950s, he had charge of exhibits in the Rotunda. A beloved figure without an enemy in the world, he retired from the company in 1963 and died in Dearborn in 1972.

Long Ago and Far Away

Back in 1909, Henry Ford stopped by a Detroit orphanage and asked the boys if they wanted jobs. One who jumped at the chance was John Moriarty, who immediately began work in the blacksmith shop of Ford's Piquette Avenue Plant.

"I was paid $1.09 a day," Moriarty recently recalled. "It seemed like big money back in 1909."

Moriarty also remembers that Henry Ford visited the shop to inspect special projects. "He especially liked to work on holidays," reminisced Moriarty, "when there weren't too many people around. One Labor Day, we repaired the engine that ran the electric generator at Highland Park. Together, we welded the driveshaft."

Moriarty spent 50 years with the company, retiring 22 years ago.

Top Banana Overseas

Because General Motors usually sells two cars for Ford's one in North America, we often overlook the fact that Ford has outsold GM overseas for many years.

Ford has made a big splash abroad since the Model T's introduction in 1908. In 1913, for example, it was producing more cars (6,319) in Europe than any other European auto company including runner-up Peugeot (5,000), and Renault (4,704), Benz (4,500), Opel (3,200), and Fiat (3,050).

The Ford name, moreover, has long been the world's best-known auto brand, partly because of Henry Ford's fame, partly because Ford subsidiaries and products bear the name Ford, whereas many of General Motors' subsidiaries and vehicles don't bear GM's name, e.g., Opel (Germany), Vauxhall (Britain), and Holden (Australia).

British Veteran Dies

Sir Patrick Hennessy, 82, former chairman of Ford Motor Co., Ltd. (England), died in March. He went to work for Henry Ford in London in 1920 and headed the British operations from 1956-68.

Your commentator met Sir Patrick in 1956, shortly after his promotion to his chairmanship, at London's big motor show. That day, Britain's Prime Minister, Sir Anthony Eden, opened the show and visited the Ford exhibit over which Sir Patrick presided.

Sir Patrick, as I recall, was aglow with the prospect of his exhibit being visited by the PM. But the PM, sleepless from having conferred through the previous night with the French premier over the Anglo-French invasion of Suez, had his mind elsewhere, and his visit and opening speech struck me as perfunctory, to say the least.

Sir Patrick generally is credited with having done a fine job with Ford of Britain, despite many obstacles. In any survey of Britain's great automotive figures, he would be rated highly.

Let Memories Lie

Ford's big stamping plant at Mariveles, on the tip of the Bataan Peninsula overlooking Corregidor Island, was built on the site of the marshalling area for World War II's Bataan Death March, according to word given to Stan Cousineau, of Ford's Public Relations Staff, during a recent visit to that area. During excavation for the plant's foundations, many human skulls and other bones were turned up.

Ford considered mentioning the site's historic connection during the plant's dedication ceremonies, then decided not to in view of the large number of Japanese tourists who visit the Philippines. "It was figured best," Cousineau was told by Ford's public relations man in the Philippines, "not to stir things up."

Exit Ford-South Africa

For the first time in six decades Ford no longer is an independent producer of cars, trucks, and tractors in South Africa. The Dearborn firm has merged its operations with the South African conglomerate, Anglo American Corp., with Ford becoming 40 percent owner of a new company called South African Motor Corp. (SAMCOR), which also assembles cars for France's Peugeot and Japan's Mazda and Mitsubishi.

Ford's decision, said a spokesman, has nothing to do with protests in the U.S. against apartheid. Rather, he added, it's because the South African car market is "highly fragmented" among 11 car and 17 truck companies; and being an independent manufacturer is no longer prudent. Ford, South Africa's second-largest automaker, produces about 40,000 cars annually, half Toyota's output. Most of Ford's 6,000 employees work in Port Elizabeth, the firm's headquarters. SAMCOR is headquartered in Pretoria, more than 600 miles away.

Ford of Canada began shipping cars to South Africa in 1906 through the New York export house of Arkell & Douglas, which, with its Montreal office, dealt not only in automobiles, but also in machinery, tools, electrical appliances, chemicals, and other products. The exporter had branches in Johannesburg, Port Elizabeth, and Capetown, and appointed Ford dealers in most important towns and cities.

By the early 1920s Ford Canada was ready to cut its ties with Arkell & Douglas, principally because the automaker, after selling its cars to the export house, had no further control over merchandising. Vehicles were being marketed at excessive prices, thus cutting down the volume of sales without benefit of the home company. Also Arkell & Douglas was selling Maxwell, Columbia, and Clydesdale cars as well as Fords; Canadian Ford wanted exclusivity.

In 1923, Ford Canada replaced the export house with a wholly-owned subsidiary, Ford South Africa. Car and truck assembly was begun at Port Elizabeth in 1924, and vehicles soon were being shipped to many African points south of the equator including Kenya and the Gold Coast. A new Port Elizabeth plant - said to be the largest in Africa under one roof - was completed in 1948.

Ford South Africa, once a jewel in Ford Canada's crown, has been losing money in recent years. Now the subsidiary, the first of many set up by Canadian Ford throughout the old British Empire, is a junior partner in a separate enterprise.

Toyo Kogyo Investment

Ford Motor Company plans to buy a 25 percent interest in Toyo Kogyo, the fourth largest Japanese automaker. Kogyo builds Mazda cars and trucks and supplies Courier pickup trucks to Ford. The $135 million deal also involves a merger of Ford Industries into Toyo Kogyo. Ford Industries, founded in 1925, prepares Ford's exports to meet Japanese government requirements.

Ford has been the only Big Three automaker without ownership in a Japanese firm. General Motors owns 34.2 percent of Isuzu Motors, and Chrysler Corporation holds 15 percent of fast-growing Mitsubishi Motors. Toyo Kogyo's Mazda's ranks sixth among imports in the U.S. The vehicles' rotary engines got the reputation of being gas-guzzlers in the 1974 gasoline crunch, and the company went through some lean years before making a recent recovery.

Going Out In Style

Ford vehicles have been used for decades as funeral cars (reikyu-sha) in Japan, reports the *Detroit News*.

The first motorized reikyu-sha was a Model T. Before the advent of the flivver, funeral carts were pulled by animals or carried on human shoulders. Today customized Lincolns and Cadillacs are the most prestigious funeral cars.

A passenger car is converted into a reikyu-sha by cutting away the upper portion of the vehicle's rear half, then installing atop the auto an ornate, half-ton wooden temple, five feet high, 11 feet long. A reikyu-sha is replaced every six years, after logging an average of 70,000 miles. Its final resting place - a scrap heap.

A problem looms. "Americans keep making their cars smaller," laments Yasuo Oka, president of a leading reikyu-sha supplier. "At the same time, our people are getting bigger."

To Protest Cork Closing

Irish cabinet officials plan to visit Dearborn to protest the closing of Ford's Cork Plant. The company has set a July closing date for the factory, which employs 800 and is the firm's only plant in the Irish Republic.

"It is not acceptable that Ford should walk away from Cork," Industry Minister John Bruton said, adding that he and Foreign Minister Peter Barry will go to Michigan to plead for a change of heart.

When in Dearborn the Irish officials no doubt will stress that Henry Ford's forebears immigrated to America from Cork, and that his company has had a presence in the city since 1917. That year, Ford acquired a beautiful, 136-acre tract along the southern bank of the River Lee. Giving up this land to Ford was no casual act for the inhabitants as it contained a large city park and the local racetrack, the latter especially dear to many citizens. But Irish support for a Ford tractor plant was fervent, the *Cork Examiner* hailing the project as marking "the true industrial development of Cork City and port, and indeed of the whole of Ireland generally."

Fordson tractor production began in 1919, but was discontinued because of poor sales in 1922. Meantime, the production of Model T parts for Ford of England was started in 1920, and the complete engine was being produced by 1921. By 1923, the Cork facility, with assets of $7.3 million, was larger than any of Ford's European operations except for Ford of England ($14.8 million in assets).

The Cork Plant again produced Fordson tractors from 1928 until 1932, when manufacture was shifted to Dagenham, England.

At present the Cork operation, still operating under the name "Henry Ford and Son Limited, Cork (Ireland)," assembles Escorts and Cortinas.

Ford In Mexico

"I notice that Ford and its Japanese affiliate, Toyo Kogyo, plan to start building small cars in Mexico to be sold in the U.S. and Canada," writes Eldon Rawson, of Milwaukee, Wis. "Sending Fords here may be new, but hasn't the Ford company been building cars in Mexico for a long time?"

Sure has, since 1926, when assembly of Model Ts was begun in a rented warehouse in Mexico City. At the time there were only 299 new cars registered in the city, among them 111 Fords, 57 Buicks, 20 Dodges, and eight Chevrolets. Ford assemblers were paid $3 per day, more than double the going rate.

Ford in 1932 opened a new Mexico City Assembly Plant with a capacity of 100 units daily. The building was located on Calzada de Guadelupe, near the famous shrine of that name; and Ford workers annually made a pilgrimage to pay tribute to the Virgin.

Henry Ford never visited Mexico, or any of his other Latin American operations. But Henry Ford II visited Mexico, Brazil, and Argentina in 1959, dining with the presidents of each nation.

No. 1 In Australia

Ford of Australia's Falcon for the third straight year is the island continent's hottest-selling car. "But its run to the top," notes the *Frankston* (Victoria) *Standard*, "has been a long time coming."

"It started back in 1960," says the newspaper, "when Ford here took over an American design and set out to tackle (GM's) all-conquering GM-Holden. That first Falcon was a fizzer. Fine for smooth U.S. highways, it was too weak-kneed and fragile to take on Australia. Then the long process of making the Falcon Aussie-tough began."

Gradually, observes the publication, the Falcon began to make a name for itself in motorsports, after which it offered everyday motorists their first taste of V-8 power. Finally, it became perhaps the fastest four-door production car in the world. In the aftermath of the Iranian oil crisis, the Falcon found itself the only big car still produced in Australia, and in 1982 it outsold GM-H's Commodore, and ended the GM subsidiary's 31-year reign as the country's leading automaker.

More than 1.4 million Falcons, including the current XF, have been sold. The line's success, concludes the *Standard*, "looks unstoppable short of World War III breaking out."

Ford cars have been sold in Australia for 80 years, and assembled there since 1925.

Thanks to reader Glen McClelland, Lagwarrin, Vic., for keeping us current on the Aussie Falcon.

Ford of Canada

Most readers are aware that Ford is one of the U.S.A.'s largest companies, whatever yardstick is used. But not everyone may be aware that Ford Motor Co. of Canada, in sales, is its host nation's third largest industrial firm.

Based in Oakville, Ont., Ford of Canada is outpaced only by No. 1, General Motors of Canada Ltd., and Canadian Pacific Ltd. Among top Canadian industrials, Chrysler Canada Ltd. is eight-ranked.

Ford of Canada, 90 percent owned by its U.S. parent, is ranked 11th by net income, 32nd in assets. GM of Canada, headquartered in Oshawa, Ont., is ranked second in net income, 21st in assets. Chrysler of Canada, based in Windsor, Ont., is 22nd in income, 83rd in assets. Both the GM and Chrysler subsidiaries are 100 percent owned by their parent firms.

Thanks to Mike Skinner, Detroit, Mich., for forwarding the [Toronto] *Financial Post*'s ranking of Canadian industrials.

No Water, No Plant

Henry Ford insisted that his overseas plants be on water - no compromises, as the manager of his Ford Holland plant learned in 1930.

That year Ford was to lay the cornerstone of a new factory at Rotterdam. Dignitaries had gathered at the foundations for the ceremony. When the auto king arrived on the scene with his manager, he asked, "Where is the water?" The manager explained that it was only a kilometer away.

"No water, no plant," said the unbending Ford, and there wasn't. The crowd went home, and Ford Holland abandoned its Rotterdam site. Later, in 1932, a Dutch plant was built at Amsterdam - on water.

This vignette perfectly illustrates a basic difference between Ford Motor Company in Henry Ford's day and its competitors, none of whose heads could have made such a decision without a meeting of the executive committee or board of directors. Ford Motor Company decisions were made inside Henry's hat.

Changes On Mack Avenue

Detroit's Mack Avenue, on which the Ford Motor Company first made cars in 1903, is now in the heart of the Motor City's black community. The street once was a main artery of Detroit, teeming with life and small businesses including the 250 by 50-foot renovated wagon shop which served as Ford's first factory.

Urban renewal and decay has blighted Mack Avenue. A few businesses remain. Harvey's Fish & Poultry sells fresh coon and wild rabbits, mullet, and catfish. A house doubles as a beautician's shop. Churches with names such as the Original Glorious Church of God in Christ No. 1 and the True House of God of the State of Michigan still attract a few of the faithful. One minister cooks and sells spareribs inside his storefront church. A handful of social agencies and hospitals also line the street.

A scaled-down reproduction of the Ford factory, ordered built by Henry Ford during his lifetime, stands in Greenfield Village. No historical marker designates the site of the Mack Avenue Plant.

Aubrey H. Robson

Cash On The Line

"I worked in the Highland Park (Mich.) State Bank (after the introduction of Henry Ford's $5 day)," recalls Aubrey Hastings Robson, Rock Island, Ill. "It made up (Ford's) weekly payroll - all in small bills and silver! One million dollars, plus! Have you any idea how big a pile a million dollars makes, in small bills? Over a foot deep, spread out on a table about 20-feet long. People on both sides would pull out bills and silver and stuff it in small 'pay envelopes' carrying an inscription of name and amount ...

"Workers emerged from the factory line where the pay envelopes were passed out, and moved in a solid mass down the street to the streetcars. Pickpockets would zip thru the crowd and the police (peering from windows of the plant) would spot them, dash down to a back door, out into the mob, and 'impound' the pickpockets. What happened to the thieves, in the alley behind the bank, is best omitted from print.

"In the meantime, each worker was 'conditioned' by Ford to bank a certain amount of his pay in the bank. But unable to write, many of them used their fingerprints as signature. Darned if most of the bank tellers didn't memorize those prints and their source bodies. Incredible!"

Thanks to Carmelita Smirnes, of the Engineering Society of Detroit, for passing on a copy of Robson's recent letter to her.

On paydays police officers stationed themselves on the second floor of this Highland Park assembly building to spot pickpockets moving among newly-paid Ford employees waiting to board streetcars on nearby Woodward Avenue. (Photo from the Collections of the Henry Ford Museum and Greenfield Village.)

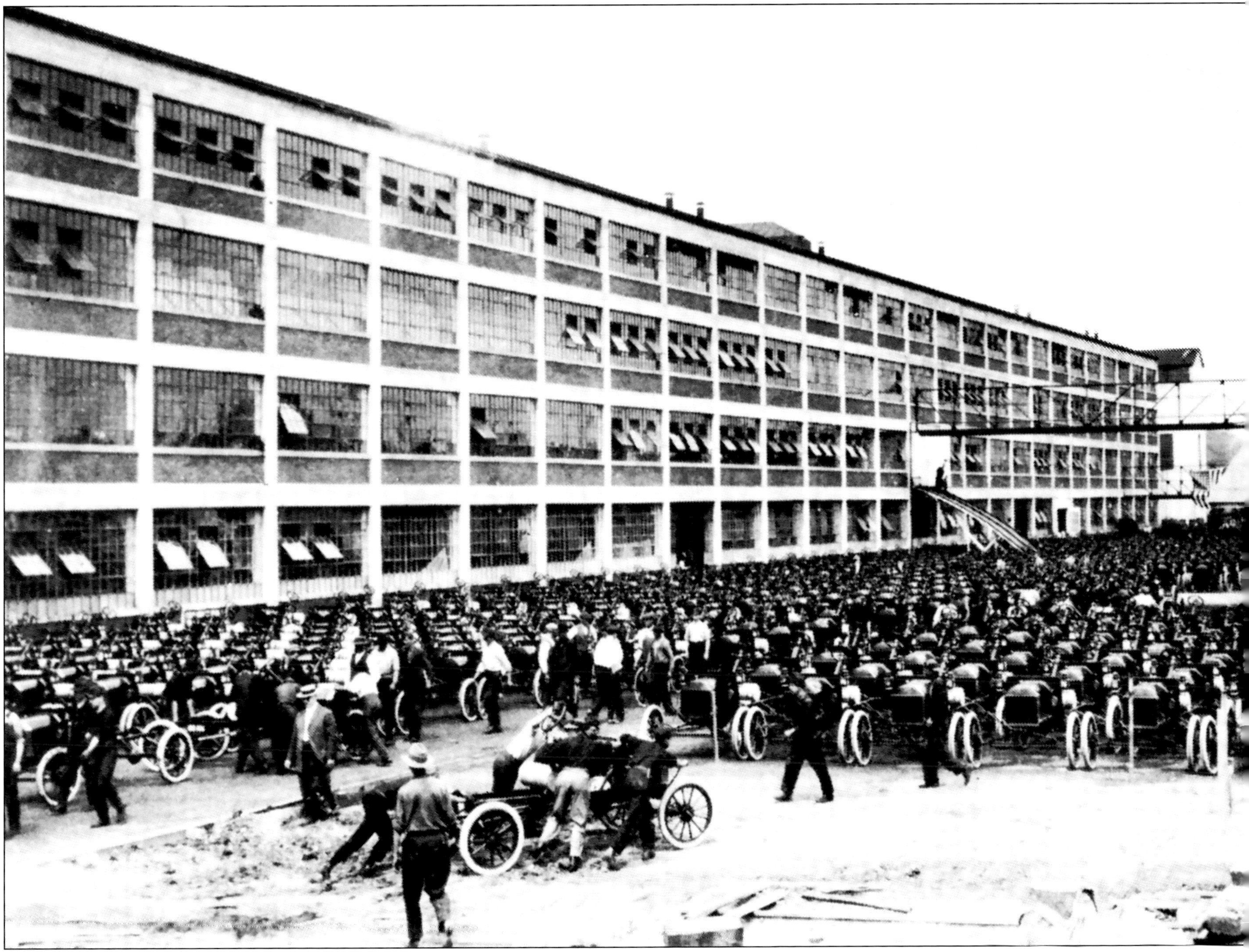

Piquette Plant

Recently I drove by the birthplace of the Model T, Ford's second factory, the Piquette Plant, at Piquette and Beaubien streets, Detroit. Built in 1904, the three-story Piquette Plant was 402 by 56 feet. A business office, presided over by Henry Ford's principal partner, James Couzens, occupied a small part of the first floor. The rest of the floor was devoted to a machine shop, electrical department, and shipping room.

On the second story, Henry Ford, Model T designer C. Harold Wills, and others had their quarters, adjoining several experimental rooms. Farther to the rear were the designing and drafting rooms and a second machine shop. Room later was made here for assembly work, and body painting and trimming. The third floor in 1904 housed the painting, trimming, and varnishing operations, and the general assembly of cars and storage space.

Recalling Highland Park

"I was employed in the Ford Highland Park Plant during 1916-17," writes Wilbert W. Ohlemacher, 91, of Sandusky, Ohio, "and some things stand out in my memory.

Ford's historic Highland Park Plant as it looked from the air in the 1950s. The powerhouse and administration building to its right were demolished in 1958; most of the remaining buildings survive. The factory recently was sold to three Michiganians who plan to convert the property into an industrial park. (Photo courtesy of Ford Archives, Henry Ford Museum, Dearborn, Mich.)

"The big office building faced Woodward Avenue. Just a short distance beyond was the power plant building. This building had very large glass windows and was a wonderful display of power generation equipment. Utility power was available, but it was not as reliable a source of supply as it is now. Then it was not unusual for a company to make its own power.

"Mr. Ford wanted power which was available at all times, so he made it himself. It was a beautiful sight to see the horizontal engines with the big flywheel belted to the electric generators. The way I remember it, these engines were unique, being driven by both steam and gas. I think they were built by an Ohio company.

"A short distance beyond the factory building on Woodward Avenue was a recreation park for all Ford employees. This park contained baseball diamonds, tennis courts, picnic tables, grills, and facilities for croquet and horseshoes. It was all well maintained, and was used by many employees. This, in itself, was a bit unusual at the time."

Highland Park Plant Sold

Ford's Highland Park Plant, birthplace of the moving automotive assembly line, has been sold for an undisclosed price to HFP Associates, a partnership of three Detroit area men with backgrounds in real estate and merchandising.

The purchasers plan to convert the historic 103-acre property into an industrial park featuring manufacturing, warehousing, and retail operations.

The Highland Park Plant began producing Model Ts in 1910 and was the cornerstone of the Ford empire until the mid-1920s. Attaining a peak employment of 68,285 in 1924, the factory for 15 years was ranked as the world's largest automobile plant. This fact, coupled with Highland Park's fame as the "birthplace of mass production," enabled the factory from 1912 to 1927 to attract more visitors than any other industrial institution in the country. An average of 124,000 guests toured the plant annually between 1922 and 1927. By comparison, the second most visited plant in the Detroit area, the Dodge factory, drew 50,000 persons during its best year, 1927.

Highland Park was eclipsed in size by Ford's River Rouge Plant in 1925. Two years later, when the company started to produce the Model A, Highland Park's final assembly line was transferred to the Rouge. Thereafter the older factory declined in importance. From 1928, when space was leased to the Briggs Body Corp., the number of Ford employees at Highland Park decreased rapidly. The plant had but 30,507 Ford workers in 1928 and only 18,231 in 1929.

During the years prior to its virtual abandonment in 1973, Highland Park turned out tractors, military and postal vehicles, and small industrial engines. Upon transferring these operations to new plants, Ford announced plans to raze most of the factory buildings except for structures, which could be converted into a trim plant or preserved for historic purposes. But Ford's downturn during and after the recession of 1973-74 stalled plans to demolish most of the buildings and to equip a trim plant and open a museum.

Long a white elephant, Highland Park now faces an uncertain future. If its buyers can lease its old buildings, fine. If not, they will face the almost prohibitive cost of tearing them down, or letting them decay over the years. The city of Highland Park, in all candor, is nobody's dream of paradise, and the area around Highland Park already has many old, abandoned factory buildings (some ancient Packard structures among them) begging for lessees.

Henry On The Job

A retired Ford welder-maintenance man recalls that the most remarkable aspect of his 40 years of service was Henry Ford's presence around the Rouge Plant.

"In the 1930s," reports Edward F. DePue, "he was around all the time. He would come into the plant to look around and check on things, even in the middle of the night. Imagine that! A billionaire and there he was in the middle of a dirty factory."

To Russia With Tires

The River Rouge's tire-plant equipments, America's most modern tire-making machinery when shipped to the Russians in 1942, has been the subject of too little research, says Melvin G. Chase, of Newark, Del. The equipment remained in the crates in which it was shipped to Russia all through and even beyond World War II, according to Secretary of the Navy James V. Forrestal. The Russians, apparently because they did not have raw rubber with which to operate a tire plant, thus got no benefit from the equipment during the conflict. Whether the machinery eventually was uncrated, rebuilt, and put into operation nobody knows, except maybe the Russians.

Executives Visit Rouge

Ford Motor Company Executive Committee Chairman William Clay Ford and President Philip Caldwell recently visited the River Rouge Plant to review progress on maintenance and repair work and to talk with workers. Naturally, they made a hit with their fellow employees, who described them as being "as pleasant and nice as anybody you'd ever meet. They seemed interested in our work."

The duo's visit marks the first time in recent memory that a member of Ford's top brass has visited the huge Rouge factory, which Henry Ford until the early 1930s often prowled through every workday for weeks on end. The auto king stopped making his daily rounds when the Great Depression curtailed sales and production, making the Rouge, in his words, "no fun anymore."

Henry Ford II chatted with hundreds of Rouge workers during his early association with the company, and he, like his grandfather before him and William Clay and Caldwell after him, made friends wherever he went.

Although Ford executives truly can't afford to spend much time in factories, and no fair-minded person, or Ford shareholder, would expect them to do so, an occasional visit seems to pay rich dividends in terms of improved employee relations.

Rouge Tours Suspended

Ford's popular River Rouge Plant tours were suspended indefinitely in 1981 because of the company's poor sales. The suspension will cut annual costs by $1.5 million.

Free tours of the Rouge were begun in 1924. During most of the 1960s and 1970s more than 200,000 persons annually visited the facility. All told, more than 7 1/2 million people took the two-hour tour. The tour route varied, but visitors usually went through the assembly plant and the steel strip rolling mill.

Some Detroiters, dismayed by the tour's discontinuance, have suggested that the company charge for the tours, rather than stop them. Ford doesn't think that's a better idea, but won't predict when the tours will be resumed. "We haven't said there will never be another tour," said a company spokesman. "It depends on what the economy will do."

Rouge Painting

"Classic Landscape," a painting inspired by artist Charles Sheeler's photographic assignments at Ford's River Rouge Plant in 1927, recently was sold for $1.87 million, the highest price ever paid for a painting by a 20th century American artist.

The painting, auctioned in New York by Sotheby's was bought by Edsel Ford, son of Henry Ford and father of Henry II, in 1932 for an undisclosed sum. It hung for more than four decades in Edsel and Eleanor's home in Grosse Pointe Shores, Mich. Edsel died in 1943; his widow in 1976.

The painting, sold by the administrators of Eleanor's estate, was bought by a consortium of three art galleries. They probably will sell it to a client and share the profit, in accordance with customary practice.

Sheeler was invited by Edsel to execute his memorable series of Rouge photographs. His artwork, based on the plant's utilitarian geometry, is generally regarded as the finest ever associated with factory architecture.

Mill Again For Sale

The historic Rouge Steel Co., a cornerstone of Henry Ford's realization of a fully integrated auto firm, is again for sale.

The company unsuccessfully tried to sell the 60-year-old Dearborn facility to a Japanese consortium in 1982-83. After the talks failed, Ford wrung $40 million in concessions from plant employees while agreeing to spend up to $350 million on modernization.

"I think Rouge Steel is being very well managed," says Ford Chairman Donald Petersen, "and given all the circumstances, is doing a fine job. But it's really struggling because of the overall problems in the steel industry."

Ford has not set a price tag on the mill, which occupies 350 acres of the 1,200-acre Rouge complex. A UAW official within the plant believes the mill's 1985 losses approached $100 million.

Wheels Needed

Is Ford's River Rouge Plant big? If in doubt, consider the following story by reader John C. Jackson of San Jose, Calif.:

"I was selling graphic arts equipment and Ford was one of my major accounts," recalls Jackson, age 66. "I did a lot of business with the purchasing departments ... I had with me a man from our factory in Elizabeth, N.J., and we were to make a series of calls within the Rouge Plant. I parked at Gate Four and we went across the Miller Road overpass down to the security station, and I obtained a vehicle pass. The man from New Jersey kidded me by saying I was getting too lazy to carry my 35-lb. satchel on these calls.

"We got back to my car, and I had him note the odometer reading. Then we went on our way, made the calls, and returned to the guard station at Miller ... Traveling from the old Navy buildings at the south end of the property to the north end of the B Building, we had driven a little better than four miles within the Rouge!"

Jackson's comments recall my employment with Ford's News

Alexandria Plant Sold

In August an Alaskan developer bought Ford's former Alexandria, Va. plant from the federal government for $14.2 million.

Purchaser of the Potomac River property is Cook Inlet Region, Inc., of Anchorage. The firm, which owns about 500,000 acres of Alaskan land, plans to redevelop the 52-year-old factory into commercial, office, and residential space. "We like the marina-type atmosphere," said a Cook spokesman.

Although 700 developers from across the nation requested bid packages for the General Services Administration's auction, only eight made bids. "The price," said Alexandria's city planning director, "was higher than what we expected. I guess the surprise also is that (the purchaser) is from Alaska."

Designed by famed industrial architect Albert Kahn and boasting an art deco facade, 30-foot ceilings, and a saw-toothed roof, the building initially was used for parts distribution and the shipment of cars overseas. Sold to the government in 1942, it assembled torpedoes for the Navy during World War II. In 1958 the Navy relinquished control over the nine-acre site to the GSA. During the past quarter-century the factory, which is being considered for nomination to the National Register of Historic Places, has been used as a storage area for several federal agencies.

Thanks to Willard Prentice, of Timonium, Md., for forwarding news stories on the sale.

Department from 1952-54, a time when I accompanied many reporters through the Rouge. We never carried anything heavier than a pencil and a notepad. But we too drove among the 34 factory buildings, which made up the huge Rouge maze.

FORD COUNTRY **101**

Old Atlanta Plant

Ford's former Atlanta Assembly Plant, which is listed on the National Register of Historic Places, will be converted into an apartment building with retail shops.

The plant, built in 1914, assembled Model Ts, Model As, and V-8s before becoming a tank factory in World War II. Later it was used as an armed forces induction center, and was known as the War Assets Building.

Real estate developers Richard H. Bradfield and Marvin L. Singer, of Atlanta, plan to convert the building's upper three floors into 123 apartments renting from $400 to $600 monthly. "The building has a natural atrium," Bradfield said. "We are going to keep it open, and, in fact, all of our apartments are going to open up on the atrium." Fifteen to 20 stores, including a restaurant, are projected for the ground floor.

The Ford Factory Square Project, as the development is called, will cost about $7 million, with most of the money to come from low-interest revenue bond financing. The developers also will take advantage of federal tax incentives for historic preservation.

The building's exterior, which features the architectural touches common to all Ford assembly plants of the early teens, will remain unchanged.

Our thanks to reader Edward A. Abercrombie, Statesboro, Ga., for providing this update.

Twilight Time?

Ford's historic Dearborn Assembly Plant may be closed, and torn down.

The 64-year-old facility, first to be built in the River Rouge complex, now assembles Mustangs and Capris. One of the company's oldest factory buildings, it employs 2,900 workers.

Because of the plant's age, recently observed a Ford executive, "there aren't many future possibilities for its use. We could just discontinue using it, or we might tear it down."

Dearborn Assembly was designed, like almost all other Ford structures of its day, by Albert Kahn. Rushed to completion in 1918 for the construction of submarine chasers (Eagle boats), the building was 1,700 feet long, 350 in depth, and 100 feet in height. Its first boss was William S. "Big Bill" Knudsen, later GM's president.

After the war, the B (for boat) Building, as it was called, was remodeled for auto body manufacturing. The first body, for a touring car, was turned out on Aug. 5, 1919. Production of open and closed bodies reached 800 per day by November.

New Life For Old Plant

The front of Ford's former Cleveland Assembly Plant, looking up into the Glass Department of the Cleveland Institute of Art, which has renovated the pre-World War I building. In addition to housing various departments of the institute, the structure rents space to a design firm, an art supply store, a Social Security Administration office, a ceramist, and Case Western Reserve University's School of Medicine. The building, located at 11610 Euclid Avenue, was used by Ford until the early 1930s, and acquired by the institute in 1981.

Kansas City Plant

Ford's original Kansas City Assembly Plant, above, the world's first auto branch assembly facility, recently was sold by Armco, Inc. to Sheffield, Inc. Sheffield, as did Armco, makes nuts and bolts in the factory.

The core of the plant was built in 1909, and later expanded. Ford sold the property to Armco in 1957, after opening a new assembly operation suburban Claycomo.

Des Moines Plant

Ford Motor Co.'s former Des Moines Assembly Plant has housed the Des Moines Technical High School for the last 30 years, reader Jim Harrigan, of that city, informs us. The school board is trying to phase out the institution, adds Harrigan, who figures that its quarters will be razed when vacated. The plant was used for aircraft production during World War II.

The Des Moines Plant was built in 1915 at a cost of $420,000. Henry Ford made the decision to build the factory, bypassing his board of directors, including John and Horace Dodge, who complained about Ford's imperiousness. The auto king, when questioned later about the irregularity of his action, admitted it. His lawyer, Alfred Lucking, added, "That is the way they did business always up there."

Such complaints prompted Ford to buy out his fellow shareholders in 1918. After that, Henry could build plants in Des Moines or anywhere else with drugstore quarterbacking.

Kearny Plant Recalled

Ford's Newark Meadows (Kearny), N.J. Assembly Plant, built in 1918, is the subject of a March, 1931 article in *Western Electric News* forwarded by reader Will S. Burns, a Western Electric engineer living in Shreveport, La.

The plant, the article states, was taken over by Western Electric, A.T.&T.'s "telephone factory," in 1929. Meantime Ford was moving to its new plant at Edgewater, N.J., which continued in operation until the 1970s.

The Kearny plant had unusual origins. It was built not as an auto plant, but to work on Ford's submarine chasers, later called "Eagle" boats. Hulls of the boats were built in Dearborn's Rouge Plant, then towed through Lake Erie, the Erie Canal, and the Hudson and Passaic rivers to Kearny for outfitting. The war ended just as the plant was geared up for full production. Through the 1920s the factory served as one of Ford's 35 assembly plants.

Louisville Plant

Yet another old Ford assembly plant which has neither died nor faded away is the company's ex-Louisville factory (photo) owned by the University of Louisville since 1958. The Albert Kahn-designed plant, at Third Street and Eastern Parkway, was opened on Jan. 2, 1916, and assembled Model Ts until 1925, when operations were transferred to a larger building at 1400 Southwestern Parkway. The successor plant, now owned by Mead Container Co., is used for the manufacture of paper boxes.

Ford's former Louisville plant.

Ford Motor Company's original Minneapolis Assembly Plant, as it looks today.

The original plant, abandoned for 15 years, was acquired in 1940 by Reynolds Metals Co. Used for the manufacture of aircraft parts until 1947, it was converted into an office building and housed the 700 employees of Reynolds' general sales division until 1958. Valued that year at $1.1 million, the building was the largest private gift made to the University of Louisville up to that time. "One student of the university's physical plant maintains that the Reynolds Building (the old plant's present name) provides a highly effective visual backdrop for the district's southwest corner," reports Dwayne Cox, assistant university archivist, "while others believe that it is downright ugly." (Photo courtesy reader Mike Martin, Louisville, Ky.)

Norfolk Old-Timer

"What's Ford's oldest active assembly plant outside of Dearborn Assembly?" asks Fred McCall, Durham, N.C.

The Norfolk Assembly Plant built in 1924 and opened for business the following year, I'd guess. The plant built Model Ts, Model As, and V-8s before World War II, then housed 1,000 sailors and repaired landing craft during the war. Over the years it has assembled 3.8 million cars and trucks; F-Series light trucks exclusively since 1974.

The work force is exceptionally stable, the average age of the hourly employees being 45.6 years, the average seniority 20.4 years.

Ford's oldest assembly operation, Dearborn Assembly, which first produced Eagle boats in 1918, began making Model T bodies in 1919.

Minneapolis Plant

Ford's original Minneapolis Assembly Plant, one of the company's largest pre-World War I assembly buildings, has been put up for sale by its owner, Honeywell, Inc.

Ford built more than a half-million Model Ts in the 10-story plant from 1913 until 1925, then abandoned it in favor of its present-day Twin Cities hydroelectric plant on the Mississippi River. The original plant was shuttered until 1943, when bought for $150,000 by Honeywell.

The old factory produced military equipment during World War II, and made a variety of parts, including thermostats, sensors, timers, and other controls, for Honeywell's Residential Division from 1946 until 1983. During the 1950s, employment rose to 2,427, and during the 1980s ranged from 700 to 1,086. In 1983, the factory's 700 workers were moved to newer facilities in Golden Valley and Plymouth, Minn.

Ford employed as many as 1,000 workers in the building, located at 420 Fifth Street, only five blocks from the heart of downtown Minneapolis. Thus during the Model T era, center city workers could conveniently inspect Tin Lizzies in the new-car showroom. In turn, Honeywell employees in 1983 said the thing about the building they'll miss most is its proximity to and view of downtown Minneapolis.

A 1943 Ford brochure on the plant shows that its square footage was 265,000, and its showroom floor was of tile, its office floors of cork.

"The building has not been sold," says the Honeywell official who is responsible for selling the facility, "but because of its location, it has generated interest for a variety of uses."

University Gets Ford Plant

Ford's former Milwaukee Assembly Plant, below, now belongs to the University of Wisconsin-Milwaukee. Now called the Kenilworth Building, the structure houses a print shop, a motor pool, a storage area, and is used for research projects. Ford built the plant in the mid-teens, and operated it until the 1930s. The building was acquired by the federal government which sold it to the university in 1973. (Photo courtesy of University of Wisconsin-Milwaukee)

St. Louis Plant

Ford Motor Company's first St. Louis Assembly Plant still stands at Forest Park Boulevard and Sarah Street as shown in this photo taken by reader Dante Carretti, of St. Charles, Mo. During World War II, the building was used by McQuay-Norris to manufacture proximity fuses for the Navy. At present it is occupied by Missouri Goodwill Industries, a charitable organization. The building remains substantially unchanged since its construction in 1912, although many windows have been replaced by glass blocks or covered by plywood. The building is similar in almost every respect to 16 other pre-World War I Ford assembly plants. The St. Louis plant employed 200 "mechanics" and was capable of assembling 5,000 Model Ts per year.

FORD COUNTRY

Ex-Omaha Plant

Ford's former Omaha (Neb.) Assembly Plant, today owned and occupied by Faberge's Tip Top Division, is shown as it looks today. Ford produced Model Ts, Model As, and V-8s in the building from 1916 until 1933, then used the structure as a parts depot until the mid-1950s. During the Ford years the part of the first floor with the covered windows was used as a showroom; much of the second floor housed offices, and the three top floors were used for assembly operations and parts storage. Tip Top, a manufacturer of hair care accessories, bought the building in 1959 from Western Electric. The structure is located at 16th and Cumming Street.

Turning Back The Clock

Say it isn't so - that Ford, for the first time in 70 years, won't be assembling cars in California. But that's the way it'll be by June 1, 1983, when the company will close its last West Coast assembly operation, a 27-year-old San Jose facility. The plant produces the Ford Escort, Mercury Lynx, Ford EXP, Mercury LN7, and F-Series pickups.

Why the closure? Imports have taken almost 50 percent of the California market and 70 percent of the small-car market. Ford's sales don't justify keeping the plant open. So it, like the firm's Pico Rivera facility, shuttered in 1980, will be closed. GM's in much the same boat, having boarded up its assembly plants in Fremont and South Gate, Calif. last February, and having recently eliminated a shift at its last West Coast assembly plant, in Van Nuys, Calif. Chrysler hasn't made cars on the coast for years.

Henry Ford built assembly plants in Los Angeles, San Francisco, Portland, and Seattle before World War I, and since that time the company has maintained West Coast operations. Now the once mighty U.S. auto industry is retreating east of the Rockies, and will henceforth ship cars to the coast as did Henry Ford before the Model T got into volume production and the auto king figured it'd be cheaper to ship parts around the country than to transport completed cars. The strategy remains sound, if one's cars are in considerable demand.

Still Going Strong At 70

One of Ford's oldest operations, the Twin Cities Assembly Plant, recently marked its 70th birthday, and more than 50,000 persons attended the seven-day celebration. Tours of the factory, located on the St. Paul side of the Mississippi River, were conducted by retirees.

Predecessor plants of the current Twin Cities facility were built in 1912 in both Minneapolis and St. Paul. In 1912-13, Ford also started assembly operations in Kansas City, Long Island City, Los Angeles, San Francisco, Seattle, Portland, Denver, St. Louis, Chicago, Memphis, Boston, Philadelphia, Dallas, Houston, and Columbus.

The present Twin Cities Plant was erected in 1924, at which time Henry

106 FORD COUNTRY

Ford's Twin Cities Assembly Plant from the air. The powerhouse is near the center of the picture, the factory to its left.

Ford damned the Mississippi and began generating electric power. When the river is high, Ford's generators can produce more than twice the amount of power needed by the factory. The hydro unit, virtually maintenance free and manned by only three persons, also supplies free power to nearby government locks and sells its surplus to the Northern States Power Co. Conversely, when the river is low, Ford has to buy as much as 70 percent of its power needs from Northern States.

The Twin Cities operation is the biggest of the two dozen hydroplants built by Henry Ford and is the only one still generating power under Ford auspices. Although the factory's recent birthday party was well attended, it attracted fewer than half the 107,000 visitors who trooped through the plant during a weeklong open house in 1926. At that time guests were guided through the premises by employees, dealers, and salesmen.

All Ford Mills Intact

"Today," the February-March 1981 issue of prestigious *American Heritage* informs us, "most of (Henry Ford's) mill plants have vanished, though a few survive as residences and small office buildings."

The magazine then tells us that Ford's Northville, Mich. Plant has been "lovingly restored - though not to the uses to which Henry Ford put it more than two generations ago (and) is one of the few surviving from the time of the Motor King."

It's distressing when a magazine of *American Heritage*'s excellence can, and in such matter-of-fact manner, be so inaccurate. One might expect it of *Time* or *Newsweek*, or almost any newspaper. But *American Heritage*? What's left?

The fact is, every single one of Henry Ford's water-powered plants and mills is still standing, and nearly all of them are in active use as manufacturing units, antique shops, community/youth centers, county maintenance facilities, and the like. Moreover, several of the factories continue to generate hydropower.

As for Northville, the original gristmill was replaced by a small factory building in 1936, and the plant continues to make valves for Ford cars just as it has since it opened in early

FORD COUNTRY   **107**

Henry Ford's "village industries" included facilities at Nankin Mills, Flat Rock, Phoenix, Waterford, Plymouth, Ypsilanti, Rawsonville, and Northville, all on tiny Michigan streams. Each of the buildings still stands, except for the Northville Mill, which Henry Ford himself replaced in 1936 with a one-story building, also still standing.

1920. This facility, the last operating under Ford auspices, will be abandoned by Ford in the fall, however.

The rest of *American Heritage*'s article is generally accurate and illuminating. "Ford," says the essay, "whose factory, an urban industrial plant, wanted to decentralize American manufacturing, take it out of the cities and put it back into the rural setting in which it had begun. The theory behind what he called his 'village industries' was that they would give farm families the opportunity to earn money during the long months between plantings and harvest and stem the pernicious flow of young, able-bodied workers from towns to the industrial warrens of the cities - many traveling in Model T Fords, of course. 'With one foot on the land and

108 FORD COUNTRY

one foot in industry,' he declared, 'America is safe.'

"Being a man of action," the article continues, "as well as of theory, and rich, and in full control of his own company, Ford first implemented his notion in 1919 by converting a small mill on the River Rouge ... into a plant producing valves for Ford cars. Employing a comparative handful of workers and operating with electricity generated by its large wheel, the River Rouge Plant was typical of those that followed - and by the end of the 1930s there were eighteen of them turning our valves, starters, gauges, springs, generators, ignition coils, headlights, and other small parts for Ford products. Each plant site was personally selected by Ford himself, who also supervised the conversion of the old mills, and as late as 1938, he was happily going over a list of 212 additional possibilities."

Most of the tiny factories were profitable until the company recognized the UAW in 1941. Afterwards, work specialization took the profit out of the plants, and, as far as Henry Ford was concerned, a lot of the fun as well.

A cost-conscious Ford Motor Co. closed most of the plants after Henry Ford's retirement in 1945. But five of the factories continued to make Ford parts until the mid-1950s; three into the early 1960s.

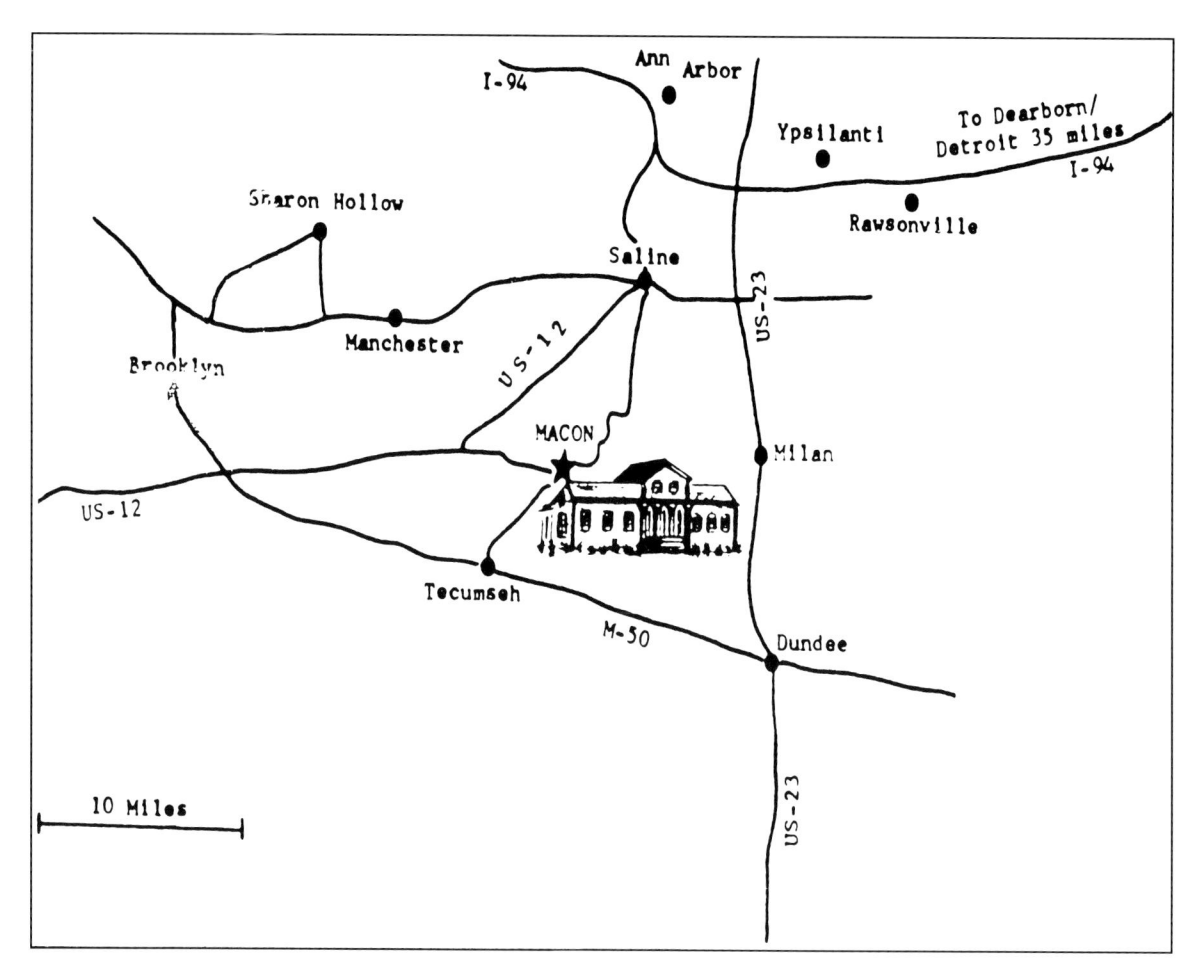

Down By The Old Millstream

Things-to-do-when-in-the-Dearborn/Detroit-area: a tour of Henry Ford's "village industries," as shown on the above map. The trip meanders through a region, which encompasses more old hydro mills than any area of comparable size in America. The building shown on the map depicts Henry Ford's format country home at Macon, Mich., once the capital of the auto magnate's rural empire. If you like a pretty countryside dotted with old mills and little plants down by the old millstream, try this tour. You'll like it.

Mixed Feelings

Proceeds from state-licensed bingo games are helping to finance renovation of Henry Ford's former Dundee, Mich., hydroelectric plant; and one can only wonder how Ford, who hated gambling, would feel about that. Profits from the games (held in the mill), along with a modest annual stipend from the village government, are enabling community-spirited citizens to renovate the handsome century-old Greek Revival structure. "We haven't got the place looking nearly as good as it looked when Mr. Ford was alive," said civic leader Frank Stukenburg, "but we've got it looking better than it did before he came along in 1935-36."

The mill made copper welding points for the Ford Company from the mid-1930s until 1954, after which it had varied manufacturing and other uses. Sold to the village for $1.00 in 1970, the mill now is used as a community center. Its River Raisin dam is the widest of any of those built for Ford's more-than-a-score hydro plants in southeastern Michigan; and its setting in the village of 2,200 is a pretty one.

Change At Clarkston

Henry Ford's ex-"village industry" at Clarkston, Mich., has recently been enclosed in brick, and soon will house a complex of 15 shops and two restaurants. The plant was built by Ford in 1941, and its dam backs up a pretty millpond. The original generator is being restored to power the development's exterior light. A natural land bowl behind the building serves as an amphitheater for local theatrical productions.

Flat Rock Plant Vacated

Henry Ford's 56-year-old Flat Rock, Mich. hydroelectric plant, which for years made most of the Ford Company's head, rear, deck and dome lamps and horn buttons, has been abandoned since August 1979, and is awaiting a new tenant.

In 1950, Ford sold the plant to Flat Rock's Moynahan Bronze Co., which made aircraft components in the facility. Moynahan was acquired in 1964 by Federal Engineering Co., Detroit, which the next year also bought Stearns Manufacturing Co., Adrian, Mich. Stearns built cement blocks and airport baggage handling conveyor systems in the factory until moving these operations to Missouri and Texas, respectively, last year.

A price tag of $1.8 million has been put on the 23-acre property, according to Dan Levine, president of Federal Engineering. Levine says several parties are interested in the facility, and not least because of the big cranes and bays which Henry Ford built into the structure. Levine adds that the plant's turbines seem to be in place, although the generators were removed years ago. He has all of the buildings blueprints.

In Henry Ford's day, Flat Rock's turbines generated enough power to keep 440 men at work, and provide additional power for the Rouge Plant, 15 miles to the north. Ford often visited the Huron River facility, usually paying as much attention to the dam and powerhouse as to the manufacturing facilities.

Flat Rock old-timers like to recall Ford's visits. On one occasion, the magnate was miffed about a big walnut tree having been cut on parkland a couple of miles north of the factory. After walking to the site, he issued a plea that such trees be spared. On another occasion, Ford's wife Clara, accompanying her husband, was said to have been outraged over the shooting of pigeons around the plant by employees. Old-timers also remember that Ford provided tractors and other equipment for the gardening that he expected of his employees, and took an interest in an old flax mill in the vicinity.

The Detroit, Toledo & Ironton Railroad, owned by Ford between 1920-29, still runs by the plant. Still to be seen along its tracks are bases of a few of the hundreds of sturdy arches which the auto king built to power the electric trains that he had in mind, but never operated.

Green Island Plant

Employees of Ford's historic Green Island, N.Y. plant above are pleading with the company to keep their facility open past a scheduled July, 1988 shutdown. The factory is now a part of the Engine and Foundry Division.

Members of UAW Local 930 point out that they were among the first to make concessions when the company needed help during the early 1980s and also helped pioneer union-management programs to make quality "Job 1" and to promote Ford products.

Henry Ford first visited the Green Island power site in 1919 while touring upstate New York and New England with Thomas A. Edison, Harvey S. Firestone, Sr., and John Burroughs. His plant, opened in 1923, utilized a federally-built dam developing 10,000 hp, making it the Ford Co.'s second-largest hydropower facility. In its heyday, the factory employed more than 1,000 workers.

Macon Memories

Old-timers in Macon, Mich., the "capital" of Henry Ford's southeastern Michigan rural empire in the 1930s and 1940s, are fond of spinning stories about Ford's influence on the community of 150 to 200 persons.

Ford owned several thousand acres of Macon-area farmland, devoting most of it to the raising of soybeans, which, in turn, were used for the production of plastic auto parts. Ford also built, in 1941, the community's only commercial enterprise, a general store, still the village's only business.

Ford's country home still stands in Macon, as does his former sawmill and high school, now a residential care agency for delinquent youths from 13 to 17 years of age. Also nearby is Ford's "Dynamic Kernels" gristmill, the last of the many hydropowered mills built by the auto king. Ford's Macon chapel was later moved to Trenton, Mich.

Shop classes at the high school were advanced, according to 52-year-old Robert Bush, an ex-student who now farms in the area. Tractors were torn down and rebuilt. Clocks were made in the woodshop. Chains were repaired and plowshares sharpened in blacksmith classes.

"Ford was a nice guy," recalls 88-year-old Clarence Hall, who once cared for Ford's home and fried steaks for the magnate and his guests. "He liked to sit by the stove and ask questions about the countryside."

Ford's Macon holdings were sold or given away after the founder's death. But the industrialist's legacy is an important part of the community's history.

House For Sale

A 130-year-old Macon, Mich. farmhouse restored by Henry Ford in the 1930s is priced for sale at $220,000.

The 4,200 square-foot house is one of several restored by the auto king during the Depression Decade, when he grew soybeans on thousands of acres in the Macon area, about 50 miles southwest of Dearborn. Today, the house stands on 27 acres of farmland.

Homes restored by Ford are highly prized in the area, for it's common knowledge that the industrialist made use of the best workmen and materials available. Like Ford's plants, they were built to last.

Macon Vault

This "vault" was built in Macon, Mich., 40 miles southwest of Dearborn, by Ford Motor Company during World War II to house company records which, it was feared, might be destroyed by an enemy air attack on Dearborn. The vault now is a storage area for Boysville, a home for wayward youths. The Archdiocese of Detroit acquired Henry Ford's Macon sawmill and educational buildings in the early 1950s.

Dynamic Kernels Mill

Henry Ford's "Dynamic Kernels" mill, completed in 1944 and the last of the hydropower plants built by the auto magnate, recently exchanged hands.

Buyer is Henry "Hank" Bednarz, Ann Arbor, Mich., who is in the natural foods business and plans to grind whole wheat flour at the mill. Bednarz also is thinking of using the 11 1/2-acre property as a setting for holistic health

112 FORD COUNTRY

workshops and retreats for business meetings.

The Macon, Mich. mill was purchased for "close to $200,000" from Eugene and James Eldridge, brothers and old-car collectors who maintained the mill and an adjacent house in excellent condition. Bednarz and his son, Jason, 11, occupy the house.

Ford's "Dynamic Kernels" mill, nestled in a natural amphitheater protected by cottonwood trees.

Henry Ford's former Manchester, Mich. "village industry," as it looks following renovation by its new owner, Hoover Universal. "I don't think Henry would appreciate the fact that we have replaced his two-way windows with one-way mirrored glass," says Hoover executive David J. Skala, "but then again, given the fact that it is now an office building and not a production facility, he probably would be glad that we are hiding the administrative overhead."

Happy Ending

Henry Ford's former Manchester, Mich. hydroelectric plant, abandoned for several years, recently was acquired by Hoover Universal, an Ann Arbor, Mich. based firm.

The River Raisin facility, which produced Ford instrument clusters from 1941-57, now houses the Marketing and Technical Service Center of Hoover's Plastics Machinery Division.

In renovating the plant, Hoover preserved the two-story building's integrity except for the addition of a mezzanine and the replacement of windows with two-inch tempered Thermopane glass with a mirror finish that gives off a 70-percent reflection.

The plant's original generators are still in excellent condition, and supply power for the building. The generator room houses exhibits which illustrate Hoover's involvement in mechanical technology.

Hoover is a nationwide, diversified manufacturing company with more than 7,000 employees and sales exceeding a half-billion dollars annually. It permits groups to tour its Manchester building, if arrangements are made in advance.

FORD COUNTRY **113**

Nankin Mills In Disrepair

Nankin Mills, a post-Civil War gristmill restored by Henry Ford, is in need of paint and in a state of disrepair, as revealed in the above photo.

The mill, in which Ford produced engravings, carburetor parts, rivets, and bearings from 1921-48, for more than three decades has been owned by Wayne County, which encompasses Detroit. The county's road commission housed a nature center in the mill from 1956 until the early 1980s, when financial stringencies prompted its conversion into office space. Earlier this year the facility was assigned to the park and recreation department, which also uses it for offices.

Your commentator's recent letter of protest regarding the building's peeling paint and general deterioration drew the following response from Assistant County Executive, James A. Meyers, also director of the Office of Public Services:

"There is no question that the condition of the building is not good. However, a coat of paint would not be sufficient; what we must do is sandblast the building and repair it, then apply a decent coat of paint ... We have found that we cannot do everything that needs to be done, immediately ... All our facilities are run-down, mostly due to the lack of funding and attention during the past 10-year period. We are in the process of trying to correct that. Our cash flow is minimal, and we are looking for alternative sources of funding."

Translated, the reply seems to say that the county will repair the building, if and when it can get state, federal, or private money to do so. Meantime, the old mill, a state historic site, continues to rot away, a victim of financial and bureaucratic neglect.

Northville To Reopen

The last of Henry Ford's "village industries" to operate under Ford auspices, the Northville, Mich. plant (photo) which produced valves from 1920 until its closure in November 1982, will reopen in early 1983 to make fuel tanks and shipping racks.

The factory will operate under a unique cost-saving plan in which its 52 hourly employees will work under an honor system with minimum supervision; there will be only four salaried employees, including one secretary. The plant employed 250 unionists when phase-out operations began last year. By November it had 81 hourly and 22 salaried personnel.

Future workers will be trained to perform several different jobs, giving management the flexibility in work scheduling that was commonplace in Henry Ford's day.

Hydro Plant Still Producing

Henry Ford's old Rawsonville, Mich. hydroelectric plant still stands on the banks of the Huron River southeast of Ypsilanti, Mich. The powerhouse, built in 1932, was given by Ford to the Joint Ypsilanti Recreational Organization and is now known as the Jyro Hydro Station. The plant once produced power for Ford's Ypsilanti factory and now generates power for the city and township of Ypsilanti. The facility looks much as it did in Henry Ford's days, except that the curb and concrete railing in the foreground are crumbling, and the lamp bulb has disappeared from one of the two posts located in front of the building. The original entrance canopy may be seen over the front door, just above the car. The roadway in front of the building runs over the dam which backs up Ford Lake.

Inactive for many years, Ford's Rawsonville hydroelectric plant resumed power production in 1983.

Rusticity Sacrificed

Rusticity was sacrificed when an old bridge, top photo, near Henry Ford's Sharon Hollow, Mich. mill, was razed to make way for a new superstructureless crossing, foreground of lower photo. Sharon Hollow, restored by Ford in 1939, was the automaker's smallest "village industry," employing 14 persons who made cigar lighters. The mill now is an antique shop. Original hydroelectric equipment provides the mill with electricity.

FORD COUNTRY **115**

The first page of Ford World's *April issue featured the story of Henry Ford II's retirement as chairman of Ford Motor Co.*

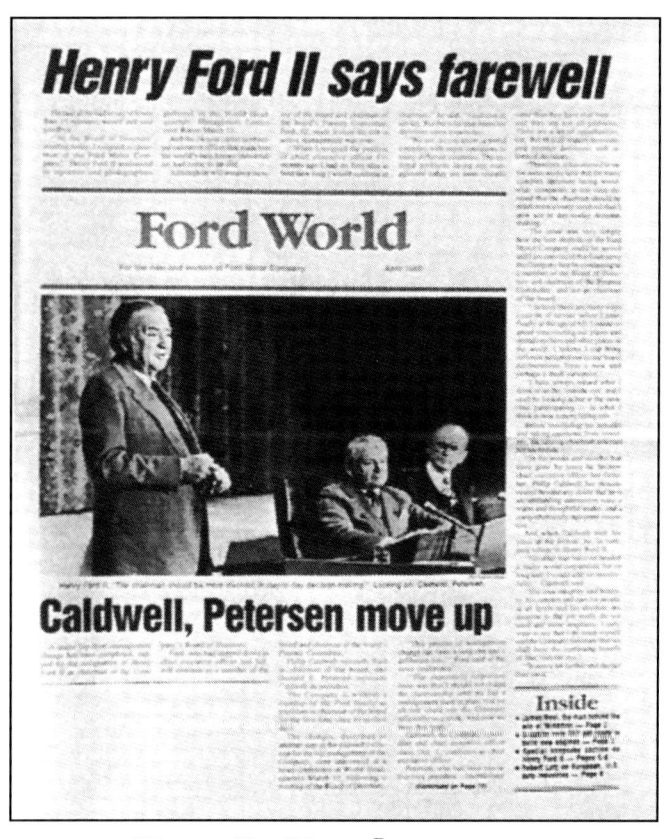

Tops In Employee Publications

Few companies can match Ford's long and distinguished record in the area of employee publications.

The company entered the field with *Ford Times* in April 1908, just a few months before the Model T's debut. A semimonthly, 16-to-40 page slick for Ford home office and branch personnel and for dealers and their employees, the *Ford Times* within a few years acquired the largest circulation of any industrial publication in the country. By early 1910 the magazine was reprinted in French, Spanish, Portuguese, and Russian, and, on the basis of being sent to 2,100 dealerships around the world, claimed the widest geographical circulation of any American publication.

Starting in 1910, *Ford Times*' circulation was expanded to include Ford owners and prospective customers. By mid-1914, the internal-external house organ had become a publication aimed at "the automobile public in general, and to Ford owners in particular." The publication was suspended with America's entry into World War I in April 1917.

Ford Times did not resume publication after the war. But another magazine, *Ford News*, was distributed among employees during the 1920s, and was published during the early and mid-1930s.

Ford Times was revived as an employee publication in April 1943, but by 1946 had evolved into the motoring magazine, which it is today. In 1946, the company also began publishing the *Rouge News*, which soon was supplemented by 30 plant newspapers.

The *Rouge News* was circulated among southeastern Michigan employees and concentrated its coverage on the Rouge industrial complex and company headquarters until 1963, when it began to include news from facilities outside Michigan, including overseas. In 1964, the paper's name was changed to *Ford World*. In the late 1960s, for budgetary reasons, the plant newspapers were disbanded and *Ford World* became a national publication.

Today, the tabloid-sized *Ford World* is mailed to the homes of the company's approximately 310,000 U.S. employees and retirees. The 12-page publication is supplemented by a locally-produced regional insert or section.

The eight-page Ohio Section covers some 44,000 readers and 14 company locations. The eight-page South Section serves 22,000 employees in 15 locations and eight states; the four-page Midwest Section, 16,000 readers in eight locations in four states; the four-page Central Section, 15,000 readers in four locations and three states.

One of the finest publications of its kind, *Ford World* ably carries on the great tradition of Ford employee publications.

Ford's famous flowing script, as pictured on a Model T brass radiator.

THE MODEL T RADIATOR

Ford Script

C. Harold Wills "penned the Ford script (and) had a style of handwriting that was both old-fashioned and pleasing."

That's what I recently read, for about the dozenth time in one version or another, in a leading old-car publication.

But the famous Ford script does not reflect Wills's handwriting. It is based on the type in a printing set which Wills had used as a boy of 15 or 16 to make calling cards, which he then sold. The type first came into use as follows:

When the Ford Motor Co. first thought of advertising itself, nobody was satisfied with the print suggested. Wills rummaged an attic for his old printing outfit, and lettered the name "Ford" in its familiar style. The design, accepted at once, endured for almost half a century. It was replaced a couple of decades after World War II by block letters, then made a comeback in the late 1960s in the company's new corporate identity program.

But, to repeat, the flowing script isn't based on Wills's handwriting, rather the handwriting of the designer of the type in his printing set. It would be interesting to know the identity of that designer, who, when you think about it, is responsible for writing which has spun on tens of millions of hubcaps and become more familiar around the world than the writing of any other brand name besides Coca-Cola.

Ford Times

Ford Times, edited and published between 1908-17 and from 1944-86 by Ford Motor Co., is now being outsourced.

The magazine, which has a monthly mailing list of 1.2 million, is being edited by the Chicago office of Hill & Knowlton, a public relations firm. "We're going to miss doing it," says ex-editor Arnold Hirsch. "There was a little sadness, but we have to adjust and go on."

"Money was not the overriding interest in farming out the *Ford Times*," adds Publications Services Manager Roland (Bud) Williams, who declined further comment.

Missed The Boat

"My Dad, if he were living, would be 98," writes reader Robert R. Rockwell, Pittsburgh, Pa. "He told me that many years ago Henry Ford himself came to the Monongahela Valley and our hometown of Charleroi (population 10,000), trying to sell Ford stock. Dad had several friends who could have bought, but no one wanted any!

"I have just finished reading *The Edsel Affair*, and noted Ford stock went public Jan. 17, 1956. What confuses me is if my Dad's story were true, wouldn't Ford stock really have been a public offering years before? And even if Ford sold no stock in Charleroi, he must have had some success elsewhere. I'm guessing that we are talking in the Model T or pre-Model T period here."

If Ford sought to sell stock in Charleroi - and Rockwell's letter marks my first awareness of it - he would have had to have done so between August, 1902, when he and his chief backer, Alexander Malcomson, agreed to form the future Ford Motor Co., and June, 1903, when the firm was chartered. During that time, Ford, Malcomson, and the latter's clerk, James Couzens,

FORD COUNTRY **117**

solicited funds from numerous Detroit area residents, and lined up nine investors in addition to themselves. After June, 1903, no further efforts to sell stock were made.

Ford and Couzens bought the shares of Malcomson and several lesser shareholders in 1906-07. The stock, by terms of the company's bylaws, forbade any stockholder to sell shares to an outsider without the approval of the other shareholders, and without giving these associates an opportunity to purchase, in proportionate amounts, at the price offered. As a consequence, stock only exchanged hands internally.

Henry Ford bought out the remainder of his fellow shareholders - Couzens, the Dodge brothers, Horace Rackham, John Anderson, and the Gray Estate - on Dec. 31, 1918. From then on, Ford held 55.2 percent of the stock, his son, Edsel, 41.7 percent, and his wife Clara, 3.1 percent. The stock remained in family hands until Edsel's death in 1943, when large holdings were bequeathed to the Ford Foundation. The company then went public in 1956.

Drat Superstition

Many a Detroiter has claimed that he turned down an invitation to invest in Ford Motor Co. in 1903. In the instance of Dr. Frederick Zumstein, however, it was Henry Ford who rejected the investor, rather than the other way around.

The Ford Co.'s first president, banker John Gray, had talked Dr. Zumstein into investing $500 in the firm, and the physician had the money in his pocket the night the investors met to organize the enterprise. But Henry Ford, observing that 12 investors already had been lined up, refused Zumstein's money, saying that a 13th stockholder would be unlucky. His compatriots agreed.

Gray bought the five shares Dr. Zumstein intended to purchase. When Gray's shares were sold to Henry Ford in 1919 they fetched $17,750,000.

A Zumstein footnote recently was furnished me by Whitman C. Daly, 80, of Berkley, Mich., who wrote that the physician had delivered the Daly's daughter, Virginia, in a Detroit apartment in 1934. After the delivery, Daly asked the doctor, "Would you happen to be the Dr. Zumstein whom Henry Ford turned down?" He looked at me and nodding his head said, "Yes, I am that man!"

We don't know whether Henry Ford's hunch about 13 investors was correct. But who can doubt that the figure 13 was unlucky for Dr. Zumstein.

Charles H. Bennett

Sold Out Too Soon

"Did Daisy Air Rifle Company ever own a part of Ford Motor Company?" asks Merritt Hampton, Glenview, Ill.

Daisy didn't, but its president, Charles H. Bennett, Plymouth, Mich., was one of 12 charter stockholders, acquiring 50 shares and a 5 percent interest in Ford for $5,000 in 1903.

Bennett became acquainted with the Ford car in the spring of 1903 when shopping for a vehicle. He had thought of buying an Oldsmobile, but had been advised by a cousin of Ford's partner, Alexander Malcomson, to look at the model produced by Ford & Malcomson, a partnership set up in August, 1902. Ford demonstrated the car to Bennett, and explained its advantages. Bennett, impressed by Ford's expertness, promised to wait for the formation of the Ford Motor Co. and one of its new cars.

Malcomson and Ford then sought to bring Daisy Co. into their enterprise. "We'd have a name sufficiently well-known for credit." Ford visited Daisy's Plymouth factory, and proposed that when the Ford Motor Co. took the place of the partnership, Daisy should underwrite half the stock, he and Malcomson keeping the rest.

Bennett and his partner, Ed Hough, inspected the Ford engine at the Dodge works where it was being made, and concluded that it was better than any on the market. But their lawyers said that Daisy's charter did not permit the air rifle company to buy stock in another concern and that if the two firms became partners, Daisy's stockholders would be liable for any Ford losses. The upshot was that Bennett invested $5,000 of his own in the Ford Motor Co.

Bennett, closer to Malcomson than to Ford, sided with the coal dealer in 1905 when the two principals fell out over the formation of a manufacturing subsidiary in which Ford froze out Malcomson. Malcomson, after threatening a lawsuit, sold his 25.5 percent interest in the company to Henry Ford in 1906, and Bennett sold his 5 percent interest to Ford and James Couzens, another charter shareholder, in 1907. To the last, Ford exhorted Bennett to keep his stock. "Don't sell. You'll be taken care of; I'll see to that," he insisted.

Bennett received $25,000 for his 50 shares. Had he retained them until 1919, when Ford bought out the remaining shareholders, he would have gotten $12.5 million, plus rich dividends along the way. (Photo from the Collections of the Henry Ford Museum and Greenfield Village.)

Thank You, Horace

One of my favorite buildings financed with Ford money is the Horace H. Rackham Building on the University of Michigan campus. The building, which houses the University's Graduate School, was put up with $2.4 million furnished by one of the Ford Motor Company's 12 charter shareholders, Horace H. Rackham.

Rackham lived until 1933, and the philanthropic fund which his will set up gave $6.5 million to the U-M in 1935, a year in which that kind of money went a long, long way. Income from the bulk of the fund continues to support research and fellowships at the university.

Built of Indiana limestone with a granite base, the handsome Rackham Building has bronze windows and door frames, a copper roof, and 155,410 square feet of floor space. For me, it contains many happy memories. In it I passed French and German languages exams en route to a Ph.D. degree, and won a faculty recommendation for a Fulbright Scholarship at the London School of Economics. Rackham also awarded me the University's top scholarship at a time when scholarships were not to be confused with financial aid by virtue of need. Now, years later, as a U-M faculty member, I occasionally roam the Rackham Building, savoring memories, standing on the rooftop, looking at the fountains and mall beneath, and the library beyond, and listening to the chimes of the nearby campus carillon. Thank you Horace, wherever you are.

Apt Inscription

A book inscribed by one of Ford's 12 original shareholders, John Wendell Anderson, recently came into your commentator's possession. The book, *Combustion on Wheels: An Informal History of the Automobile Age*, was written by David L. Cohn in 1944. Anderson's undated inscription, to a Mr. Arvidson, read, "We saw it happen."

John Wendell Anderson, as caricaturized in a 1905 publication, "As Our Friends See Us." The sketch depicts Anderson, a partner in the Detroit law firm, Anderson & Rackham, expounding at the city's University Club. (From the Collections of Henry Ford Museum and Greenfield Village).

Indeed Anderson did see auto history unfold. He was the attorney for his cousin, coal dealer Alexander Malcomson, along with Henry Ford the driving force behind the formation of Ford Motor Co. The lawyer in 1927 recalled Malcomson bringing Ford to his law office on Aug. 16, 1902.

"Mr. Ford," said Anderson, "it developed from the talk, has designed a motor car, an engine along rather novel lines; and Mr. Malcomson, who was then driving a Winton car, and was interested in automobiles, had become interested in Mr. Ford's idea, and thought it was a good one, and was willing to back his faith by advancing money to supply materials and pay the labor necessary to create a car based upon the designs which Mr. Ford had made."

As a result of the conference, Anderson drew up a contract which led to the formation of the present-day Ford Motor Co. on June 16, 1903. Moreover, the lawyer, after borrowing $5,000 from his father, invested that sum in the new firm, acquiring a 5 percent interest in return. He also became one of five charter directors, along with Ford, Malcomson, president John S. Gray, and John F. Dodge. Ford paid Anderson $12.5 million for the latter's stock in 1919.

"New" Benson Ford

The *Benson Ford* will sail on, although the lake carrier which bore the name from 1924-82 will be scrapped or used as a barge.

The "new" *Benson Ford* is the old 10,606-ton *John Dykstra*, named for the man who served as Ford's president from 1961-63. The *Dykstra*, originally named the *Joseph Wood*, was bought by Ford in 1966 from Northwestern Mutual Life Insurance Co.

The original 13,000-ton *Benson Ford*, 612 feet in length, 62 feet in beam, and 32 feet in depth, and its sister ship, *Henry Ford II*, were exceeded in capacity by only 18 vessels operating on the Great Lakes during the 1920s. With speeds up to 14 knots, Ford's lakers were chiefly used to carry Ford-mined Kentucky and West Virginia coal from Toledo to the company's River Rouge Plant in Dearborn and to Lake Superior ports and to haul iron ore from Minnesota, Wisconsin and Northern Michigan. In recent years, the Ford fleet has hauled pelletized iron ore and limestone from Wisconsin and Northern Michigan to the Rouge, in addition to coal.

The old *Benson Ford* is anchored in the Rouge slip. The pilothouse and cabin section on the stern have been removed, as have furnishings and most equipment other than the inoperative diesel engines. Thus, those who might wish to buy life rafts and other souvenirs are out of luck. Some of the equipment has been transferred to the *Henry Ford II*, which was converted into a self-unloading vessel in 1974.

One prospective buyer of the old *Benson* wants to use it as a barge, a sad ending for a once-proud craft. But even that firm's offer failed to meet minimum bid requirements.

The new *Benson Ford* recently was leased to a Toledo company for grain storage. But it's now back in Ford service.

Ford's fleet now consists of the *Henry Ford II*, the renamed *Benson Ford*, the 19,000-ton *William Clay Ford*, commissioned in 1953, and the *Ernest R. Breech*, built in 1952, although acquired by Ford in 1962. Breech was Ford's executive vice-president from 1946-55 and its chairman from 1955-60.

Watch The Ford Go By

Ford's venerable laker, *Henry Ford II*, built in 1924, is one of the ships "freighter freaks" most like to see glide by, according to a *Monthly Detroit* article forwarded by reader Mike Skinner, of Detroit.

"The power, the gritty majesty of a 600-foot bulk carrier ponderously moving up the (Detroit) river has for (freighter buffs) the same inexplicable excitement that old clocks or guns or cars have for their aficionados," declares the magazine.

Ships of the *Henry Ford II*'s 600-foot class first appeared on the Great Lakes in 1906, and were considered the behemoths of their time. Even today they are reminiscent of an exuberant age, raw American industrial power, steel trusts, and robber barons or heroic entrepreneurs, call them what one will.

The older ships are now being displaced by 1,000-foot vessels which can carry loads equal to three loads transported by the older lakers. The newer ships "are functional," sniffs Kathy McGraw, a guide at Detroit's Dossin Great Lakes Museum, "but they don't look as good."

Ship spotters look for lakers that are long, and have clean decks uncluttered by machinery, brightly colored smokestacks with unusual company logos, and bits of trim and finish that dress up a boat - things like mahogany railings or shiny brass fittings. To help identify the ships, buffs consult reference books which list vessels by name and owner, and give such data as the year the ships were built, length, tonnage, and various noteworthy features (one of the better books is *Know Your Ships*, Marine Publishing, Box 68, Sault Ste. Marie, MI 49783).

McGraw and other Motor City freighter enthusiasts find out which ships are near Detroit by monitoring radio messages between vessels and a mailboat operating out of the Motor City. McGraw's favorite ship is the *Henry Ford II*, which despite the installation 10 years ago of an unsightly loading/unloading boom, still maintains a style and beauty associated with lakers built a couple of generations ago.

When the *Henry Ford II* is due, McGraw and her fellow buffs gather on the riverbank. If the day is foggy or misty, they'll first see the big *Ford*'s prow peeking through. On early clear mornings, they can see the white superstructure glowing incandescently in soft, diffused sunlight. In addition to admiring the ship's beauty, they can sense its power through the throb of mighty diesels resonating through the water. And they'll know why Henry Ford, who sailed many times on the *Henry Ford II* between Detroit and his Northern Michigan properties, asked to be taken to see the vessel on the last day of his life, April 7, 1947. Upon being driven along the big laker, tied up at the Rouge Plant's boatslip, he proudly exclaimed to his chauffeur, "that's my yacht."

The William Clay Ford *at the Rouge Plant. (Photo from the Collections of the Henry Ford Museum and Greenfield Village.)*

Pilothouse Preservation

Named for Henry Ford's youngest grandson, the *William Clay* was built in 1953 at the Great Lakes Engineering Works Shipyard at River Rouge. She spent her lifetime carrying bulk cargoes on the Great Lakes for the Ford Co.'s Rouge Plant.

The pilothouse was donated to the museum by the Erwin Robinson Co. of Detroit so as to preserve a lasting example of Michigan's shipbuilding heritage. An interpretive exhibit describing the vessel's construction and operation from 1953 to 1984 will be placed alongside the pilothouse.

Your commentator remembers the maiden voyage of the *William Clay*, having been a member of the company's News Department in 1953. One of his colleagues that year was assigned to accompany journalists on a cruise between the Rouge and Lake Superior. The trip was made in August, and didn't we all wish we had been chosen for such a favored assignment. The guy selected, Bill Goodell, is now a Ford public affairs executive.

Leading Motown Employer

Dearborn's Ford Motor Company, not Detroit-based General Motors, nor Chrysler, headquartered in Highland Park (which is surrounded by Detroit), is the Detroit area's largest employer, according to a recently published *Short Book of Detroit Lists*. Ford has 120,000 employees in the Detroit area, General Motors 92,500, and Chrysler 82,500. The book also notes that the year-old Detroit Plaza Hotel, centerpiece of Henry Ford II's Renaissance Center, is the city's tallest building, topping out at 730 feet.

Ford Big Factory Builder

Over the past seven decades, Ford has built some of the world's biggest factories. Its Highland Park Plant was the world's largest automotive facility from 1910 until the early 1920s, when the River Rouge complex became the world's largest single-company industrial concentration. Ford's Willow Run Bomber Plant was the world's largest building upon completion in 1942. Now the *Guinness Book of World Records* informs us that "the greatest ground area covered by any building in the world is that by the Ford Parts Redistribution Center, Brownstown Township, Mich. It embraces a floor area 2,100,000 square feet or 71.16 acres." The parts center, adds *Guinness*, was opened on May 20, 1971, and employs 1,400 people. This facility obviously is of a size that would have pleased Old Henry were he still around.

Pioneer Ford Supplier

When someone writes a history of Ford Motor Co.'s suppliers - and the volume should read like a listing of who was who and is who in the auto business - it will chronicle the auto giant's relationship with the little-known General Industries Co. of Elyria, Ohio.

General Industries, according to a recent Associated Press story, has served Ford for all of the 78 years of the automaker's existence. The supplier was founded as Dan Electric Co. in 1903 and for years produced auto horns and lighting systems.

Henry Ford had special shipping requirements, said Jim Callihan, GIC's director of marketing and the firm's self-appointed historian. "Wooden boxes to ship horn buttons had to be of a special length, supposedly so Ford could use the tops of the containers for running boards of the Model T."

Much later, GIC began selling plastic-enclosed heaters and electric seat motors to Ford. The company, still housed in its original building, now employs 1,300 workers, while another 300 in auto-related operations are temporarily laid off.

Among other early Ford suppliers were the Dodge brothers (engines, transmissions and axles), Holley Carburetor, C.R. Wilson Carriage Co. (bodies), Hartford Rubber Co., Prudden Co. (tires), U.S. Steel, Hyatt Roller Bearing, Firestone, and Kelsey Wheel.

World Headquarters

Several readers have expressed an interest in seeing a picture of Ford's present World Headquarters Building. Here 'tis. The structure, originally called the Central Office Building, was completed in 1956 on a 90-acre Dearborn site. Henry Ford II's dining room and six bedrooms for executives are located in the penthouse.

FORD COUNTRY **123**

III

FORD PRODUCTS

Ford products, like the company which makes them, have long been a force to be reckoned with. During the Teens and Twenties, almost half of America's motor vehicles were Fords. Today, Ford-built vehicles account for one out of five vehicle sales in America, one out of seven worldwide.

In addition, Ford, more than any other automaker, has produced a succession of history-making models. The most famous of Fords - indeed the most influential car of all time - remains the Model T. Shortly after its demise it typically was said to have performed a service to the people "greater by far than that of the telegraph, the telephone, rural free delivery, the phonograph, the radio, or electric light and power." The passage of time has done little to diminish that assessment - at least in terms of impact on America's psychology, manners, and mores, or the national economy - television, computers, and the commercial application of atomic power and space exploration notwithstanding.

Hardworking, commonplace, heroic, the Tin Lizzie patently was the sort of thing that could happen only once. It was the first people's car, the first world car. Now a part of American folklore, and regarded with bemused affection, it continues to generate goodwill for the Ford Company.

The T's successor, the Model A, also stands out. The A's gestation alone generated interest and publicity unparalleled in the annals of business - *and* the car lived up to expectations. "Even the most godless scoffer," editorialized the *New York World*, at the time of the A's launch, "must realize that the magnum opus thus offered for sale is worth all of the commotion it is causing." "Every Ford dealer," added the *New York Times*, "is so pleased with his new product that, if stroked gently, he would purr." Some old-car enthusiasts say the A is the best car ever built, pound for pound, dollar for dollar, while others rhapsodize as did a journalist attending a Model A meet: "The lump in my throat was so big I had to unbutton my collar. It was like stumbling on your old school sweetheart after a quarter-century lapse and finding her still slender and sweet, young in heart and fun to know and - can such things be - lovely beyond recall."

The Model A enabled the Ford Company to regain in 1929-30 the market leadership lost in 1927-28 following the T's abandonment. In turn, as A sales flagged, Henry Ford brought out in 1932 his last mechanical triumph, the V-8. The V-8 outsold Chevrolet in 1935, and came close to doing so again in 1937, then lost ground during the remaining prewar years. Its bread-and-butter car on the skids, the company's market penetration also sagged - from 30 percent in 1935 to 19 percent in 1941.

Although Fords accounted for the vast bulk of company sales during the prewar era, the firm produced a handful of Lincolns from 1922 onward, and launched the medium-price Lincoln Zephyr and Mercury in 1935 and 1938, respectively, and the luxurious Lincoln Continental in 1939. The latter, built to Edsel Ford's specifications, has been ranked as the sixth best-designed mass product of modern times.

The post-World War II sellers' market bought time for Ford to bring out its first postwar products. The highly-salable '49s remain the cars Henry Ford II is "most proud of because the 'new' Ford Motor Company brought them out. They weren't the best cars we ever produced," he adds, "but they started the ball rolling for our organization."

The company's sporty Thunderbird, unveiled in 1955, broke new ground, and has become a classic. The compact 1959 Falcon, the company's first import fighter, set a record for first-year sales. Another winner was the brilliantly-styled Mustang, which broke the Falcon's record and gave its name to a generation. The company also had a noteworthy loser, the Edsel, which cost the firm more money than its executives care to remember and whose name eventually became synonymous with colossal mistake. For these reasons, the Edsel today is probably the most publicized of old cars.

The 1970 Pinto was advertised as a modern Model T, and Henry Ford II expressed the hope that its longevity might match that of the flivver. But adverse safety-related publicity hastened its 1980 demise. Meantime, the company launched the European-built Fiesta in 1976 and the Escort in 1980. The latter, during the first half of the 1980s, was the world's best-selling model. A word about Ford trucks, always a major company asset, albeit little publicized until recently. Today the company's F-Series is the nation's best selling motor vehicle, car or truck, and highly profitable as well.

Ford's current market penetration and profitability are fueled by some cars old, some cars new. The oldies are the Lincoln Town Car and Ford LTD/Mercury Grand Marquis, which have continuing appeal for the "big-car set." The hottest newcomers are the aerodynamic Taurus/Sable, which have given the company design leadership plus driveability unmatched by previous Ford production cars. Taurus/Sable have, in fact, given the company a boost reminiscent of that provided by the Model T, the Model A, V-8, and Mustang—and, in the view of Fordophiles, they couldn't happen to a better company at a better time.

Fords Among Top 100 Cars

A new medallion series, the Centennial Car Mini-Ingot Collection, pays tribute to the "100 greatest cars of the first century of automobiling." Among the 100 cars are seven made by Henry Ford/Ford Motor company including the founder's 1896 Quadricycle, 1909 Model T, 1928 Model A, 1932 V-8, 1932 Lincoln, 1941 Lincoln Continental, and the 1965 Mustang. Six GM-produced cars also were designated; two of Chrysler's.

Ford Cars Rated Highly

Ford-built cars scored well in a recent poll of six Detroit-area automotive experts to determine the five best post-World War II U.S.-built cars. The 1965 Mustang and the 1955 Chevrolet tied for first place, each being named by five of the electors.

Other best cars were the 1955 Thunderbird, 1978 Ford Fairmont, 1959 Rambler, and the 1976 Oldsmobile Cutlass. Chevrolets led the worst-car category, the 1959 model and Vegas (all models) each receiving four votes. Others rated worst were the 1958 Packard, the 1950 Nash Airflyte, and the 1949 Ford.

Those who made the selections were Tom Kleene, automotive writer for the *Detroit Free Press*, John Conde, curator of the Henry Ford Museum's Transportation Collection, James Bradley, curator of the National Automotive History Collection, Len Barnes, editor of *Motor News*, Jerry Flint, the *New York Times*'s Detroit correspondent, and Pat Bedard, executive editor of *Car and Driver*.

Fords Top-Rated

Four Fords were named among the "most important and influential cars of all times" in

FORD COUNTRY **125**

a recent *Detroit News* article.

Designated were the Model T, Model A, 1932 V-8, and 1949 Ford. The T was described as "the car that put America on wheels," the A as an "innovative" vehicle, and the '32 Ford as "the first high-volume low-priced car to have a V-8 engine, laying the groundwork for the hot rod culture and, two decades later, the horsepower race." Of the '49 Ford, it was said, "if it had not been as right as it was in both styling and mechanical attributes, Ford Motor Company might not have survived."

The other six cars on the *News*' list include the 1895 Duryea, 1903 Buick, 1912 Cadillac, 1927 Cadillac La Salle, Volkswagen Beetle, and Volkswagen Rabbit.

10 Most Romantic Cars

A recent advertisement by Hudson's, the Detroit area's largest department store, lists the 10 most romantic automobiles. Two of the cars are Ford products, the Lincoln Continental and the 1955 Thunderbird.

T, Edsel Are Best, Worst

Ford products - the Model T and the Edsel - were designated the best and worst American cars, respectively, in the September, 1973 issue of *Life*.

Two other Ford products were cited in the article - the Model A, named the seventh best car, and the 1957 Mercury Turnpike Cruiser, rated the sixth worst.

Runner-up to the Model T was the 1901-04 Curved Dash Olds, followed by the 1932-33 Duesenberg SJ, 1911-14 Mercer T Head Raceabout, 1936 Cord S10, 1915-18 Pierce-Arrow, the Model A, 1955 Chevy Bel Air, 1930-34 Packard, and 1930 Cadillac V-16.

Trailing the Edsel was the Chevy Vega, 1959 Cadillac, 1957-58 Packard with Studebaker body, 1957 Mercury, 1958 Buick, 1938 Graham Sharknose, 1939 Crosley, and 1957 Nash Ambassador.

Life's judges were 11 automotive historians, designers, and collectors, one of whom at least unsuccessfully prevailed upon *Life* to select the "greatest" and "most disappointing" cars, rather than best/worst. *Life*, true to its journalistic colors, opted for best/worst.

Oldest Production Ford

The oldest surviving production Ford made and sold by the Ford Motor Company is not in the Henry Ford Museum, where one might logically expect to find it, but in the Harold Warp Pioneer Village in Minden, Neb. Alongside its 1903 Model A, Pioneer Village displays a 1903 Cadillac, also designed by Henry Ford.

Pioneer Village was founded by Harold Warp, a native of Minden who ran up a fortune in 43 years of inventing and plastics-making in Chicago.

Five Major Changes

If you were to guess how many times Ford has made a major engineering and design change in its standard-size car over the past 70 years, you'd probably estimate a higher figure than actually exists: five. The Model T gave away to the Model A in 1927, and the A was superceded by the 1932 V-8. The next big change came with the first post-World War II offering, the 1949 Ford, and then there wasn't a major change until the 1965 Ford. The fifth big change was made in the 1979 product.

The company's all-time record-holder for longevity remains the Model T, produced from 1908-27. For many years it was believed that the T would always remain the title-holder in this department, as well as in total sales, but a number of models have been built longer including Volkswagen's 1200, Volvo's PV444, Citroën's 2CV, and Fiat's 1100 (Rolls-Royce's Silver Ghost matched the T's life span).

Longer Is Better

In 1903, the year of the Ford Motor Co.'s founding, Henry Ford was sweating the details, as recalled by Charles E. Hulse, a longtime Flint, Mich. car collector.

"In 1933," recalls Hulse, "there was an article and photo of a Curved Dash Olds in the [Detroit] *Adcrafter* magazine, and the article referred to an old artist in Detroit who illustrated early auto advertisements. I found his address, and he had a small office in one of the downtown buildings in Detroit.

"We visited, and ... he mentioned the first Ford catalog, and said, 'old Henry looked at the sample drawing of the car [1903 Model A] and said, "stretch it out, it looks too short." So I made it look longer and Ford was satisfied. He was the only one who ever complained about my work.' "

The 1903 Model A was indeed short, having a wheelbase of only 72 inches. In requesting the artist to make his car appear longer, Ford may have once again pioneered a practice in the auto industry. Most subsequent auto advertising sought to convey the impression that cars are longer (and seats wider) than facts warrant.

Search For 1903 Models

One of the brightest and most provocative publicity stunts engineered by Ford Motor Company during its 75th anniversary year is the search for as many 1903 Model As as can be found.

During the first 15 months of the company's existence, Ford built 1,708 of the cars, billed as the "most reliable machine in the world." In an effort to locate those extant, Ford has sent letters to museums, antique auto clubs, and private collectors. Owners will be invited to an anniversary luncheon in Dearborn. At present, the company knows the whereabouts of about 40 of the As, including two on display at the Henry Ford Museum. It is hoped that more will turn up, and, thanks to the worldwide publicity that has accompanied the search, the company has been hearing from a good many people who think they've got an A.

The car, which came in red only, had a short wheelbase, stiff springs, and no shock absorbers. It had a two-cylinder eight-horsepower engine which, if pushed could hit a top speed of 30 miles an hour. The vehicle had other problems too. Owners who forgot to retard the spark when cranking could suffer broken arms, and despite company claims to the contrary, the brakes tended to disappear when needed. The car initially sold for $750, and for an extra $100 a buyer could purchase a detachable tonneau (a bucket-shaped back seat).

"Breakthrough" Car

Model T hobbyists have long debated those aspects of the Tin Lizzie which made it different from other cars produced at the time of its 1908 introduction. Commenting in 1928, the U.S. Board of Tax Appeals - which was appraising the Ford Company's value, and setting forth reasons for its worth - cited the T's "distinguishing features" as follows: ... "a planetary transmission, a rear axle of unusual design, a magneto built into the flywheel as an integral part of the motor, the use of vanadium steel, and relative lightness and power. Incorporation of the magneto as part of the motor reduced the weight of the car. Vanadium steel was used in the car to make it stronger and lighter, increasing the ratio of horsepower to the weight and making the car cheaper to operate. The car was simple of design, making it easy to operate and easy to maintain and repair. The parts were so precisely manufactured that a number of cars could be disassembled, the parts mixed, and the same number of cars rebuilt from the parts. It is said that this could not be done with any other car in the low-priced field as late as 1913."

The Model T was, of course, a "breakthrough" car, perhaps the closest thing we've seen to a "reinvented" auto before or since its time. As one reflects on the flivver, he cannot but wish that a reincarnated Henry Ford (minus a few warts) would come back to "reinvent" a 1980's-style counterpart to the T.

Easy To Drive

Today, almost any motorist would regard learning to drive a Model T as difficult, since there's considerably more to driving a Tin Lizzie than modern cars. But the Ford Motor Co. in 1913 emphasized how easy it was to drive a flivver. So easy, said the firm, it seemed "especially adapted for the use of the lady driver."

"There is no complex shifting of gears to bother the driver," said Ford, "in fact there is very little machinery about the car - none that a woman cannot understand in a few minutes and learn to control with very little practice. At no time in the operation of the Ford car is it necessary to remove the hand from the steering wheel. Starting, stopping and reversing are controlled by foot pedals, leaving the hands of the driver free at all times for the more delicate operation of steering the car. This feature for safety will be recognized as a great advantage to men and women drivers alike."

Ford also extolled the virtues of the T's left-hand drive. "Many American manufacturers have blindly followed European customs by placing the driving wheel upon the right," noted the company. "In Europe, however the rule of the road is to turn to the left when approaching a vehicle. But in America, where we keep to the right, there is a distinct advantage in a left-side drive. The driver may more easily see the road ahead - and watch his clearance in passing other vehicles. Also he does not have to get out in the dirt or mud when he properly stops the car at the curb."

Finally, Ford boasted that the T had but four constructional units - the powerplant, frame, front axle and rear axle. Each, said the company, was easily accessible and could be quickly removed for adjustment or replacement. "All of these simplifying features go to make the Ford a silent running car," boasted the firm. "Its perfect mechanical adjustment and the elimination of all unnecessary parts minimize noise in Ford operation. The Ford is as silent as machinery can possibly be made."

The Model T as silent as machinery can possibly be made? Anyone who believes that will believe anything.

Favorite Picture

Every Model T enthusiast has his favorite flivver picture - and here's mine. This photo was taken in a California barnyard in 1952, and of course its appeal lies as much in the jacked up left rear wheel and the two chickens as in the superb composition and lighting.

Sex In Model T?

One of the more interesting letters that has come to the attention of James J. Bradley, Curator of the Detroit Public Library's National Automotive History Collection, deals with Henry Ford's alleged views on sex as it concerns the Model T. Carl E. Ott, Berkeley, Mo., wrote Bradley that his father, a Michiganian who died in 1955, had told him the following story several times:

"In 1924 or 1925, while driving a Model T on a Michigan road, the car developed engine trouble. My father stopped and raised the hood. While working on the engine, trying to ascertain the cause of the trouble, a large car (not a Ford) passed, slowed up and pulled to a stop. A man got out of the car and came back to offer assistance. My father recognized the man as Henry Ford."

"Mr. Ford was curious about the engine trouble and also about my father's opinion of the Model T. My father mentioned the only objection to the car which came to his mind at the moment - the small seating capacity of the front seat. According to my father, Mr. Ford replied that the length of the seat, which I have found to be 38 inches, was adequate and one merit of the length was the inability of a man and woman to engage in intercourse while in the seat of the car. Mr. Ford said that for this reason he would not make the seat any longer ... I recently told an acquaintance of my father's conversation with Mr. Ford. The acquaintance said that if such was Mr. Ford's intention, that Mr. Ford was in error - that intercourse was possible in the front seat of a 1924-1925 Model T."

Personally, given the Model T's seven-foot height, I should think that a short couple could embrace standing up.

The Cat's Pajamas

The discovery of King Tutankhamen's tomb in Egypt had recently been in the news and "Lizzie lables" were in vogue when young William T. Cameron, Minocqua, Wis., and his pals drove their Model T, dubbed "King Tut's Kiddie Kar," to the Indianapolis "500" in 1924. An old streetcar gong was mounted under the rear floorboards and, Cameron recently recalled, "was extremely helpful in getting us through traffic lines at the Speedway." Added Cameron, "I was working for an electric company at that time, and brought home a large enameled reflector which we mounted upside down on the back of the front seat with a hose leading beneath the car. This saved a lot of time looking for 'rest stops.' " The sign on the rear of the car reads "King Tut's Kiddie Kar Fresh from the Tomb," on the rear door "Stage Entrance," and on the front door "Queen Tut's Bathtub Step In." Legends on the left side read "Family Entrance" and "Sealed Entrance to the Tomb" (in front where there was no door). No doubt about it, this flivver, in its day, was the berries, the razzmatazz, hotsy-totsy, copacetic, jake, swell, and the cat's pajamas and the cat's meow as well.

Expression Of Art

Richard Cooper can't afford a Model T, so he did the next best thing: he painted one on his garage door, adding three-dimensional realism by making and putting on tires, fenders, grille, and headlights which stick out in front of the door. Cooper, an industrial truck repairman, at Ford's Woodhaven (Mich.) Stamping Plant, spent 11 days of his 1974 vacation fashioning the parts and painting the door. He made fenders, headlights, and hubcaps from stovepipes. The grille formerly was a window screen, and the hood ornament a wooden table leg. The front tires are real, but are actually one tire cut in half and made to look like two. Why did the Monroe, Mich., citizen do it? "Because Model Ts are my great love. But with four kids from 8 to 18 years old, I just can't afford to have the genuine car parked in my garage ... but I can dream." (Photo courtesy *Monroe* (Mich.) *Evening News*.

A "T" Under The Tree

A tyke, her toys and a T pose in this 1920s-era photo submitted by reader John C. Walters, Jr., 803 Woodland Avenue, Millville, NJ 08332, who bought the print at a yard sale. Was the T also a Christmas present? We'll likely never know.

Wood For Model Ts

"What woods were used in the Model T?" asks Ron Halley, of Allentown, Pa.

The T's body was framed with spruce and hemlock; the wheel spokes were made of ash or hickory; and the front seat framing of the gasoline tank was pine. Wood for the T was lumbered from Henry Ford's forests in Northern Michigan and sawed in his mills at Kingsford (Iron Mountain), L'Anse, and Pequaming.

Model T Radio Pioneer

A Model T was the first car to be fitted with a radio, according to the British-based *Book of Firsts*. The radio was installed on a passenger door in May, 1922 by 18-year-old George Frost, president of Chicago's Lane High School Radio Club.

The first commercially-produced car radio was the Philco Transitone, introduced by the Philadelphia Storage Battery Co. in 1927. By 1933 more than 100,000 U.S. cars were equipped with radios.

FORD COUNTRY

Good Old Days

Model T lovers will find few pictures more pleasing to the eye than this one of a 1917 T touring owned by Dave Chambers, West Lafayette, Ind., and taken on Oct. 3, 1948. Lizzie is coming off the Hoffman Iron Bridge - built about 1884, torn down about 1956 - which crossed the middle fork of Wildcat Creek in Tippecanoe County, Ind. *(Photo courtesy Dave Chambers)*

Model T Bus Stamp

A picture of a Model T school bus is featured on a new 3.4-cent coil stamp, above, issued by the U.S. Postal Service. The 3.4-cent denomination meets the new basic minimum per-piece rate for carrier route third class bulk mailings by nonprofit organizations.

The T body shown on the stamp was built in 1927 by Bluebird Body Co., Fort Valley, Ga. The vehicle, also restored by Bluebird, is now displayed in Fort Valley.

The green stamp, part of the Transportation Series initiated in 1981, has two lines of type: "School Bus 1920s" and "3.4 USA."

Ignorance Pays

You're a contestant on the television game show, "Trivial Trap," and the host, Bob Eubanks, asks, "Were all Model Ts painted black?"

Contestant: "Yes."

Eubanks: "Correct!"

But as every Ford enthusiast knows, the answer is no. Fords were painted various colors until 1913, and again from 1926-27.

At times, it obviously pays to be ignorant, especially on a game show whose host is equally uninformed.

Thanks to well-informed Mrs. Gary Custer, Harrisonburg, Va., for sharing this tidbit.

Farewell To E.B. White

The author of "Farewell to Model T," the most delightful essay ever written about the Tin Lizzie, died recently in North Brooklin, Maine. He's E.B. White, who wrote about the flivver under the pseudonym Lee Strout White.

Copies of the *New Yorker*'s May 16,

1936 edition, which originally published White's touching little story, were worn out within months of publication, prompting G.P. Putnam's Sons to reprint the essay in book form. On the jacket of the book, which sold for 75 cents in 1936, the publisher described *Farewell to Model T* as "the perfect gift book - the perfect book to read aloud." Still true, although the price of any 1936 edition (your commentator is fortunate enough to have two) is somewhat more than 75 cents, and the book is difficult to find.

"I see by the new Sears Roebuck catalogue," the essay begins, "that it is still possible to buy an axle for a 1909 Model T Ford, but I am not deceived. The great days have faded, the end is in sight. Only one page in the current catalogue is devoted to parts and accessories for the Model T; yet everyone remembers springtimes when the Ford gadget section was larger than men's clothing, almost as large as household furnishings. The last Model T was built in 1927, and the car is fading from what scholars call the American scene - which is an understatement, because to a few million people who grew up with it, the old Ford practically was the American scene.

"It was the miracle God has wrought. And it was patently the sort of thing that could only happen once. Mechanically uncanny, it was like nothing that had ever come to the world before. Flourishing industries rose and fell with it. As a vehicle, it was hardworking, commonplace, heroic; and it often seemed to transmit those qualities to the persons who rode in it. My own generation identified it with Youth, with its gaudy, irretrievable excitements; before it fades into the mist, I would like to pay it the tribute of the sigh that is not a sob, and set down random entries in a shape somewhat less cumbersome than a Sears Roebuck catalogue.

"The Model T was distinguished from all other makes of cars by the fact that its transmission was of a type known as planetary - which was half metaphysics, half sheer friction ...

Published in the last week of May, 1927, this cartoon laments the passing of Henry Ford's "Tin Lizzie," sometimes also referred to as "Elizabeth." (Photo from the Collections of Henry Ford Museum and Greenfield Village.)

Because of the peculiar nature of this planetary element, there was always, in Model T, a certain dull rapport between engine and wheels, and even when the car was in a state known as neutral, it trembled with a deep imperative and tended to inch forward ... In this respect it was like a horse, rolling the bit on its tongue, and country people brought to it the same technique they used with draft animals.

"Its most remarkable quality was its rate of acceleration. In its palmy days the Model T could take off faster than anything else on the road. The reason was simple. To get under way, you simply hooked the third finger of the right hand around a lever on the steering column, pulled down hard, and shoved your left foot forcibly against the low speed pedal; the car responded by lunging forward with a roar ...

"The driver of the old Model T was a man enthroned. The car, with top up, stood seven feet high. The driver sat on top of the gas tank, brooding it with his own body. When he wanted gasoline, he alighted, along with everything else in the front seat; the seat was pulled off, the metal cap unscrewed, and a wooden stick thrust down to sound the liquid in the well ... Directly in front of the driver was the windshield - high, uncompromisingly erect. Nobody talked about air resistance, and the four cylinders pushed the car through the atmosphere with a simple disregard of physical law ...

"The purchaser never regarded his purchase as a complete, finished product. When you bought a Ford, you figured you had a start - a vibrant, spirited framework to which could be screwed an almost limitless assortment of decorative and functional hardware ... A Ford was born naked as a baby, and a flourishing industry grew up out of correcting its rare deficiencies and combating its fascinating diseases ...

"Repairs? ... Having 'fixed' it, the owner couldn't honestly claim that the treatment had brought about the cure. There were too many authenticated cases of Fords fixing themselves - restored naturally to health after a short rest. Farmers soon discovered this, and it fitted nicely with the draft-horse philosophy: 'Let 'er cool off and she'll snap into it again'.

"The days were golden, the nights were dim and strange. I still recall with trembling those loud, nocturnal crises when you drew up to a signpost and raced the engine so the lights would be bright enough to read destinations by. I have never been really planetary since. I suppose it's time to say good-bye. Farewell, my lovely!"

Butch's "Git Car"

Those of us who saw the movie, *Butch Cassidy and the Sundance Kid*, have the impression that Butch and the Kid were gunned down in South America in 1909. But Butch's sister, Lula Parker Betenson, in a new book, *Butch Cassidy, My Brother*, says that the desperado survived the shootout and in 1925 made his way home from Juarez, Mexico, to Utah - in, what else, a Model T.

T Tied To Advertising

Ever notice how often various companies tie in the Model T with their advertising? A few years ago the Mennen Company's advertisements featured a Model T filled with men's toiletries; and Auto Union (Audicars) and Universal Oil Products Company pictured Tin Lizzies in their ads, while noting that their products antedated even the flivver. Volkswagen has frequently carried pictures of T's in its ads, comparing the Ford's finer qualities with those of the Beetle. At present, RCA's ads show how easily the firm's AM/FM-stereo push-button radio can be installed under the dashboard of a 1915 T.

Thrill of a T

The gift of a Model T must have excited many a person, but perhaps none so much as Henry A. Wallace, vice-president from 1940-44.

On his wedding day in 1914 Wallace was given a Tin Lizzie by his father, a secretary of agriculture under two presidents. Wallace and his bride came out of the church after the ceremony, and the bridegroom was so pleased with the sight of the Ford that he ignored congratulators, went immediately to the car, and drove off. It was thought odd, but people said he was testing the car for his bride's comfort. A half-hour passed, and then another. Toward late afternoon Wallace returned, and called out from the driver's seat, "Get in, Ilo, I'd forgotten you."

Wallace's wife told the story years later.

Capt. Harry Truman poses in his World War I uniform in front of his Stafford car. (Photo courtesy of Truman Library, Independence, Mo.)

Truman's Ford Connection

Harry Truman generally looked down his nose on Model Ts. But he did momentarily consider establishing a Ford dealership, as brought out in the 1983 book, *Dear Bess: The Letters from Harry to Bess Truman 1910-1959*.

After racing with a Model T owner in 1914, Truman wrote, "He had a half-mile start on me, and just when I got within about a hundred yards of him one of my lights jarred out and I had to stop. He'll never get done blowing about beating my Stafford with his little old Ford ... You can imagine that I was rather hitting the high places when I tell you I gained the half-mile in driving two and a half."

Truman's estimate of the Tin Lizzies also is offered in the following lines: "Dreamt I was taking you to the show last night. Had a new machine (not a Ford either)."

The future president's sole favorable reference to a Model T was prompted by loneliness while awaiting his return to America after World War I. Writing from France on December 14, 1918, he told Bess, "I am frankly homesick and very, very lonesome ... I'm hoping to have just enough of this world's goods [upon my return] to make it pleasant to try for more, to own a Ford and tour the U.S.A. ..."

Truman toyed with the idea of entering the auto business in 1916, with a partner in a lead and zinc mine near Commerce, Okla. "I may go into the auto business down here if I can make the old mine produce even a reasonable amount," he wrote. "There is no Ford agency here. One would pay about $5,000 a year. They sell about 200 cars every year here, besides supplies and tires." But Truman's mine failed, and, after a flyer in the oil business, he joined the Army.

History Repeats Itself

Computer clubs are being organized around the country much in the manner of auto clubs in motordom's early history.

More than 400 clubs for owners of Commodore computers are listed in a recent issue of *Commodore Computers*, and similar clubs have sprung up for users of Apple, Atari, Texas Instruments (now an orphan make), and other hardware. Members of the clubs learn how to use computers, try out new software, and read computer magazines.

The first club formed by the owners of any one make of car was organized by Ford's St. Louis branch manager in mid-1908, after a group of Ford owners proposed the idea. The manager asked the city's 300 "Fordists" to be his guests at a nearby resort, where a club was organized, membership and tourist committees appointed, and an identifying radiator emblem selected. Runs of up to 150 miles were planned for summer and fall Sunday afternoons. The *Ford Times*, advised of these arrangements, found "the idea to be an excellent one, for it promotes sociability among members, boosts the automobile generally, and assists in Ford sales in particular."

Taking their cue from the St. Louis branch, Ford branches and dealers during the next few years organized owners' clubs in hundreds of American communities. Some of the sociability runs and parades brought together as many as 1,200 Model Ts and 5,000 Ford owners and members of their families.

The first outing of the first auto owners club, organized by Ford's St. Louis branch manager in mid-1908. All of the cars are pre-Model T Fords, the outing preceding the Tin Lizzie's introduction by four months. (Photo from the Collections of the Henry Ford Museum and Greenfield Village)

Ford Joke Recalled

"One major factor in the achievement of the Fuller Brush Company," notes an article on the firm in the April 1982 issue of *Yankee*, "was the flood of cartoons and jokes that popularized the Fuller Brush Man as the Model T Ford was popularized a generation before with barbs about the Tin Lizzie."

Quite true, and the same may be said of the Nash Rambler and the Volkswagen "Beetle."

The Ford joke flourished during much of the period in which the Model T was made. It is impossible to precisely determine the origins of Ford humor. It may have been an offspring of the "automobile joke," which was a stock-in-trade of vaudeville performers after 1902. The Essex, Saxon, and even the high-priced Pierce-Arrow were among the targets of comedians during the early automobile period. One gag that always brought a laugh at the Franklin's expense was the description of a bucktoothed girl: "She wouldn't be so bad-looking only she's got Franklin teeth - they're 'air-cooled.'"

Another view was that the jokes were started in Ford's early years by competitors. "It's not a car," rival salesmen allegedly told potential buyers, "it's just a Ford." Credence is given this opinion by some of the company's 1907 advertising. "The Ford 4-cylinder ($600) runabout owes half its unparalleled popularity to the misrepresentation of jealous rivals," stated one advertisement, while another remarked: "Had you ever noticed that it is a weakness inherent in disciples to disparage their leader? Some makers affect to discount the achievements of FORD."

Perhaps another source of the Ford joke was the Ford owner himself. Out of a desire to forestall or avert criticism, some Ford owners resorted to the psychology of the defense mechanism. By joking about the car's smallness, its low price, and so on, the Fordist could laugh off any joshing the owner of a bigger and higher-priced car might be disposed to give him.

The Model T itself, because of its very cheapness, versatility, and toughness, encouraged many Ford jokes. Almost everyone knew that more than half of the pieces that made up the Ford engine sold for 10 cents or less. News stories frequently told of a stationary Model T providing power for motors which did everything from running newspaper presses and telephone exchanges to pumping water and exterminating gophers.

The car's toughness also was widely discussed. A Texan had to abandon his T to escape Mexican bandits, who hacked and burned the car until it was

FORD COUNTRY **135**

a wreck. However, the owner returned and was able to drive the T away. Another Ford, although buried for six years in the muck of a California riverbed, still had gas in the tank and ran "as good as new" after starting wires were installed.

Such stories made the public feel that almost anything was possible for a Model T - hence the countless jokes which, though bordering on the ridiculous, had a trace of plausibility about them. No doubt many of the people who invented or repeated Model T jokes fully shared the opinion expressed by author/reformer Ida Tarbell in 1915: "I have never in all the world ... seen so much to cause me to laugh and weep, to wonder and rejoice, as I have at the Ford."

Advertising men believed that Ford jokes helped sales until the early 1920s. After that time, however, as the Chevrolet, Dodge, Hudson-Essex, and Willys-Overland moved rapidly to the fore and the Model T became an anachronism, the Ford joke boomeranged too frequently to be considered an asset. Now Ford owners realized that their critics were in dead earnest and fewer of them could laugh off the jokes. The nationwide Keith-Albee vaudeville organization, perhaps the country's leading arbiter of street-corner humor, issued a mandate that Ford jokes, because they were not funny anymore, were to be barred from the stage.

For practical purposes the Ford joke died with the Model T. The Model A, introduced in December 1927, was too highly regarded stylistically and mechanically to lend itself to humor. "With her," observed the *New York Sun*, "he who goes to josh remains to praise." The Ford joke never completely died out, however. In 1953, an owner of a 1908 Model T was fined for speeding. His widely publicized courtroom comment was in keeping with the Lizzie tradition: "It was only hitting on three. If it had been hitting on all four I doubt if you would have caught me."

Ts Average 34.5 MPG

In an increasingly fuel-oriented society, we old-car owners frequently are asked what kind of mileage our buggy gets. Many of us, unequipped with fuel gauges and odometers, don't know how many mpg we get - or how many mpg our cars got when new. But if you are a Model T owner, and are asked the question, you might keep in mind that 205 stock Model Ts averaged 34.5 mpg on a Denver tour in January 1927. The winning car, as noted in an article by Les Burg in *Vintage Ford*, attained 56 mpg - not bad for a windy, snowy day with the temperature at 10 degrees.

The economy run was sponsored by Ford and the *Rocky Mountain News*, a Denver daily; and one of the judges was Floyd Clymer, later a major automotive publishing figure.

Sticking To One Model

There are quite a few 1916 Model Ts around. But Samuel Treon, Red Cross, Pa., has one that's rather special, for he has driven it since the day it was bought, June 16, 1916.

Treon was 12 years of age when the man who reared him, Harry Latsha, bought the flivver for $440. "You paid another $17.50 for freight. That was it. There was no this and that," Treon recently informed the *Sunbury* (Pa.) *Daily Item*.

Although he was too young to obtain a license, Treon drove the T on the roads near his home and remembers riding in it many times to church and market. Today, the car is shiny and worth a lot more than $440. "There's no end to offers," observes the retired insurance agent. "But I just say it's not for sale."

Ford Joke Books

Covers of two of the numerous Ford joke books which appeared during the heyday of the Model T. (Photo from the Collections of the Henry Ford Museum and Greenfield Village.)

Don't Be Seen In One

A Model T didn't do much for a young man's image in the mid-1920s. Prof. Harold E. Kubly of the University of Wisconsin recently recalled a 1925 trip which he and a friend took to the East in a Tin Lizzie. "In Detroit," he said, "we got on a ferry to Buffalo, and upon arrival a host of fancy cars came out of the hold - Cadillacs, Packards, Pierce-Arrows and the like - and much to the amusement of the citizens, our Model T. This evoked a number of supposedly funny remarks - and it was only after the other cars had been claimed that my friend and I took over our car.

All went well until we were headed home when mountain driving did us in. We burned out the brake and low gear bands and got to Hagerstown, Md., only by driving up a mountain in our only good gear - reverse. There we sold the car, got on the B & O Capitol Limited and finally arrived home."

That Green Pill

All the talk about "gasohol" has revived the 1914 story about Henry Ford having looked into a scheme to use water as a fuel.

A 70-year-old inventor, Louis Enricht, claimed he could make a car run on water and a mysterious green pill. The press was abuzz with stories about Enricht's substitute for gasoline, and an intrigued Ford sent the inventor a Model T for use in a test on Enricht's estate in Farmington, Long Island. After observing the T's engine turnover and run on the doped water, Ford issued a careful statement to the press: "I don't know yet what to think of Enricht's discovery, but if tests work out I will buy the process. I understand he is trying to disguise the mixture so he can get a patent."

Enterprising reporters soon discovered that Enricht previously had been arrested for fraud in England, and had paid a $500 fine. Later, chemists discovered that Enricht's pill contained acetylene. By using acetone to take up

FORD COUNTRY **137**

the acetylene and then dissolving the acetone in water, an explosion was carried to the cylinders. The reaction was the same as if one poured oil on ashes. So Enricht had developed a gasoline substitute, one which could be made for a penny a gallon, but which would destroy expensive engines upon consuming a few tankfuls of the stuff. Ford naturally dismissed the "invention," one of thousands of crank panaceas he was to receive during his lifetime.

Perennial Harvester

A 1917 Model T truck has participated in every harvest for 57 years on the Ernest Duhachek farm near Newman Grove, Neb. Duhachek bought the truck's engine, frame, and wheels for $495, then added the cab, seat, and cargo box. The truck's a homebody; it's never been more than a few miles from Newman Grove.

1918 T Still On The Job

One of the nation's oldest working Model Ts is a 1918 panel truck still occasionally used for deliveries by Callandar Cleaners, Columbus, Ohio. The flivver was bought by C.E. Callandar, who founded his firm in 1906 and at first used a horse-and-buggy for deliveries. C.E.'s son, Don, is now head of the firm.

Ford Country, Dutch Style

Was the Model T popular in Holland in the early 1920s? Yes, if the photo (above), taken in Amsterdam, is any indication. Nine of the 10 trucks shown are Ts, the exception being the vehicle at far left. A Fordson tractor also appears second to end, far right.

Yankee Ingenuity

"Back in 1922," a *Detroit News* reader recently wrote the paper's editor, "a friend and I bought a Model T Ford and headed for Chicago to look for work."

"We had four flat tires, and no money to fix them. But a Model T could be driven on flat tires if the tires were stuffed with weeds. That's what we did, and that's how we got to Chicago."

5,000 Ts in Uruguay

There are more than 5,000 Model Ts on the roads of Uruguay, many used for everyday travel, according to the *Detroit News*. Souped up flivver engines also are regularly used in racing events.

T-Rail Ambulance

The use of a converted Model T in the Queensland Ambulance Transport Brigade is reported in a recent article in *Restored Cars*, an Australian publication.

Beginning in 1917, ambulances began operating on rails during Queensland's wet season, during which service was bogged down in isolated areas. The T unit was used by the Goondiwindi and Baralba "centres" of the Brigade. Its engine was placed at a right angle to the brake, and chain drive was used to provide traction. Because of the T's unique transmission, the unit did not have to be turned around at the destination, but simply put in reverse, while the driver faced in the return direction. The vehicle was "rather expensive at 436 pounds complete."

"The main trouble with railcars using a chain drive," observes Robert Scoon, Arcadia, Calif., who forwarded the article, "was that the links would break or skip off the cogs; this happened when the chain stretched. An idler was needed."

We're familiar with Ts having been used as ambulances; 6,000 of them were built for the Allied forces during World War I. And we're equally familiar with the Tin Lizzie having been mounted on rails for a variety of purposes. But Brian Nelson's article, "Ambulance Transport in Australia," is the first mention we've seen of the T being used as an ambulance on rails.

Model Ts In Japan

Model Ts were used to teach Japanese to drive cars in the 1920s, according to a recent story in *Vintage Ford* by Col. Kenneth R. Baird.

Semma Iguchi, 83, owner/operator of a Kobe driving school for more than 60 years, has maintained his interest in Ts, and plans to open a museum devoted to them.

Iguchi, says Colonel Baird, used Model Ts during the 1920s because the flivver was Japan's most popular car during that decade. He obtained his Ts from Ford's Yokohama assembly plant and Tokyo's used-car market. Iguchi and his staff performed all repair work, making use of Japanese-language shop manuals. Replacement parts were brought from Ford's Kobe dealer. The most vexing problem associated with the car: starting. Iguchi used horse blankets and hot water to facilitate starts.

Iguchi still had Ts in his inventory at the outset of World War II, but some of his cars went to scrap dealers, and others were damaged by bombing.

The collector's first acquisition was a well-restored 1926 T. He recently visited the U.S. in search of a 1914 model.

First Tokyo Taxis

Six Model Ts provided Tokyo's first taxi service in 1912, according to *Mazda World*, published in Hiroshima, Japan.

Tin Lizzie meters registered 0.60 yen for the first mile, 0.10 yen for each additional half mile, and 0.10 yen for every five minutes of waiting time. In 1912, a yen would buy two dozen eggs; today it's worth about half a U.S. cent. Only the well-to-do could afford T taxi service, and they had to pay an extra 0.10 yen per quarter-mile, if traveling late at night, in the rain, or through muddy streets. (Thanks to reader Charles W. Reich, of Jacksonville, Fla., for forwarding *Mazda World.*)

Low-Price Heritage

Lynn A. Townsend, ex-chairman of Chrysler Corporation, credits the Model T, Model A, and V-8 with paving the way for the Ford company to outsell all other firms, including General Motors, in the low-price field. "The company's heredity was the quality, low-priced car, and they still live with that heredity," noted Townsend with a hint of envy.

Model T Invasion

"Ford is conquering Japan," proudly declared the Ford Times *in 1913. This photo shows a Ford dealership and taxicab garage complete with uniformed driver. (Photo from the Collections of Henry Ford Museum and Greenfield Village.)*

Somewhere In Time

Used Model Ts, as we all know, didn't command premium prices during their heyday. Even so, I found surprising the following advertisement from a 1915 edition of the Waterbury (Conn.) American: "For sale - Tribune bicycle, cost $60, will sell cheap or will trade even for Ford touring car." A pre-1915 Ford touring in good shape fetches many thousands these days. Wonder what a pre-1915 Tribune bike is worth?

Restored In Russia

This car is represented as the first Model T to have been restored in Estonia, a province of the U.S.S.R. Margus H. Kuuse, engineer and automotive journalist, sent the photo to a friend and ex-General Motors associate of mine, Karl E. Ludvigsen, now vice-president-governmental affairs, Ford of England. Kuuse's note to Ludvigsen said that a second T, with a Tudor body, will be restored in time for vehicle rallies in 1983.

Pleasant Rattle

During the teens, the Pierce-Arrow was regarded as the car to own; and the Model T was looked upon by jokesters as the car not to own. Consequently, innumerable jokes were spun involving the two cars. My favorite is the following: "Along a country road came a $6,000 Pierce-Arrow. As it caught up to a Ford car, the owner of the big car looked patronizingly at the owner of the Ford, and said: 'Heavens, man, what is there about your car that makes such a dreadful rattling noise?' "

" 'That is the $5,500 jingling in my pocket,' replied the Ford owner."

Henry Outfoxes Billy

Henry Ford was a hard man to beat when it came to pricing, as William C. Durant, the founder of General Motors, learned in 1923.

"Durant," writes Whitman C. Daly, of Berkley, Mich., who was working for a Detroit body builder at the time, "ran ads in the three Detroit newspapers that his new car, the Durant Star, would be the lowest-priced car on the market. The Star touring was supposed to sell for $10 less than a Ford touring. About three or four days before the Star's debut, Henry Ford cut his price $25 so that when the Star was introduced, the Ford touring was selling for less than Durant's car.

"Two fellow employees bought Stars," added Daly, "and one allowed me to take his car for a spin. I would say that it was a much easier car to handle than the Model T."

But the Star never sold for less than the Tin Lizzie, nor has any other regular-size car.

Endurance Runs

Advertisements heralding a Model T Ford Endurance Run in Death Valley, Calif., on February 16-20 bring to mind the endurance runs in which Tin Lizzies were entered in years of yore.

During the period 1907-12, the Ford Company, some of its factory branches, and many of its dealers participated in hundreds of endurance contests. Flivvers were frequent winners in their classification and occasionally showed up well in the sweepstakes competition of important tours. A Model T finished second in the 1910 Munsey Tour, and a team of three Fords ranked fourth, ahead of the Cadillac, Marathon, and Flanders in the prestigious Glidden Tour in 1941. Perhaps the T's greatest victory came in Russia, where it was the only one of 45 European and two American cars to receive a perfect score in a 1,954-mile test conducted by the Imperial War Department. Czar Nicholas II personally inspected the winning T and recommended Fords for the Russian army. Ford dealers often conducted special endurance tests to show that their cars could withstand the roughest kind of treatment. A Rochester, N.Y., dealer annually sponsored January tours of Ford cars over hundreds of miles of snow.

Actually, the Ford Company never worked up quite the enthusiasm for reliability-endurance runs that it did for racing and hill climbs. Perhaps it regarded the former as being too tame. "Endurance runs," complained the *Ford Times*, "are that only in name; in actuality they are joyrides that accomplish nothing except a holiday for the contestants and advertising orders for the newspapers." The publication also complained that many of the contestants who finished with perfect scores had cheated, and suggested that each car should be equipped "with a moving picture machine and a talking machine to see what the driver and observer are up to."

Model T 500s

Model Ts, which years ago burned up dirt tracks all over the country, are still being raced in annual 500-mile "performance runs" in California, Montana, and Colorado. Top T driver is M.R. "Dutch" Watters, a 65-70 year-old Coloradoan, who won all three events in 1978 at average speeds of 52.06, 53.83, and 51.91 mph. Watters is the third driver to win the "Triple Crown" of racing Ts, according to an article by Harold H. Wilson in *Vintage Ford*.

The Montana race is the oldest of the three, having been run for 17 successive years. It is also the biggest of the three 500s, usually attracting drivers from four or five states. The Montana race is held in late June; the California event in late February; and the Colorado run in August or September. To be eligible, Ts must be stock with the exception of the outside oil line running from the transmission cover to the front of the engine.

T Named Greatest Car

The Model T was selected as the "world's greatest motorcar" by *Motor Trend*'s readers, who have named 24 autos to the magazine's Hall of Fame. Ranked second and third in the poll were the Porsche 356 (1950-64) and Mercedes-Benz 300 SL (1954-67). Four other Ford products were designated among the top 24: Model A (1928), Ford (1949), Thunderbird (1955-57), Mustang (1964-67), and Pinto.

Model T Is Fashionable

The Model T has lent its name to the world of fashion? For years *Webster*'s and other leading dictionaries have defined "Ford" as a design that repeats and repeats in sales, as "a highly successful fashion designer," or as a "low-priced copy of a successful high-priced style in woman's dress." It likely won't be long until dictionaries begin describing an "Edsel" as a colossal mistake, putting the Ford Company two up on other automakers.

Detroit Commemorates T

As part of its celebration of the national Bicentennial, Detroit is issuing this commemorative coin which on one side shows a replica of a 1909 Model T, honoring the city's past, and on the other side shows a finished concept of the Renaissance Center (now under construction on the riverfront), symbolizing the future. Made of antique bronze and about the size of a half-dollar, the coin is on sale for $3.50.

Model T Talk

It's surprising how much the phrase "Model T" continues to pop up in the public prints. Over a recent five-week period, for example, I noted a United Press International story which said that the cooling plan for the Three Mile Island nuclear reactor "will use the same natural circulation process Henry Ford used to cool the Model T engine"; a *Detroit Free Press* article which reported that the owner of a Birmingham, Mich. shirt printing company aspires to be "the Henry Ford of T-shirts" and is well on his way "to becoming Mr. Model T"; and a *Detroit Free Press* advertisement for a Japanese typewriter which boasted that the machine is "jampacked with quality like the Model T Ford and just as simple to repair." The memory of the Tin Lizzie thus has become a part of America's thinking and lexicon.

Most Influential Cars

Ford's Model T and Volkswagen's Beetle were named the "most influential cars" in world history by an auto-oriented group recently surveyed by the *Detroit News*.

The T was built between 1908-27. The Beetle, first produced in West Germany in 1946, was sold in the U.S. through 1977, and continues to be assembled in Mexico, Peru, Brazil, and Nigeria.

Trailing the Tin Lizzie and the Bug were Ford's Model A (1927-31), Packards in general, but especially the 1928-40 models, the 1924 Chrysler, 1939-40 Oldsmobile, 1922-24 Essex Coach, 1932 Ford V-8, the Nash Rambler and its successor, Rambler American, and the 1964 Mustang.

The poll's panelists included John Conde and Randy Mason, retired curator and associate curator of the Henry Ford Museum's Transportation Collection, respectively; Bob Lienert, editor *Automotive News*, Ralph Nader, consumer activist; George Romney, ex-president of AMC; Arvid Jouppi, auto analyst for Collin, Hochspin Co.; Roger White, curatorial assistant, National Museum of American History; Dick Teague, AMC vice-president for styling; Ross Roy, head of the Detroit advertising agency which bears his name; Richard Kughn, auto collector; Tom Northrup, manager of the Detroit Branch of the Society of Automotive Engineers; and the author of this column.

Catalogs, Barrels, and Ts

The Big Three in the Pantheon of Americana: "The Sears catalog, the cracker barrel, and the Model T," according to columnist George Cantor of the *Detroit News*.

McDonald's is seeking entry into the pantheon, reports Cantor, as evidenced by its use of nostalgic ads. But nostalgia, as Cantor points out, connotes a yearning for something that no longer exists, and a McDonald's outlet can be found "on every suburban intersection." The same can't be said of old catalogs, cracker barrels, and Ts.

Model T In Select Company

A Model T touring car is among the three "things" and four personalities appearing on the cover of *TV Magazine*'s Jan. 8-14 issue, which features the documentary film, "A Walk Through the 20th Century with Bill Moyers."

A motion picture camera and an atomic cloud also are shown on the cover, along with sketches of Franklin D. Roosevelt, Adolf Hitler, John F. Kennedy, and an astronaut.

"Walk Though the 20th Century" is a highly-acclaimed documentary "exploring the major events, personalities, and more which shaped our century," and represents journalist Moyers' personal attempt to rediscover, in his own words, "the vivacity of the past." Given the plot, it's easy to see why the Model T is one of the show's stars.

Unroyal Welcome

Won't you come home, Bill Bailey, won't you come home?

Bill Bailey, 18, of San Jose, Calif., brought his 1919 Model T speedster "home" all right - to Dearborn's Greenfield Village - but was unceremoniously told to move on by Village security officers. After rebuilding the chassis and engine, found in an abandoned northern California gold town in 1972, Bailey and a pal, 19-year-old Martin Ginnett, made the run from San Jose to Dearborn in six days as "sort of a pilgrimage." Their disappointment was keen when they received less than the warm welcome they had expected. "The guards weren't too impressed, and they kept telling us to get out," said Ginnett. "It was kind of terrible."

The Village, putting it mildly, blew it.

"Heck of a Good Time"

Among the longer "Bicentennial runs" of old cars was a 5,400-mile jaunt made by a 1917 Model T touring car owned by Jim and Donna Reed, of Seattle, and their children, Kelly, 11, and Kris, 10. The Reeds averaged 260 miles per day on the first leg of their journey, Seattle to Dearborn; and their only problems were a flat tire, an out-of-gas experience, and a shortage of luggage space. Jim spent two years restoring the car, then decided to give it a "make or break" Bicentennial run. "We got awfully sunburned," said Donna, "but we had a heck of a good time."

Tears For VW

The crocodile tears which Volkswagen Beetle aficionados have been shedding over the Bug's recent abandonment of the U.S. market after 28 years reminds me of the discontinuance of Model T production in 1927.

A Detroit newspaper recently devoted half a page to Beetle owners' laments and love affairs with their cars. All ignored the fact that Beetle sales decreased from 423,008 in 1968 to 27,009 last year.

Similarly, in 1927 Model T loyalists ignored the Tin Lizzie's obsolescence

FORD COUNTRY **143**

and sharp sales decline.

Hearst editor, Arthur Brisbane, adding a new Ford sedan and Ford truck to the several of each he already possessed, telegraphed Henry Ford that he should keep one plant running indefinitely to make 500,000 Model Ts a year, for, he thought, they could easily be sold at increased prices by mail order. A Ford dealer in Newark sought to arrange for its manufacture and/or assembly in New Jersey, whose citizens, he assured Ford, would finance the proposition. One elderly lady of means in Montclair, N.J., purchased and stored away seven new Model Ts so that she would not be without one during the remainder of her life. A Toledo man bought six of the cars finally wearing out the last one of them in 1967.

But Henry made almost everyone forget the Model T - at least in terms of believing that it couldn't be improved upon - with his vastly improved, still inexpensive Model A.

Ts, Beetles & Successors

Comparisons of Ford's Model T and Volkswagen's Beetle are commonplace, especially with respect to the cars' production numbers and longevity. More than 15 million Ts were built; more than 20.6 million Beetles, and the latter, which observed its golden anniversary in 1985, still is being produced in Mexico, Brazil, and Nigeria.

Both cars look as if they need a friend; their owners want to take care of them. Both have "personalities" whereas most other cars are simply cars. Both are simple machines repairable by shade-tree mechanics. Both inspired die-hards to insist that their manufacturers resume their production.

In time the T and the Beetle were outmoded, and had to be replaced if their parent companies were to survive. But their immediate successors impacted differently on their respective firms. The highly-successful Model A enabled the Ford Co. to shed its Model T image overnight. In contrast, Volkswagen, the corporation, has had difficulty moving away from its Beetle image, which continues to stand in the way of the Bug's successor, the Golf. Sold in the U.S. as the Rabbit until a year ago, the Golf has never established the same respect, much less rapport, among its owners as did the Bug.

The Model A, on the other hand, to this day is regarded by many old-car enthusiasts as the best car ever built for the money. The A also continues to warm the hearts of owners and others in a way that the Rabbit/Golf hasn't, and likely will not.

Model T Chapel

The Rev. Milton Strebel of Green Bay, Wis., is building himself a "chapel on wheels" - specifically on a Model T chassis. He got the idea from the above picture of a similar vehicle which appeared in the 1970 issue of the *Model T Times;* the picture first appeared in a 1922 edition of the *Fordson Farmer*. The original chapel on wheels was built on a Model T chassis by the Rev. Branford Clarke, of New York City, who gained fame as a poet-painter-preacher. His chapel had arched stained-glass windows, and contained a small organ upon which Mrs. Clarke played. The steeple atop the chapel, complete with cross, folded down when the Rev. Clarke put his car

144   FORD COUNTRY

in the garage. The Rev. Clarke did most of his preaching to throngs along Broadway.

The Rev. Strebel, a tireless researcher, has found that the Rev. Clarke died in 1952, and that his church and its records were destroyed in the 1960s after being hit by a plane. Thus the modern-day chapel on wheels will have to be rebuilt from the above picture and the Rev. Strebel's imagination. The Green Bay minister reports that he has blasted his flivver chassis, and has found new wainscoting for the outside of the chapel and some beautiful maple and cherry flooring which must be 70 to 100 years old. "I now have all the materials I need to build the chapel," he reports. "If I don't run into any unforeseen problems, I should have my project on the road by next summer. The Model T should be an attention-getter." *(Photo, Ford Archives, Henry Ford Museum, Dearborn, Michigan.)*

Longest Tow

A Model T was involved in the longest tow on record, according to the 1977 edition of *The Guinness Book of World Records*. The 4,759-mile tow was made from Halifax, Nova Scotia, to Canada's Pacific Coast by Frank J. Elliott and George A. Scott, of Amherst, Nova Scotia, to win a $1,000 bet. The pair persuaded 168 passing motorists to tow their engineless T; and the trip took 89 days, ending on October 15, 1927.

VW Has Better Idea

As one watches the gradual phasing out of the Volkswagen Beetle, he cannot but compare this car's slow, sensible demise with the overnight death of the Model T.

Volkswagen's management plans to milk the last possible sale and ounce of profit out of its product, whereas Henry Ford discontinued profitable manufacture of the Tin Lizzie at a time when he had yet to design, much yet tool up for, a successor vehicle. VW has stopped selling cars in the U.S. except for a limited number of convertibles; but only because it became too expensive to tailor them to American fuel and emissions standards. More important, a worthy successor, the Rabbit, is on the market. WV also has stopped making the car in West Germany. It will, however, continue to produce them in Mexico, Brazil, South Africa, and Nigeria. VW obviously plans to keep on making the car as long as there is a demand for it, and an honest Deutsche mark can be turned by doing so.

Henry Ford, in one of the biggest boneheads of his career, lost $101 million in 1927-28, the years in which he cashiered the flivver and brought out the T's successor, the Model A. More than 19.2 million Beetles have been sold to date; more than 15 million Model Ts found their way to market.

Flivver-Cooled Tank

Seeing is believing, otherwise I'd have trouble believing that a Ford Model T radiator could have been used on Britain's World War I modified Mark I tank. But without question, it's a flivver radiator that incongruously adorns the big lizardlike vehicle pictured in *British and German Tanks of World War I*.

The tank was not powered by a Model T engine, however; rather by a Daimler. The Mark series of tanks was the type first used in action by anyone, in 1917, and the vehicles were designated Male or Female depending on the amount of armament they carried.

For the above piece of intelligence we are indebted to Frederick D. Roe, 837 Winter Street, Holliston, Mass., who explains, "I don't care what I read so long as it is about something that moves and is not fiction!"

FORD COUNTRY 145

Model T RV No. 1

The title, "Recreational Vehicle Number One" has been claimed for a 1921 "housecar" mounted on a Model T one-ton truck chassis in an article in *Vintage Ford*.

The article states that the first owners drove the housecar, whose dimensions are only five by 11 feet, from Connecticut to Florida and back six times between 1922 and 1929. The car was acquired in 1929 by a Clinton, Maine couple who actually lived in it for 34 years. As author James F. Fenske observes, the couple's devotion to their little home - and to each other - must have been considerable.

Since 1972, the vehicle has been owned by Homer Johnson, of Dover-Foxcroft, Maine. He began restoration last year, and hopes to have it back on the road within another year or two.

Model T - Balloon Rally

During the Model T era the Ford Company and its dealers and owners engaged in almost every imaginable kind of sporting event. But one they didn't dream up was a Model T Ford-Hot Air Balloon Rally - which recently was sponsored by the Central Ohio Chapter of the Model T Ford Club of America, the Greater Ohio Balloon Club, and the Marysville, Ohio (locale of the event) Chamber of Commerce.

Twenty-one Tin Lizzies and an equal number of balloons participated in the rally. Each flivver was assigned to chase a balloon sent aloft for an hour. The balloonists tried to land as near as possible to a road and their waiting Fords, then jumped into the Ts and raced back to the finish line in town. Winners of the race were Jim and Jody Davis of Columbus, Ohio, driving a 1925 depot hack. The Davises' balloon landed only fifty feet from the road where the T was waiting.

Balloons which traveled fewer miles than others gave their T chasers an advantage (one went as far as 40 miles). Some balloonists thus skulked at treetop level or descended into valleys to stay out of the wind. One balloon touched down in the Scioto River before ascending again. In addition to the Ts, many Marysville citizens followed the balloons by motorcycle, truck, and tractor. Farmers often pointed out little-known roads to help people get closer to the balloons they were chasing.

Model T Railcar

A Model T railcar still plies the tracks of California's Sierra Railroad, although in recent years it's been used only in the filming of television commercials.

The little Ford, according to a recent *Vintage Ford* article by Jack Smith, initially transported the railroad's superintendent and paymaster. Built in Sierra's Jamestown shops in 1925, the vehicle has a 1922 Model T roadster body and a 1923 flivver engine, along with railcar underpinnings including flanged wheels.

The Jamestown facility, home base for the T railcar, long has been a favorite with moviemakers, and has been the locale of many films and TV commercials including *High Noon* starring Gary Cooper. Tours of the roundhouse and shops are available on weekends. Jamestown is located on California Highway 108 about five miles south of Sonora, in Tuolumne County.

T For Tow

A Model T engine powered the nation's first ski tow, according to a historical marker located near Woodstock, Vt.

The marker reads as follows:

"In January, 1934, on this pasture hill of Clinton Gilbert's farm, an endless-rope tow, powered by a Model 'T' Ford engine, hauled skiers uphill for the first time. This ingenious contraption launched a new era in winter sports."

A photo of the marker, published in the December 1983 issue of *Yankee*, was forwarded by Glenn W. Helm,

Lockport, Ill. The magazine also published a photo of the engine and tow apparatus, and reported that Ford Motor Co. would reenact the T-driven first tow at Gilbert's Hill on Jan. 14, 1984.

Going Out In Style

"Do you know of any cases in which somebody was taken to the cemetery in his Model T?" writes Hanson Waltz, St. Paul, Minn. "I like the idea, but my family thinks it's not right to do it."

Every now and then one reads about a T owner who takes his last ride in his Tin Lizzie. In 1979, for example, the body of Albert C. White, Detroit, Mich., was carried to its grave in a 1927 depot hack. The entire funeral procession was made up of cars from White's collection, among them the lead car, a 1923 T, in which the deceased's widow and grandson rode.

Worth Getting Loaded

The Model T, not surprisingly, was "a favorite among early trippers," (transporters of illegal whiskey), according to an article, "That Good Old Mountain Dew," in the October, 1983 issue of *USAir* magazine.

The T, says the piece, "could carry 90 gallons of whiskey in demijohns and Mason jars." Since moonshine sold for about $40 a gallon after passage of the Volstead Act, a T-load of hootch could fetch around $3,600. Not a bad day's haul for those who could outrun or outditch the revenuers.

1919 T Fire Truck

A 1919 Model T fire truck was the first vehicle to provide fire protection at the Wayne County (Mich.) General Hospital, located in Eloise, Mich., west of Detroit. The Ford pumper was supplemented by new equipment in 1932. Present plans call for the T to be put on long-term display at the City-County Building in downtown Detroit.

Official Portrait

This picture of Abraham Lincoln is not your run-of-the-mill photo of Honest Abe; it's the one the Lincoln Motor Company sent to Lincoln aficionados when founders Henry M. and Wilfred C. Leland ran the firm from 1917-22. It was given to me by Wilfred's elderly widow during a 1966 interview. At the time Mrs. Leland was living in an apartment in Detroit's inner city.

FORD COUNTRY   **147**

Lincoln Statue

A statue of Abraham Lincoln (above), which once graced the front of the Lincoln Motor Car Co.'s plant at Livernois and Warren, Detroit, now stands behind the Downtown Branch of the Detroit Public Library despite many neighborhood changes. Among the changes is the recent abandonment of nearby Hudson's, long the Motor City's largest department store. The library itself, located at 121 Gratiot Avenue, is open only part-time because of Detroit's financial stringencies.

The statue's granite pedestal is inscribed, "Let Man Be Free." Its left hand holds a scroll bearing the words "Proclamation of Emancipation" on its unfurled edge. Its right hand is relaxed and open, palm forward, in a gesture of friendship to those it faces.

The life-size statue is one of six duplicates of an original designed in 1898 by a German immigrant, Alfonso Pelzer, Salem, Ohio. The work was commissioned by Henry M. Leland, an admirer of Lincoln and founder of the Lincoln Motor Car Co. Installed in front of Lincoln's new factory during World War I, the statue was moved in 1959 after Ford which bought Lincoln in 1922, abandoned the building. Detroit's Junior Chamber of Commerce paid for the move.

In 1968, vandals pushed over the 300-pound statue, leaving only its feet atop the base. The sculpture was restored and remounted in 1969, after workmen removed the head to reinforce the body. Today the statue looks out over a small grassy triangle, once part of a bustling Detroit, now a quiet backwater.

Continental Connection

The Ford Motor Company has been delving into its rich history to promote its new Continental Mark V, as shown in the above publicity photo of a prewar Continental and the front end of the new offering. Ford's news releases are stressing that the Mark V's, "uncluttered design reflects the classic styling tradition begun by its ancestor." Ford publicists also are emphasizing Edsel Ford's contribution to the original Continental's design.

148   FORD COUNTRY

1940 Zephyr In Japan

A 1940 Lincoln Zephyr sedan formerly owned by the U.S. ambassador to Japan and subsequently used by the Imperial family has surfaced in Japan, according to Chad Coombs, writing in the *Way of the Zephyr*, publication of the Lincoln Zephyr Owner's Club. The car, now owned by the Chuo University Auto Club, is in excellent condition. It has right-hand drive, one of 311 Zephyr sedans so equipped during the 1940 model year for sale in Japan and the British Empire. This Zephyr may be the only car of its marque in Japan, perhaps in the entire Orient.

Lincoln Brochure

If you were the curator of Detroit's National Automotive History Collection, a fire broke out in the institution, and there was time to grab only one item on your way out, which one would you save?

Curator James J. Bradley says that item would be a sales catalog produced by Lincoln for its 1937 or 1938 cars. The catalog, 20 by 16-1/2 inches, is entitled, "The Lincoln V-12 with Suggested Colors and Upholsteries." It has a thickly padded cover into which is sunk a greyhound medallion. Inside are swatches of upholstery, plus body color samples complete with striping. There also are lush color photographs of the various body styles offered by coachbuilders Le Baron, Willoughby, Brunn, and Judkins.

The catalog was given to the Detroit Public Library, of which the collection is a part, in 1953 by Oscar E. Baumann, about whom nothing is known. Bradley feels that the catalog is as valuable as any that might be acquired, adding that he'd not hesitate to ask "between $2,000 and $3,000" for it. It's difficult to determine whether the catalog refers to '37 or '38 Lincolns, or perhaps both, inasmuch as the two models are so similar; also because the bodies, being custom-built, are so dissimilar.

Last Big Lincoln

The last of the "dinosaurs" - a white two-door Continental Town Coupe with a brown vinyl roof - recently completed its one-hour, 24-minute crawl down Ford's Wixom, Mich. assembly line. The car, 19-feet, 5-inches long and weighing more than 4,800 pounds, was the last of the huge personal cars to be built in America except for Cadillac's limousine. It lists for retail sale at $11,467, and gets 12 miles per gallon in city driving, lowest of any U.S. model. Lincoln's 1980 downsized model will be about two-feet shorter and 500 pounds lighter than its predecessor.

The name of the buyer of the last big Lincoln was not revealed. The work ticket was blank except for the computer-printed words "The End." But the purchasers of the last of the special-trim "Collector's Series" were on hand when that car also recently came off the line. A $21,452 midnight blue Mark V, it went to Seattle old-car restorers, Omar Throndsen, and his son, Larry. "We're going to hold on to this one," said Larry. "Maybe we'll drive it only on Sundays."

"Popemobile"

Pope John Paul II's white Lincoln Continental Town Car - dubbed the "Popemobile" by some - recently was sent to Rome from Ford's Wixom Assembly Plant, near Detroit. The four-door sedan was bought for the Pope by friends and alumni of Orchard Lake (Mich.) Schools, a complex of Roman Catholic facilities with close ties to the Pontiff.

The Pope's Lincoln is loaded. It has the usual big-car equipment - automatic transmission, power steering and brakes, air conditioning, tinted glass, and automatic temperature control. It also has a "moon roof," opera windows, illuminated entry system, AM-FM-tape stereo, and a white leather interior with red trim. The Town Car, with a 400-cubic-inch engine, has one of Detroit's last big V-8 car engines. Pope John Paul can expect to shell out 705,600 lire ($900) a year to fuel the car. Although Ford did not install bulletproof glass or tires, a company spokesman said the Vatican might do that later. Ford gave the papal Lincoln VIP treatment mostly because Henry Ford II took a personal interest in it.

HFII received regular reports on the car as it moved from assembly to shipment. The vehicle was priced at $17,500.

Bring Back Model A

Some attitudes don't change, especially those concerning Model A Fords.

For instance, E.B. White, who wrote many years for the *New Yorker* and authored the delightful 1936 book, *Farewell to Model T*, had the following to say in 1958 about the Model A:

"In the New England village I live in, the automobile is used chiefly for getting to and from a job and a store. The one car for which there is always a brisk demand in my town is the Model A Ford, now about thirty years old. Whenever a Model A comes on the market, it is snapped up in no time, and usually there is a waiting list.

"The reason the A is going strong today is simple: The car is a triumph of honest, unfussy design and superior materials. It doesn't look like a turbojet or like an elephant's ear, it drinks gasoline in moderation, it puts on no airs, and when something gets out of adjustment the owner can usually tinker it back to health himself.

"The car is not long; it is not low, but it works and it is extremely durable. It wouldn't fit the bill today for high-speed travel over superhighways, but I am quite sure of one thing - if Ford could suddenly produce a new batch of Model A's and put them up for sale some morning, at about double what they cost originally, they'd be gone by nightfall. I'd be strongly tempted to buy one myself. It isn't exactly what I'm looking for, but it's close."

Long Haul

Most recent acquisitions of Britain's National Motor Museum at Beaulieu are 1928 and 1930 Model As which were driven by Britons Don Yorke, 28, and Jim Blun, 25, from New Zealand to England. The cars were uncovered in a junkyard - one had a tree growing through it - while the Britons were vacationing down under. For a lark, they restored the vehicles, with the help of six New Zealanders, then drove them across southern Asia and Europe. The trip was virtually incident-free.

"Hot" Model A Returned

Mike Dooley, according to the Associated Press, probably got back his stolen 1929 Model A because it was impossible to fence. Dooley distributed 50,000 fliers offering a $1,000 reward for information leading to the car's recovery after it had been stolen. "I just kept the heat on and made it so hot it was the hottest car in the United States," the Chicagoan said. The 35-year-old IBM typewriter repair specialist added that the thieves had him playing musical phone booths for five days before the car was returned to its original parking spot.

The car was in perfect condition when brought back, and now is chained to a lightpost in front of his North Side house with the wheels locked. Dooley said he also plans to install a burglar alarm. "I'm not going to lose it again," he said, adding that he had wanted to own an A since the age of five. He values the car at $6,000.

Model A Recordholder?

Frederick F. Bauer, Princeton, Ill., who styles himself a " 'nit-picker' by avocation," questions a statement in our January column to the effect that "first-year sales (of the Mustang) were 418,812, the highest ever for any new car ever introduced by Ford."

That statement came from Ford's News Department; and your columnist accepted it at face value. Bauer says that the first-year sales of the Model A exceeded those of the Mustang, and although we can't come up with precise figures for the first 365 days of A sales, he's probably right. We do know that 4,186 As were produced in 1927; 713,528 in 1928 (see Ray Miller's *Henry's Lady*, whose figures are based on statistics originally compiled by Ford expert Les Henry for Floyd Clymer's *Henry's Fabulous Model A*). Sales and production figures aren't one and the same, and one must keep in mind that the A was produced in small numbers late in 1927 and during the eight months of 1928 (only 275,000 had been delivered to buyers by the end of August, 1928). Still, the evidence suggests that by December 2, 1928, the first anniversary of Model A sales, more As had been sold than first-year Mustangs.

All Model A Fords Black?

It's commonplace to read that the Model T was painted only black, in line with Henry Ford's oft-quoted statement, "The public can have any color it wants so long as it's black." Actually, the Model T was painted in various colors during both the first and last few years of its 19-year production run.

But now we read, in *The Day the Bubble Burst: The Social History of the Wall Street Crash of 1929*, that all Model As were painted black. One is tempted to write authors Gordon Thomas and Max Morgan-Witts about the error of their ways. But they have made so many mistakes in writing about Ford and other auto moguls of the late 1920s, it's likely they could care less.

Look Again

A reader recently informed this column that U.S. $10 bills picture a Model A sedan tooling past the U.S. Treasury Building, and we dutifully reported same. Not so, retorted another reader, "The car is a 1927 Hupmobile ... a new, crisp note and magnifying glass help." Another reader said "the automobile is so small it is hard to define, but it is a Model T."

These divergent views inspired a letter to the Treasury Department's Bureau of Engraving and Printing which elicited the following reply:

"A careful examination of the vignette on the reverse side of the $10 note will show that four automobiles are included in the design. While the cars are similar in appearance to those manufactured in the 1920s, none represents a specific make or model of a particular company. This was done in keeping with the established policy that no feature depicted on currency should be identifiable with the product of a particular manufacturer, thus avoiding a claim of preferential treatment."

Model A Prototype

"We put the Model A prototype together by hand using 16-gauge black iron," recalled Thomas Alexander on a recent visit to Detroit. "We worked in the 'white room' at the Highland Park Plant. It was called that because it was a top security project, and we were surrounded by white curtains."

Alexander joined Ford in 1923 as an inspector of Model T camshafts. Four years later he was one of four men tapped to build the first Model A. He later worked in Ford's Rouge, Ypsilanti, and Wixom plants and the Ford Rotunda, finally returning to the Highland Park factory before his retirement. He now lives in Reddington Shores, Fla.

Model A On Tour

A 1929 Model A is being used by Eldon D. Wigton, to drive across the country blindfolded.

The 34-year-old Wigton, of Kilbourne, Ohio, is making the 2,600-mile trip to promote his career as a professional magician. He hopes his stunt will earn him a spot on the television program, "That's Incredible."

Wigton's A has been restored to look like a medicine-show vehicle. Of his blindfolded driving, he simply says, "It's magic," and that his training and knowledge will keep him from going left of center. "I worry about the other guy," he adds. Still, a friend's car is driven in front of Wigton's A for insurance purposes.

Model A Going Strong

A 1931 Model A pickup continues to meet some of the transportation needs of Lyle Skinner, Twin Lakes, Wis., whose family bought the car new for $450.

"It was depression times when I saw her for sale at the Walworth County Fair," Skinner recently told the *Kenosha (Wis.) News*. "The dealer dropped the price from $500 to $450, providing you paid cash, and you should have seen my dad running around looking for some money."

The Skinner family milked 22 cows at the time, and loaded seven eight-gallon cans onto the trunk each day for delivery to a nearby train depot. "I remember because it was my job to deliver the milk each day," Skinner continued. "The roads around here weren't paved, but it didn't matter because we didn't drive very fast anyway." ... One reason Gertie (the car's name) lasted so long "is we took awful good care of her. She was always parked in a shed."

The car has a manifold heater, but no windshield defroster. In wintertime, Skinner often sticks his head out of the side window to see where he's going. On the other hand, the truck has a hand crank, and can be run on kerosene, if need be. Gertie's speedometer cable broke in the car's second year, so Skinner has no idea how many miles the truck has traveled.

Thanks to G.D. Sytkowski, Kenosha, Wis., for acquainting us with Gertie.

That's Incredible

Not even the watch company that boasts "it takes a lickin' and keeps on tickin' " can match the comeback of a 1929 Model A recently recovered from the bottom of a lake where it lay submerged for 47 years, according to *Ford World*, a Ford Company employee publication.

The A plunged through the ice of Idaho's Lake Coeur d'Alene in 1936, and came to rest 130 feet below. Two hours after it had been pulled up and its battery had been replaced, the car's horn, engine, clutch, brakes, and one headlight performed flawlessly.

New owner Tom Butterwield bought the car for $500, and plans to restore it with the help of his son-in-law and stepson.

'A' Anticipation

Some measure of the excitement engendered by the debut of Ford's Model A in 1927 can be gleaned from an article appearing in the November 18, 1927 issue of a British publication, *Autocar*, the article having been forwarded by reader Marsh Hesler, La Mesa, Calif.

The magazine sent a member of its staff to report on the new model, which was to be introduced on December 2. He cabled back that the delayed introduction of the new car had brought on a sharp slump in motor vehicles sales in September and October as buyers waited to learn about the new Ford before buying a 1928 model. The correspondent also noted that Edsel Ford had been seen driving one of the new cars through Detroit's streets in October.

Observers, it was reported, said the car resembled a "smaller Little Marmon, with low body of streamline appearance and a flying-goose emblem on the radiator, deep crown mud wings, front and rear buffers and wire wheels. Men in the know who have been permitted to drive the new car attest that it is capable of a top speed of more than sixty miles an hour."

Autocar's reporter also noted that Ford had received 125,000 American orders accompanied by a cash payment, not to mention 250,000 additional orders unaccompanied by cash. "It is safe to say," observed the correspondent, "that no other company in America could book £36,000,000 worth of business on an article of merchandise none of the buyers has seen or - to put it bluntly - knows anything about."

Model A Driveaways

After the Model A was introduced in December, 1927, many of the cars were driven by dealers' representatives (rather than shipped by train or trailer truck) to the dealership where they were to be displayed and sold.

Among those who drove the first five As from Dearborn to Indianapolis was a reader, Leland Q. Clapp, who at the time was a Butler University freshman. Clapp recalls that he was "stuck in an upper berth going up there, and I didn't sleep and couldn't tell where we were or what time it was." Of the Ford assembly plant, he says, "I can still smell the banana oil." On the way home, he recalled that "we acted much as a miniature parade with our caravan. All the small-towns' people turned out to see the new Fords. Wish I had one now!"

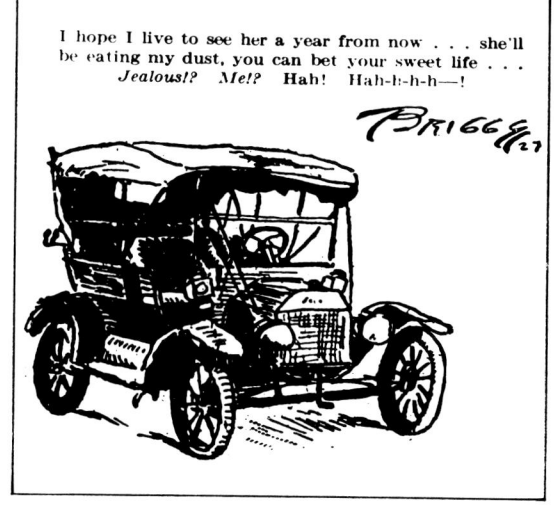

HIS NEW SCOOTER
—Evans in the Columbus *Dispatch*.

LIZZIE'S GOT A LITTLE SISTER
—Kirby in the New York *World*.

I caught a glimpse of her the other day—and honest, it isn't that I'm *catty* or jealous, but *really* I can't see anything to rave about! I think she's *common* . . . all painted and rouged . . . It's *disgusting!*

I hope I live to see her a year from now . . . she'll be eating my dust, you can bet your sweet life . . . Jealous!? Me!? Hah! Hah-h-h-h—!

Copyright, 1927, by the New York Tribune, Inc.

Birth of the Model A

Fifty years ago this month Henry Ford introduced his Model A, regarded by many old-car enthusiasts as the best car ever built, pound for pound, dollar for dollar. At the time of the A's debut, many newspapers ran cartoons dealing with the new Ford and the "Model T's reaction" to its successor. Here are four of them.

FORD COUNTRY   **153**

Model A Engine Power

A 40 hp Ford Model A engine powers the above biplane once owned by renowned aviator Wiley Post, who was piloting comedian Will Rogers when the pair crashed to their deaths in Alaska in 1935. The plane, rebuilt by John A. Bouteller, Jr., is displayed by the Oklahoma Aeronautics Commission in Oklahoma City.

Advertising The Model A

The announcement that N.W. Ayer ABH International will reopen offices in Detroit in 1980 recalls that agency's association with Ford Motor Co. between 1927-40. Ayer was hired by Henry Ford in 1927 to advertise the Model A. Ford disliked advertising, and during many of the Model T years remained aloof from it. But before abandoning the Tin Lizzie, he had committed himself to a large-scale introductory and continuing advertising campaign in behalf of the T's successor.

"They kept at me about it," he told a writer in 1927, "until I was sick of the subject. At last I said, 'All right. If you have to have that kind of doctor, get the best one you can find.' "

During the spring of 1927 several agencies submitted presentations for the Ford account, and N.W. Ayer & Son was retained. Founded in Philadelphia in 1869, Ayer was then, as now, the oldest continuing advertising firm in the country, having as many advertising "firsts" to its credit as Ford had manufacturing "firsts."

During the Model T-Model A interregnum, the company and its agency planned an introductory advertising campaign that in sheer size of appropriation and breadth of coverage dwarfed any previous effort of its kind ever conducted in America. For five straight days, from Monday, Nov. 28, through Friday, Dec. 2, 1927, full-page advertisements were run in all of the nation's 2,000 English-language daily newspapers. The ads cost the company $1.3 million.

The first ad, signed by Henry Ford, discussed the new car only in general terms. The second and third ads promised that the vehicle would sell at a low price and disclosed mechanical specifications. The fourth ad, published on the eve of the public showing, supplied a photograph of the Model A and quoted its prices. The fifth ad summarized the four previous ads.

The series was cited by the president of the Advertising Club of New

York as "the most soundly coordinated advertising campaign in America's advertising history." The ads were certainly among the most widely discussed in advertising annuals. As many commentators pointed out, "everyone who can read is reading them."

Ayer ably served Ford until 1940. But the agency was constantly harassed by Henry Ford and his chief satrap, Harry Bennett, and at times hardly knew from one week to the next whether it would continue handling the Ford account.

Ayer's difficulties with Ford, according to the company's advertising manager, A.R. Barbier, began when the agency's president, George H. Thornley, misadvised Henry Ford on the outcome of the Presidential election of that year. Thornley told Ford that Hoover would win, and the auto magnate, later claiming that he had acted on Thornley's prediction, came out in strong public support of the Republican nominee. Embarrassed and angered by Hoover's overwhelming defeat, Ford never forgave Thornley or his agency. At times the industrialist made no effort to conceal his contempt.

"How many Ayer men have you got with you today?" Ford once asked Barbier in the presence of an Ayer executive.

"Just one, Mr. Ford," replied Barbier.

"That," said Ford belligerently, "is one too many."

Bennett was also derisive of the Ayer organization and, acting in Ford's name, on various occasions insisted that the agency hire at least five of the magnate's relatives and friends. The last of those demands led to an abrupt termination of the 13-year-old Ford-Ayer relationship. Ayer refused to hire the Ford relative, who was to be paid even without the expectation that he would appear for work, and immediately lost the Ford account.

Ayer later took over Chrysler's Plymouth account. Since 1971, the agency has handled General Motors' public affairs advertising out of a New York office. Ayer was one of the two largest agencies in the country when it took over the Model A account and is now the nation's 14th largest advertising firm.

First Model A Ad

This advertisement, first in a series of five, was one of the best read ads in U.S. history inasmuch as almost everyone was gasping for Model A data when it appeared. (Photo from the Collections of the Henry Ford Museum and Greenfield Village.)

A For Advertising

Living the life of Riley, according to New England Life's recent advertising, means owning a Model A.

"Riley really knows how to live," runs the ad, which features a color photo of a "regular" young man, his pert wife, and their redheaded, freckle-faced kid, each applying spit and polish to the family's A. A long-eared, sad-eyed dog sits in front of the car, the ad agency going all out to make the ad as American as apple pie.

"Riley really knows how to live," proclaims the ad's text. "He's got his family, his home, and his car. And a few days ago, he found out he could increase the value of his life insurance policy without increasing his premium."

Forget increasing the value of the policy. But we'll take the A, with or without the mutt.

Ads Highlight Model A

Volkswagen has been running ads featuring the Model A, explaining that motorists who liked and kept the A for years also would like the Beetle, and for the same reasons. Sears, Roebuck has pictured the A in its ads, and proclaimed that it still sells parts for the car. Republic National Life Insurance Company, of Dallas, is conducting an ad campaign declaring that "two great ideas were born in 1928" - the Model A and Republic National [actually the A was launched in 1927].

"Needlepoint" Ads

These "needlepoint" designs, featuring the Model A, are handed out to customers in the form of postcards, wall posters, and car floor mats by the 140 dealers of the Newark Ford District Dealers' Association. Similar designs also have been used in outdoor billboard advertising. Theme of the nostalgic, colorful series, developed by Ketchum, MacLeod & Grove, Inc. is "Come Home to Ford." To tie-in with the campaign, many Newark dealers over the past four years rented Model As to display in their showrooms. The needlepoint art has inspired numerous requests for reproductions, and a commercial poster company has been authorized by the dealers to make prints of the ad and sell them.

18-Plus MPG

A recent column reported that the Ford Company ran a test on a prime-condition 1930 Model A, and found that it got less than 15 miles per gallon. The figure surprised me, and I asked "can that be?"

In response, Fred Bauer, Rural Route 5, Princeton, IL 61356, dusted off records he had kept some four decades ago for a 1929 Model A sport coupe. Bauer was given the car by his parents in June, 1933, when he started his first job, and kept it until 1936. In 1934 he drove the car 17,857 miles using 953 gallons of gasoline costing $151.26; and that figures out to 18.7 mpg at 15.9 cents per gallon. In 1935 he drove 13,200 miles using 705 gallons, costing $116.37, figuring out at 18.9 mpg at a cost of 16.5 cents per gallon.

The meticulous Bauer's records show that he had installed a rebuilt engine for $49. The replacement, he figures, did not affect mpg. His last notation regarding the car was at 85,630 miles for six gallons of gas costing 97 cents. He then sold the car to a fellow next door for $75, and bought himself a Chevy.

So there you have it - one A which did better than 15 mpg. Still, 18.7-18.9 mpg doesn't compare favorable with the mileage of many of today's light cars.

Model A Jitney

This pink 1930 sedan, owned by Detroit's Shelby Hotel, is perhaps the only Model A jitney in the country. It shuttles guests between the hotel, in front of which it is parked, and Detroit's convention center, Cobo Hall.

Speed Makes Difference

During a recent visit to the Ford Archives I had occasion to glance through the famed little black statistical book kept by P.E. Martin, one of the company's two top manufacturing executives from 1908-41. An entry noted that a Model A Ford tested by the firm in November, 1927 (the A was publicly introduced in December), got 32.8 miles per gallon of gas at 15 miles per hour; 29.2 mpg at 25 mph, and 21.8 mpg at 40 mph, the car was run over regular roads with a driver and three passengers.

Parks Car Inside Home

How many people keep a Model A in the living room? One such person is Elmer Duellman, Fountain City, Wis., who parks his 1929 phaeton in his home. An auto graveyard operator, Duellman says his parking spot keeps his prize car from becoming like the junkers he sees at work everyday."

Long Honeymoon Trip

In recent years a good many couples have taken honeymoon trips in old cars. But perhaps the longest trip of them all has been completed by a New Zealand couple who shipped their car to the West Coast, then toured the U.S. and Canada in a 1930 Model A. By the time they were the guests of Greenfield Village in mid-October, they had been on the road 16 weeks and traveled 10,500 miles. During their trip they had eight flat tires, one blowout, and two major mechanical problems. But Oliver Midgely, 27, a mechanical engineer, repaired the car's timing gear, which broke in the Nevada desert, and rewired the ignition when its wires caught fire in Banff National Park in Alberta, Canada.

"We wanted to do something exciting for a honeymoon," said Mrs.

FORD COUNTRY **157**

Midgely, "and our trip has been far better than we could have imagined." Many people, the couple reported, reminisced with them about the "good old Model A and Model T days," and some told of taking their own honeymoon in a Model A.

Bringing Back Salad Days

A Detroit area retirement complex provides a 1930 Model A for the residents' amusement. In addition to riding in the car, the senior citizens "love to tinker with the engine and keep it shining," according to car and complex owner Bob Gillette.

Gillette, 38, says he operates his complex "as if my own mother were living here," and that's why he bought the Model A.

"Ramblin' Wreck" = Model A

Many readers are familiar with the phrase, "Ramblin' Wreck from Georgia Tech," but few may be aware that since 1961 the wreck has been a 1930 Model A cabriolet sport coupe restored and maintained by Ford Motor Co.

The Model A was Tech's first *official* Ramblin' Wreck, but a Model T was the first car to be so described, according to the *Whistle*, Tech's alumni magazine. The T, a 1914 model owned by Dean of Men, Floyd Field, was referred to by the student newspaper in 1925 as "the oldest Ford on campus" and in 1927 as a "Ramblin' Wreck."

In the latter year, Dean Field considered trading his Tin Lizzie for a new car. The student newspaper protested: "The old Tech traditions must be upheld whatever the cost, and besides, there are too many miles yet left in the old Ford for it to be casually discarded." Nonetheless, in September, 1928, Dean Field traded his T for a Model A.

In 1929, the students began sponsoring an annual race of student-owned cars from Atlanta to Athens, the event being variously called the "Old Ford Race" and the "Flying Flivver

Georgia Tech's "Ramblin' Wreck," a 1930 Model A cabriolet sport coupe.

Race." Eligible entries had to be "worn out." Over the years, as vehicles became faster, the race evolved into today's "Ramblin' Wreck Parade," held during Homecoming Weekend and featuring both "wrecks" and special-interest autos.

In the late 1950s, Tech officials decided to designate a pre-1940 car as the institute's official "Ramblin' Wreck." About that time James Dull, then dean of students, now vice-president/dean of student affairs, noticed a restored 1930 Model A near his apartment building. Leaving a note on the car, he later heard from the owner, Capt. Ted J. Johnson, a Delta Air Lines pilot. Johnson had newly restored the coupe with his son, Craig, for whom it was a gift.

At first Johnson was unwilling to part with the car, then agreed to sell it for $1,000. He later returned the $1,000, fulfilling a desire to go on record as having donated Georgia Tech's "mascot."

"Over the years," states the *Whistle*, "the Ford Motor Company has taken great pride in keeping the 'Ramblin'

Georgia Tech's Centennial "Wreck," a 1930 Model A, which is being raffled by institute fund-raisers. The car was donated by alumnus Pete George, manager of Ford's Hapeville, Ga. Assembly Plant, and restored by plant employees.

Wreck' in top condition. In 1982, under the supervision of Tech alumnus Pete George, manager of the company's assembly plant in Hapeville, Ga., the 'Wreck' was completely restored."

More recently, George donated another 1930 Model A, also restored by the Hapeville Assembly Plant, to the Georgia Tech Athletic Assn. on the occasion of the school's 100th anniversary. The Centennial Wreck, as this car has been named, is being raffled by institute fund-raisers.

Thanks to Charles A. Kistler, Jr., Marietta, Ga., for acquainting us with Tech's Ford-related traditions.

50 Years Of Wagons

The year 1979 marked the 50th anniversary of station wagon production by Ford, one of the first of the domestic automakers to build the vehicles. Station wagons date to horse-powered "depot wagons" or "depot hacks" used by turn-of-the-century vacation resorts to pick up people at train stations. They also were dispatched by wealthy folk to collect arriving guests at the depot.

Ford's first wagons, Model As, were remarkably like those of their horse-drawn ancestors. They were made of wood and had canvas curtains. Their paneling was made of birch and the roofs were supported by hard maple. The company's 1929 wagons retailed for $650, and were classed as commercial vehicles. Ford listed its wagons in its truck catalog and a number of states required that wagons bear truck licenses.

These early wagons generally weren't considered family vehicles, and often performed the duties of the earlier, horse-drawn depot wagons. Those that survived intact became the famous "woodies" that carried surfboards instead of wealthy tourists. The use of wood bodies continued through the 1930s and the 1940s even though postwar families and suburbanites started turning to the wagon as a family vehicle.

Unable to shake off their heritage, automakers kept real wood trim on the sides of their wagons for a few years. But maintenance problems associated with exposure of the wood to the elements led to the use of "woodlook" metal. The wagons haven't had the same character since.

Ford Kept Wagon Alive

Henry Ford's fondness for the out-of-doors perhaps kept the Ford station wagon alive, according to the *Woodie Times*, monthly publication of the National Woodie Club. Although Ford's wagon sales sharply declined in 1932, Ford continued to produce the vehicle. By doing so, says the *Times*, he "kept the whole wagon concept alive and ultimately made the wagon an important part of the American way of life. It certainly made Ford the leader in wagon production and sales - the undisputed 'wagon master.' " Ford assembled 1,516 wagons during the 1932 model year. They sold for about $600 new, and survivors now sell for about $11,000. Ford and Mercury wagons account for about half of the vintage wagons produced.

Woodies

Sixty-five percent of extant wood-bodied cars are Fords and another 10 percent are Mercurys, according to estimates of the National Woodie Club.

Chrysler-made woodies account for 12 percent of existing woodies, GM products for 11 percent.

Club members own 1,015 woodies, including 646 Fords, 95 Mercurys, 56 Chryslers, 45 Plymouths, 42 Chevrolets, 27 Buicks, 25 Pontiacs, 23 Dodges, 15 Packards, and 11 Oldsmobiles. Among the Fords, the 1947 model is the most popular; there are 77 of them.

Watch Out for Termites

Whereas most old-car club publications run articles on how to control rust, the *Woodie Times* published by the National Woodie Club, whose members own wood-bodied Fords (and other makes), carries tips on how to spot and deal with termites. If you're a member of that club, you avoid visiting folks with termite-infested homes, or parking your car next to trees plagued with wood boring beetles or rot fungi.

V-8 Devotee Memorialized

The Depression Decade's most notorious outlaw, John Dillinger, who wrote Henry Ford in praise of the V-8's getaway qualities, is memorialized in a Nashville, Ind. Museum.

The museum, located in a large Victorian house, features Dillinger memorabilia, including his guns, good luck charm, the trousers he wore when gunned down in 1934 by the FBI outside a Chicago theater, his original headstone, and the "wooden gun" that the desperado used to escape jail in 1934, fleeing in the sheriff's 1934 V-8.

A V-8 is on display, along with a copy of Public Enemy No. 1's letter to Ford; the letter's original is in the Henry Ford Museum's Ford Archives.

The document reads as follows:

"Hello Old Pal. You have a wonderful car. It's a treat to drive one. Your slogan should be drive a Ford and watch the other cars fall behind you. I can make any other car take a Ford's dust. Bye-bye."

The museum is open from 10 a.m. to 6 p.m. in spring, summer, and fall; from 1 to 5 p.m. in the winter, closed Tuesdays. Admission is $2.25 for adults, $1.25 for children.

V-8 Hearse

A recent clipping from the *Capetown* (South Africa) *Argus*, sent by Rolph Fairchild, Fremont, Calif., notes that a South African church has put up for sale a 1936 Ford V-8 Model 67 hearse with a "side-valve engine that is as silent as a graveyard." The car has been driven so seldom that it still has the original tires, and the only maintenance ever required was replacement of the air filter and the addition of a turn signal. The vehicle, as the article notes, has seldom been driven fast, and no back-seat passenger has ever complained about the ride.

V-8s In Logging

"When the first flathead V-8s were put on the market in 1932," writes Robert B. Kennedy, Klamath Falls, Ore., "my love for Fords really began. I was very young, they were very smooth and fast. With the straight pipe, they put out the most beautiful sound."

Kennedy says he has been a logger and roadbuilder all of his life, and that "as a very young man it was my true pleasure to drive Ford trucks in the logging woods of the State of Washington in the 1930s." He recalls that loggers used so many Ford V-8 trucks from 1933 through World War II that "it is said Henry Ford came to the West to observe how the industry used his trucks."

"Basically," he observes, "it started with the standard Ford truck with a single-axle trailer and grew from there. Eaton 2-speed axles replaced the standard Ford axle. Some (had) much more capacity than the standard Ford axle or even the standard replacement Eaton axle ... Various companies also built tandem drives that were added along with dual axle trailers to give added carrying capacity." After describing the various options available on the trucks, Kennedy notes that "all of these units were characterized by terrific gear reductions so that the little V-8 could start loads of G.V.W. (gross vehicle weight) of over 40 tons. "These trucks were used up to and through World War II," he adds. After that, the hauls became longer and nearly everyone turned to diesels ... Some companies bought new (V-8) fleets yearly and treated them as if they were expendable. Others, of course, took very good care of them and ran them for several years."

Fond Ford Memories

"My family," recalls James Roosevelt, son of President Franklin D. Roosevelt, "has always had an interest in the Ford family because it was the Ford Co., founded by Henry Ford, that made life so much more enjoyable for my father by providing him with a Ford touring car in both Hyde Park and Warm Springs, Ga. which he could drive with the controls, using only his hands. Without the Ford car, my father would have been unable to drive himself and enjoy and accomplish many of the things which a Ford made possible." FDR's 1936 phaeton, on permanent display at Hyde Park, is shown above.

"Incidentally," added Roosevelt, "my first car in college (1926-30) was a (Model T) Ford nicknamed 'Ebenezer,' and it was the best ever."

V-8 "Fathercar" Of Computer

If a Ford V-8 hadn't started at 20 degrees below zero, reader George L. Hamlin, Clarksville, Md., informs us, "the computer would not have been invented."

The first electronic digital computer, writes Hamlin, was conceived and completed by Dr. John Vincent Atanasoff in 1937 and 1939, respectively. Atanasoff's story, as told by Hamlin, is as follows:

"A physics professor at Iowa State University (Ames) who had some sympathy for his students, Atanasoff

FORD COUNTRY **161**

noticed that the time required of them to do various calculations for their studies was getting out of hand. In the late 1930s, 'calculator' meant 'an operator with a Marchant' [machine] and some of the calculations needed for graduate work in engineering and physics ran into the tens of days. Atanasoff began searching for some means to lighten the burden of his graduate students.

"He considered and discarded dozens of ideas, even at one point considering lining up 30 identical Marchants or Monroes and driving them off a common shaft. But it was obvious that the progress he wanted would not come from clunky adaptations of then-current technology. The breakthrough he needed would not come. Finally, one winter night in 1937, he stormed out of his office, threw on a coat (it was something like 20 below) and 'did something that I had done on such occasions, got in, and started driving - I went out to my automobile on the good highways of Iowa at a high rate of speed ...' Taking his mind off the original problem ... he was able to relax. Eventually, and it would have taken four or five hours, he found himself in Illinois.

" 'I said to myself,' he remembers, 'I've got to stop this foolishness.' So he pulled off into a tavern, ordered a drink, and sat down to think. At that point the ideas came; he decided during the evening on the four basic principles still used in electronic digital computing (base 2, electronics as media, regenerative memory, computation by direct logical action). He got back in the car ('Cold! The heater could barely keep up'), went back to Ames, and finished his design.

"What kind of car did Atanasoff have?" asks Hamlin. "A V-8 Ford, with a South Wind heater. Iowa State made a documentary film about the computer's invention, and wanted the correct car to shoot out of. [But] the film does not show the exterior of the car.

"I knew you Ford maniacs would want to know about this," concludes Hamlin.

Father Of Sportsman

The Ford Company has introduced many innovative cars during the thirty years Henry Ford II has been president of the firm. Yet Henry II, unlike his grandfather, Henry, and father, Edsel, is not thought of as being personally responsible for putting innovative vehicles on the market. At least one exception to this generalization, however, is the Sportsman line, a brainchild of Henry II and originally intended as a one-off design for his personal use.

The "prototype" of the Sportsman (Model 71), according to the Seventy-One Society, an organization comprised of Sportsman owners, was built at Ford's Iron Mountain, Mich., plant, the wood body being placed on a 1931 Model A chassis, creating a Sportsman-like "convertible station wagon." Henry II ordered a similar version to be built on a 1946 chassis, and the Sportsman was born. After being driven by Henry II and displayed in Dearborn, this car was sold to actress Ella Raines in Hollywood on Christmas Day, 1945. Regular Sportsman production began in July, 1946, and continued until November, 1947. Only 3,692 of the vehicles were built.

The Sportsman is a convertible coupe which has had the door, rear quarter, and trunk area sheet metal removed. A hand-formed steel skeleton was attached, over which the finished wood panels were placed. Bodies were constructed and finished at Iron Mountain, then shipped to assembly plants. The car was expensive and difficult to maintain, and it would appear that fewer than 100 of them survive.

V-8 Engine Top Rated

Ford's 1932 V-8 engine is rated by Alex Mair, vice-president in charge of GM's technical staffs, as one of the "six car engines so innovative for their time that they changed the course of engine design."

"Henry Ford wanted to beat Chevrolet," Mair recently told the *Detroit News*. "So he told his engineers to develop a V-8 with a single-piece block. They said it couldn't be done. He said he'd get someone else to do it if they couldn't. This engine really made the V-8 accessible to every man."

Mair's other engine choices included the 1930 Cadillac V-16, the 1937 Chevrolet "Blue Flame," 1949 Cadillac Kettering, 1949 Olds Rocket, and 1955 Chevrolet small-block V-8. The list strikes one as being top heavy with GM power plants, but Mair is entitled to his opinion same as everyone else.

1955 Thunderbird

T-Bird Takeoff

"It was an instant classic," declares Tom Case, product development manager for the original Thunderbird, now a Ford leasing executive.

When starting work on the T-Bird in August 1952, recalls Case, the company sought to "create an 'image' car - a car that would appeal to youth and draw people into our showrooms. It wasn't expected to sell in large volume or make money. Jaguar, MG and other popular foreign sports cars were expected to be Thunderbird's chief competition. So their photographs were hung in the styling studios as guides. The goal was for Thunderbird to outperform those cars in zero to 60 and zero to 100 mph tests. And it did."

"The car started out as a clean, simple, very basic sports car," says Case. "But it had developed into a personal sports car by the time it reached the showroom."

The two passenger car was a winner, although only 48,910 were produced during its three-year production run. "We never made enough to satisfy the market demand," notes Case. "But it did its job in building Ford's image as an innovator.

Over the past 25 years, more than 2-1/4 million Thunderbirds have rolled off the line at the Dearborn Assembly Plant. Case has bought a number of them.

Silver T-Bird

Can it be 25 years since Ford introduced the Thunderbird? Must be, for the company is introducing a silver anniversary T-Bird to help combat the auto sales slump.

FORD COUNTRY 163

As for the day of the Bird's press preview, I remember it well, having been a Ford Motor Co. publicist at the time. The unveiling took place behind the company's Rotunda Building, the "gateway to the Rouge," which was destroyed by fire in 1963. Presiding at the ceremony was William Clay Ford, youngest of Henry Ford's grandsons, then group director of the Continental and Lincoln Divisions and a rising star in the Ford firmament.

The car drew the ooohs and aaahs that it deserved and all present thought that the company had a winner, and how right we were. But the most memorable part of that day, to me, was some pettiness on the part of Ford's vice-president of public relations, Charlie Moore. He was miffed because one of his subordinates, Jim Danaher, who had gone to prep school with William Clay, was laughing over old times with his ex-schoolmate. Moore told Danaher to stay away from William Clay; Charlie would look after Bill himself.

Thunderbird Thief

Many people have a love affair with the Classic Thunderbird, but Wylie Carhartt III's passion for the 1955-57 beauties has gone too far: his obsession led him to steal 22 of the cars, according to a recent Associated Press report.

When The Edsel Was New

A reminder of the Edsel which plucks the heartstrings of Edsel lovers driving east on East Warren near St. Jean, in Detroit, is this fading Edsel advertisement on the wall of an apartment building. The sign was put up by Simms Edsel, Inc., 7440 Gratiot, located three blocks north of Seven Mile Road, a location four or five miles northwest of Warren and St. Jean.

Carhartt stole T-Birds exclusively during a three-year binge, restored them, then sold each for a bargain price of $3,000. An electronics technician, Carhartt, 32, was sentenced to serve three years' probation, repay his victims, and seek counseling to curb his uncontrollable desire for T-Birds.

Edsel Stars In Film

One of the stars of the box office smash, *American Graffiti*, is a '58 Edsel Corsair four-door hardtop. The film features the drive-in set of the early 1960s, and much of the action is focused on cars dragging the main stem of a Southern California town.

Ba-a-ad Memories

Former Ford executives once associated with the Edsel car can laugh off their connection with the ill-starred car. They can afford to; they're no longer with the Ford Company. Eugene Bordinat, Jr., Ford's vice-president-design since 1961, however, can't afford that luxury.

In a *Detroit News* article which reviewed his career and talents, it was noted that "Mention of Ford's Edsel design disaster of the late '50s causes the slightest of bristling in the Bordinat eyebrows, followed quickly by an expression akin to flashing bright headbeams into the eyes of an oncoming driver on a very treacherous country road."

"There are more checks and balances in the design and car development process today," replies Bordinat with the calmness of a Ford auto designer who was involved only briefly with the ill-fated oval-grilled vehicle. "Such things are not likely to happen again."

A few years ago, Lee A. Iacocca, the company's recently-deposed president, said, in response to a question about the Edsel, that he was "trying to forget it."

Forecast Edsel's Failure

Hindsight is wonderful, isn't it? Nowadays, lots of people can claim to have known that the Edsel would come a cropper, and why. But Louis B. Cheskin, founder of Chicago's Color Research Institute, claims he was the only consultant who, in the 1950s, said the Edsel would flop.

Cheskin says that only 9 percent of those whom he surveyed at the time of the Edsel's debut liked the styling, and only 7 percent liked the name. "They told me that the Ford fortune would be behind the car," he recalls, "and I told them that Fort Knox could be behind it and it would still fail."

Edsel, Ky.

An old shanty in an old shantytown? Actually, it's the former post office building in Edsel, Ky., the only community in the world named for Henry Ford's son.

A close look at the picture reveals an old-timer in the center of the porch, flanked by firewood at left and a go-cart at right. Above the door is a wooden sign which says "Edsel, Kentucky 1926-1960 Wade Blevins, Postmaster." The sign on the porch's floor, installed by Edsel owners who visited the town in 1981, says, "Welcome to Edsel, Ky."

The village was named for Edsel by Postmaster Blevins, an admirer. Blevins served as postmaster until the office was discontinued in 1960. He died in 1974.

Today, the community, sustained by tobacco farming, consists of only the boarded-up postal building complete with a two-hole outhouse, a grocery store, a two-story house, and a Church of God edifice. The boarded postal building is occupied weekends by hunting dogs. Its owners are Jewell Blevins Greene, Wade's daughter, and her husband, Guy. (Photo courtesy Jack J. Whipple, Russellville, Ky.)

Too Valuable To Be Joke

The Edsel car now is too valuable to serve as the butt of jokes, in the view of a *Philadelphia Bulletin* columnist, David Diamond.

In a story entitled, "Sorry Edsel," Diamond says that the Edsel must move over for more worthy failures, among them DuPont's Corfam leather, which would last almost forever, but didn't stretch with the foot; Real Cigarettes, whose manufacturer was so confident of success that vital test marketing was skipped; and Ideal Toy's Jesus doll, which did not sell because parents feared that it might be mistreated by their children.

First Edsel Off The Line

Everyone wanted to pose with the first production Edsel at the Edsel Owners Club's recent annual meeting in Dearborn. Gathered around the green 1958 four-door Citation hardtop, on display in the Henry Ford Museum, are (left to right): the author of this column; Perry Piper, a cofounder of the club; Randy Mason, acting curator of the museum's Transportation Collection; Shelley "Shamrock" Cleaver, president of the club; and Douglas A. Bakken, director of the Edison Institute's Archives and Research Library. A placard next to the Edsel describes the vehicle as being representative of the chrome-laden, gas-guzzling autos of its era.

Poking Fun At the Edsel

Under the title, "The Edsel Makes Its Mark in Film," Tom Champion, writing in the March 1981 issue of the *Edseletter*, publication of the International Edsel Club, lists the numerous motion pictures and TV programs in which the Edsel is featured.

"The Munsters," notes Champion, "seems to have been written by former disgruntled Edsel dealers. In one episode, Herman went into another room to talk to strangers. Lily said that she ought to go with him because the last time he talked to somebody by himself he ended up buying a used Edsel.

"In another episode, Spot, the pet dragon which visited wrecking yards to eat leftovers, was sick for three days after consuming an Edsel. In another program, a professional race driver, after looking over the Munsters' car, was told by Herman about the ten two-barrel carburetors and high speed cam installed in the vehicle, 'Oh,' said the driver, 'for a moment I thought they had brought back the Edsel.'

"In yet another episode, the chairman of the board of Amalgamated Motors displayed an emerald with which he allegedly put a curse on accessories of competitors' cars, i.e. make gas gauges inaccurate or have radios play only commercials for his own vehicles. Grandpa Munster asked if he had ever put a curse on an entire car. 'Yes,' was the reply. 'Of course you have heard of the Edsel.' " Ad infinitum.

Russians Zap Edsel

The Edsel's failure has been blamed on many factors including its timing; it was introduced as the 1958 recession was getting under way.

Timing was indeed a major problem, according to ex-Ford employee Rudolph E. Hirsch, specifically the fact that the Russians "within days of the Edsel's launching, fired their first intercontinental missile ahead of the Americans. That caused a great outcry that America was spending too much on nonessentials such as the Edsel [Ford had trumpeted its expenditure of $250 million to bring the car to market], and not enough on training scientists.

"The Edsel is probably the only product to have been done in by a *New Yorker* magazine cartoon," continues Hirsch. "The cartoon read, 'Well, it's been a great week. The Russians got the ICBM, and we got the Edsel.' Driving an Edsel promptly was viewed as unpatriotic, something Ford obviously could not have anticipated."

Hirsch adds that he was offered a supervisory position in Edsel Division's

Market Research Department at the time of the car's introduction. "I declined," he concludes, "and instead joined IBM to learn programming. My resume looks the better for it."

Speaking Of Edsels

"The 1958 Edsel is the most distinctive of the Edsel models," reports Editor David R. Babb in the *Edseletter*, "and the 1959 is more reliable, but the 1960 is rarest.

"My idea of a practical Edsel collection," adds Babb, "is a fine 1958 for show purposes, a usable 1959 for everyday, and a 1960 in any condition as an investment."

"If you have a restorable Edsel," continues Babb, "acquire now all of the parts you will need. If you have a fine complete car, keep it that way - there won't be any more ... If you have a convertible, you're in a class by yourself. An Edsel convertible is the best of two worlds and has two separate markets. It has paradeability that no closed car can achieve, and undoubtedly is the only Edsel that has returned a meaningful profit to its owner."

Babb also questions rumors of high selling prices for Edsels. "Where, oh where, are all of the $4,000, $5,000, $6,000, and $10,000 sales reports that we hear about? Is there a secret, unknown Edsel club somewhere where people trade Edsels at fantastic prices? Does Kruse have unreported auction statistics? We know of a few people who have sold excellent Edsels at undisclosed prices - but very few, and we suspect both buyer and seller often would like us to think the price was higher than actually paid."

Edsels Generate Publicity

No other car clubs generate as much publicity as the two national Edsel organizations - International Edsel Club and Edsel Owners Club. Each inspires a tremendous amount of local and national print and electronic publicity during its annual meet. Here, in Nashville, Tenn., International Edsel Club member David R. Babb, Belvidere, Ill., left, is interviewed by Nashville's WSM-TV, (the Grand Ole Opry station). Each of the major TV networks also carried excerpts on the meet.

Avid Edsel Collector

One of the country's most avid Edsel collectors is Hugh Lesley, who has 80 of the cars scattered throughout the woods and crowded into two buildings on his farm five miles northwest of Oxford, Pa.

"Lesley's Lemon Grove," as some call his place, also houses another 70 cars. "I have a preference for any Ford

FORD COUNTRY   **167**

product from the 1960s on back," observes Lesley. He still has his first car, a 1940 Ford V-8 sedan bought in 1950; and has driven the car all over the country, even using it on his honeymoon in 1955.

20,000 Edsel Survivors

In a recent issue of the *Edseletter*, published by the International Edsel Club, President David R. Babb speculates that about 20,000 Edsels exist. Of this number, he believes about 13,000 are parts cars, or junkers "beyond restoration." Of the 7,000 others, he reasons that about 3,000 are 1958s, 3,000 1959s, and 1,000 1960s.

Babb also believes that about half of each of the "good cars" left are now, or might some day, be owned by a restoration buff. Of this number, about two-thirds already are complete, and need no parts. These figures, Babb suggests, point up the problem of making Edsel parts reproductions pay off. There are many parts cars still around; there aren't all that many restorable Edsels out there; and the bulk of the restorables already are in good shape. Still, a few Edsel parts have been reproduced, and more likely will be as time goes by.

Edsel "Schnoz-Mobile"

The above photo of the Edsel may be transformed into a "Schnoz-Mobile" by poking one's nose through an open space in the grille. "This is the most ridiculous thing I ever saw," says Mike Skinner, of Detroit, who forwarded the card, "but I had to buy a few for my Ford friends."

The car was designed by Bette Levine and is sold by Intra-Dynamics, Inc., of Santa Barbara, Calif. Other cars in the series feature President Ronald Reagan and movie stars.

In addition to the hole for the nose, a couple of small triangular openings in the windshield permit one to see the finished work of art. It's difficult not to chuckle upon doing so.

Time Capsule For Cars

Among the cars offered for sale at one of Syria's two permanent used-car "swap meets" was a 1958 Edsel, according to a recent article in the *Los Angeles Times*.

"I understand this car is very famous in your country," the owner remarked to an American tourist. The vehicle, painted red and white, was said to get about six mpg. When asked how many miles it had traveled, the owner indicated that the odometer had gone around twice: 200,000 miles.

Syria's troubled economy does not

allow the importation of many new cars, and imports are priced at $40,000 up. Consequently, the nation's capital, Damascus, has become "the elephant graveyard of American cars ... a sort of time capsule for thousands of perfectly maintained old American cars." Prospective buyers don't kick tires; they pound the hood.

Dream Come True

It has taken 27 years, but, says Frank Caliendo, Wichita, Kan., the Edsel is finally becoming the singular sensation it was supposed to be at the beginning.

"I was eight years old when my father was selected as an Edsel dealer," Caliendo recently wrote *Green Line*, news bulletin of the Edsel Owners Club. "My dad took me to a small old garage in the center of town to show me the new car that he would be selling within a month. He required me to refuse to tell anyone any of the details of the car. This was the first time that my dad had really given me a sense of responsibility ...

"I was really awed by this large and very different looking automobile ... I recall standing face-to-face with the grille of a Citation two-door hardtop with a two-tone black/white body. The car was quite impressive, and to this day is one of a few vivid memories of my boyhood. My dad explained to me that the car was so new and different that it would be a great trendsetting car that was to foretell the future in automobiles to come ... I was mesmerized because I was responsible for not letting anyone know this creation until it was transferred to the showroom and the lowly public was shown this amazing new car that would become the ultimate form of transportation of the future.

"My memory of the Edsel is about as encompassing as that. It fades after this introduction, and maybe I'm lucky. I don't recall any details of my dad's horror stories [about trying to sell the car]."

Caliendo recently bought an Edsel Corsair which "definitely does not blend into traffic. It is very well received and of great interest to everyone who happens to be around when it's parked. Usually people express disbelief, then smile, and after an inspection, become awed, impressed, and ultimately hypnotized. This is why my dad said the car would do to the public in 1957. After 27 years, this car is doing what it was supposed to have done when introduced. If it had met Ford's and my dad's expectations, I would probably be selling them today."

1958 Edsel Citation.

Little Orphan Edsel

"As a designer I'm proud of the car," insists Roy Brown, chief stylist of the Edsel. "There is not a bad line on the car."

Brown, the subject of an article in the December, 1985 issue of the *Edseletter*, scrapped the tailfins common to the 1950s, and gave the Edsel scalloped fenders, an unusual two-tone design, and lines that made the car look longer than it actually was. But the car's most unusual feature was its vertical grille, accented by a pair of oval chrome rings. Brown says the vertical shape, suggested by one of his staff, was a throwback to classic cars: "It was so old it was new."

When Brown unveiled his design to Ford's board of directors, according to the article, "Henry Ford II led a standing ovation." But the car, introduced at the start of a recession, didn't sell, and fingers soon pointed at the economy, the advertising, the car's performance - and its appearance. "A lot of people said, 'Hey, it's Roy Brown's fault," said Brown. "They wouldn't even talk to me for awhile."

As sales faltered, people began to compare the vertical grille to a horse collar, a toilet seat, and worse. "There are people that have toilet-seat minds," retorts Brown.

Still, the criticism hurt. "It was a blow to my ego," he admits, "which taught me a bit of humility, which I needed to learn," continues Brown. "I did what I was told and I did a good job of it."

Brown, in retrospect, blames the car's failure on economics, not aesthetics. It was aimed at a part of the market already well served by competitors. "A similarly-priced car that had been a success for years, the DeSoto," he notes, "went down the tubes in 1958."

After presiding over the Edsel's first annual model change, Brown was assigned to another division at a rank two rungs lower in pay: "I cried in my beer for two days and then said the hell with it. Enthusiasm got me where I was, and it'll get me back."

After six months, recalls Brown, his attitude convinced management to give him another chance. He became design director for Ford of Britain in 1960, eventually supervising 120 employees. "Every car I worked on over there," he says, "was quite successful." The Cortina, he notes, outsold any previous Ford of Britain product, and "probably made more money than the Edsel lost."

In 1963, Brown attended a company party in Detroit. At the time, Henry II walked up to him, complimented him on his work in England, and said, "It's a helluva lot different than it was three years ago, isn't it? Sometimes we're judged more by how we handle what looks like failure than success. It looks like you handled it well."

Brown returned to the U.S. in 1965, and during the following 10 years worked on designs of various Ford cars including the 1972 and 1973 Lincoln interiors. Today, living in Fort Lauderdale, Fla., he leases a Mercury from the Ford Co. During visits to Michigan, he drives an Edsel. People often stop him, he says, and offer to buy the car. Brown's response:

"Where the hell were you in 1958?"

Mustang Paternity Suit?

The Mustang "was developed seven months before [Lee Iacocca] ever saw it," ex-Ford styling chief Gene Bordinat recently informed the *Detroit Free Press*. "That car would have made it to the marketplace without Lee."

"I'll never put Lido down," says Bordinat. "He was a hell of a talent. But ... he surrounds himself with a Christlike aura."

"I don't like people pecking away at the Ford family," adds Bordinat. "You just don't put your finger in the eye of people who make you rich. Henry Ford granted [stock] options to 108 guys [in the mid-1950s] and made them instant millionaires. Lee's somehow forgotten 60,000 shares."

Bordinat, 65 who served 19 years as Ford's design vice-president, worked for eight presidents. Compared with such frequent turnover, the salty retiree declares, "having piles removed is nothing."

Pantera Discontinued

A future collector's car, the Pantera, has been killed by the Ford Company. The $10,000 sports car has been sold since 1971 by Lincoln-Mercury dealers as competition for the Maserati and Ferrari. Fewer than 4,000 of the cars have been sold in the U.S. Ford had hoped to sell 2,500 annually, but the car peaked at 1,831 registrations last year.

The car was done in by "escalating costs to meet government regulations for safety, damageability, and emissions, to the company. There are enough '74 models around, it's figured, to sell the cars into 1975. In its May issue *Motor Trend* ran a coupon which readers could send to the company in an appeal to keep the car alive. More than 1,800 readers responded.

8N, 9N Tractors

The Fordson tractor, produced in the U.S. from 1917-28, generally is cited as Henry Ford's greatest contribution to agriculture. "But Ford's greatest contribution," according to reader Joe R. Hainline, Ft. Lauderdale, Fla., a former GM public relations executive, "was in the massive production of the 8N and the 9N models back in the 1940s. These models," says Hainline, "to this day are the standard of performance and command prices many times their original cost. Restoring N series tractors is a big business and there is an eager market for them regardless of their condition. They are almost indestructible and regardless of their state of disrepair they can be made operable by even the most awkward mechanic."

Hainline adds that he has owned several of these tractors and "found them better workhorses than any of the new models, dependable and easy to operate. Most recently I owned a Ford Golden Jubilee [NAA] which was made to celebrate the fiftieth anniversary [1953] of the Ford Motor Company. The dealer told me it probably cost about five hundred dollars when it was new in 1952. He called me in 1973 to tell me my machine was old enough to vote, and would I sell it back to him. He paid $2,500 for it."

Tractor Reorganization

Ford recently announced the reorganization of its venerable tractor operations, effective Jan. 1, 1987. The reorganization stems from the company's 1985 acquisition of Sperry Corp.'s New Holland farm equipment business, for which Ford paid $330 million and assumed $110 million in liabilities.

Ford's new wholly-owned tractor subsidiary will be called Ford New Holland, Inc. The company's United Kingdom tractor operations, wholly owned by Ford Motor Co. Ltd., will be known as Ford New Holland Ltd. The two firms are expected to do business in about 100 countries, employ 18,000 workers, and generate revenues in excess of $2 billion. Ford's tractor units now employ about 9,000 workers.

Ford's tractor operations, based in Troy, Mich., were marginally profitable in 1985, worldwide sales totaling 83,848 units, of which 36,061 were in the U.S. The worldwide tractor business has been in the doldrums since 1979, when Ford marketed 133,628 units.

Ford's present-day tractor operations may be traced to a partnership forged by Henry Ford and Harry Ferguson in the late 1930s.

IV

OTHER PEOPLE, PLACES, AND THINGS

Henry Ford, left, and Charles A. Lindbergh. (Photo courtesy Archives and Research Library, the Edison Institute, Dearborn, Mich.)

"Ford Country" focuses on the Ford family and the company and products that bear its name. But it has carried many stories that cross family/company/product lines, or don't fit neatly into any pigeonhole. That's unsurprising, much of the column being based on casual reading, whimsical thought, and ideas and materials tossed through the transom by readers and others. This section therefore presents a trifle of what's left over, plus the kitchen sink. Enough potpourris remains to fill a book.

Flying With Lindy

One occasionally reads that Henry Ford took his first flight on Aug. 11, 1927 with Charles A. Lindbergh in the *Spirit of St. Louis*, in which Lindy made the first solo transatlantic hop. One seldom reads that Ford took two flights with Lindbergh that day. Here's the way it happened, according to Cole Morrow, aviation historian and writer.

"When Lindbergh visited Detroit after his Paris flight," recalls Morrrow, of McLean, Va., "he asked Mr. Ford if he would like to take a ride in the *Spirit of St. Louis*. Much to the surprise of everyone, including Lindbergh, Mr. Ford said he would be delighted.

"The *Spirit* had never carried a passenger before. Lindbergh supervised the rigging of a temporary seat just behind the pilot, and gamely, Ford climbed in and they took off. So, on Mr. Ford's first flight he also became the first person other than Lindbergh to fly in the *Spirit*. Lindbergh then took Edsel for a ride, and next he took his mother up for a ride. I was living in Detroit at the time, and I was at the Ford Airport that day and witnessed all of the flights.

"After Lindbergh finished the flight with his mother, Mr. Ford invited Lindbergh to fly one of the shining new Trimotors sitting on the ramp. Mr. Ford went along with the other passengers, who were Edsel, William B. Mayo,

William Stout (leading figures in Ford's aviation program), Maj. Tom Lanphier, and some newspapermen. Upon landing, Mr. Ford said, 'I wouldn't mind taking a spin every day.' "

"Only one other person ever flew as a passenger in the *Spirit* - Anne Morrow, when Lindbergh first met her in Mexico City. A short time later they were married.

Henry Indulged Edsel

I recently gave a talk on "Henry Ford and Aviation" before a women's organization in Dearborn. Afterwards, a woman who knew Ford personally and also knows a great deal about his personality, character, and activities, told me that Ford himself never was greatly interested in aviation. He went along with the manufacture of planes, construction of Detroit's first airport, pioneering in air routes, etc., to indulge his son, Edsel, who was an ardent aviation enthusiast.

Reflecting on my informant's appraisal of the matter, I agreed with it. Even so, the father's willingness to sink millions into aviation and permit his company to lead the way in several important aspects of aviation is much to his credit. Without the elder Ford's backing, the Ford Company would not have made aviation history.

Dressing To Impress

Henry Ford's most important contributions to aviation are cited in a Michigan Historical Commission marker outside the Dearborn Inn. The marker notes that Ford ushered in a "new era of flight embracing the all-metal airline, radio control devices, air mail, scheduled flights, and the airline service that the generation of the 1930s came to expect."

The sign might also have noted that Ford was one of the first airline operators to dress his pilots in uniforms. The automaker, according to an article in the *Dearborn Historian* by Richard L. Hagelthorn, believed that a uniformed pilot, like the uniformed captain of a ship, would be reassuring to passengers. Before Ford's day, pilots were casually attired in windbreakers or jackets, scarves, and helmets.

Ford also was one of the first to employ cabin stewards to see to his passengers' comfort. They too sported natty uniforms.

Trimotor In Smithsonian

Is it a bird? Is it a plane? Or is it "Superplane?" Truth is, it's a Ford Trimotor hung from the ceiling of the Hall of Air Transportation of the Smithsonian Institution's National Air and Space Museum. The Trimotor is one of only six planes on display, so it's considered special, if not exactly super.

The Ford Trimotor's significant niche in aviation history is amply borne out in the Hall of Air Transportation of the Smithsonian Institution's new National Air and Space Museum. The Trimotor is one of only six planes on display, the others being the Boeing 247D, Douglas DC-3, Fairchild FC-2, Northrup Alpha, and Pitcairn Mailwing. These craft are cited as "examples ... of transport aircraft ... which have helped mold the air transportation and air cargo industry."

The Trimotor on display, one of only a handful extant, is the N9683, formerly owned by American Airways, Inc. It occupies the foremost location in the display, and its placard reads as follows:

"The Ford Tri-Motor, affectionately known as the 'Tin Goose,' was an important American airplane. It combined a ruggedly handsome appearance with genuine utility and unusual longevity. The Ford was the largest civil aircraft in America when it started passenger service on August 2, 1926. Its all-metal construction and the prestigious Ford name made it immediately popular with passengers and airlines. It featured wicker seats for the 14 passengers who traveled at 175 kilometers per hour (about 110 miles per hour)."

Although Fordophiles might like to think that the Trimotor was the Model T of aviation, that distinction lies with the Douglas DC-3. The Smithsonian aptly describes the DC-3 as "the important single aircraft type in the history of air transportation."

Honk Of Tin Goose Unheeded

Island Airlines, the last commercial line to fly a Ford Trimotor, is trying to sell its "Tin Goose," but has no takers.

"We had a lot of response to our advertising, but when it came to our auction, we didn't have any buyers," lamented Dave Haberman, owner/operator of Island, based in Port Clinton, Ohio. Haberman initially asked $950,000 for the

The author, left, and Island Airlines owner/chief pilot, Harold Hauck, stand next to Island's Ford Trimotor in 1970. In those days the line's pilots disdained uniforms, and runways were covered with grass and dandelions. Hauck's successor has the Trimotor up for sale.

plane, but says he'll consider $750,000. Island, which bills itself as the "world's shortest airline," flies between Port Clinton and several of Lake Erie's islands. It has flown Fords since 1935.

Flying on one of Island's Trimotors was a memorable experience, never to be forgotten. In 1970, I traveled the island circuit in a 1928 model with semibald tires. The control cables on the outside of the fuselage slapped against the washboard metal skin of the plane, setting up vibrations. The pilot was as busy as a one-armed paperhanger, steering with one hand, regulating the plane's three throttles with the other, while watching the instruments.

The plane cruised at 85 miles per hour, and covered the 34-mile circuit in 45 minutes taking off and landing 12 times. A 13-year-old passenger agent manned the "terminal" on one of the islands.

On the way back, I asked the pilot, "What would you do if I pointed a gun at you and said, 'take me to Cuba?'"

He laughed and said, "I'd laugh."

"Really, what would you do if I insisted on going to Cuba? How far would we get before we had to refuel?"

"Columbus, Ohio, about 120 miles distant, maybe." And, he chuckled, "by that time, at our rate of speed, I think you'd say, 'Oh, forget it.'"

"Queen Of The Airways"

A sketch of a Ford Trimotor airplane (above) was featured in United Airline's recent Executive Air Travel Program.

An information card which accompanies the sketch notes that the Trimotor, the "Queen of the Airways," flew "The Friendly Skies" of United from 1926 until 1933, when it was replaced by newer and faster equipment.

United's Trimotors carried two crew members and 14 passengers, plus a half-ton of mail/baggage. The plane had a cruising speed of 122 mph, a range of 475-625 miles and a ceiling of 18,050 feet. Each plane cost about $50,000.

Visual Aid

As a guide to aviators, Ford ordered its U.S. dealers to paint the names of their hometowns on their dealerships' roofs, according to the May 20, 1930 edition of an Olney, Ill. newspaper.

One of those complying with the directive was D.A. Piper, Olney's Ford dealer. Piper was the uncle of Perry E. Piper, a founder and leading light of the Edsel Owners Club, who forwarded the news clipping.

McGinny's Tin Goose

This large, attractive painting of a Ford Trimotor adorns Mr. McGinny's Tin Goose restaurant, 24366 Grand River Ave., Detroit. Inside, the decor is tied to Henry Ford's famed airplane, the nation's leading passenger craft in the late 1920s and early '30s.

Mile-High Wedding

A Ford Trimotor was the setting of the first airplane wedding in Oklahoma and the third in the United States, according to a recent *Detroit Free Press* obituary on Fern H. Green, 81, Royal Oak, Mich.

The mile-high ceremony was part of a 1929 promotional campaign sponsored by an Enid, Okla. jeweler. Mrs. Green, taking her first airplane ride, dropped her bridal bouquet on the "thousands" of gawkers below. She never knew who caught the bouquet, said a surviving daughter.

Thanks to Detroit's Mike Skinner for forwarding the article.

Black Leaders Loved Ford

One of the more interesting aspects of the Dearborn/Detroit celebrations marking Ford's 75th anniversary was the tribute paid to the Ford family and company by leaders of Detroit's black community.

The three black speakers at a Ford marker ceremony in Detroit's Renaissance Center - Detroit Mayor Coleman A. Young, Detroit Common Council President Erma Henderson, and Detroit Common Councilman Rev. Nicholas Hood - all spoke of the Ford family and company in glowing terms. One could not conceive of these leaders speaking in similar terms about any other Detroit company, or, for that matter, any other nationwide firm. In turn, they told of how Old Henry and his company offered jobs - some of them white-collar and skilled - to blacks at a time when most firms wouldn't permit them to work except in foundries or on the end of a broom; of how much and in so many ways the Ford family has contributed to the Motor City's cultural heritage; and of Henry II's and the company's key role in the revitalization of Detroit through construction of the Renaissance Center.

Ford, it seems to me, enjoys better public relations among blacks than any other firm in the country, and for good reason. It has done more for them since Henry Ford hired the first Negro in 1914 - than any other company. Little wonder that the *Journal of Negro History*, after Ford's death in 1947, observed that "He endeavored to help humanity by offering men work at living wages and making it comfortable for them in his employment. In this respect he was a great benefactor of the Negro race, probably the greatest that ever lived."

Joe Louis's Better Idea

Joe Louis's employment in Ford's Rouge Plant in the 1930s was mentioned in recent obituaries of the ex-heavyweight boxing champion. One of the stories also noted that Louis was slated to work for Chrysler, not Ford. John Conyers, Sr., father of a Detroit congressman, recalled lending Louis $6 to outfit himself for an amateur fight. The elder Conyers, an ex-Chrysler employee, said he gave Louis the money with the understanding that the young fighter would join Chrysler and represent the company in athletic competition. Instead, Louis accepted a Ford offer.

Conyers said Louis later apologized, and, after his career took off, offered his benefactor two tickets to one of his matches as repayment for the $6. Conyers told him not to worry about it: "I said, 'You made it man. That's the important thing.' "

Jesse Owens, Ex-Fordman

The late Jesse Owens, 66, who won four gold medals in the 1936 Berlin Olympics, was employed by Ford during World War II.

Owens was assigned to the company's Rouge Plant personnel office. His boss was another black man, Willis Ward, now a Detroit judge. "He helped me," recalled Ward, "but he didn't speak (to groups). He couldn't. That was something that came later." Owens, Ward adds, eventually became an inspired lecturer and was in great demand on the dinner circuit and at school assemblies.

Henry Ford's hatchet man, Harry Bennett, remembered Owens in a different light. When I interviewed Bennett at his home in Las Vegas in 1973, he had the following to say of Owens: "He had a lot of ideas, maybe too many, on how we should run the place."

Of Ward, Bennett said, "He was smart, educated, very intelligent. I put him in charge of black employment. He got our problems cleaned up and the fellows liked him."

During World War II, Ford's Rouge Plant employed approximately 100,000 workers, about 4,000 of them black. "It was a very early affirmative action program," as Ward put it.

The late Lawrence J. Washington (left) listens to a foreman in the Rouge Plant's iron foundry in 1953. Washington, for years Ford's highest paid black employee, had charge of labor relations for the foundry's 9,000 workers.

Veteran Black Executive Dies

Lawrence J. Washington, 67, of Detroit, one of the first blacks to rise to high position within Ford Motor Co., died recently.

Washington joined Ford as a Rouge Plant

foundry worker in 1939. "The first thing I saw was a guy being carried out from exhaustion," recalled Washington. "I wondered if I was going to live to see my potential."

In 1941, Washington became an employment clerk, then got into labor relations. By April 3, 1954, when your commentator interviewed him in connection with a study on black employees at Ford, he was supervisor of the foundry's hourly personnel, with labor relations responsibility for more than 9,000 black and white workers. His annual salary of $12,000 was higher than that of any other black employee at Ford.

Washington recruited black employees for Ford after Detroit's 1967 race riots. In 1973 he was promoted to community affairs manager for Ford Motor Land Development Co., and held this position at the time of his death. He also was president of the Detroit chapter of the National Assn. for the Advancement of Colored People.

Ex-Fordist Motown Mayor

Detroit Mayor Coleman Young, left, Henry Ford, center, and UAW President Leonard Woodcock laughing together at a Detroit banquet. Young worked for Ford during his youth. Woodcock, after retiring from the union, became U.S. ambassador to China.

Detroit's Mayor Ex-Fordman

Many of Detroit's black political leaders worked for Ford during the 1930s, a decade when only Ford among auto companies hired blacks, except in menial or dirty jobs.

Many of Ford's blacks thus were embroiled in the labor-management strife of the Depression Decade. Although most remained Ford loyalists, in deference to Old Henry's willingness to give them decent jobs, others were in the forefront of the UAW's efforts to organize company workers.

Among those helping the union organize Ford was Detroit's present mayor, Coleman Young, then 22, who was fired by the company for hitting a racist white foreman on the head with a steel bar.

178 FORD COUNTRY

Receiving His Due

Although accused by Lee Iacocca of calling blacks a derogatory name, Henry Ford II has been honored many times by black organizations. Above, in 1973, he receives the Founder's Gold Medallion Award from the United Negro College Fund for "excellent and meritorious service." Presenting the award is the fund's founder and honorary president, Dr. Frederick D. Patterson.

Neither Hank Nor Bill

The late Bill Harrah, owner of the world's largest auto collection, is described by the author of a newly-published biography as being an individual of great contradiction - and as being rapacious, ambitious, materialistic, uncommunicative, oblique, and socially narrow-minded.

"In short," notes reviewer Charles Betts, Jr. in a recent issue of *Antique Automobile*, "one who might fit into the same sort of niche as that reserved for Henry Ford, Sr."

I largely agree with Charlie and the author of *William Fisk Harrah: The Life and Times of a Gambling Magnate*, Leon Mandel, who knew Harrah personally. Indeed, I was struck by the many similarities between Ford and Harrah while spending a week studying Harrah's collection in 1973.

Perhaps the most apparent similarity between the two men was the deference that subordinates paid to each. Just as associates never called Ford "Henry," others didn't call Harrah "Bill." Each came on quietly, but his presence diminished others in size when he entered a room. Each was shy, but immodest. Neither was a public speaker. Ford struggled through fewer than 20 public addresses during his lifetime. Harrah may have given more, but was no more at ease at the podium than Ford. The list of similarities could go on and on.

Like many other old-car enthusiasts, I saw Harrah at a number of meets, especially at the Hershey meet and Franklin and Wills-Ste. Claire rallies at Cazenovia, N.Y. and Marysville, Mich., respectively. Between marriages Bill would be accompanied by a young beauty. People respected his privacy, while circling about. I once asked an aide, a bodyguard I suppose, if his boss minded having his picture taken. I was told he didn't mind, so I took quite a few.

Undoubtedly there was much more to Bill Harrah than met the eye. He didn't get to be Nevada's No. 1 casino operator by being an ordinary guy. But the side of him seen by hobbyists was likable. He loved old cars and he did right by them. That went a long way with most of us.

Advice From Henry

Like many others, I knew that Detroit's great old car collector, Barney Pollard, had stashed like sardines hundreds of antique vehicles in makeshift sheds on his construction company's property. But despite several chats with Pollard, I learned only recently that Henry Ford had advised Barney to store his cars in this fashion, and why:

The story goes back to World War II, according to Whitman C. Daly, 80, of Berkley, Mich., a veteran auto painter who assisted Pollard with restorations. "During the early part of the war," Daly wrote me, "Mr. Pollard had his large yard in Detroit filled with antique cars, some dating back to 1902. Some members of the War Department demanded that he sell them for scrap. He said that he contacted Henry Ford (whom he knew), and Mr. Ford advised him to put up makeshift buildings and store the cars on their front ends leaning against each other after oil was poured into the cylinder heads and the leather upholstery was brushcoated with neat's-foot oil."

"Being a contractor," Daly added, "Mr. Pollard had access to wood materials and metal sheeting, so he took Mr. Ford's suggestion and had all of his collection under cover in a short period." That done, Pollard convinced the government that he was a car collector, not a gatherer of scrap iron, and his magnificent array came through the war unscathed. Pollard died in 1981. His family still has about 200 of the approximately 1,000 cars collected by Barney, according to Daly.

Evangeline Dahlinger

Evangeline Côté Dahlinger, whose son, John, claims that Henry Ford is his natural father, died November 4, 1979 in a Port Huron, Mich. nursing home at age 86. She had been in poor health since suffering a stroke in 1976. John's claim was made in a book, *The Secret Life of Henry Ford*, published in 1977, after Mrs. Dahlinger's senility made it impossible for her to learn about or comprehend her son's revelation. Mrs. Dahlinger herself never said that Ford was John's father.

Mrs. Dahlinger joined Ford Motor Co. in 1909, working in a secretarial pool. She became secretary to C. Harold Wills, the firm's brilliant metallurgist and designer, and in this capacity attracted Ford's attention. In 1917, she married a company test driver, Ray Dahlinger, who later bossed Ford's farms. Evangeline worked closely with Ford in planning and developing the Edison Institute (Henry Ford Museum and Greenfield Village), and eventually cared for Ford and his wife, Clara, in their declining years. Her role in Henry Ford's life was so important that, quite apart from any romantic involvement she may have had with him, I designated her as one of the 10 persons who had the most influence on the magnate, (Harry Bennett, who died earlier this year, was another).

Your commentator had been investigating the Dahlinger/Ford story for more than a dozen years before John published his book and had long since concluded that circumstantial evidence would convince any open-minded person that Henry and Evangeline were more than platonic friends, and that John likely was fathered by Henry. John's book corroborated some of my information, and added additional circumstantial evidence. But of course the only persons who knew all there was to know about the Evangeline/Henry relationship were Evangeline and Henry, and both are gone.

I met Mrs. Dahlinger just once, and very briefly, on Sunday afternoon, May 5, 1974. Bob Smith, who had been given Henry and Clara Ford's "Honeymoon House" by the Fords and had worked closely with Mrs. Dahlinger in Greenfield Village years ago, took me to see her. After our brief encounter, I wrote a note to myself, as is my wont after such meetings. Here it is unaltered even as to a final sentence which I rather wish I had omitted:

"Bob and I went to the house (in Dearborn) on foot. We saw a light upstairs, and a boy mowing the lawn; otherwise no signs of life or habitation around the place. The place looks run-down on the outside. It is of stone, sizable, and impressive, with wooden balconies, at least two of them. Was in need of repair and general picking up outside. We thought it might be unoccupied, except for the light. Bob rang the bell, and we heard a dog bark. Then Mrs. D. came to the door on the second floor, and we talked to her from downstairs. Bob identified himself, but she didn't recognize him or his name. She then said, 'What is it you want?'

and Bob said he'd like to pay her a visit. She didn't invite us in, saying she was having lunch (it was about 2 o'clock), and that she was watching the baseball game on TV. She was dressed in a red dressing gown, had gray hair, was semitoothless, and, if she's in her 80s didn't altogether look that old. She looked as if she was in her 70s however. Her voice was strong, her mind seemed clear in every respect, even though she didn't recognize Bob, who said he hadn't seen her for at least 15 years. She also easily controlled the sizable dog. She was not friendly, but not abusive. She wore black horn-rimmed glasses. There is now a bit of the crone about her."

Ah, but there was a time when she was young and passing fair, and much more saucy, coquettish, pert, impertinent, and if not precisely the kind of girl who married dear old Dad, the kind of girl dear old Dad might have liked to have known, and known well. Too, the thought of the youthful Evangeline always reminds me of the song, "Who Wouldn't Love You," whose lyrics run like this:

Who wouldn't love you,
Who wouldn't buy,
The west side of heaven,
If you'd winked your eye...

Evangeline winked, and Henry, methinks, bought. Some say he may have bought $50 million worth. That figure strikes me as high, but it certainly went into the millions even in pre-1947 dollars. And from all that I have heard of Mrs. D. in her prime, Henry likely considered any amount well-spent. Although no great beauty, Evangeline was, as the English would say, some package.

Springwells Park Sold

Springwells Park, a Dearborn community created by Henry and Edsel Ford, was sold recently to an investor group headed by two Birmingham, Mich.-based real estate developers. The 25-acre area contains 300 rental apartments and town houses, as well as a small shopping village sometime referred to as America's first shopping center.

Henry Ford and his wife, Clara, gave the site to the newly-established Ford Foundation in 1937. The Ford interests

Dahlingers

Mrs. Ray Dahlinger, shown above at age 50 presiding at a ship christening in 1943, died on November 4, 1979, at age 86. She was one of Henry Ford's closest friends for more than three decades.

Her bearded son, John, 56, claims that he was fathered by Henry Ford. John is shown at the reunion of Edison Institute alumni in August, 1979.

The Ford-financed Springwells Park (part of Dearborn) shopping village as it looked in the early 1970s. Between the two wings is a stone dedicated to Henry and Edsel Ford by Springwells Park residents in 1948. Atop the memorial is a metal strip (right) which reads, "The Shadow Passes - Light Remains."

then created a development combining single-family homesites with apartments as well as a commercial shopping area, a visionary concept that came to be known in the 1970s as planned unit development.

The Foundation gave the property to the Founders Society of the Detroit Institute of Arts in 1959. The Founders sold the property to an investor group headed by Henry Ford II's close friend, Max Fisher, in 1965.

Residents of the area erected a stone memorial to Henry and Edsel Ford in 1948. Atop the memorial is a metal strip which reads, "The Shadow Passes - Light Remains." The memorial may be seen between two wings of the tiny shopping center.

Railroad Sold

Henry Ford's old railroad, the 588-mile Detroit, Toledo & Ironton, will be acquired by the Grand Trunk Western Railroad, if, as expected, the Grand Trunk's purchase bid wins approval from the Interstate Commerce Commission. The Grand Trunk has offered to pay $25.2 million for the D.T. & I., and plans to spend about $12 million improving its track and signal equipment.

Ford bought the railroad in 1920, which year it had shown a deficit of $1,896,523. Its roadbed was defective, its rails badly worn, its locomotives and cars inadequate in number and in poor condition, its stations and shops in disrepair, and the morale of its employees low.

The auto king poured millions into a program of improvement, and slashed the number of employees while increasing the pay of those remaining. He also reduced freight rates by 20 percent.

When Ford retired from railroading, he could look back on his experience as

Proud Of Native Son

Dearborn takes justifiable pride in being Henry Ford's hometown, and even police headquarters advertises the fact, as this sign attests. In addition to noting that the "City of Dearborn Michigan" is the "Home Town of Henry Ford" and was settled in 1795, the sign's emblem features a sketch of a youthful Henry Ford, his 1896 quadricycle, and the Henry Ford Museum. Signs at all major entrances into Dearborn note that the community is the "Home Town of Henry Ford."

182   FORD COUNTRY

a rewarding one. He had made money, sold at a profit (just in time to escape the Depression), and reaped a harvest of publicity which enhanced his reputation as the world's leading industrialist.

Experimental Concrete Ties

One of Henry Ford's most interesting - and unsuccessful - experiments involved the use of concrete, rather than wooden, railroad ties on his Detroit, Toledo & Ironton Railroad. Veteran railroaders warned the automaker that trains needed the "give" of the track to avoid derailment. Unconvinced, Ford ordered a stretch of track relaid with concrete ties. Sure enough, his locomotive jumped the track. Ford ordered the engine put back on the track, backed 'er up, and ran it forward again. Again derailment. End of experiment; the concrete ties were replaced with conventional wood. This 1925 photo shows a stretch of the experimental track. (Photo, courtesy of Ford Archives, Henry Ford Museum, Dearborn, Mich.)

Chinese Concrete Ties

In the 1920s Henry Ford built and laid concrete ties, hoping they'd replace wooden ties. But his experiment failed, apparently because of improper ballasting. Today, in China, much of the mainline rail system makes use of concrete ties, as shown in this recent photo taken at a station stop. The white lines indicate to the engineer where his locomotive should pull up.

FORD COUNTRY **183**

Ghosts Out Of The Past

Like ghosts out of the past, these arches, once used to help power electric trains on Henry Ford's Detroit, Toledo & Ironton Railroad, march down the track as far as the eye can see. Although many of the arches - erected by Ford during the 1920s - have been torn down, hundreds still can be seen along the D.T.&I.'s tracks southward from Dearborn. This picture looks north as the tracks cross Northline at Empire in Taylor, Mich. The D.T.&I.'s trains are now powered by diesel engines.

Origin Of Five-Dollar Day

There are numerous versions as to the origin of the fabled five-dollar daily wage paid Ford workers in 1914, and to this day no one can say for sure which story is correct.

One version, recently passed on by George May, Ypsilanti, Mich., was chronicled in Royce Howe's *Edgar A. Guest: A Biography*. Guest, a Detroit newsman, wrote homespun poetry greatly admired by Ford, and consequently had access to the motor king.

One day, before 1914, Guest recalled that he was in Ford's office, as the magnate looked out the window at a line of job seekers outside.

"Do you know why we can hire a man for $1.85 a day?" Ford asked an aide in Guest's presence. The aide said it was because that was the prevailing wage for factory work. Ford replied, "No, that isn't the reason at all. It's because every fellow in here can look out the window and see another fellow who can take his job."

Ford, according to the biography, began to wonder how the workers were doing with the $1.85 wage scale. From inquiries made of doctors and the work of investigators, the magnate learned of the hardships his workers and their families endured.

"How much would it take to fix it to make them secure?" Ford asked his investigators, who came up with a figure of $5 a day. That response, Guest claimed, was the origin of the $5 day.

The story is plausible. Ford, during the teens, was an enlightened, compassionate employer, a man who lived up to his personal and his company's motto, "Help the Other Fellow." Alas, the industrialist was hardened and embittered by press attacks in the wake of the announcement of his five-dollar day, the sailing of his ill-fated Peace Ship, and his libel suit against the *Chicago Tribune*.

Downtown That Never Was

Henry Ford's fabled five-dollar day and the auto industry's relatively high wages and fast growth doubled Detroit's population between 1914 and 1920, and made the Motor City America's fourth-largest city, the nation's industrial capital, and a marvel of the world.

But those phenomena kept Detroit from developing a healthy downtown business district, according to Detroit Planning Director Corinne Gibb and real estate tycoon A. Alfred Taubman, a close friend of Henry Ford II. "A healthy downtown needs a high proportion of white-collar workers packed into vertical buildings," observes Taubman. "But the high wages of the auto plants, even as they lured thousands from around the country and overseas to Detroit kept service industries away. Henry Ford paid $5 a day. Insurance workers and accountants got $4; (their employers) built elsewhere."

Detroit's population peaked at 1.8 million in the early 1950s. The city has less than 1.2 million people today, and is now the nation's sixth largest municipality. The downtown area held its own until the late 1960s, but, except for the flashy Ford-sponsored Renaissance Center, today is but a shadow of its former self.

Henry's Way

As some workers are being described as overpaid and asked to accept wage cuts, Henry Ford's 80-year-old five-dollar day is being increasingly discussed by those concerned with the long-term effect of lower pay.

"What Ford did was to pay his workers enough money to be able to buy the cars they produced," typically states a *New York News* columnist, "and he wound up selling more Model Ts than any other cars in history. He may have been the first industrialist to look at his employees not as mere wage-slaves but as potential customers. Putting more money into their pockets would help his business and business in general."

"Ford," continues the columnist, "was denounced in boardrooms and pulpits across the land for violating a basic law of nature: pay your help as little as you can get away with. Ford said he simply wanted to share his profits with his workmen."

"Today we're headed in the reverse direction. The economic trend is to hammer the wage earner back into submission. But let us ask: how many new cars will a flight attendant buy when she earns $15,000 a year? How many flights, even at cut-rate fares, will an auto worker take when he is knocked back to subsistence-level wages?"

Foundation Sells Ford Stock

The Ford Foundation has severed its last financial link with Ford Motor Company by selling its remaining Ford stock.

Established in 1936 by Henry and Edsel Ford, the foundation held 87 percent of the company's capital stock in 1956. That year, when the company began selling shares to the public, the foundation also started disposing of its Ford securities. In early 1974, the foundation owned only 6.4 percent (value $250 million) of the company's stock. Thanks to Ford dividends, the foundation has distributed $4,000,000,000 to scientific, educational, and charitable causes, some of which likely had Old Henry spinning in his grave.

Henry Ford II and his brother, Benson, will remain on the foundation's board of trustees, but otherwise the company and foundation no longer have ties.

HFII Blasts Foundation

Henry Ford II resigned from the Ford Foundation's board of trustees with a blast at the huge institution.

Noting that the foundation is a "creature of capitalism," Henry added that "it is even difficult to find a recognition of this fact in anything the foundation does. It is even more difficult to find an understanding of this in many of the institutions, particularly of the universities, that are beneficiaries of the foundation's grant program. I must suggest ... it is time for the trustees and the staff to examine the question of our obligations to our economic system and to consider how the foundation, as one of the system's most prominent offspring, might act most wisely to strengthen and improve its progenitor."

Ford noted that as the "son and grandson" of the foundation's founders, he has "a uniquely special reason to want the foundation to be effective."

Three Banquet Survivors

This column reported in September of 1979 that the late Cleveland industrialist Cyrus Eaton was one of the last survivors of the Light's Golden Jubilee banquet staged by Henry Ford in the Henry Ford Museum in October 1929.

We now know of at least three other banquet survivors - Theodore Miller, one of Edison's sons, and his wife, Ann, who reside in West Orange, N.J., and John Edison Sloane, an Edison grandson.

Some observers would add to these three Henry Ford II, who is pictured in a huge mural at the banquet scene commissioned by Henry Ford and painted during the 1930s by the magnate's artist-in-residence, Irving Bacon.

But HFII had the measles at the time of the banquet and remained at home in quarantine. His brother, Benson, and his parents, Edsel and Eleanor, also stayed at home. Henry Ford, who figured that the foursome should have been there, had his artist paint them into the banquet anyway. The mural occasionally is displayed at the Henry Ford Museum.

Better Times At Village

New marketing techniques, stock diversification, belt-tightening, and an aggressive promotion campaign have reversed a seven-year decline at Greenfield Village/Henry Ford Museum, according to the *Detroit News*.

"I think we've turned the corner," said Harold K. Skramstad, president of the Edison Institute, which administers the museum complex. Attendance rose 11 percent in 1983 over 1982, the first increase since 1976, while the institute lost about $1 million, half the previous year's deficit. "We are looking to break-even in 1984," observed Skramstad.

The museum and village, founded by Henry Ford in 1929, attracted approximately one million visitors in 1983, far short of the 1.7 million who toured the complex during the Bicentennial year in 1976, but the first increase since then. The institute has cut its work force by 15 percent during the last two years, and now employs 300 full-time and 600 part-time persons.

Skramstad says the institute has been hurt by the popular perception that its operations are subsidized by Ford Motor Co. The institute receives no direct subsidy from Ford, but has had the income from an endowment now totaling $40 million - left by the Ford family. "Seventy percent of our endowment used to be in Ford Motor Company stock," institute spokesmen Peter Logan told the *News*. "And that hurt us when the value of the stock declined and dividends went down. Now we have diversified our investments and

Entrance to the historic Henry Ford Museum in Dearborn, Mich.

Ford stock represents about 7 percent of our endowment."

The institute is still battling to convince the public that its $8 adult admission price is fair. The price was raised in 1981 as the institute sought to cut losses, and the backlash is still felt. Skramstad maintains that the price is a "bargain" compared to other tourist attractions, and your commentator agrees.

Hitching Up At The Village

More than 250 weddings are conducted annually in Greenfield Village's Martha-Mary Chapel, named for Mary Litogot Ford and Martha Bryant, the mothers of Henry and Clara Ford.

The 52-year-old, 150-seat chapel may be rented for $300, plus a $40 membership fee in the Friends of Greenfield Village and Henry Ford Museum. The membership entitles the couple to unlimited village/museum visits throughout the year.

"Couples like to get married in the chapel," reports Shirley Miller, who handles arrangements, "because they remember earlier visits with their families, and it brings back such pleasant memories. It has a special sense of history for them."

An average of six weddings per weekend are performed in the nondenominational chapel, which features the ringing of a bronze bell cast in 1834 by a son of Paul Revere. Ceremonies are scheduled for Fridays at 6 and 8 p.m., Saturdays at 10 a.m., noon, and 5 and 7 p.m., and Sundays at 5 and 7 p.m. Call (313) 271-1620, Ext. 445, if in the market.

School Daze

One of the most delightful features of Greenfield Village is the one-room Scotch Settlement School in which visitors may experience instruction in the 19th century manner.

After the classroom is filled, the schoolmaster begins the lessons, not so much readin' and writin' as arithmetic, history, and geography. The questions generally are easy, and those who think they know the answers raise their hands, recite, and, if correct, receive due praise. But those who answer incorrectly are scolded, ordered to the dunce's stand, and made to feel that the next lesson will be taught to the tune of a hickory stick.

It's all great fun, and your commentator, bright lad that he is as long as questions concern neither algebra nor chemistry, dazzled his schoolmates by correctly reciting that Copenhagen is the capital of Denmark.

Scotch Settlement School, built in 1860 in the rural area of Dearborn, was moved to the village by Henry Ford in 1923. The building was part of the village's school system between 1929 and 1969, when the schools were closed.

Sikorsky Helicopter

One of Edison Institute's more significant artifacts, Igor I. Sikorsky's first helicopter, has been loaned for a year to United Technologies Corp.'s Sikorsky Aircraft Division, Stratford, Conn., for refurbishing and display. The VS-300 chopper, which Sikorsky first piloted in 1939, will not be restored to the point of flying condition, however.

Henry Ford and Sikorsky first met on April 16, 1938, at the institute's dedication of the house and cycle shop in which Wilbur and Orville Wright had lived and built their first airplane. Sikorsky was one of more than 200 airplane designers, manufacturers, explorers, Army Air Force officers and aviation pioneers assembled for the occasion.

Sikorsky initially offered his helicopter to the Smithsonian Institution, which rejected the craft because of lack of storage space. Following a recommendation from Charles A. Lindbergh, Sikorsky then gave the chopper to the Edison Institute.

The presentation ceremony, held on Oct. 7, 1943 before 5,000 persons, also was memorable for 26-year-old Henry Ford II. Accepting the gift in his grandfather's behalf, the Ford scion gave his very first speech as a Ford Motor Co. executive. He wrote the talk himself, and it was not bad.

Thanks to Glenn Heim, Frankfort, Ill., for acquainting us with the loan and restoration of the helicopter. Heim adds that his firm, Heim Corp., a manufacturer of punch/stamping presses, makes "the lowest-price press, the Model T of the press industry."

Pioneer Helicopter

This column's December, 1984 issue noted that Igor I. Sikorsky's first helicopter, owned by the Edison Institute, had been loaned for a year to United Technologies Corp.'s Sikorsky Aircraft Division, Stratford, Conn., for refurbishing and display. The pioneer VS-300 chopper, first flown in 1939, is shown above in its salad days. Henry Ford and Sikorsky first met in 1938; the aviation pioneer donated his craft to Ford's Edison Institute in 1943. (Photo courtesy United Technologies Corp.)

HFII New Chairman

Henry Ford II, carrying on a family tradition has accepted the board chairmanship of Detroit's Henry Ford Hospital. He succeeds his brother, Benson, who served as chairman from 1974 until his death last July. Three other Ford family members are on the board; HFII's youngest brother, William, his sister, Mrs. Walter B. Ford II, and his sister-in-law, Mrs. Benson Ford.

The hospital has been associated with the Ford family since 1914, when Henry Ford assumed full responsibility for financing construction of an institution for which funds were being solicited. After its completion the auto king administered the institution and worked out a type of hospital different from that which had originally been contemplated. The institution was "closed"; that is, although any doctor could bring patients to the hospital, once inside, they could be treated only by staff physicians and surgeons. Furthermore, laborers and millionaires were charged the same amount for the same service. The fact that Ford permitted certain of his bedridden employees to earn regular wages by screwing nuts on bolts by hand also created a stir and prompted innumerable Ford jokes.

One of the best publicized medical institutions in America during the teens and 1920s, the hospital contributed considerably to Ford's worldwide reputation as a humanitarian. For decades the institution has been rated by health authorities as one of America's leading hospitals.

The idyllic 19th century setting of Greenfield Village hardly seems compatible with unionization. But craftpersons who work in the outdoor museum and its companion institution, Henry Ford Museum, recently voted to join the UAW by almost a 2 to 1 margin. (Photo from the Collections of Henry Ford Museum and Greenfield Village)

Village Unionized

Once again Henry Ford's body has rolled over in its grave: the blacksmith, glassblowers, candlemakers, and others who portray life styles of yore in Henry Ford Museum/Greenfield Village have voted by almost a 2 to 1 margin to join the United Auto Workers.

Ford despised unions, and his company was the last to be organized by the UAW, in 1941. In setting with the union, however, the magnate gave it the most generous contract it had won up to that time.

Ford likely couldn't imagine that employees of his beloved museums of Americana would ever wish to be represented by a union. But now 136 of them, by a vote of 68 to 36, are card-carrying members of the UAW. "From now on," declared UAW Vice-President Stephen Yokich, "not only the spirit of American ingenuity, but also the spirit of American trade unionism will be on display at Greenfield Village."

Ford Hospital's "Super 7"

A new book, *The Best Doctors in the U.S.*, lists seven Henry Ford Hospital physicians among the 2,500 leading doctors in the U.S. and 50 leading medical figures in Michigan. Henry Ford Hospital, on which its founder spent $11,167,024 between 1914 and 1926 and to which the Ford Foundation pledged $100 million in 1973, was rated as the nation's sixth best hospital by leading health authorities in 1967.

Old Henry administered the hospital during his lifetime, and decreed that the institution be "closed," which meant that any doctor could bring patients to the hospital but once admitted, they could be treated only by staff physicians and surgeons.

Moreover, laborers and millionaires were charged the same amount for the same service, and the hospital contributed substantially to Ford's worldwide reputation as a humanitarian.

Duryea No. 1

What is the "most significant" car in the Henry Ford Museum's marvelous collection? A Ford? Not in the view of Randy Mason, assistant curator of the collection; it's an 1896 Duryea, America's first production car. The museum's vehicle is the third of the 13 cars built by Charles E. and J. Frank Duryea, and it is the only one known extant.

"In 1971," notes Mason, "we celebrated the diamond jubilee (75

FORD COUNTRY

years) of the automobile industry, and the thing we were celebrating was the 1896 Duryea." The prototype of the 1896 Duryea won America's first race, a 50-mile run in the Chicago area sponsored by the *Chicago Times-Herald* on Thanksgiving Day, 1895.

Oldest of the museum's cars is an 1863 Roper steam carriage; newest is the 1967 Ford Mark IV GT race car which Dan Gurney drove to victory in the Le Mans 24-hour race that year. "We don't usually display a car until it's 25 years old," said Mason, "but the 1967 is especially significant and does add a great deal to our stable of racing cars."

Mason's personal list of the museum's gems include the Roper which, he explained, "is significant because of its extreme age, and because it was designed as a passenger-carrying vehicle and not an agricultural vehicle with technology evolving from the carriage trade."

Other non-Ford Motor Company cars to look for when touring the collection, according to Mason, include an 1897 (approximately) Haynes-Apperson, probably the second successful production car in the country, a 1904 Packard Model L, the first production car produced in Detroit; a 1923 Stutz Bearcat; a 1949 Ford, the first post-World War II Ford; a 1930 Model J Duesenberg Victoria, "generally considered the epitome of American classic cars"; President Roosevelt's 1939 "Sunshine Special"; President Eisenhower's "Bubble Top"; and, of course, Henry Ford's race car, "999," and Ford's 1896 quadricycle.

Power Section Boring?

Henry Ford Museum's hot air engines exhibit is included in a *Detroit News* listing of the "10 most boring places in and around Detroit."

"It's not that we don't like progress," says the *News*. "It's not even that we don't care for hot air engines. But we would like to know what they do (did?), and, as the plaque is missing, our question remains unanswered."

Hot air engine enthusiasts might disagree with the *News'* assessment of the interest level in their beloved engines. But it's a fact that the museum's collection of dynamos, generators, electric motors, and traction, steam, marine, and portable engines is one of its least popular sections.

In any event, Henry Ford had a special liking for old-time power equipment, gathered and installed it by the megaton, and there it is, and there it will remain. Actually, I rather like to wander through the area from time to time.

A Notable V-8

Henry Ford and his wife, Clara, seated in the magnate's last personal car, now displayed in the Henry Ford Museum. The Fords were watching the razing of the company's dirigible mast at Dearborn's Ford Airport in 1946. (Photo from the Collections of the Henry Ford Museum and Greenfield Village.)

Ford's Last Car

Henry Ford Museum's more knowledgeable visitors continually point out that the vehicle marked as Henry Ford's last personal car - a 1942 four-door sedan - has a 1946 grille, engine hood, trim, and trunk lid. The fact is, the motor magnate frequently updated his personal cars; all of them were hybrids. He also had new parts put on vehicles given to his friends.

The 1942 sedan has a two-way radio that permitted Ford to maintain contact with his plants and key executives. The automaker and his crony, Harry Bennett made many trips in the car to the Willow Run Bomber Plant and Ford's village industries. Ford was driven around Dearborn in this car on the day he died, April 7, 1947.

Kennedy Limo On Display

The 1961 Lincoln convertible in which President John F. Kennedy was assassinated has gone on display at Henry Ford Museum.

The 21-foot-long car was custom-built from a stock 4-door convertible at a cost of more than $200,000 to Ford Motor Co. It was leased to the Secret Service for a token $1 a year until retired from White House service in 1977.

Your commentator had a sneak preview of the car when it was transferred from Washington into museum storage in 1977. At the time, the late James J. Bradley, curator of the Detroit Public Library's national Automotive History Collection, was appraising it for megabucks, something like $750,000, as I recall. The museum had accepted the car on condition that it would not be displayed until the President's children, John and Caroline, had reached maturity.

The museum's Presidential exhibit includes Teddy Roosevelt's 1902 Brougham, William Howard Taft's Baker Electric, Franklin D. Roosevelt's 1939 "Sunshine Special," and Dwight D. Eisenhower's 1950 "Bubble-Top."

Botsford Inn

The Botsford Inn, as it looked in 1925, a year after being bought and restored by Henry and Clara Ford.

The ballroom in the Botsford Inn, Farmington, Mich., was unheated for as long as Henry and Clara Ford and the Ford Motor Co. owned the property.

The Botsford, one of Michigan's two oldest operating inns, was built as a home in 1836, and converted into a tavern and Detroit/Lansing stagestop five years later. Milton Botsford acquired the inn in 1860, and Henry and Clara often danced there while courting in the 1880s. Ford, according to the inn's present owner, John Anhut, didn't heat the ballroom because of his belief, "if you dance properly, you don't need heat."

The Fords bought the run-down inn in 1924, when the widening of Grand River Avenue, out front, threatened the old buildings survival. After restoration, the property remained in Ford family/company hands until sold to Anhut in 1951. Today the inn's public rooms display photographs of and clippings on Henry Ford as well as antiques from the Fords' estate, Fair Lane.

FORD COUNTRY 191

The Botsford is described in the August issue of *Michigan Living*, monthly publication of the Automobile Club of Michigan, as a "country inn in the city" with a "comfortable sipping-hot-cocoa-in-front-of-the-fire atmosphere." The inn's 65 guest rooms offer modern amenities such as cable television, air conditioning, and clock/radio alarms, while featuring solid wood furniture, thick Laura Ashley print comforters, feather pillows, antiques, "Greenfield Village" print wallpaper, and vases filled with "sweet william" plucked from the gardens. In winter, the inn's seven fireplaces are kept blazing.

Dearborn Inn Marker

A new marker was recently erected adjacent to the Dearborn Inn by the State of Michigan's History Division. Its text reads as follows:

"Henry Ford built the Dearborn Inn in 1931 to accommodate overnight travelers arriving at the Ford Airport. Located opposite the inn on Oakwood Boulevard, the airport opened in 1924. The 179-room inn, designed by Albert Kahn, was the world's first airport hotel. The Georgian-style structure features a crystal-chandeliered ballroom and high ceilings. Its rooms are decorated with reproductions of furniture and fabrics of the eighteenth and nineteenth centuries. The guest quarters along Pilots Row originally were used by the airline's crews. The inn and the adjacent colonial homes reflect Henry Ford's fondness for American history."

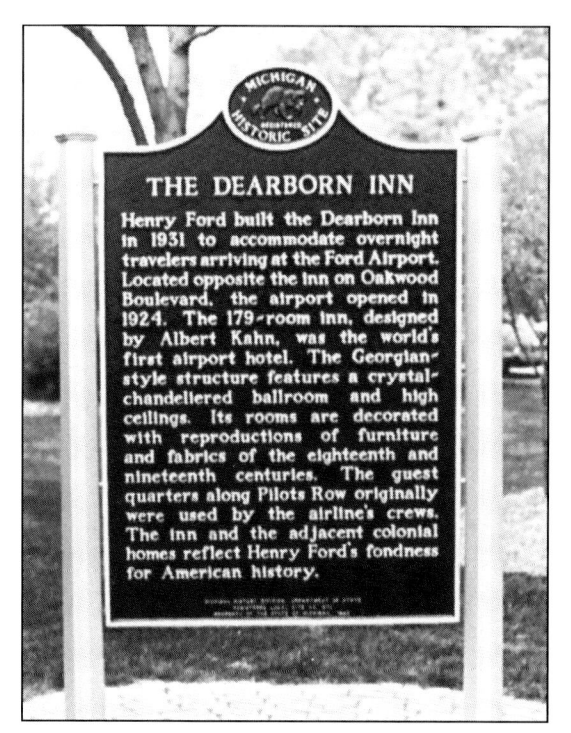

The new marker supplements a state marker erected in front of the inn in 1958. The older marker is entitled "The Ford Airport" on one side, and "Ford Tri-Motor William B. Stout 1880-1956" on the other. Surprisingly, the new marker repeats a mistake on the original marker: "For the first time in the world: A hotel, the Dearborn Inn, was designed and built for the air traveler." Untrue, although the inn qualifies as one of the first half-dozen airport hotels.

The first airport hotel, according to aviation historian William R. Larkins, of Pleasant Hill, Calif., writing in *Ford Life*'s January-February, 1973 edition, was opened at Oakland Airport on July 15, 1929; and the building still stands. Subsequent to the Dearborn Inn's opening reception on July 1, 1931, continued Larkins, "airport hotels were opened at Roosevelt Field in New York; Minneapolis, Minnesota; and Montgomery, Alabama, in 1930.

"In addition," added the historian, "the 50-room hotel at Croydon Aerodome, in London, was opened July 20, 1928. Since this is described in one source as 'replacing one more like a shack' during its construction in 1927, it seems possible that there was an airport hotel four years before the opening of the Dearborn Inn.

"The Dearborn Inn's claim," concluded Larkins, "has been on all of the Dearborn Inn literature and is immortalized in bronze in a huge plaque outside the inn. All that really proves, as we all should know, is that bronze plaques often create false history."

The new marker also refers to "the airline's crews." What airline, one might ask, since the marker gives no clue. Presumably the reference is to Ford Motor Co.'s airline or Stout Air Services.

192 FORD COUNTRY

Ford Buys Dearborn Inn

The Dearborn Inn, shown as it looked in 1962, has been reacquired by Ford Motor Co. from the Edison Institute (Greenfield Village/Henry Ford Museum).

The Ford Co. donated the inn to the institute in 1953 to provide operating capital for the institute. The inn has been a moneymaker through the years ($200,000 in 1982), but has not generated enough income to finance much-needed renovation and expansion. The 179-room facility has an assessed valuation of $6.5 million, and it is believed to have exchanged hands for about that figure.

"We will want to do some refurbishing and improvement," said Ford Chairman Philip Caldwell. "But we want the inn to be a place where people appreciate the heritage of the past and can feel the warmth and hospitality of the kind of company we'd like to be."

The inn's 24 acres are surrounded by a 700-acre tract on which are located Ford's principal design, engineering, product development, and testing facilities. (Photo courtesy Archives and Research Library, The Edison Institute, Dearborn, Mich.)

The Fords' Table

If you wish to dine at Henry and Clara Fords' favorite spot in the Dearborn Inn's Early American Room, ask for Table 16. That's where the Fords dined most Sundays at 1 p.m. From that vantage point, next to the window nearest the entrance, they could watch other guests come and go.

Nowadays Table 16 is open to anybody, and Sunday dinners are brunch/buffet style, rather than served. Moreover, contrary to the Fords' druthers, smoking and drinking are permitted. But the décor of the room is unchanged and the fare is still American.

The room's interior is Georgian. The windows, tall and arched, are flanked by rose draperies; the walls are flowered with wallpaper and bordered with gray wainscoting. Chippendale chairs, sturdy tables, and starched linens elevate the atmosphere to one of dining, not merely "eating out."

Friendly Rivalry

"You say the Wayside Inn purchased by H. Ford is America's oldest," says A.J. Cerilli, Rhinebeck, N.Y. "We have the Beekman Arms in Rhinebeck which also boasts it's the oldest. Who is right?"

Inquiries sent to the keepers of the two inns produced the following response:

"We feel our hotel is the oldest in the United States," commented Charles A. LaForge, Jr., the Beekman Arms' innkeeper, "as we are still operating in the original structure. It is my understanding that the Wayside Inn was completely rebuilt and restored by the Ford Foundation years ago. We both make the same claim as to our heritage but we feel we qualify 'as we are still doing business at the same old stand.' "

FORD COUNTRY **193**

The Wayside Inn, centerpiece of a 2,577-acre colonial preserve set aside by Henry Ford in the mid-1920s. The hostelry provided the inspiration for Henry Wadsworth Longfellow's epic poem, Tales of a Wayside Inn. (From the Collections of Henry Ford Museum and Greenfield Village.)

Master industrial architect Albert Kahn. (Photo courtesy Albert Kahn Associates, Architects & Engineers, Detroit, Mich.)

"We have no question as to their (Beekman's) date," says Wayside's innkeeper, Francis Koppeis. "As to calling themselves an inn, we suggest a review of the early laws where the provision of Food, Drink, and Lodging for Man, his Horses, and his Cattle were the requirements of an inn (Massachusetts Bay Colony laws and regulations of 1647). We have no question as the Arms being the oldest Hotel. [But] we can and do provide for man and beast. Chuck and I have had some fun with the so-called rivalry. I did call his hotel to inquire as to provision for a horse and the charming lady who answered was horrified at the thought of a horse stabled in the middle of town at a hotel."

The Beekman Arms was built around 1700. Wayside's core can be traced to a farmhouse constructed in 1686. But the structure did not become an inn until the 18th century. Wayside was mostly destroyed by fire in 1955, and was restored with a $500,000 grant from the Ford Foundation.

Ford And Kahn

A new book, *Architecture in Michigan*, by Wayne State University Professor Wayne Andrews, devotes a chapter to Henry Ford's architect, Albert Kahn.

In addition to describing Kahn as "the ablest factory designer of all time," and discussing Kahn's work, the chapter refers to the architect's religion - Jewish - and Ford's anti-Semitism.

"Insensitive when it came to the feelings of Jews," says Andrews, "Ford peddled anti-Semitism for years without considering the effect his stand would have on Ford sales or what Kahn's reaction might be."

Kahn studiously ignored Ford's anti-Jewish blasts, none of which was directed at the architect personally. But Kahn felt insecure. Even in 1923, as his organization was doing more work for Ford Motor Co. than ever before, he wrote his vacationing wife, "Whether we can hold them is, of course, always a question. We'll try our darndest." He held them, by not rocking the boat and through brilliant work, until his death in 1942.

Henry Ford baffled Kahn to the last. "He is a strange man," said the architect shortly before he died. "He seems to feel always that he is being guided by someone outside himself. With the simplicity of a farmhand discussing the season's crops, he makes vast moves."

Didn't Pay To Work Hard

We like to think that, in the good old days, every workman truly worked, and nowhere more so than in a Ford plant. But Bill Paton, employed at Ford's Piquette Plant as a 17 year-old in 1907, tells a different story. Paton, a University of Michigan professor emeritus, tells of having come off the farm and finding a job in the four-year-old Ford Company's Milling Department. Eager and naive, Paton did the work assigned to him as fast as he could, then asked the foreman for more work. The foreman was nonplussed; and Bill's coworkers were angered. One of them told the youth, "if you keep up that monkey business, a monkey wrench will be bounced off your head, only it may not bounce."

Bill got the message, but, disgusted with an environment in which employees were supposed to work at reduced speed, found employment elsewhere. After the introduction of the moving assembly line in 1912-13, Ford workers no longer worked at their own pace, and the eventual "speed up" on Ford's lines elicited innumerable employee complaints. Bill, it appears, came along a few years too soon.

Coming Full Circle

"Here's a familiar complaint," writes reader Al Gaines, West Des Moines, Ia., upon forwarding the following early-Model T-era story for *Motor Age*'s March 11, 1909 issue.

The article, datelined Detroit, reports that "The Detroit Federation of labor at its last meeting listened to a pathetic but eloquent statement from the lips of John Hancock, delegate from the Horsehoers Union, in which he made no secret of the fact that the Detroit trade has been all but wrecked by the advent of the motor car and motor truck."

" 'Work is scarcer, horses are fewer, our trade's shot to pieces and more shops are being deserted every month,' lamented Hancock. 'There will soon be nothing for us to do but to go to work in a motor car factory.' "

"The more things change, the more they seem the same," adds Gaines. But one difference between the horseshoers of 1909 and auto workers of today is that the former had a new, lusty industry to turn to for employment. Many of today's workers can only wish for a similar opportunity.

Proud to Be An Employee

In recent years, employees of many companies have taken to wearing "company ties," i.e. ties woven with a shamrock for Kelley Girl Services, a big M of McDonald's, or Avises for the car-rental company. These and other companies present their ties as gifts to employees, or award them for a job well-done. All this reminds me of Ford employees in the wake of Henry Ford's doubling of their wages in 1914. In the same spirit in which an athlete wears a well-earned letter, Ford workers proudly affixed to their Sunday suits big, non-Ford furnished badges stating, "I Work for Ford."

Harleys OK

"After I went to work in late 1931 at the Memphis Ford Assembly Plant," recalls reader Edward V. Sheely, Jr., Memphis, Tenn., "I heard of an unofficial company policy that Ford employees' automobiles were expected to be Fords only."

"I did not have an automobile," continues Sheely, "but I had a motorcycle which I rode to work. To be

FORD COUNTRY **195**

on the safe side (as jobs were scarce in 1931) I told my immediate boss that I did not own an automobile; and asked him if it would be permissible for me to ride my motorcycle to work and park it in the employees parking lot."

"After a short deliberation, he told me that this would be permissible, and that he didn't think I would be prejudiced against by doing so. Consequently, I rode the motorcycle to work for the duration of my employment there. I presume it was figured there was no competition between Harley-Davidson and Ford."

Snitching A Smoke

Although smoking was forbidden in Ford plants until 1946, some employees circumvented the ban, as reader Edward V. Sheely, Jr., Memphis, Tenn., informs us.

"I worked as a stock checker in the Memphis Assembly Plant in 1932, the year that the Model B and Model 18 (V-8) came out. Smoking was forbidden in the plant's manufacturing and similar areas, but the boys had a way to beat it, as follows:

"The toilets were located on mezzanines at several locations. Workers who wanted to 'snitch' a smoke would go to a toilet area, get in one of the stalls, puff on a 'fag,' and blow the smoke into the commode bowl, and then flush the commode after each puff of smoke. The rushing water would effectively carry the smoke down the drain. I was not a smoker, but I did see that done on occasions. I don't know whether anybody got caught or not."

The flushing technique, it may be added, was used throughout the Ford empire. Culprits occasionally were caught by company spies, and were variously fired, suspended without pay or otherwise punished. Offhand, it would seem punishment enough just to blow the smoke from each drag down a toilet bowl.

Henry's Way

Chrysler Corp. announced in November that it might assign production in its struck Canadian plant to outside firms, if strikers didn't return to their jobs. The announcement recalls Henry Ford's reaction to a strike of his workers in 1912.

In September of that year, employees of Ford's Buffalo Stamping Plant struck over dissatisfaction with piecework rates on outside contracts the company was performing. The plant's managers, one of whom was William S. "Big Bill" Knudsen, later GM's president, conferred with Ford by phone.

"That suits me," said Henry. "If the men don't want to work, get some flat cars and move the presses and machinery to Highland Park." Knudsen, much distressed, tried to talk to the strikers, who jeered him. So loyal machinists tore down the presses and other machinery, and loaded them on flat cars. Knudsen, followed by a gang of mechanics, installed them at Highland Park. Three days later, the old gang and Highland Park millwrights began work, the familiar machines turning out familiar crankcases.

In Buffalo, the stamping factory was converted into an assembly plant. The strikers lost their jobs.

Job Security Precarious

During the Henry Ford era, job security at the Ford Motor Company was precarious, putting it mildly. Bob Lusk, who joined Ford's Greenfield Village school staff in 1946, recently recalled his first meeting with Irvin Bacon, the auto king's artist-in-residence. Bacon informed Lusk that he never brought his lunch to work, despite his wife's urging. "Mother," Bacon would say to his wife, "I've only been there 30-some years, and I'm not sure I'll be there at lunchtime to eat it."

All Is Fair In ...

A humorous episode in the UAW's bitter 1941 strike against Ford recently was recalled by Jim Sullivan, 68, in a *Detroit Free Press* interview.

"The first two days (Dearborn's mounted police, who backed Ford) were working us over," recalls Sullivan, who started to work in the Rouge in 1936 ... "I knocked a policeman off his horse on the second or third day ... This policeman was swinging his club at me, trying to hit me, and I was ducking. And I was down low, and all I could see was the horse's two front legs. I didn't dare raise up because I was scared I'd get hit on the head.

"I said to myself, how in the hell am I going to get out of this? So I reached behind the near leg and I grabbed the off leg of the horse. I went that way and the horse went in the other direction with the policeman.

"The next day, the same policeman had me against the fence, the horse's butt against me. He had me pinned, wasn't a thing I could do ... I had a cigarette lighter. I said to myself, what'll happen if I light the horse's tail? So I did ...

"They took me to court on that. [The judge] said, 'Did you do what this policeman says you did?' I said 'Yes sir.' He said, 'Why?' I told him that the horse was leaning against me with his butt, the policeman was pinning me against the fence, the horse's hoofs were all over my feet, and I said it was either me or him. And this federal judge said case dismissed. It was self-defense."

Ford-Related Magazines

The five national bimonthly magazines prepared for Model T, Model A, and V-8 owners are among the best of the magazines published by marque clubs. They not only keep club members and other subscribers up-to-date on club activities, but also delve regularly into many aspects of Henry Ford's life and the Ford Motor Company's and their car's history.

Thanks to the size of the sponsoring clubs, among the largest of marque-club organizations, the T, A, and V-8 magazines are adequately financed and well edited. All have color covers, are approximately 8-1/2 x 11 inches (except for the *V-8 Times*' 7 x 10 inches), have slick pages, and use artwork to good advantage. All also welcome manuscripts and black and white photos from would-be contributors, and all accept advertising.

Oldest of the publications is the *Model T Times*, launched 22 years ago. The *Times* is published by the Model T Ford Club International, the most venerable of all marque clubs. The magazine usually runs 48 pages; its circulation is not revealed by the club. The *Times*' regular features include a lengthy reprint from an original *Ford Service Bulletin*, a service and repair question-and-answer column, and a page of readers' favorite Model T pictures. Howard Gustavson edits the magazine.

Vintage Ford, started in 1966, is published by the Model T Ford Club of America. Usually running 56 pages, its circulation exceeds 5,000. *Vintage Ford* is noted for its cover photography, most of it shot by Glenn Embree. Although the magazine focuses on the Model T, it also discusses pre-T Fords, Fordson tractors and once even devoted most of an issue to the Chevrolet. Many readers approved of the "Chevy issue"; many others howled that treatment of the Chevy was out of place in a Ford magazine. Nonetheless, the magazine's editor, Bruce McCalley, is not sounding out reader sentiment on the feasibility of running articles on Models A and B, the V-8, and other non-Fords. "After all," says McCalley, "the *Vintage Ford* was so named because it was not the desire of the founders of the Model T Ford Club of America to limit its scope to just the Model T." *Vintage Ford*, which may soon begin paying for editorial contributions, prides itself on being a magazine about the *car*, rather than of the activities of the club and/or its chapters. "Our feeling," points out McCalley, "is that, for the most part, readers in say, New York could care less about most of the activities of those in say, California."

Model A enthusiasts are served by two magazines, the *Restorer* and the *Model "A" News*. The *Model "A" News*, now in its twenty-first year, is published by the Model "A" Restorers Club. The *News* runs 28 to 44 pages; its paid circulation exceeds 6,100. Strong on comprehensive, restoration-copy, its editor is George DeAngelis, the Ford employee who handbuilt two replicas of Henry Ford's 1896 quadricycle.

The *Restorer*, now in its seventeenth year, is published by the Model A Ford Club of America, Inc. It runs from 32 to 44 pages, and has a circulation of more than 13,000, largest of any of the Ford marque publications. New editor of the *Restorer* is Lorin Sorensen, also editor/publisher of *Ford Life*.

The 11-year-old *V-8 Times* is published by the Early Ford V-8 Club of America, which devotes itself to Ford vehicles from 1932 to 1948. Running 48 pages, the *Times* has a circulation of 5,500, and is growing at the rate of 100 each month. The magazine has improved greatly the last year under the editorship of Roger Neiss, formerly editor of the Classic Thunderbird Club International's *The Early Bird* and the Milestone Car Society's *The Milestone Car*. The magazine sometimes devotes most of a single issue to products of a single model year.

Ford Life, a nonclub publication founded in 1970, is published and edited by Lorin Sorensen. *Ford Life* deals with all aspects of Fordiana through the Edsel, and runs from 50 to 58 pages. Its especially strong on artwork, circulation is 7,500.

Numerous other publications — *Fork & Blade*, *The Way of the Zephyr*, *Continental Comments*, *Castor Oil Fumes*, *Forties Spirit*, *The Early Bird*, and *The Big E*, to name a few - serve owners of other Ford marques.

Three's Company

One of the pleasant things about being a Ford historian is that one gets to meet nice people. Here, for example, your commentator is flanked by two of Henry Ford's great-granddaughters, Lynn Ford Alandt, left, daughter of the late Benson Ford, and Sheila Ford, daughter of William Clay Ford, chairman of the family firm's executive committee. The photo was taken last year in the Henry Ford Museum following a speech I gave on Henry Ford's life. Lynn and Sheila are trustees of the Edison Institute, of which the museum is a component.

198 FORD COUNTRY

Edsel Publications

Edsel enthusiasts are served by two magazines, the *Big E* and the *Edseletter*. The *Big E*, now in its fifth year, is published by the Edsel Owners Club, Inc. Usually consisting of eight pages, the perfectly-typed, well-edited *Big E* has a circulation of more than 2,000, of which about 1,500 represents club members. The illustrated quarterly has an usual page size - 7" by 9-1/2". Strong on chapter news, the *Big E* carries a variety of items about the membership's favorite steed and a page and a half of Edsel exchange ads. The new editor is Don Franklin, successor to the first editor, Perry Piper, who keeps his hand in as the magazine's printer.

The *Edseletter*, published by the International Edsel Club, was launched in 1968 as a one- or two-page mimeographed organ. Published spasmodically for a time, it has since grown to five pages (just inside the 10-cent first-class postal rate) and, according to club founder and editor, Mr. Jean Leonard, has become a "monthly more or less publication."

Written and typed by Leonard in a style reminiscent of old country editors who wrote stories at their Linotype machines, the *Edseletter* is informal and chatty; and one never quite knows what he'll come across in the next paragraph, much less the next page. The most recent issue started out, for example, with the following remarks: "This issue is being typed on a Sat. morning - not very early for we 'slept in' - until about 10:00 a.m. We hope - by working thru to Monday a.m. - to get the issue into the mails - and on to you." "On our wages" (0), notes Leonard in another issue, "we seldom take Edsel affairs too seriously."

If the club's members find the publication lacking in finesse, it undoubtedly finds it interesting and informative; and it also serves as a free advertising medium for the membership. The *Edseletter*'s circulation is 750.

Facts Of Ford Life

Many Fordophiles have lamented the demise of *Ford Life* magazine, edited and published by Lorin Sorensen, from 1970-74. I asked Lorin recently why he had discontinued publication of *Ford Life*, and whether he had made or lost money on the venture. He replied that editing of the publication - putting together the articles and the photographs for which it was noted - was enjoyable, but that production and circulation problems were a constant headache. "For example," he said, "if the post office delayed or made errors in deliveries, *Ford Life*, rather than the post office, would be blamed; and we had to spend a lot of time apologizing for and straightening out such matters."

Financially, Lorin maintains that he'd been better off during the *Ford Life* era had he remained on his previous job as head of the security force of a big Sears store. The true reward, he added, was in putting out a magazine which attracted thousands of devotees and launched him into a publishing career. Lorin printed 100,000 copies of his latest book, *The Ford Road*, published in conjunction with the Ford Motor Company's 75th anniversary. At latest count, more than 70,000 of the books had been sold, mostly to Ford units, about 15,000 of them overseas.

Assembly Line Shaped America

Only five of the 356 events which historians and editors recommended for inclusion in *Life* magazine's recent special report on "The 100 Events That Shaped America" were unanimously agreed upon - and one of them was Henry Ford's assembly line. Other unanimous choices include the framing of the Constitution, 1787; the linkup of the first transcontinental railroad, 1869; the stock market crash, 1929, and the Supreme Court's desegregation decision, 1954. If I had been asked, I'd also have voted for the introduction of the Model T, 1908, and Ford's five-dollar day, 1914.

Take Your Choice

Henry Ford, in his autobiography, *My Life and Work*, and elsewhere, repeatedly stated that the idea for his moving assembly line "came in a general way from the overhead trolley that the Chicago packers use in dressing beef."

But now a new book, *Initiative in Industry: Dresser Industries, Inc. 1889-1978*, informs us that Ford attributed the assembly line idea to articles he had read about the conveyor system used in Thomas A. Edison's New Jersey iron-ore processing plant.

Well, maybe he got the idea from both places - or from somewhere else.

Henry Showed The Way

Much is being made these days of the "innovative" Japanese "fast inventory system" - delivery of auto parts to assembly lines as they are needed sans stockpiling. Nissan's Smyrna, Tenn. plant will use such a system, and American manufacturers are being exhorted to adopt a "just-in-time" parts schedule so that assembly plants won't be used as parts warehouses.

The idea is fine, but scarcely innovative. Henry Ford conceived and made use of it from the early 1920s onward. As Ford wrote in his autobiography, *Today and Tomorrow*, published in 1926:

"The extension of our business since 1921 has been very great, yet in a way all this great expansion has been paid for out of money which, under our old methods, would have lain in piles of iron, steel, coal, or in finished automobiles stored in warehouses. We do not own or use a single warehouse ...

"Our finished inventory is all in transit. So is most of our raw material inventory. The average shipping time between the factory and the branches is 6.16 days, which means that there is an average of a little more than six days' supply of parts in transit. This is called the 'float.' If production is at the rate of 8,000 cars a day, there are parts enough in transit to make more than forty-eight thousand complete cars. Thus, the traffic and production departments must work closely together to see that all the proper parts reach the branches at the same time - the shortage of a single kind of bolt would hold up the whole assembly at a branch. The exact status of the float may be determined at any hour of the day.

"Our production cycle is about eighty-one hours from the mine to the finished machine in the freight car, or three days and nine hours instead of the fourteen days which we used to think was record breaking."

Henry Ford, wherever he is, must be laughing up his sleeve (one of his favorite expressions) at the way modern manufacturers are reinventing his truly innovative "inventory float."

Ford In North County

"I can clearly remember seeing Henry Ford walking up-and-down the main street of L'Anse and Pequaming (Mich.) in the mid-Thirties," writes Thomas R. Emblad, a L'Anse native who now is president of the Whiting Corporation, Harvey, Ill. "He always seemed to have a Panama straw hat with his shirt-sleeves held up by a black garter band. All the kids referred to him as the man who owned the sawmill - we didn't know that he owned most of the State of Michigan!" Emblad also recalls visits to the Ford "bungalow" in Pequaming. "We were always impressed with its state of readiness," he says. "Apparently the Ford officials would show up unexpectedly and Mr. and Mrs. Westman (the caretakers) kept everything in first-class order at all times."

Mr. Emblad's father was a Michigan

Conservation Department official who at times in the 1930s and 1940s "logged on the side of the Ford mills."

"Dearborn North"

Iron Mountain, Mich., in which Ford maintained large-scale operations from 1921 to 1951, probably is the home of more retired Ford workers, per capita, than any other community except Dearborn. Many of the workers remain fanatically loyal to the company, as attested by a recent letter from retiree Charles R. Edmond, 75, who worked for the firm between 1925-51.

Edmond, who recalls that he had only 16 cents in his pocket when hired, owns four Ford products - a car, pickup truck, dump truck, and Ford tractor. His six children own 10 cars and trucks, plus a tractor; and his two brothers and sister drive four more Ford products.

Recently, said Edmond, a real estate man asked him what he did for a living. Edmond replied that he had a Ford pension and Social Security. The realtor questioned whether Edmond drove a Ford product. Edmond responded emphatically, "Yes sir. My conscience would bother me if I didn't, and also I wouldn't bite the hand that's feeding me."

Ford's Racing Twins

Henry Ford's big twins, 999 and Arrow, are among the 18 "most significant racing cars of all time," according to *Auto Racing History*, quarterly journal of the National Auto Racing History Society.

The top cars were named by racing history enthusiasts, each asked to designate 12 vehicles in a survey conducted by Editor Tom Saal. Seven of Saal's respondents put the 1926-27 Miller 91 supercharged front-drive on their lists, five the 1912 Peugeot L76, the 1936 Auto Union C-Type, and the 1967 Indy turbine car; and four the 999, the 1946-53 Novi, the 1952-54 Fuel Injection Special, and the 1951-54 Hudson Hornet. The Arrow was one of 10 cars placed on three ballots.

The 999 is identified with both

The racing vehicle which was called the 999 in 1904 Ford advertising and the Arrow in Ford's 1922 autobiography, My Life and Work, *in the shop of the New Baltimore (Mich.) powerhouse in January, 1904. The vehicle's flywheel, which had flown off during a trial run, was being repaired before Henry Ford's successful assault on the speed record for the mile. (From the Collections of the Henry Ford Museum and Greenfield Village.)*

Henry Ford, its builder, and Barney Oldfield, who won his first race in the vehicle on Oct. 25, 1902. With Oldfield at the wheel, the 999, as respondent Charles L. Betts, Jr. noted, was the first car "to average 60 mph or better for one lap on a circular mile track (flying start, Indiana State Fairgrounds, July 19, 1903)." The Arrow was the machine in which Ford set a world's record for the mile - 39.4 seconds - on the ice of Michigan's Lake St. Clair on Jan. 12, 1904.

Barney Oldfield is shown at the tiller of 999 in one of the few photos picturing Oldfield without a cigar in his mouth. (From the Collections of the Henry Ford Museum and Greenfield Village.)

Ford As Racing Driver

"How many times did Henry Ford actually drive in competition?" asks longtime reader Jack Kissling, Warrentown, N.J. "Aside from his land speed record, did he ever drive the 999 or the Arrow in competition? When did Frank Kulick die? When was he last interviewed?"

Ford drove only once in competition - on Oct. 10, 1901 at the Grosse Pointe race track, near Detroit. His machine was entered in the 10-mile sweepstakes event, in which America's champion, Alexander Winton, was heavily favored. Winton opened up an early lead but as his car faltered because of overheated bearings, Ford shot ahead and won going away.

After the triumph, Ford developed racing fever, as evidenced in a letter he wrote to a brother-in-law concerning a challenge he was issuing to the French champion, Henri Fournier.

"If I can bring Mr. Fournier in line there is a barrel of money in this business ... I don't see why he won't fall in line ... if he don't I will challenge him until I am black in the face ... My company (Henry Ford Company in which Ford held a one-sixth interest) will kick about me following racing, but they will get the Advertising and I expect to make $ where I can't make ¢ at Manufacturing."

But Ford raced neither Fournier nor anyone else, partly because racing against competition scared him, partly because he found first-rate drivers such as Barney Oldfield and Frank Kulick to compete under his colors. But he raced

Frank Kulick, above, at age 78 in 1959, at the wheel of a duplicate of the Model T he drove in the 1909 New York-to-Seattle race. At right Kulick at the wheel of Ford No. 1 in 1909, accompanied by his racing partner, H.B. Harper, Ford's advertising manager and editor of the Ford Times. *(From the Collections of Henry Ford Museum and Greenfield Village.)*

against time, setting a world's record for the mile in the Arrow on the ice of Lake St. Clair, northwest of Detroit, on Jan. 12, 1904. Also, he tried unsuccessfully to set new records for the mile at Cape May, N.J. in 1905 and at Ormond Beach, Fla. in 1906.

On the strength of his victory over Winton, his mile record, and his expertise in building race vehicles, Ford has been elected to the Helms Athletic Foundation Automobile Racing Hall of Fame in Los Angeles, the Michigan Sports Hall of Fame in Detroit, and the American Auto Assn.'s Auto Racing Hall of Fame in Indianapolis.

As for Frank Kulick, I don't know when he died. He was 78 and living at 200 Interlochen Avenue, Route 2, Orchard Lake, Mich., (with a winter home at 1929 Hayes Street, Hollywood, Fla.) when requested in 1959 by Ford Motor Co. to pose with a duplicate of the Model T he drove in the 1909 New York-to-Seattle race. When interviewed, Kulick continued to insist, and with excellent reason, that he would have won the race had he not, on two occasions, been misled by guides in western states. The 1959 interview is the last of which I am aware.

Big Bay Inn

The Big Bay (Mich.) Inn, shown in this recent photograph, was restored by Henry Ford at a cost of $550,000 in 1944 and sold by Ford interests in 1951. After being closed for 12 years, it has been reopened by Mr. and Mrs. C.B. Stortz. Henry and Clara Ford maintained a suite, now called the Henry Ford Suite, on the second floor of the hotel, front left. The wing was built in 1959 by director Otto Preminger as a set for the movie, *Anatomy of a Murder*, starring James Stewart, Lee Remick, Kathryn Grant, Eve Arden, and Duke Ellington. The hotel, a pale pink for many years, has been painted yellow. But the beds, if the one in which I recently slept is any indication, is a holdover from Ford days, and perhaps beyond. Still, the hotel is a good place to stay, and the price is right — $25 for the Ford Suite, $18 for any of the other 16 rooms.

Only Make Believe

"Once, when Cape May rivaled Saratoga and Newport, President and Mrs. Ulysses S. Grant came up from humid Washington. [Actress] Lily Langtry arrived on her private railway car. On the hardpacked beaches Henry Ford raced his Model T, but lost to a fellow named Chevrolet."

That's what we're told in a recent *Town & Country* promotional piece. "Did Henry Ford ever race Louis Chevrolet?" asks Mike Skinner, Detroit, who forwarded the literature. "If so, it's news to me."

To me, too. The fact is, Ford, in a racing car based on his big Model K, in 1905 (three years before the T was introduced) tried to set a speed record for the mile at Cape May, but failed to do so. He never raced Louis Chevrolet at Cape May or anywhere else.

Sad Ending

This sad photo of the shell of the powerhouse at Henry Ford's Pequaming, Mich. sawmill was furnished by M.L. "Pete" Rodgers, Mequon, Wis., just before its boiler was removed and the building was demolished. The powerhouse and adjacent mill were acquired by Henry Ford in 1922, and operated by the automaker until 1942. Ford and his wife, Clara, also maintained a summer home in Pequaming. The house still stands.

Views Inconsistent

Henry Ford was an inconsistent man. If you have any doubt of it, consider his views on racing.

Writing in 1922 in his autobiography, *My Life and Work*, of the events which led him to build his first racer in 1901, he said that he could "hardly imagine any test that would tell less" about the merits of a car than racing. In 1907, as he was pleading for a reduction in the size of racing engines, he told the *Cleveland Plain Dealer* that "track racing is of inestimable value to the trade and to the development of the art of automobile building." A few months before he reentered racing in 1909 (he had stopped in 1907) he was quoted by *Horseless Age* to the effect that "automobile racing is a thing of the past, and it is a good thing for the industry that this is so. It takes time and money ... that could be better spent in improving the car as a commercial, not a sporting proposition."

In 1911 Ford told the *New York World*, "The question of automobile racing has become the subject of criticism by some manufacturers who seemingly overlook the possible benefits that may be derived by successful competitors ... There was never inaugurated an enterprise that did not carry with it its portion of those who sacrificed their lives in contribution of its glory and ultimate success."

Ford's policy, it's clear, was dictated by expediency.

Transcontinental Race

"This year is the 75th anniversary of the New York-to-Seattle transcontinental race," writes Thomas Catlin, Buffalo, N.Y. "Do you have a photo of the two Model Ts that were entered?" Here's one, showing Ford's mud-splattered entries pausing briefly on the main street of Goodland, Kan. On June 11, 1909. One of the cars finished first, but later was disqualified for having illegally changed an engine en route. (Photo courtesy Archives and Research Library, The Edison Institute, Dearborn, Mich.)

Fast Fords

Fast cars are a part of Ford's heritage. Among such cars displayed in the Henry Ford Museum are (clockwise from top left): The 1962 Mustang I, an experimental forerunner of the popular commercial Mustang of 1964; the 999 with Barney Oldfield at the wheel and Henry Ford standing alongside; the 1967 Ford GT Mark IV, winner of the 1967 24 Hours of Le Mans, driven by A.J. Foyt and Dan Gurney; and the 1965 Lotus Ford, driven by Jimmy Clark to victory in the 1965 Indianapolis 500. (Photo from the Collections of Henry Ford Museum and Greenfield Village.)

Dynamic Duo

Barney Oldfield, who sped to fame and fortune as the driver of Henry Ford's racing car, 999, was full of good stories. The one I've always liked best was his oft-told tale of how he and Ford had made each other, "but I did much the best job of it."

Another anecdote which invariably left them laughing was Barney's explanation of his frequent, off-the-track car accidents: "I can't think clearly if I'm traveling less than 100 miles per hour."

Oldfield's former home is still standing on the southeast corner of Chandler and John R streets, Detroit.

FORD COUNTRY **205**

Piloting Pace Cars

A reader inquires if Henry Ford, racing champion and enthusiast that he was, ever drove the pace car at the Indianapolis "500." The answer is no. But his son Edsel drove the pace car in 1932, his eldest grandson, Henry Ford II, in 1946, his second grandson, the late Benson Ford, in 1950 and 1964, and youngest grandson, William Clay Ford, in 1953 and 1968.

There was talk that Edsel II, now assistant managing director of Ford of Australia, would drive the Mustang which served as this year's pace car. But it was piloted by ex-world champion Grand Prix driver, Jackie Stewart, who for years has been associated with Ford's motorsports activities.

T Bests Edsel In Race

The Edsel, it seems, just can't win - not even over a Model T. In the annual Baja 1000 (875-mile) race, through Mexico's Lower California, a Model T driven by Larry Streeter and Ed Archer, who entered the competition for a lark, got 200 miles further down the road than an Edsel driven by a professional stock car driver who was trying to win. The T was within 200 miles of the finish, and had passed more than 100 dropouts before being forced out of the race by a broken steering spindle arm. The flivver's engine didn't miss a beat on the entire trip, nor did the drive train give any trouble over the rough roads.

Lum Passes On

One of the first entertainers to advertise Fords on radio, Chester H. Lauck, died recently in Arkansas at age 79. Lauck played "Lum" on one of the America's most popular radio programs, "Lum & Abner."

Lauck and his high school chum, Norris Goff, who died in 1978, were on radio from 1931 to 1955. The success of their program, which featured country store humor, was second only to "Amos and Andy" among shows of its kind.

Ford dealers, rather than the company, sponsored "Lum & Abner" in 1933 over 19 eastern and midwestern stations of NBC's Red network. They paid for the program from funds provided by the company, which allocated $3 per car sold for advertising.

Waring Stays In Harness

Fred Waring, the first entertainer to be sponsored on network radio by Ford,

Fred Waring, left, and the author in Sturgis, Mich. in 1976.

conducted his farewell tour last year, but this fall will launch his "first anniversary farewell tour."

Waring's refusal to quit doesn't surprise me. A couple of years ago, when I asked him when he planned to retire, his response was a slightly indignant "retire to what?"

Waring, 81, had the highest-rated show in radio in 1933 when Ford stole him away from tobacco manufacturer P. Lorillard Co. by offering him $10,000 a week. His orchestra, called the Pennsylvanians, began performing for Ford over the largest network in the history of commercial-program broadcasting - 86 American and Canadian CBS stations.

In deference to Henry Ford's lifelong

aversion to blatant advertising, commercial messages on the Waring show were restrained compared to those of most other sponsors. In the first of Waring's broadcasts, Edsel Ford, who shared his father's distastes for "hard-sell" advertising, informed the audience that "our dealers do not intend to spoil this program by intrusive advertising. I know they will be glad enough to talk Ford V-8 to you whenever you wish, but they don't expect me to press on that subject while you are guests on this program."

Under Ford sponsorship, Waring's orchestra was among the top radio programs, and was acclaimed by radio editors and critics. But a cutback in the company's radio advertising budget for 1937 forced the show's cancellation.

Orchestra Hall

Detroit's historic Orchestra Hall is reputed to have the best acoustics of any major auditorium in Detroit. The initial home of Ford's nationwide pre-World War II symphonic broadcasts, in recent years it has been restored to its old grandeur.

Historic Hall

Detroit's Orchestra Hall, from which the "Ford Sunday Evening Hour" was broadcast from 1934-36, recently was designated a Michigan historic landmark.

The "Sunday Evening Hour" featured the music of the Detroit Symphony Orchestra, and was presented over the 86 stations of the CBS network. The program was moved from the 2,000-seat Orchestra Hall to the 5,000-seat Masonic Temple, largest auditorium in Michigan, in order to accommodate additional in-house listeners.

The "Hour" was Ford's longest-running pre-World War II radio program even though it appealed only to a "longhair" audience. Henry and Edsel Ford liked the show, and that was that - until the war forced its cancellation in early 1942.

Ford's Dance Program

This column occasionally receives letters from those who own records made by Henry Ford's old-fashioned dance orchestra. But it recently heard for the first time from someone who listened to the Ford orchestra "live" on radio. The gentleman is James W. Cranick of Harbor Springs, Mich.

Between January, 1944-July, 1945, Ford's orchestra, consisting of a dulcimer player, a cymbalist, a violinist, and a bass violinist, broadcast a half-hour program, "Early American Dance Music," from the Ford Company's recording studio in Dearborn Engineering Laboratory. Henry Ford took a personal interest in this show, often commenting on its quality and making suggestions for its improvement. The only reference to the auto king on the show was the opening statement: "Mr. and Mrs. Henry Ford present early American dance music." In January, 1945, the Fords asked that their names no longer be associated with the program; the opening line was then changed to "The Ford Motor Company, builder of cars and trucks, presents early American dance music by the Ford Early American Dance Orchestra."

The program attained a fair audience rating, ranking fourteenth among the twenty orchestras on network radio during the 1944-45 season. But most of its listeners, according to its fan mail, were retired or inactive people, many of them hospitalized - scarcely a car-buying audience. Acknowledging that the program was "not suitable for advertising automobiles," the company dropped it upon resuming civilian vehicle production in July, 1945.

Ford Hour Conductor Dies

Eugene Ormandy, above, conductor of the Philadelphia Orchestra for 44 years and the highest-paid guest conductor on Ford's symphonic radio program, the "Ford Sunday Evening Hour," died on March 12 at age 85.

In addition to being the highest-paid conductor on the Ford Hour, broadcast over the CBS network from 1934-41 and the ABC network from 1945-46, Ormandy also was one of the Hour's most frequent guest artists. Typically, he appeared eight times during the 1936-37 season, six times during the 1940-41 season, and was scheduled for nine appearances on the 1941-42 program, canceled shortly after the start of World War II.

Ormandy's fee, $1,500, never varied, despite considerable inflation between the time he started commuting to Detroit during the Great Depression and the post-World War II period. His fee was rarely matched by any of the Ford Hour's other big-name conductors, and was more than double that of the lesser lights.

Resuscitating RenCen

Henry Ford II has found it so difficult to rent space in his new Renaissance Center that he will transfer approximately 1,750 Ford Motor Company employees from Dearborn to the downtown Detroit office complex during 1977.

Many of the employees, as they contemplate commuting into Detroit and paying the Motor City's income tax, are decidedly against the move; and not a few, especially secretaries, are quitting their jobs rather than work in the crime-ridden city.

The Renaissance Center now has renters for about 60 percent of its available office space; and nobody seems to know where the remainder of the tenants will come from. RenCen thus may be the biggest white elephant in Michigan's history. It reminds me of the "peace ship" which Henry Ford chartered in 1915 in a vainglorious

Detroit's Renaissance Center towering above the Dodge Fountain and a marker commemorating Ford Motor Company's birthsite.

Renaissance Center

"Has Detroit's showcase Renaissance Center been a drain on Ford Motor Company's finances?" asks reader William James, Winterhaven, Fla.

"Ford's original investment was $100 million," it was revealed at the firm's 1984 annual meeting, "and the company's losses have exceeded this amount."

Ford now owns about a third interest in RenCen I, comprised of the 70-story Westin Hotel and four 39-story office towers, and about a 50 percent interest in RenCen II, two 21-story office buildings. The company says most of RenCen's office space is occupied, while admitting there are vacancies in the retail areas and hotel bookings are less brisk than anticipated. "Nevertheless,"

Model T Casino

Not all of Nevada's casinos have glitzy names, as suggested by this photograph of Winnemucca's Model "T" Casino. Asked why the den had the name, a waitress said that the former owner had displayed a Model T outside as a lure for customers. Both ex-owner and flivver are gone, but the name lingers on. The casino, on Winnemucca's main street, is advertised east of town by a big billboard featuring a sketch of a flivver.

effort to mediate an end to World War I. Ford tried to stop the war at a time when others simply wrung their hands. He failed, but the fact that he tried endeared him to the common people.

Henry II is trying to resuscitate downtown Detroit with his huge office/hotel complex. If he succeeds, all hats will be doffed to him. If he fails, he, like his grandfather, will be looked upon as "God's Fool" - a man who unsuccessfully sought to save a city at a time when many others are giving up on it.

the company maintains, "Phase I - where the real problem was - no longer is a drain on the company."

RenCen represents a magnificent effort on the part of Henry Ford II to restore life to downtown Detroit. It has helped, especially along the riverfront

FORD COUNTRY **209**

which stretches from RenCen to the Joe Louis Arena, site of the GOP's 1980 national convention. But much of the rest of Detroit resembles more a seedy capital of a Third World country than the vibrant Motor City of yesteryear.

A Place Called Edsel's

Perhaps it had to happen: a restaurant/nightspot named Edsel's (exterior sign shown in photo).

A restaurant by day, Edsel's, located at 8557 Research Boulevard, Austin, Tex., is a dance hall at night, featuring '50s music. The hall's disc jockey presides behind the front end of a pink 1958 Edsel Pacer convertible.

Owner Steve Rose decided that an Edsel theme would be perfect for his new place, then bought an Edsel and had it chopped apart for his decorative needs.

"Henryburgers" Live On

Joe Bernardi (photo) and his wife, Helma, owners of Pepino's restaurant, Walled Lake, Mich., report many requests for "Henryburgers" since Lee Iacocca's book noted that Joe, formerly executive chef at Ford's World Headquarters, made mouthwatering hamburgers for Henry Ford II.

Ford's dining room, according to Iacocca, served anything from oysters Rockefeller to roast pheasant. But Henry II's standard request was a hamburger, which Ford's chairman regarded as superior to any burger his domestic chef or any commercial restaurant could make. Joe's secret, Iacocca discovered, was the ingredient, an inch-thick New York strip steak. "Amazing what you can cook up when you start with a five-dollar hunk of meat," Joe said.

The Bernardis' restaurant serves a $3.25 hamburger which Joe admits is not up to Henry's standards. "I wouldn't stay in business very long if it was," he says. If customers insist on a "Henryburger," Joe quotes a price of $15. He's had no takers.

Ford The Educator

Henry Ford was not a professional educator, but there are some who believe that, if he had devoted his insight and energy to education, he might have been almost as effective in this sphere as he was in industry.

Ford operated schools in Dearborn, Southeastern Michigan, Northern Michigan, Georgia, Massachusetts, and England, and certain principles were common to all of them. Recognizing that most of his students would not progress beyond high school, Ford insisted that high school education should emphasize "education for living," rather than mere preparation for college. He also believed in a wide "activity" program, and thus encouraged students to participate in chapel services, social training, organ lessons, blacksmithing, weaving classes, and the like. He advocated small schools with a favorable student-to-faculty ratio. He was not greatly concerned about school buildings, for to him children were the school, and buildings were incidental. Structures around town were used for instruction. After all, figured Ford, there was no better place to teach homemaking than in a house, nor agricultural training than on a farm.

Were Ford's students happy with their training? Your commentator has talked with many of them, and also has seen the findings of several public opinion studies made among them. The consensus: They felt they received a superior education - a much better education than they could have gotten at any conventional public school.

Some School

Students in Henry Ford's Greenfield Village schools constantly were entertained by celebrities who were visiting Henry Ford - and Ford himself spent more of his time in the Village than any other place during the 1930s and 1940s.

On Thursday, October 4, 1934, for example, the children's chapel service was attended by Dizzy and Paul "Daffy" Dean and Pepper Martin, stars of the St. Louis Cardinals, then in Detroit for the World Series; comedian Joe E. Brown; and a Mr. Miles, a second cousin of Abraham Lincoln. Diz gave a talk to the kids, who applauded him even though in the chapel (they later were told it was okay); Mr. Miles recited a story about Lincoln's life; and Brown told a story about a mouse and a cat. The children concluded the program by singing "Happy Days" with unusual gusto.

Ford-Related School Classes

Detroit Institute of Technology, for which Henry Ford taught a class for machinists in 1893, recently closed its doors for lack of students.

The institute began offering evening classes in Detroit's YMCA in 1877. Its enrollment, 2,600 in the mid-1960s, dwindled to 600 during 1980-81 academic year.

One of Ford's students, Oliver Barthel, later claimed that he inspired Ford to build his first gasoline engine by showing the future billionaire an article on gas motors in the Nov. 7, 1895 issue of *American Machinist*. Barthel said he regarded Ford as "just an average instructor."

Wayside Inn's School

An item on Henry Ford and Louis Varricchione, who helped Ford run his Wayside Inn school, appeared recently in the *South Middlesex News*, Framingham, Mass.

Varricchione relates that he first talked with the automaker about the school in 1929 while perched on a log outside the inn - at 5 a.m. At the time Ford was wearing a stocking cap and munching on raw carrots (which he believed were highly beneficial to his health).

The school enrolled about 100 boys ranging in age from nine to sixteen; most were orphans or products of broken homes. Upon graduation, the boys could work for the Ford Company, with a recommendation from its founder, or take a non-Ford job. Ford often would suggest that this or that boy be a chemist or an engineer, and provide additional training for him.

Varricchione, who gave young Henry Ford II a few boxing lessons, recalls that the elder Ford prized work. When Varricchione went to Ford for funds to build a playing field for an athletic field, Ford replied, "Sure, fine. Spendid idea. Tell you what. I'll get some axes and hoes and you can set the boys right to it." That's all the money Varricchione got for the project. But Ford's idea resulted in a big, handsome playfield - about six months later.

The Henry Ford Trade School as it looked in 1925. The building was located immediately north of Ford's Highland Park Plant. After the site was razed, the site was converted into a playground and park - Ford Park - by the City of Highland Park. (Photo from the Collections of Henry Ford Museum and Greenfield Village.)

Henry Ford Trade School

A doctoral dissertation on the Henry Ford Trade School is being prepared by Sam Gaft of the University of Michigan's School of Education.

Gaft, in his proposal, notes that the school was established at Ford's Highland Park Plant on Oct. 25, 1916, and remained open for 39 years. During this period the institution provided training in machining, metallurgy, engine design, and drafting for more than 8,000 boys from ages 12 to 18. Many of the graduates were hired by Ford, while others went to college, or took jobs with other firms.

The trade school concept was not original with Ford, says Gaft, but Ford's school was unique in that it provided scholarships to all students, and did not require company employment. Boys were recruited locally, and admission was based on need. At first, students were taught only trade skills, and had to take academic courses from local schools. Later, the trade school was certified to meet academic requirements for graduation and to award high school diplomas. The youngsters attended shop and other classes for three to four years, and graduated at the mandatory age of 18.

The Ford Trade School experience forged lifelong bonds among many students. An alumni association holds regular meetings and social events in Detroit and Los Angeles, and maintains a large and successful country club in the Motor City. Students' records are stored at Dearborn's Henry Ford Community College.

First Cruise Missile

Henry Ford and his top aide, C. Harold Wills, were among a select group which developed America's first cruise missile during World War I, according to Jay P. Spenser, assistant curator for aeronautics at the Smithsonian Institution's National Air and Space Museum in Washington, D.C.

"The story," said Spenser, "is a fascinating one with all the drama of a novel." Six months after the U.S. entered World War I on April 6, 1917, notes Spenser, Charles "Boss Ket" Kettering, who had developed the self-starter for Cadillac, brought together Henry Ford, Orville Wright and Elmer Sperry to build a revolutionary weapon the Allied Powers could use to attack industrial complexes and armies deep within Germany.

Also assigned to the top-secret Dayton project, according to Spenser, whose research was reported on by the Associated Press, were C.H. Wills, Ford's top engineer, and Edward Deeds, who worked with Kettering at Delco. Ford and Wills were assigned by Kettering to produce a lightweight powerplant; Wright the fuselage; Sperry the self-guidance system. The missile's cost was not to exceed $200 per weapon when mass-produced.

Work began in October, 1917. By the spring of 1918, the "flying torpedo," or "robot bomb," or "Kettering Bug," as the missile was variously called, began to take shape. It was 12 feet in length with a 14-foot wingspan. Wright designed the wings and tail assembly using pasteboard, pieces of spruce, and oiled paper. Ford and Wills built a two-cylinder engine, but vibration forced them to substitute a four-engine motor.

The Ford-Wills engine was unique - it required no carburetor. The flow of fuel was predetermined and unadjustable. The engine was to cost less than $50 per unit.

The missile made its first successful flight on Aug. 18, 1918. The following month, Col. Henry "Hap" Arnold, who would head the U.S. Air Force in World War II, was dispatched to Europe to brief Gen. John Pershing, commander of the American Expeditionary Forces. But Arnold contracted the flu aboard ship, and upon landing in France was hospitalized for weeks. By the time he recovered, the Armistice was signed. No longer needed, the missile was mothballed. Kettering pledged each man who worked on the weapon to keep it a secret, and the secret was kept for years. It was left to Adolf Hitler to reactivate the idea with his World War II VI "buzz bombs."

Our thanks to Meritt R. Marks, Clearwater, Fla., for having forwarded the *St. Petersburg Times* article on which the above account is based.

Model Ts On Western Front

The Model T received high marks as an ambulance on World War I's Western front, according to a report by an American colonel published in a recent edition of *Antique Automobile*.

The report, written in 1918 by Col. Percy L. Jones of the U.S. Medical Corps and submitted to the magazine by Frank N. Potter, states, "Without a doubt the best car for the advance [ambulance] work is the Ford car. It is small, light, easy to run, easy to maintain, simply constructed, economical in the consumption of gas, does not take much road space, and can be handled by one man when necessary. What it lacks in capacity is more than compensated for by the above advantages.

"In light of what I have seen for the last year," continued Colonel Jones, "I am firmly convinced that the Ford ambulance ... can operate in any place where troops go. It is an ideal car for advance work, the large car serving advantageously for evacuation farther back. The roads are excellent throughout France. Shell holes, however, are constantly appearing, but in no case have I known where a Ford was blocked for more than a few minutes. On account of this fact, should

FORD COUNTRY **213**

American Red Cross nurses demonstrate the way in which wounded soldiers would be evacuated from battlefields by Model T ambulances in this World War I photo taken in front of Ford's Highland Park Plant powerhouse. (Photo courtesy Archives, Henry Ford Museum, Dearborn, Mich.)

the car accidentally run into one of these holes, it may be literally lifted out with the help of a few passing soldiers."

Despite Colonel Jones' high regard for the Ford ambulance, he had a low opinion of its body.

"The superstructure ... is composed of composition material, in reality papier-mâché. When they are struck by shell they break like glass, and are very difficult to repair ... This service has let a contract which is being delivered now for 6,000 wooden bodies of more durable nature."

"It is noticed," added Colonel Jones, "that some of these cars coming from America (whether he is referring to Fords or other makes isn't spelled out) are also provided with heaters, which depend upon exhaust gases for their heat. This, as experience has shown, should not be used under any conditions."

A subsequent issue of *Antique Automobile* reports on a surviving Ford ambulance owned by Warren J. Wolloff, of Dedham, Mass. An all original antique, the 1917 ambulance has been in the Wolloff family since the year it was built.

From Cars To Bombers

A Ford engineer who was responsible for designing the upper instrument panel in the B-24 "Liberator" bomber's cockpit recently recalled his World War II employment at Ford's huge Ypsilanti, Mich. Willow Run Bomber Plant.

George Sunal, 65, who now lives in Ann Arbor, Mich., was an electrician in Ford's Rouge factory when the war broke out. "I was working on cars before the war," he recalled. "What did I know about planes?" But he and others transferred to the plant, which eventually had 42,000 employees, soon learned.

Sunal remembers that midgets, because of their small size, worked in the cramped quarters of the plane's wing sections. Women worked in many capacities. But regardless of what they did, they were all called "Rosie the Riveter." It was during this time, said Sunal, that women first began wearing slacks and hairnets, called snoods, for safety reasons.

"Working in the plant was strictly business," he remembers. "There were no coffee breaks and music wasn't allowed. Since Henry Ford was against smoking, he didn't allow smoking in the plant." Because of the size of the facility, which totaled more than 3 million square feet, Sunal often drove a scooter to get around.

Some of the bombers on which Sunal worked were later returned to Willow Run for modifications. "Many were full of bullet holes," he recalls. "Sometimes we found blood inside where the crew members had been wounded or perhaps killed during combat. It was heartbreaking. And I thought I was doing a lot. You felt you were a part of each plane made. You were at the plant so much, you practically lived there."

After the war Sunal went back to designing cars. He retired in 1970 after 35 years with Ford.

A World War II airman (the artist?) inspects sketches of a Model T and bombs denoting 42 missions on the side of a B-24, named "Fords' Folly" (the apostrophe is misplaced). Many of the Ford-built craft served as "canvases" for artists and cartoonists. (Photo courtesy Archives and Research Library, The Edison Institute, Dearborn, Mich.)

Liberator Art

The Ford-built B-24 "Liberator" probably was the most ungainly aircraft of World War II, but her slab-sided fuselage served as a made-to-order "canvas" for Army Air Force artists and cartoonists in every theater of the war, according to a recent article in the *Yankee Air Force News*, quoting from Martin Bowman's book, *The B-24 Liberator, 1939-1945*.

Much of the planes' embellishment was inspired by crew members' thoughts of home, and often took the form of comic strip characters or of shapely females with captions such as "This Above All" and "Purty Baby." As feminine figures grew more revealing, headquarters would order clean-up campaigns, and skimpy clothes and negligees would be painted over the illustrations. One nude figure completed 100 missions with the Seventh Air Force, but, typically, donned a bra for a stateside war bond tour.

A recurrent nude was based on *Esquire*'s Alberto Vargas renderings. Characters from "Li'l Abner" were perhaps the most popular comic strip characters. Walt Disney characters, including Snow White and the Seven Dwarfs, also adorned a fair number of B-24s.

Some servicemen created the art for free, others for pay. A first-rate piece of art was said to command a fee of several hundred dollars.

Last Flight of "Fords' Folly"

This column's June edition ran a photo showing sketches of a Model T and bombs denoting 42 missions on the side of a B-24 "Liberator" bomber named "Fords' Folly." The photo inspired a poignant letter from reader Philip A. Lundy, museum curator and historian for the Yankee Air Force, stationed at Ford's former Willow Run, Mich. plant.

"This particular aircraft," says Lundy, "is somewhat of a significant part of Ford-Willow Run wartime history ... (It) was the 802nd aircraft built by Willow Run (499 fly-a-ways and 303 kits). It was the second B-24 with a factory installed nose turret and the first such plane (factory built) to reach combat status. The first nose turret Ford-built B-24, serial number 7465, was retained by Ford for test purposes ..."

"Fords' Folly" was built in early July, 1943 and ... delivered to the 8th Air Force, 392nd Bombardment Group (Heavy), 578th Bombardment Squadron in Wendling, England."

"The final mission of "Fords' Folly" was on September 11, 1944 to bomb an ordnance manufacturing facility in Hanover, Germany. After releasing her bombs on the target, she turned for England and the entire mission was attacked by enemy fighters. At about 11:58 "Fords' Folly" was seen over Koblenz, Germany with #3 engine on fire. Shortly thereafter, the entire aircraft was engulfed in flames and seen to spin down and crash. No parachutes were observed."

Wanted: Affordable B-24

A B-24 "Liberator," the four-engine bomber built at Ford's Willow Run, Mich. plant, has yet to join the collection of planes gathered by the Yankee Air Force (YAF), a Willow Run-based organization which memorializes the history of World War II aviation.

"The only B-24 for sale is priced at $800,000," says YAF president Rosemary Goodes. "That price is too high." As an alternative, the organization plans to buy and restore a B-17 "Flying Fortress" priced at $280,000. The B-17 is in Mesa, Ariz.

A former B-24 pilot, Richard Bodycombe, recently commented on the Liberator's ruggedness. As a 22-year-old in 1944, he was at the controls of a Liberator struggling homeward from a bombing run over Vienna. One of the ship's four engines was gone, another was failing, the electrical and hydraulic systems were out, and fuel was low.

The crew urged Bodycombe to permit everyone to bail out over German-held Yugoslavia. He refused. "I couldn't stand to be a POW," recalled the retired Air Force major general. Dipping his plane toward the Yugoslav island of Vis, he landed the bomber on a British-built emergency landing strip. Bodycombe was the second pilot to crash a B-24 on Vis that day. Minutes afterward, a third Liberator plowed across the field. The crews eventually were returned to their units.

Forty-one years later, Bodycombe asked U.S. Embassy officials in Belgrade whether any wrecked B-24s were still in Yugoslavia. The answer was no.

Bodycombe is disappointed that the YAF's first bomber won't be a B-24. "During the war," he said, "they brainwashed us (into believing) that we had the best plane." After the war, he flew B-17s, and acknowledges that they "are aerodynamically smoother." Still, he said, "I loved the B-24. I'll never forget it - it was so tough."

The four-year-old Yankee Air Force has 1,150 dues-paying members. It has already restored one World War II airplane - a twin engine Douglas C-47, the military version of the DC-3. The organization owns 22 retired warplanes.

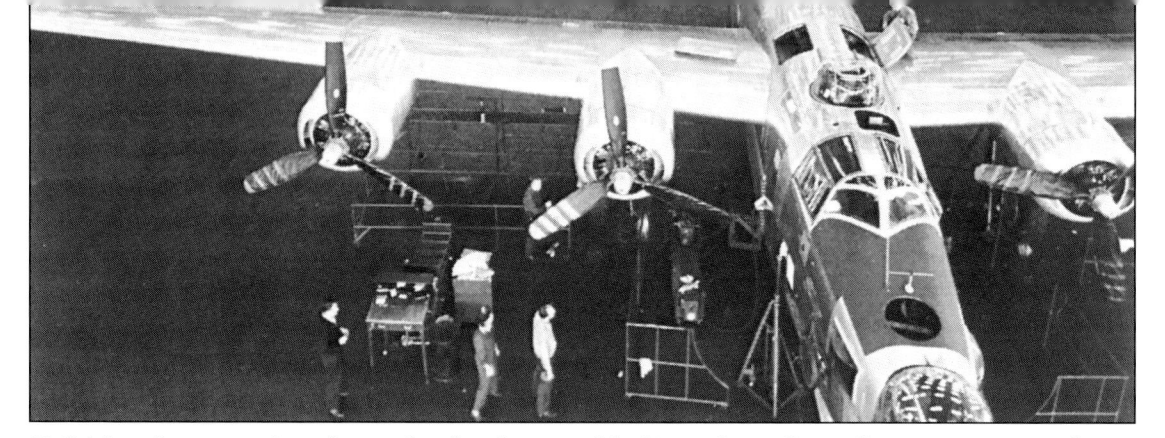

B-24 bombers moving down the final assembly line of Ford's Willow Run. At peak production the plant made 21 bombers daily. (Photo from the Collections of Henry Ford Museum and Greenfield Village.)

Ford No. 1 In Gliders

Ford was America's largest producer of gliders during World War II, as noted in an article in the most recent issue of the *Chronicle of the Historical Society of Michigan.*

The gliders were produced at the company's Iron Mountain, Mich. complex, which since the early 1920s had been producing wooden auto parts, station wagon bodies, chemicals, charcoal, and other products. The plant, Northern Michigan's biggest employer, was closed early in the war after being classified as a producer of materials nonessential to the war effort.

In March 1942, however, Ford was asked by the U.S. Air Force to build 1,000 15-seat CG-4A cargo gliders. In the summer of 1942, the Iron Mountain plant was reactivated. The average age of those hired to build gliders was an advanced 40, as younger laborers were either in the services or had already moved to other war plants.

The gliders were built of spruce, plywood, and cotton fabric around a steel fuselage. Many production innovations were introduced. A quick-dry gluing procedure, for example, simultaneously applied heat and pressure to reduce drying time from eight hours to five minutes. Special rubber tubing used in hard-to-reach wing areas was swollen with steam, allowing the glue to dry more quickly.

A total of 4,205 15-seat gliders was produced between September 1942 and Aug. 13, 1945. In addition, the company produced 87 huge 42-seat CG-13A gliders, redesigned by Ford to carry 42 armed soldiers.

Ford gliders were used in the invasions of Sicily and Normandy. Pilots praised them as "the best, the cleanest, easiest to fly, quickest to trim, and smoothest in free flight."

Iron Mountain resumed civilian production after the war, but its huge powerhouse whistle summoned Ford workers for the last time in 1951. Much of the old plant still stands, mostly in ruins.

Henry Ford's big Iron Mountain/Kingsford, Mich. factory is shown from the air during its glory days. The body plant, in which gliders were built during World War II, was comprised of three "wings." The extension to the center wing, in foreground, was the loading dock. (Photo courtesy Ford Archives, Henry Ford Museum, Dearborn, Mich.)

FORD COUNTRY **217**

Index

A

Abercrombie, Edward A., 34, 102
Academy Awards, 28
Adams, John, 22
Adams, Lisa (Mrs. Benson Ford Jr.), 7, 65
Adcrafter (magazine), 127
Addams, Jane, 44
Adenauer, Konrad, 51
Administration Building (1928-56), 50
Adrian, Mich., 110
Advanced Vehicles Development Department, 62
Advertising Age, 85
Advertising Club of New York, 154-55
Advertising, Ford Motor Company, 38, 70-74, 78, 127; institutional, 73-74; Lincoln, 38; Mercury, 38; Model A, 154; Model T tie-ins, 133; radio, 206-07; television, 70-71
African Americans, 27-28, 93, 176-78, 199; mentioned, 73
Airplanes, 154
Alabama, 192
Alandt, Paul, 2, 5, 7
Alandt, Mrs. Paul (Lynn Ford), 2, 5, 7, 66, 198
Alaska, 101, 154
Alaska pipeline, 69
Alberta, Canada, 157
Albion, Pa., 75
Alda, Alan, 21, 64
Alexander, Thomas, 151
Alexandria (Va.) Assembly Plant, 101
Allen Park, Mich., 23
Allen, Woody, 64
Allied Powers, 213
Ambulances, 139, 213-14
American Airways, 174
American Auto Association's Auto Racing Hall of Fame, 203
American Broadcasting Corporation, 55, 208
American Dream, 68
American Expeditionary Forces, 213

American Football League, 38
American Graffiti, 164
American Heritage, 86, 107-09
American Machinist, 211
American Motors Corporation, 37, 78, 142
American Red Cross, 214
Amherst, Nova Scotia, 145
"Amos and Andy," 206
Amos Press, v
Amsterdam, 95, 138
Anatomy of a Murder, 203
Anchorage, Alaska, 101
"Anchorage, The," 52
Anderson, John W., 89, 118-20
Anderson & Rackham, 120
Andreson, Wilbur, 78
Andrews, Wayne, 194
Anglo American Corp., 93
Anhut, John, 191
Ann Arbor, Mich., 82, 109, 214-15
Annual meetings, 62-63, 65, 88
Annual reports, 70
Anniversaries, of FMC, 50th, 171; 75th, 59, 70, 73-74, 80-90, 176; 80th, 74
Anthony, Susan B., 21
Anti-Defamation League of B'nai B'rith, 16
Antifreeze, 45
Antique Automobile, 179, 213-14
Appalachia, 19
Apple cider, 26
Applebaum, Stuart, 86
Apple Corp., 22, 134
Arab League, 54
Archer, Ed, 206
Arches, concrete, Detroit, Toledo & Ironton, 88, 111, 183-84
Architectural Digest, 52
Architecture in Michigan, 194-95
Arden, Eve, 203
Argentina, 95
Arkansas, 206
Arkell & Douglas, 93

Armco, Inc., 103
Armstrong, Louis, 22
Army Air Force, 83, 187, 215-17
Arneson, Winfield H., 14
Arnold, Henry "Hap," 213
Arrow racing car, 201-03
Articles of Association (incorporation), 70
Ashley, Keith, 79
"Ask the Man Who Owns One," 72
Assembly line, 199-200 (also see mass production)
Assembly plants, 101-07
Associated Press, 20, 123, 150, 213
Atanasoff, John Vincent, 161-62
Atari, 134
Athens, Ga., 158
Atlanta, 158
Atlanta Assembly Plant, 102
Atomic bomb/plant, 20, 69
Auburn, Ind., 83
Austin, Tex., 201
Australia, 95, mentioned, 66, 92
Autocar, (British), 152-53
Auto Racing History, 201
Auto Union, 133
Auto Union C-Type racing car (1936), 201
Automobile Club of Michigan, 192
Automobile Manufacturers Association, 37
Automotive Golden Jubilee, 37
Automotive Hall of Fame, 81, 84
Automotive News, 142
Avco's Crosley Division, 78
Avery, Clarence W., 12, 81
Aviation, 21, 172-76, 187-88; mentioned, 21-22, 190
Aviation Hall of Fame, 73-74
Avis, 72-73, 195
"A Walk Through the 20th Century," 143
Ayer, N.W. & Son, 70, 154-55

B

Building (Rouge), 103
B-17 bomber, 216
B-24 "Liberator," 70, 214-16
B-24 Liberator, 1939-1945, The, 215
Babb, David R., 49, 167-68
Babson College, 61
Bacon, Irving, 186, 196
Bailey, Rev. A. Purnell, 35-36
Bailey, Bill, 143
Baio, Scott, 21
Baird, Col. Kenneth R., 139
Baker Electric, 191
Bakken, Douglas, 39, 166
Baltimore & Ohio Capitol Limited, 137
Banff National Park, 157
Bangor (Maine) *Daily News*, 45
Banks, John and Lucille, 33
Bantam Books, 86
Baralba, Queensland, 139
Barbier, A. Roy, 29, 38, 48, 155
Barnes, Len, 125
Barry, Peter, 94
Barton, Bruce, 14
Baryshnikov, Mikhail, 53
Bataan Peninsula, 92
Battle of the Overpass, 82
Bauer, Frederick F., 150-51, 156
Baumann, Oscar E., 149
Bear, Fred, 22
Beatty, Warren, 53
Beaulieu, Hants, England, 150
Bedard, Pat, 125
Bednarz, Henry "Hank," 112-13
Beekman Arms, 193-94
Beetle, 84, 126, 133, 142-45, 156
Bekins, 78
Belgrade, Yugoslavia, 216
Bell, Alexander Graham, 22
Bell & Howell, 78
Belleville, N.J., 21
Bellingham, Wash., 75
Belvidere, Ill., 75
Bennett, Charles H., 89, 118-19
Bennett, Gertrude, 83

Bennett, Harry, 12, 18, 38, 82-83, 155, 177, 180, 191; castle, 82; mentioned, 6, 77
Benson Ford (lakeboat), 120-21
Benz, Karl, 22; car, 92
Benzol, 45-46
Bergmoser, J. Paul, 78
Berlin Olympics, 177
Bernardi, Joe, and Helma, 210
Berry, Martha, and College, 35-36
Bershback, Nancy, 16
Best Doctors in the U.S., The, 189
Betenson, Lula Parker, 133
Betsy, The, 49
Betts, Charles L. Jr., 179, 201
Bhattacharya, Sharmilla, 7, 67
Bhutan, 42-43
Bicentennial, U.S., 73
Bierman, Robert J., 75
Big Bay Inn, 203
Big E, 199
Big Three, 93
Birmingham, Mich., 142
Black, Fred L., 8, 13
Blanchard, James J., Gov., 35
Blevins, Wade, 165
Blimps, 71
Bloomsburg, Pa., 75
Bluebird Body Co., 131
Blun, Jim, 150
BMW, 66
B'nai B'rith, Anti-Defamation League of, 16
Board of Tax Appeals, 127
Bodycombe, Richard, 216
Bocci, Jeanne, 6
Boeing 247D, 174
Bomber art, 215
Book of Firsts, 130
Books, about Ford, 18
Boon, Arthur W., 19
Boone, Daniel, 22
Bordinat, Eugene Jr., 164-65, 170
Boston Assembly Plant, 106
Botsford, Milton, and Inn, 191

Bourke, Frederic A. Jr., 7
Bourke, Mrs. Frederic A. Jr. (Eleanor C. Ford), 3, 7
Bourke, William O., 78
Bouteller, John A. Jr., 154
Bowman, Martin, 215
Boycotts: Arab League, 17, 54; brewers and distillers, 13
Boyer, Robert, 28
Boysville (Macon, Mich.), 112
Bradfield, Richard H., 102
Bradley, James J., 125, 128, 149, 191
Brand name, 92, 117
Brazil, 95, 142, 144-45
Breech, Ernest R., and Breech School of Business Administration, 1, 53-54, 78, 84
Breitmeyer, Eleanor, 16
Brewers, 70-71
Briggs Body Corp., 99
Briquets, 45
Brisbane, Arthur, 12, 82, 144
Britain, Ford of, 43, 54, 92, 140, 170
British Empire, 93, 149
British and German Tanks of World War I, 145
Brokaw, Tom, 86
Brooklyn (Mich.) Plant, 109
Brooks, Harry, 14
Brown, Joe E., 211
Brown, Roy, 169
Brownstown Township, Mich., 122
Brunn bodies, 149
Brush Street, Detroit, 30
Brussels, 70
Bruton, John, 94
Bryan, Ford Richardson, 24, 28, 39
Bryant, Edgar LeRoy (Roy), 38
Bryant, Martha (Henry Ford's mother-in-law), 187
Bryant, Mary Elizabeth, 38
Buck, Pearl, 22
Buffalo, N.Y., 137
Buffalo Stamping Plant, 196
Buhler, Rosa, 41
Buick, David, and car and division, 41, 72, 94, 126, 160
Bulgari, Gianni, 53
Burbank, Luther, 8, 23, 44, 89

Burg, Les, 136
Burns, George, 21
Burns, Will S., 103
Burroughs, John, 8, 12, 19, 89, 111
Busch, Adolphus Jr., 27
Bush, Robert, 112
Butler University, 153
Butterwield, Tom, 152
Businesses named for Henry Ford, 209-10
Business Week, 13
By-products, 45-46

C
Caddy, Frank, 37
Cadillac, Antoine de la Mothe, 82
Cadillac car/engine, 50, 126, 137, 141, 149, 163, 213
Caldwell, Philip, 11, 55, 60, 68, 87, 100, 193
Caliendo, Frank, 169
California, 65, 106, 128, 136, 141, 143, 146
Callandar Cleaners, Columbus, Ohio, 138
Callihan, Jim, 123
Calzada de Guadelupe, 94
Cameron, William J., 12
Cameron, William T., 129
Campsall, Frank, 8-9, 12
Canada, 91, 145, 157, 196
Canadian Jewish Review, 17
Canadian Pacific Ltd., 95
Cantor, George, 143
Cape May, N.J., 203
Capetown, 93, and *Capetown Argus*, 160
Capone, Al, 47
Capri (U.S.), 102
Car and Driver, 125
Carretti, Dante, 105
Carey, Frank, 85
Carhartt, Wylie III, 164
Carroll, John, 39
Cars & Parts, v, 80
Cars, collectors, 179; greatest/best, 124-25; important/influential, 125-26; longevity, 126; romantic, 126; worst, 126

Carson City, Nev., 59
Cars That Henry Ford Built: A 75th Anniversary Tribute to America's Most Remembered Automobiles, 42
Carter, Jimmy, 21
Carver, George Washington, 8, 27-28
Case, Tom, 163
Case Western Reserve University, 102
Cassidy, Butch, 133
Castor Oil Fumes, 198
Catalog, first Ford, 127
Cazenovia, N.Y., 179
Centennial Car Mini-Ingot Collection, 125
Central America, 74
Central National Bank of Cleveland, 87
Central Office Building, 123
Ceresco, Neb., 75
Cerilli, A.J., 193-94
Chambers, Dave, 76, 131
Champine, Norm, 53
Champion, Tom, 166
Chandler, A.B. "Happy," 70
Chapels, 28, 112; on wheels, 144-45
Chapin, Roy D., Sr., 50
Chaplin, Charlie, 28-29
Charcoal, 45
Charleroi, Pa., 117
Charles, Prince, 53
Charlotte Ford for Jondel Collection, 64
Charlotte Ford's Book of Modern Manners, 63
Chase, Melvin G., 99
Chemical Plant, 28
Chemurgy, 45-46
Cherokee Indian Nation, 23
"Cherry Hill Plantation," 34
Cheskin, Louis B., 165
Chevrolet, Louis, 203; car/division/engine, 69, 94, 124, 125, 136, 156, 160, 197
Chicago, 32, 130 138, 150, 165
Chicago Assembly Plant, 106
Chicago Times-Herald, 190
Chicago Tribune, 184
Children's Fund of Michigan, 78
China, 183

Chinese imperial treasures, 40
Christ Episcopal Church, Grosse Pointe Farms, Mich., 50
Christ, Jesus 14
Christison, Richard and Sharon, 34
Christmas, 130
Chronicle of the Historical Society of Michigan, 217
Chrysler Walter P., 41; Chrysler Canada Ltd., 95; Chrysler cars, 55, 142, 160; Corporation, 78, 80, 85-87, 93, 106, 122, 125, 155, 177, 196; Walter P. Jr., 1
Chuo University Auto Club, Japan, 149
Church of God, 165
C.H. Wills & Company, 79-80
Cigarettes, 70
Citroen 2CV, 126
City County Building, Detroit, 147
Civil War (War Between the States), 20
Clairol, 72
Clapp, Leland Q., 153
Clara Ford Hall, 36
Clark, Jimmy, 205
Clark, John Henry, 56
Clarke, Rev. Branford, 144-45
Clarkston, Mich., 90, 110
Class A, B Ford stock, 3-4, 8-9
"Classic Landscape," 100
Classic Thunderbird Club International, 198
Claycomo, Mo., 103
Cleaver, Shelley "Shamrock," 166
Cleveland, 185
Cleveland Institute of Art, 102
Cleveland Plain Dealer, 204
Clorox Co., 45
Clubs, car, 134-35
Clydesdale car, 93
Clymer, Floyd, 136, 151
Coal mines, 74, 120
Cobb, Ty, 29
Coca-Cola, 69, 72, 117
Cohn, David L., 119
Cohn, Roy, 62
Collin, Hochspin Co., 142
Colorado, 141
Color Research Institute, 165

Colors, car, 127, 131, 151
Columbia Broadcasting System, 206-07
Columbia car, 93
Columbus Assembly Plant, 106
Columbus, Ohio, 138, 146
Columbus (Ohio) *Dispatch*, 153
Combustion on Wheels: An Informal History of the Automobile Age, 119
Commerce, Okla., 134
Commissaries, Ford, 24, 74-75
Commodore car, 95
Commodore Computers, 134
Computers, 69, 134, 161-62
Concrete ties, 183
Conde, John, 125, 142
Connecticut, 146
Connors, Jimmy, 53
Constitution, U.S., 20, 199
Continental, 2, 125-26, 148; greatness, 125; Mark II, 60; Mark V, 148; mentioned, 66, 70, 124
Continental Comments, 198
Continental Division, 164
Cook Inlet Region, Inc., 101
Coolidge, Calvin, 23
Coombs, Chad, 149
Cooper, Gary, 146
Cooper, Richard, 130
Copenhagen, 187
Cord car, 126
Corfam, 165
Cork Examiner, 94
Cork, Ireland, Plant, 94
Corporate identity program, 117
Corregidor Island, 92
Cortina, 170
Cosell, Howard, 55, 64
Cotswold, England, 50
Courier pickup, 93
Cousineau, Stan, 92-93
Couzens, Frank Jr., 79
Couzens, James, 1, 12, 89; philanthropy, 78-79; tomb, 50, 82; mentioned, 40, 77, 98, 117, 119
Cowling, W.C. 6
Cox, Dwayne, 104
Cracker barrel, 143

FORD COUNTRY **219**

Craig, B.J., 78
Craig, Marvin, 56
Cranick, James W., 207
Crippen, David R., 74-75
Crockett, Davy, 22
Crosley car, 126
Cross-country trips, 143, 151-52, 157-58, 202-03
Crowther, Samuel, 12, 18
Croydon Aerodrome, 192
Cruise, Glenna McMann, 19
Cruise missile, 213
Cuba, 175
Curt Sjoberg Ford, 75
Curtis, Austin W. Jr. 28
Custer, Gary, 36; and Mrs. Custer, 131
Cutlass, 125
Cycle and Automobile Trade Journal, 69

D

Dagenham Plant, 43, 94
Dahlinger, Evangeline, 12, 180-81
Dahlinger, John, 12, 180-81
Dahlinger, Ray, 12, 180
Daimler engine, 145
Daisy Air Rifle Company, 118-19
Dallas, 156
Dallas Assembly Plant, 106
Daly, Whitman C., 118, 140, 179-80
Damascus, Syria, 168-69
Danaher, Jim, 164
Dangerfield, Rodney, 67
Davis, Thomas, 59-60
Das, Ambarish (Alfred Brush Ford), 66
David Frost's Book of the World's Worst Decisions, 84
Davis, Jim and Jody, 146
Dawson, Orlie W., 90
Day the Bubble Burst: The Social History of the Wall Street Crash of 1929, The, 151
Dayton, Ohio, 74

DC-3, 216
Deakin, Michael, 84
Dealer Policy Board, 2, 59
Dealers, Ford Motor Company, 56, 75-76, 153; advertising, 156; Edsel, 169; oldest, 75; overseas, 140; Pantera, 170; radio programs, 206-07; mentioned, 38, 63, 93, 116, 134, 144, 170, 175
Dean, Dizzy; and Paul "Daffy," 211
Dean Electric Co., 123
DeAngelis, George, 198
Dear Bess: The Letters from Harry to Bess Truman, 1910-1959, 134
Dearborn, 32-35, 37, 181-82; historic plants/sites, 88, 181-82; mentioned, 19, 24, 28, 43-44, 48, 89, 94, 109, 120, 123, 126, 143, 176, 180-81, 187, 189-90, 196-97, 200, 207-08, 210
Dearborn Assembly Plant, 102, 104, 163
Dearborn Engineering Laboratory, 88-89, 208
Dearborn Historian, 24, 28, 39, 173
Dearborn Historical Commission, 39
Dearborn Independent, 16
Dearborn Inn, 14-15, 192-93; mentioned, 28, 173
Death Valley, Calif., 141
"Death Valley Scotty," 55
Decraene, Charlene (Mrs. Walter Buhl Ford III), 7
Deeds, Edward 213
DeLorean, John Z., 52
Delta Air Lines, 158
Democrats, 73
Deng (Teng), Hsiao-ping, 55
Denmark, 187
Dentch's Stoughton Ford Center, 75
Denver Assembly Plant, 106
Depot hacks, 159
Derek, Bo, 21

Desegregation, 199
Desert Hot Springs, Calif., 83
Design, car, 126, 169-70
Des Moines Assembly Plant, 103; Technical High School, 103
DeSoto, 170
Detroit/Detroit area, 82, 142, 176, 184-85; most boring places, 190; mentioned 22, 24-25, 30, 39, 46, 48-49, 63-64, 86-89, 96, 98-99, 109-10, 114, 120-22, 125-26, 137, 147-48, 154, 157, 164, 172, 179-80, 191, 195, 203, 205, 207-09, 211-12
Detroit Automobile Company, 69
Detroit Club, 8
Detroit Federation of Labor, 195
Detroit Free Press, 39, 52, 65, 73, 85, 125, 170, 176, 197
Detroit Institute of Arts, 48-49, 182
Detroit Institute of Technology, 211
Detroit Junior Chamber of Commerce, 148
Detroit Lions, 2, 60
Detroit News, 15, 23, 64, 73-74, 82, 94, 126, 138, 142, 163, 164, 186, 190
Detroit Plaza Hotel, 122
Detroit Public Library, 40-41, 80, 125, 148-49, 191
Detroit River, 89
Detroit Symphony Orchestra, 207
Detroit, Toledo & Ironton Railroad, 88, 111, 182-83
Detroit University School, 81
Detroit-Wayne County Port Authority, 53
DeWald, Tom, 83
Dewey, John, 44
Diamond, David, 165
Diamond, Florence (daughter of A.R. Barbier), 29, 48
Diehl Ford, 75

Dillinger, John, 160
Dils Motor Co., 75
Diocletian, 52
Disney, Walt, 22, 215
Disraeli, Benjamin, 55
Dodge Brothers, 123; car, 94, 136, 160; factory, 99, 119
Dodge Fountain, Detroit, 209
Dodge, John F., and Horace Sr., 12, 39, 50, 77-78, 89, 103, 118; Horace Jr., 1
Dooley, Mike, 150
Dossin Great Lakes Museum, 121
Douglas C-47, 216
Douglas DC-3, 174
Downe, Edward R. 7
Drury College, 84
Duellman, Elmer, 157
Duesenberg, 126, 190
Duhachek, Ernest, 138
Dull, James, 158
Dundee (Mich.) Plant, 110
Du Pont family, 1
Durant, William C., and Star (car), 140
DuRoss, Kathleen (see Ford, Kathleen)
Duryea, Charles E. and Frank, 189-90; car 126, 189-90
"Dynamic Kernels" mill, 112-13

E

Eagle boats, 102, 104
Earhart, Amelia, 21
"Early American Dance Music," 207-08
Early American Room, Dearborn Inn, 193
Early Bird, 198
Early Ford V-8 Club of America, 198
Easterby, Fred, 90
Eaton axles, 161
Eaton, Cyrus, 185
Eden, Sir Anthony, 92
Edgar A. Guest: A Biography, 184

Edgewater (N.J.) Assembly Plant, 103
Edison Institute, 10, 14, 187-88, 193; mentioned, 2, 37, 39, 180, 193, 198
Edison, Thomas A., 8, 12, 21, 22, 25, 89; camping, 19; mentioned, 23, 33, 45, 111, 200
Edmond, Charles R., 201
Edsel Affair, The, 117
Edsel and Eleanor Ford House, 50-51, 58
Edsel (car), 58, 126, 164-70, 199, 206; collectors, 167; dealers, 169; design, 169-70; failure, cause of, 164-65, 169-70; in film, 164; jokes, 165-66, 168, 210; mistake/disaster, 126, 141, 164-65; prices, 165; publicity, 167; survivors, 168
Edseletter, 49, 167, 168-69, 199
Edsel, Ky., 165
Edsel Owners Club, 167-68, 198
Edsel's (restaurant/nightclub), 210
Egglefield Bros., Inc., 75
Egypt, 129
Eiffel Tower, 40
Einstein, Albert, 17, 21, 44
Eisenhower, Dwight D., 21, 190-91
Eldridge, Eugene and James, 113
Electrification of nation, 21
Elizabeth (N.J.) Plant, 101
Elizabethtown, N.Y., 75
Ellington, Duke, 203
Ellis, Jack, 71
Eloise, Mich., 147
Elyria, Ohio, 122
Emblad, Thomas R., 200-01
Embree, Glen, 197
Endurance runs, 141
Engine and Foundry Division, 111
Engineering changes, Ford

cars, 126
England, 137, 210, 216
Enricht, Louis, 137-38
Erie Canal, 103
Ernie Breech: The Story of His Remarkable Career at General Motors, Ford, and TWA, 84
Ernest R. Breech (lakeboat), 121
Erwin Robinson Co., 122
Escort, European, 94, 125; U.S., 64, 74, 106, 125
Esquire, 215
Essex car, 135, 142
Estonia, 140
Ethanol, 45-46
Eubanks, Bob, 131
Europe, 16
EXP, Ford, 106

F

F-Series, 106, 125
Faberges, 106
Fairchild FC-2, 174
Fairchild, Rolph, 160
Fair Lane (see Henry Ford Estate-Fair Lane)
Fairlane (railroad car), 23
Fairlane Woods, 53
Fairmont (car), 70, 125
Fairmont, Minn., 75
Falcon (car), American, 125; Australian, 95
Falwell, Rev. Jerry, 67
"Famous Ford 'Firsts,' " 73
"Farewell to Model T," 131-32, 150
Farmington, Mich., 191
Federal Emergency Relief Commission, 79
Federal Engineering Co., 110
Federal-Mogul, 78
Ferrari car, 170
Fiat, 92, 126
Field, Floyd, 158
Fiesta car, 125
Fiftieth anniversary, FMC, iii, 171

220 FORD COUNTRY

Film, 164; film studios, 71
Firestone, Harvey S. Jr., 19
Firestone, Harvey S. Sr., 8, 12, 19, 25, 111
Fire trucks, 147
Fisher, Lawrence P., 67
Fisher, Max, 6, 54, 182
Five-dollar day, 74, 184; mentioned, 70, 195, 200
Flanders car, 141
Flat Rock (Mich.) Plant, 108, 110
Flint, Duttee, 12
Flint, Jerry, 125
Flint, Mich., 127
"Flivver skates," 15
Florida, 146
Folsom, Dick, 41
Foote, Cone & Belding, 72
Forbes, 6
Ford Airport, 14, 40, 71, 192
Ford, Alfred Brush (Ambarish Das), 2-3, 7, 66
Ford-Allen farm implements, 38
Ford, Anne McDonnell (Mrs. Henry Ford II), 3, 7
Ford, Anne (Mrs. Chuck Scarborough), 3, 7, 50, 63-64
Ford Archives, iii, 157, mentioned 8, 39, 74, 160
Ford, Benson Jr., 2-3, 7, 62, 65-66
Ford, Benson Sr., 1-3, 5, 7-8, 59, 206; mentioned, 15, 33, 35, 65-66, 185, 188, 198
Ford Benzol, 45-46
Ford, Betty, 13
Ford, Briget (Walter Buhl Ford III's daughter), 2
Ford catalog, first, 127
Ford Cemetery, 24-25
Ford, Charlene (Mrs. Walter Buhl Ford III), 7
Ford, Charlotte, 2-3, 7, 62-65; (Mrs. Edward R. Downe), 7
Ford, Clara, 1, 4, 7, 8, 12, 23, 35, 111; "Believer," 1, 48; frugality, 41; grave, 25; relatives, 1-4, 38-40, 187; servants, 41; widowhood, 47; will, 38; mentioned, 28, 30-34, 36, 118, 180, 190-91, 193, 203
"Ford Country" (column), v-vi

"Ford Country" (Grosse Pointe Farms), 5
Ford, Cristina V. Austin (Mrs. Henry Ford II), 7, 57
Ford, Cynthia Neskow (Mrs. Edsel Ford II), 7, 61
Ford: Decline and Rebirth, 1933-62, 18
Ford Division, 62, 69
Ford, Edith McNaughton (Mrs. Benson Ford Sr.), 7, 59, 188
Ford, Edsel B., 48; arts patron, 100; aviation, 173; car (personal), 37; character, 49; death/tomb, 49-50; designer, 124, 148; homes, 50-52; memorials, 164-65, 182; presidency, Ford Motor Company, 1, 68, 78; qualities, 49; Rivera mural, 48; signature, 41; youth, 90; mentioned, 5, 7-8, 12, 29, 31, 41, 70, 81, 89, 91, 118, 152-53, 162, 185
Ford, Edsel II, 2-3, 61-62, 206; ambitions, 61; career path, 61-62; and father, 61; homes, 5; name, 61; work ethic, 64; mentioned, 7, 43-44, 65, 206,
Ford, Eleanor Clay (Mrs. Edsel Ford), 1, 3-4, 7, 37, 49, 186; arts patron, 49, 100; death/tomb, 50, homes, 50-52
Ford, Eleanor C. (Mrs. Frederic A. Bourke), 4, 7
Ford, Elizabeth (Mrs. Charles Kontulis), 7
Ford Engineering Laboratory, 89-90
Ford: Expansion and Challenge, 1915-32, 18
Ford Factory Square Project, Atlanta, 102
Ford family, 7; shareholdings, 4, 117-19, inheritances, 8-9
Ford Farms, 24, 180
Ford Field, 12
Ford Foundation, 8, 50, 181-82, 185, 193-94
Ford, Gerald R., 13, 73
Ford, Henry, 7, admirers, 21-22; advertising views, 70, 127, 154-56, 205; and African Americans, 176-77; aging process, 13; agriculturist,

24, 68, 108, 111; alcoholism, views on, 13; ancestors, 94; anecdotes about, 35-36, 90-91, 95, 99, 110-12, 129, 196; antiunionism, v; anti-Semitism, v, 14, 16-17, 194; appearance (physical) 9, 12; and aviation, 68, 172-73, 187-88, 190-92, 214; birthdays, 18, 39, 47; birthsite, 14; books about/by, 18, 201; camper, 19, 45; cars (personal), 190; chapels, 28, 112; character, 6; chauffeurs, 41; people closest to him, 12-13, 181; and comic strips, 35; common sense, 1, 37; conservation, 123; dancing, 19-20, 191, 207-08;
death/funeral/grave, 24-25, 38; 41; diet/health, 16, 27-28, 46, 211; dining out, 193; dress, 37, 200; as driver, 37; educator, 210-12; employees, attitude toward, 12; engineering talent, 1; environmentalist/ecologist, 32-33, 111, 123; estate, 8-9; exercise, 13, 15, 37; experiments, 183; father of..., 45; folk hero, 22, 25-26; genius, 90; gifts, 35-37; as godfather, 27; as grandfather, 15-16; guns, 15; halls of fame, 73-74, 203; Henry Ford of..., 21-22, 142;

Homes: Bagley Avenue, Detroit, 29-30, 37; Edison Avenue, Detroit, 31; Fair Lane, Dearborn, 32-33, 58, 74; Harper Avenue, Detroit, 30; Fort Myers, Fla., 33; Honeymoon House, Garden City, Mich., 27, 49, 74; Huron Mountain Club, Big Bay, Mich., 52; John R Street, Detroit, 30; Macon, Mich. 33; Pequaming, Mich., 34, 52, 204; Richmond Hill, Ga. 34;

Humanitarian, 188; image/greatness/hero/importance/influence/popularity/rankings/reputation, 1, 6, 8, 17, 20-22, 44, 68; impishness/pixie, 35, 37, 41; individualism, 21; influenced by, 12; ingenuity, 68; innovations, 45, 74, 126, 183, 199-200; isolationist, 26; last day, 121; lawsuits, 184; literacy, 24; luck, 1; marital

relations, 1, 48; memorials, 44; mistakes, 14, 80, 145; music lover, 19, 207; overseas, 94-95; personality, 6; philanthropy, 37, 185-89; philosophy, 6; pioneering, 45-46; plant visits, 57; and plastics, 62; pricing policies, 140; prime, 1; prohibitionist, 13; psychologist, 15; publicity, 1; qualities, 1, 179; quotations, 43; racing, 201-05; and radio, 206-07; railroader, 68, 111; rumors about, 40; servants, 41; sex, views on, 129; shipper, 68, 120-21; signature, 41; skater, 15; smoking, views on, 70, 214; speeches, 12, 38, 179; spelling, 14; spirituality, 6; stamps, 42-43; statues/effigies, 43-45; village industries, 107-15; vision, 46, 73, 182-83; wealth, 14, 46-47; will, 8-9; work ethic, 1, 68, 211; and workmen, 15; World War I, 213; youth, longing for, 13; zeal, 1; mentioned, 72-77, 88-92, 103, 106, 124, 128, 143-45, 160, 162-63, 179-80, 185-87, 203

Ford, Henry II, 51-58, 169-70; and African Americans, 1-2, 176-79; annual meetings, 88; art interests, 57, 100; boyhood, 35; celebrity, 52-54; character, 52-54; criticism of, 65; and daughter Charlotte, 62-63; diet, 210; divorces, 57; and Edsel II, 61; as executive, 53-56; favorite car, 124; and Ford Foundation, 185;

Homes: Bahamas condominium, 57; Canadian shooting lodge, 57; Carlyle Hotel (New York) penthouse, 57; Edsel and Eleanor Ford House, 51; English country, 57; Lake Shore Drive, Grosse Pointe Farms, 58; London townhouse, 57; Palm Beach, 55; Provencal Road, Grosse Pointe Farms, 5; Seal Harbor, Maine, 52;

Honors, 17-18; and Lee Iacocca, 54, 56, 85-87; Jewish relations, 2, 17-18, 54; memorials, 182;

outspokenness, 55-56; overseas leadership, 53-54, 95; philanthropy, 54; popularity, 2, 56; praise of, 62-63; qualities, 1-2; quotations, 55; and Renaissance Center, 89, 208-09; retirement, 53, 55-56, 68, 116; rumors about, 87; signature, 41; speeches, 188; stature, 2, 52-53; visitors, 55; wealth, 6; wives, 7; mentioned, 8, 33, 50, 61, 68, 70, 78, 85-86, 100, 116, 150, 162, 184-85, 188, 206, 211
Ford, Henry III, 2-3, 66
Ford Industries, 93
Ford, John, 39
Ford, Josephine (Mrs. Walter Buhl Ford II), 1-5, 7-8, 52, 66, 188
Ford, Josephine C. (daughter of Josephine), 3, 7
Ford, Kathleen DuRoss (Mrs. Henry Ford II), 5, 7, 54
Ford Land Development Corporation, 27, 53, 71, 178
Ford Life, 192, 198-99
Ford, Lynn (Mrs. Paul Alandt), 2, 3, 5, 7, 65-66, 198
Ford & Malcomson Company, Ltd., 75, 118
Ford, Margaret (Henry Ford's sister, Mrs. James Ruddiman), 39
Ford, Martha Firestone (Mrs. William Clay Ford Sr.), 7
Ford, Martha P. (daughter, William Clay Ford Sr.), 3, 7
Ford, Mary Litogot (Henry Ford's mother), 13, 39, 187
Ford-Mercury, 77
Ford & Mercury Restorers Club, 79
Fordmobile, 75
Ford Motor Company, 68-123; African American relations, 176-79; assembly line, 199; assets, 68; brand name, 92; birthsite, 29-30, 209; cars, greatest, 124-25; commissaries, 75; design, 126; employee relations, 71, 74, 195-96; employees, 122, 177-78, 180, 184-85, 195-96, 201, 208, 214-15; engineering, 127; executives, 77-86, 92, 100, 177-78; founding, 69-70, 89, 117-20; global aspects, 68;

FORD COUNTRY 221

history, 69-70; importance, 68-69; innovations, 74, 217; losses, 68; manufacturing, 199-200; market share, Middle East, 17-18; market valuation, 68; plants (see Plants, Ford); officers, 77-78; overseas activities, 92-95, 170; Presidents' cars, 161; profits, 69; publications, 116-17; radio programs, 206-08; reputation, 68-69, 71-72, 74; retirees, 90; sales, 124-25, 127-28; ships, 120-22; size, 69; stockholders, 89; styling, 72; village industries, 107-15
Ford Motor Company Fund, 59
Ford Motor Credit Company, 71
Ford of Australia, 61, 66, 95, 206
Ford of Britain (Ford Motor Co., Ltd., England), 43, 54, 92, 140, 170
Ford of Canada, 93, 95
Ford of England (see Ford of Britain)
Ford of Europe, 63
Ford-Holland, 95
Ford Jokes, 135-37, 140
Ford New Holland Ltd., 171
Ford Old-Timers Club, 90
Ford Park, 212
Ford Parts Redistribution Center, 122
Ford Penny, 40-41
Ford Quadrangle, 36
Ford Road, Dearborn, 27
Ford Road: 75th Anniversary, Ford Motor Company, 1903-1978, The, 199
Ford, Robert (Henry Ford's brother), 39
Ford Rotunda, 91-92, 151
"Ford Row" (Provencal Road), 5
Ford, Sheila (Mrs. Steven Hamp), 2-3, 7
Ford-South Africa, 93
Ford Sunday Evening Hour, 207-08
Ford: The Times, the Man, the Company, 18
Ford Tomato Juice, 24
Ford Trimotors, 14
Ford Times, 73, 80, 116-17, 134, 141, 202
Ford, Walter Buhl II, 3-4, 7, 52
Ford, Walter Buhl III, 3, 7
Ford, William (Henry Ford's father), 13
Ford, William (Henry Ford's brother), 38-39
Ford, William Clay Jr., 2, 7, 62-64
Ford, Mrs. William Clay Jr. (Lisa Vandersee), 7
Ford, William Clay Sr., l-3, 7-8, 15-16, 60-61, 100, 164, 188, 198, 206; career path, 2, 16, 60-61; wealth, 6, 16; mentioned, 13, 52, 62, 65
Ford, Mrs. William Clay Sr. (Martha Firestone), 3
Ford World, 74, 90, 116, 152
"Fordists," 135
Fords, third generation, 2-3
Fords, fourth generation, 2, 61-67
Fords, fifth generation, 2-3, 66
"Fords' Folly" bomber, 215-16
"Ford's Out Front," 71
Fordson (municipality), 37
Fordson Farmer, 144-46
Fordson tractor, 70, 94, 138
Fordwatchers, 16
Fork & Blade, 198
Forrestal, James V., 99
Forties Spirit, 198
'49 Ford, 124-26, 141, 190
Ft. Knox, 165
Ft. Lauderdale, 90
Ft. Myers, Fla., 33
Fort Valley, Ga., 131
Fountain City, Wis., 157
Fournier, Henri, 202
France, 17, 19, 21
Franklin car, 135, 179
Franklin, Rabbi Leo, 8
Frankston (Victoria, Australia) *Standard*, 95
Fraser, Douglas, 52, 87
Frazier, Jack and Virginia, 42
Frederick the Great, 40
Fredericks, Marshall, 43-44
Frey, Donald, 78
From These Beginnings: The Early Philanthropies of Henry and Edsel Ford, 1911-1936, 18
Frost, David, 84
Frost, George, 130
Frost, Robert, 44
Fry, Vernon C., 89
Fuel Injection Special racing car (1952-54), 201
Fuentes, Louis, 65-66
Fuller Brush Company, 135
Fulton, Robert, 22
Funeral cars, 94, 147, 160
Foyt, A.J., 205

G
Gaft, Sam, 212
Gaines, Al, 195
Galaxie 500, 40
Gallagher Presidents' Report, 53
Gallo, Frank, 22
Gallup Poll, 21, 85
Gap Mills, W. Va., 19
Garden City, Mich. 27, 74, 90
Garner, James Nance, 91
Gasahol, 137-38
General Industries, 122-23
General Motors Corporation, iii, 71-72, 125-26, 155; mentioned, 14, 17, 68-69, 78, 84, 92-93, 102, 196
General Motors of Canada Ltd., 95
General Services Administration, 101
George, Pete, 159
George Washington Carver Laboratory 26
Georgia, 131, 161, 210
Georgia Tech, 158-59
Germany, 16-17, 92, 142, 145, 213, 216
Gibb, Corinne, 184
Gilbert's Hill, 147
Gillette, Bob, 158
Gillette Safety Razor Company, 70-71
Ginnett, Martin, 143
Giraffe Society, 21
Glass Division, 71
Glass Plant, Dearborn, 88
Glass, safety, 74
Glenn, John, 44
Glidden Tour, 141
Gliders, 217
GMC, 69
GM-Holden, 92, 95
Goff, Norris, 206
Gold Coast, 93
Golden Gate Exposition, 91
Goldenson, Leonard, 55
Golf car, 144
Good Housekeeping, 72
Goodell, Bill, 122
Goodes, Rosemary, 216
Goodland, Kan., 204
Goondwindi, Queensland, 139
G.P. Putnam's Sons, 132
Grace Cathedral, San Francisco, 44
Graham car, 126
Grand Marquis, 125
Grand Trunk Western Railroad, 182
Grant, Kathryn, 203
Gray, John S., and Gray estate, 77, 89, 118, 120
Great Britain, 21, 92, 150
Great Crash, 1929, 20, 199
Great Depression, 1930s, 20, 68, 100, 208
Great Lakes, 78, 120-22
Great Lakes Engineering Works Shipyard, 122
Greatest/best cars, 124-26
Green, Kan., 76
Green Bay, Wis., 144
Green, Fern H., 176
Green Island (N.Y.) Plant, 137-38
Green pill, 137-38
Greene, Jewell Blevins and Guy, 165
Greenfield Road, Detroit, 24-25
Greenfield Village, 143, 157, 189, 196; attendance, 186-87; employees, 189; finances, 186-87; greenhouse, 26; Mack Avenue Plant replica, 96; schools, 211; Soybean Laboratory, 46; weddings, 187; mentioned, 2, 10, 25, 28, 29, 31, 35, 39, 59, 180, 186, 190-91, 193
Greenleaf, William, 18
Green Line, 169
Greenville, Mich. 90
Greenwald, Gerald, 78
Grimshaw, Ernie, 90
Grosse Pointe Farms, Mich., 2, 5, 50, 60, 65
Grosse Pointe North High School, 6
Grosse Pointe Race Track, 202
Grosse Pointe Shores, Mich., 41, 51, 100
Guest Center, 88
Guest, Edgar A., 184
Guinness Book of World Records, 46-47, 122, 145
Gurney, Dan, 190, 205
Gustavson, Howard, 197
Gwinnett, Button, 41

H
Haberman, Dave, 174
Hagelthorn, Dick, 35, 173
Hagerstown, Md., 137
Haifa, Israel, 18
Hainline, Joe R., 171
Hale, Nathan, 22
Hall, Clarence, 112
Hallmark, 72
Halls of Fame, 73-74, 203
Hamilton, Charles, 41
Hamlin, George L., 161-62
Hammond (Ind.) *Times*, 85
Hamp, Steven, 7
Hamp, Mrs. Steven (Sheila Ford), 2, 7, 198
Hancock, John, 195
Handicapped, cars for, 161
Hanover, Germany, 216
Hapeville, Ga., 159
Harbor Beach, Mich., 52
Harding, Warren G., 23
Hare Krishna Consciousness Temple, 66
Harley-Davidson, 195-96
Harold Warp Pioneer Village, 126
Harper, H.B., 202
Harper Woods, 90
Harper's Bazaar, 53
Harrah, William Fiske, 179
Harrigan, Jim, 103
Harris & Sergeant, Inc., 75
Hart Plaza, 89
Hartford Rubber Co., 123
Hartner, Charles, 12
Harvey's Fish & Poultry, Detroit, 96
Hauck, Harold, 174-75
Hawaiian Quintette, 19
Hawke, Allen E., 90
Hayes, Walter, 87
Haynes-Apperson car, 190

Hearse, 94, 147, 160
Hebard, Charles, 34
Heftler, Pierre, 4, 66
Heim, Glenn, 188
Helm, Glenn W., 146
Helms Athletic Foundation Automobile Racing Hall of Fame, 203
Henderson, Erma, 176
Hennessy, Sir Patrick, 92
Henry VIII, 40
Henry Ford and Son Limited, Cork (Ireland), 94
Henry Ford: An Interpretation, 18
Henry Ford Centennial Library, 15, 43-44
Henry Ford Community College, 212
Henry Ford Company, 202
Henry Ford Estate-Fair Lane, iii, 8, 15, 74; mentioned, 13, 31, 59
Henry Ford Hospital, 13, 59, 188
Henry Ford Museum, 14, 166, 182, 186-87, 193; Henry Ford Room, 89; significant cars, 189-90; mentioned, 2, 20, 23, 28, 35, 39, 59, 127, 142, 180, 189-91, 198
Henry Ford Suite, Big Bay Inn, 203
Henry Ford Trade School, 60, 90, 212
"Henryburgers," 210
Henry Ford II (lakeboat), 120-22
Henry Ford II Chair in Transportation, 17-18
Henry, Les, 151
Henry's Fabulous Model A, 151
Henry's Lady, 151
Herald, 39
Hershey, Milton, 22
Hertz, 78
Hesler, Marsh, 152
HFP Associates, 99
Hickerson, J. Mel, 84
Highland Park, Mich., 122
Highland Park (Mich.) Plant, 10, 98-100, 122; commissaries, 74-75; employment, 99; historic marker, 88; size, 68, 74, 98; Trade School, 212; visitors, 29, 99; mentioned, 37, 81, 92, 151, 196
Highland Park Sales and Service Building, 88

Highland Rose cold cream, 74-75
Hill & Knowlton, 117
Hill, Frank Ernest, 18
Hill, Iden, Dr., 55
Hindenberg, Paul von, 17
Hirsch, Arnold, 117
Hirsch, Rudolph E., 166-67
Historical markers (see Markers, historical)
Hitchcock, Alfred, 83
Hitler, Adolf, 17, 143, 213
Hodges, Charlie, 41
Hoffa, Jimmy, 82
Hoffman, Dustin, 64
Hoffman Iron Bridge, 131
Hoffman, Paul, 14
Holden, 92, 95
Holland, 95, 138
Holley Carburetor, 123
Holley, George, 50
Hollister, Calif., 75
Hollywood, 71, 162
Holst, Herman V. von, 32
Holzbaugh, Geo., 77
Honeymoon House, 27, 49, 74, 180
Honeywell, Inc., 104-05
Honolulu, 66
Hood, Rev. Nicholas, 176
Hoover, Herbert, 10, 155
Hoover, J. Edgar, 22
Hoover Universal, 113
Horace H. Rackham Building, 119
Horseless Age, 204
Horseshoers Union, 195
Hough, Ed, 119
Housenick Motor Co., 75
Houston Assembly Plant, 106
How to Love the Car in Your Life, 63
Howe, Royce, 184
Hudson car, 50, 136
Hudson Hornet (1951-54), 201
Hudson, J.L., Department Store, 37, 148
Hudson, Joseph L., 22, 50
Hudson River, 103
Hughes, Russell, 83
Hulse, Charles E., 127
Hungary, 42
Hupmobile, 151

Hupp, Robert C., 50
Huron River (Mich.), 111
Hyatt Roller Bearing, 123
Hyde Park, N.Y., 161
Hydroplants, 106-15

I

"Iacocca: An American Profile" (film), 86
Iacocca, Lee A., 78, 85-87, 165, 170; admired, 85; autobiography, 86, 210; bitterness, 85-86; celebrity, 52; compensation, 86-87; and Henry Ford II, 56, 85-87, 210; dismissal, 54, 85
IBM, 85, 167
ICBM, 166
Idaho, 152
Ideal Toy, 165
India, 74
Indiana State Fairgrounds, 201
Indianapolis, 203
Indianapolis "500," 129, 153, 205
Indy turbine car (1967), 201
Ingle, John W., 7
Ingle, Mrs. John W. Jr. (Josephine Ford), 7
Iguchi, Semma, 139
Initiative in Industry: Dresser Industries, Inc., 1889-1978, 200
Innovations, FMC, 74
Inns: Big Bay 203; Botsford, 191; Dearborn, 14, 192-93; mentioned, 28, 173; Wayside, 15, 19, 193-94, 211
Interdec, 34
International Dull Folks Unlimited, 67
International Edsel Club, 49, 166-68, 199
International Harvester, 78
International Jew, The, 16-17
Interstate Commerce Commission, 182
Intra-Dynamics, Inc., 168
Invention Time Chart, 69
"Inventory float," 200
Iowa State University, 161
Iranian oil crisis, 95
Ireland, 94
Iron Mountain, Mich., 201

Iron Mountain Plant, 162, 217
Iroquois Theater, 70
Iron ore, 120
Islamic Center of Detroit, 24
Island Airlines, 174-75
Israel, 18, 54
Israel Institute of Technology, 17
Isuzu Motors, 93

J

Jackson, John C., 101
Jackson, Mich., 86
Jackson, Reggie, 53
Jagger, Mick, 64
Jaguar, 163
Jamestown, Calif., 146
Japan, 94, 139-40; mentioned, 21-22, 64, 100, 142, 149
Japanese, 93, 200
Jefferson, Thomas, 22, 73
Jensen, Jens, 50
Jesus doll, 165
Jets, 69
Jewett, Harry, 50
Jews, 14, 16-17, 194-95
Jim McKain Ford, Inc., 75
Jitney, 157
Jobs, Steven, 22
Joe Louis Arena, 210
John Dykstra (lakeboat), 120
John Paul II, Pope, 149-50
Johnson, Lyndon Baines, 22
Johnson, Ted J., and Craig, 158
Jyro Hydro Station (Ypsilanti, Mich.), 115
Jokes, Ford, 47, 78, 135-37, 140
Jones, Tom, 22
Jones, Percy L., 213-14
Journal of Negro History, 176
Joseph, Matt, 14
Joseph Wood (lakeboat), 120
Jouppi, Arvid, 142
Joy Road, Detroit, 24
Juarez, Mexico, 133
Judkins bodies, 149
Jung, Paul, 22
Junkers, Erhardt, 27
Just-in-time production, 200

K

Kahn, Albert, 12, 50, 102-03, 192, 194-95
Kailimai, Henry, 19
Kaiser, Henry J., 21-22
Kansas City Assembly Plant, 10-11, 103, 106
Kanzler, Ernest C., 78
Karman, Joseph, 37
Kearny (N.J.) Assembly Plant, 103
Keith-Albee, 136
Kelley Girl Services, 195
Kellogg's, 22
Kelsey Wheel, 123
Kenilworth Building, 105
Kennedy, Caroline, 191
Kennedy, John F., 21-22, 84, 143, 191
Kennedy, John "John John," 191
Kennedy, Robert B., 160-61
Kenosha (Wis.) *News*, 152
Kentucky, 74-75, 120
Kenya, 93
Ketchum, MacLeod & Grove, Inc., 156
"Kettering Bug," 213
Kettering, Charles, 14, 213
Kilbourne, Ohio, 151
Kimes, Beverly Rae, 42
King, Martin Luther Jr., 22, 73
Kingsford, Mich., 45, 130, 217
Kingsford Chemical Co. (also Kingsford Co.), 45
Kipling, Rudyard, 55
Kissling, Jack, 202
Kistler, Charles A. Jr., 159
Klamath Falls, Ore., 160
Klann, William C., 81
Kleeber Motor Sales, Inc., 75
Kleene, Tom, 125
Kmart, 61
KMS Industries, 82
Know Your Ships, 121
Knudsen, Semon E. "Bunkie," 2, 78
Knudsen, William S. "Big Bill," 12, 54, 102, 196
Kobe, Japan, 139
Koblenz, Germany, 216
Kontulis, Charles, 7, and Mrs. Charles Kontulis (Elizabeth Ford), 7

FORD COUNTRY **223**

Koppeis, Francis, 194
Kornfield, Lewis, 22
Kroll, Richard, 90
Kruse, 167
Kubly, Harold E., 137
Kughn, Richard, 23, 143
Kulick, Frank, 202-03
Kuuse, Margus H., 140

L

Labor, 74, 96, 177-78
Lafayette, Ind., 76
LaForge, Charles A. Jr., 193
Lake Coeur d'Alene, 152
Lake Erie, 103, 175
Lake St. Clair, 58, 201-03
Lake Superior, 52, 120
Lane High School, Chicago, 130
Langellier Motor Co., 75
Langtry, Lily, 203
Lanphier, Maj. Tom, 173
L'Anse (Mich.), 130, 200
Lansing, Mich., 86, 191
Lapeer, Mich., 90
Lapeer Metal Products, 90
Laredo, Tex., 75
Larkins, William R., 192
Las Vegas, 177
Last Billionaire, The, 18
Latin America, 95
Latsha, Harry, 136
Lauck, Chester H., 206
Le Baron bodies, 149
Lee, John R., 80
Leland, Henry M., 147
Leland, Wilfred C. and Mrs., 147
Le Mans, 190, 205
Leonard, Jean, 199
Leonard, Sugar Ray, 21
Lesley, Hugh, 167-68
Levine, Bette, 168
Levine, Dan, 110-11
Lewis, David L., iii, v-vi, 18, 39-40, 41-42, 44, 81, 84, 90, 92, 114, 119, 122, 147, 164, 166, 173-75, 180-81, 187, 191, 198, 206
Lewis, John L., 44
Lewis, Ted, 92
Liberator bomber, 215-16

Liddy, Terrence, 82
Liebmann Breweries, Inc., 70-71
Liebold, Ernest G., 12
Lienert, Bob, 142
Life, 126
Light's Golden Jubilee, 185
"Li'l Abner," 215
Limericks, 26-27
Lincoln, Abraham, 8, 10, 21-22, 73, 147-48, 211
Lincoln cars, 94, 124-25, 149, 170; Continental, 124-25, 149; '32, 125; Town Car, 125, 149; Town Coupe, 149; V-12, 149; Zephyr, 124, 149
Lincoln Division, 164; Lincoln-Mercury Division, mentioned 2, 59, 61
Lincoln, Ill., 75
Lincoln Motor Car Co., 148
Lincoln Zephyr Owner's Club, 149
Lindbergh, Charles, 21-22, 25-26, 172-73, 187, and Mrs. Charles Lindbergh (Anne Morrow), 26
Lindside, W. Va., 19
"Little Orphan Annie," 35
Litton Industries, 78, 83-84
Livingstone, William, 12
Livonia (Mich.) Transmission Plant, 56
"Lizzie labels," 129
LN7, Mercury, 106
Logan, Peter, 186
Logging, 160-61, 200-01
London, 40, 92, 192
London School of Economics, iii
Longevity, cars, 126
Longfellow, Henry Wadsworth, 22, 40, 194
Long Island City Assembly Plant, 106
Lorillard Company, P., 206
Los Angeles, 203, mentioned 26, 71, 212
Los Angeles Assembly Plant, 106
Los Angeles Studio-TV Car Office, 71
Los Angeles Times, 168
Lotus Ford, 205
Louis Ferdinand, Crown Prince, 27
Louis, Joe, 177
Louisiana Purchase, 21
Louisville Assembly Plant, 103-04
Lovett, Benjamin, 13, 20

Low-price cars, 139
LTD, Ford, 125
Lucking, Alfred, 103
Ludvigsen, Karl E., 140
"Lum & Abner," 206
Lundy, Philip, A., 215-16
Lusk, Robert, 196
Lutheran High School, Detroit, 24
Lynx, 64, 74, 106

M

MacArthur, Douglas, 21-22
MacDonald, Rachel, 35
MacDonald, Ramsay, 17
Mack Avenue Plant, 69, 96
Mack, Harry, 77
Macon, Mich., 33, 42, 109, 112
Magazines, Ford Club, 197-98
Maine, 146
Mair, Alex, 162-63
Malcomson, Alexander Y., 12, 77, 89, 117-19
Malkasian, Nazar, 90
Mallast, Roberta, 41
Manchester (Mich.) Plant, 109, 113
Mandel, Leon, 179
Manhattan, 63
Manhattan Beach, N.Y., 8
Manley Motor Sales Co., 75
Mannheim, Germany, 22
Manufacturers National Bank of Detroit, 79
Maplegrove, 13
Marathon car, 141
Marchant machine, 162
Marine Publishing, 121
Mariveles Stamping Plant, Philippines, 92
Mark II, 60; Mark IV, 190, 205; Mark V, 148-49
Markers, Historical, 14-15; Aviation, 173, 192; Bagley Avenue, 27; Dearborn Inn, 192; Detroit, Toledo & Ironton Railroad arches, 88; Edsel and Eleanor Ford House, 50; Flat Rock (Mich.) bridge/dam/structure, 88; Ford [Dearborn] Engineering Laboratory, 88; founding site, Ford Motor Company, 89, 209; Highland Park Plant, 88; Highland Park Sales and Service Building, 88; Honeymoon House, 27; Orchestra Hall, 207; Piquette Plant, 88; Rouge Glass Plant, 88; Rouge Plant, 88; Rouge Tire Plant, 88; C.H. Wills & Company, 79-80
Marks, Meritt, 213
Marmon car, 152
Marquis, Samuel S., 13, 18
Marshall, Thurgood, 44
Martha-Mary Chapels, 187
Martin, Jack, 60
Martin, Pepper, 211
Martin, Peter E. "Ed," 12, 78, 81, 157
Martin, Steve, 21
Mary Ford Hall, 36
Mary Had a Little Lamb, 35
Marrying Up, 54
Marysville, Mich. 79-80
Maserati, 170
Mason, Randy, 142, 166, 189-90
Masonic Temple, Detroit, 207
Mass Production, 1, 74, 81 (also see assembly line)
Massachusetts, 210-11
Massachusetts Institute of Technology, 64
Matsushita, Konosuke, 22
May, George, 184
Mayo, William B., 172
Maxon, Inc., 38
Maxwell cars, 93
Maxwell House, 72
Mazda, 64, 93
Mazda World, 139
McArthur and Son, 76
McCall, George, 16
McCalley, Bruce, 197-98
McCallum, Robert, 56
McCardell, Archie, 78
McCarthy, Joseph, 62
McClelland, Glen, 95
McDonald's, 143, 195
McDonnell, James, 64
McGraw, Kathy, 121
McGuffey, William Holmes, 8
McMann, Stanley/Mrs. McMann, 19
McNamara, Robert S., 78, 84

McQuay-Norris, 105
Mead Container Co., 103-04
Medici, 52, 66
Mein Kampf, 17
M-E-L (Mercury-Edsel-Lincoln) Division, 87
Melbourne, Australia, 66
Memphis, 76
Memphis Assembly Plant, 106, 195
Mennen Company, 133
Mercedes-Benz SL, 141
Mercer car, 126
Mercury cars, 77, 124-26, 159-60, 170; Mercury and Special Product Division, 59
Meseke, Marilyn, 91
Metal Stamping Division, 47
Methanol, 45
Metro Airport, Detroit, 86
Metropolitan Detroit, 63
Metropolitan Museum of Art, 60
Metzger, Bill, 50
Mexico, 94, 133, 135-36, 142, 144-45
Mexico City, 91, 94, 173
Meyers, James A., 114
MG, 163
Michigan, 20, 189, 192, 200, 207-08
Michigan Building, 29
Michigan Living, 192
Michigan Register of Historical Sites, 33
Michigan Sports Hall of Fame, 203
Middle East, 17
Midgely, Oliver and Mrs., 157-58
Midgets, 214
Midland, Mich., 81
Milan, Mich., 27; plant, 109
Miles, Mr., 211
Milestone Car Society and *Milestone Car*, 198
Milestone cars, Ford 27,000,000, Ford 28,000,000, 91
Milkweed, 28
Miller, Arjay, 78, 83
Miller, Arjay Arboretum, 50
Miller, James F., 90
Miller 91 (1926-27) racing car, 201
Miller, Ray, 151
Miller Road (overpass), 101

Miller, Shirley, 187
Miller, Theodore, 186
Milwaukee Assembly Plant, 105
Minden, Neb., 126
Mines, 74
Minneapolis, 192
Minneapolis Assembly Plant, 104
Minnesota, 120, 192
Minocqua, Wis., 129
Missile, 213
Mississippi River, 104, 106-07
Missouri Goodwill Industries, 105
Mitchell, Jerald, 31
Mitsubishi, 93
Model A (1903), 43, 70, 89, 127
Model A, 74, 124, 150-59;
  advertising, 154-56; affection for, 124, 150; dealers, 153; gestation, 124; greatness, 126, 142; launch, 124, 127, 152-56; mileage, 156; prototype, 151; sales, 124, 151; trucks, 152; unusual uses, 157-58; mentioned, 70, 89, 99, 102, 104, 125-26, 136, 139, 144, 197-98
Model "A" News, 198
Model "A" Restorers Club, 198
Model B, 196-97
Model K, 203
Model S, 43
Model T, 74, 123-47; abandonment, 14, 144; advertising, 133, 154; affection for, 124, 130-33, 143, 161; ambulances, 213-14; best car, 126; birthplace, 90; breakthrough car, 127; bus, 131; colors, 131, 151; cross-country trips, 143; design, 128, 141; dimensions, 129; disparagement of, 134; driving, ease of, 128; emblem, 117; engineering, 127-28, 132-33; fifteen millionth, 89; folklore, 124, 131-33; funeral cars, 94, 147; "gitaway car," 133; greatness/impact/importance/influence/ranking, 1, 20-21, 124-26, 131-33, 114; jokes, 26, 135-37; launch, 74, 116; left-hand drive, 128; longevity, 126, 136, 144; mileage, 136; Model T of..., 142, 174, 188; nicknames, 161; noise level, 128; overseas, 94, 138-39;

personality, 144; prices, 139-40; production, 92, 144; quality/qualities, 132, 142; racing, 134, 141, 202, 204-06; radio, 130; on rails, 138-39; as "restroom," 129; sales, 141; sex in, 128-29; stamps, 42, 131; taxis, 139; trucks, 138; unusual uses, 144-46, 158; wood used in, 130; mentioned, 15, 25, 42, 45, 68, 70, 76, 99, 102, 104-06, 151, 185, 200
Model "T" Casino, 209
Model T Ford Club of America, 146, 197
Model T Ford Club International, 197
Model T Ford-Hot Air Balloon Rally, 146
Model T Times, 144, 197
Moekle, Herman L., 78
Monaco, 42-43
Moynahan Bronze Co., 110
Monongahela Valley, 117
Monroe machine, 162
Monroe (Union, W. Va.) *Watchman*, 19
Montana, 141
Montclair, N.J., 144
Montgomery, Ala., 192
Monthly Detroit, 121
Montreal, 93
Moon landings, 20
Moonshine, 147
Moore, Charlie, 164
Morgan-Witts, Max, 151
Moriarty, John, 92
Morris Motors, 22
Morris, William R. (Lord Nuffield), 22
Morrow, Anne, (Mrs. Charles Lindbergh), 173
Morse, Peter C., and Mrs. Morse (Martha P. Ford), 7
Morton Salt, 73
Moscow, 48
Motor Age, 195
Motor News, 125
Motorsports, 62, 70, 95, 141, 190
Motor Trend, 141, 170-71
Moving assembly line, 74, 81, 195 (also see mass production)
Moyers, Bill, 143

Mr. McGinny's Tin Goose Restaurant, 176
Munsey Tour, 141
"Munsters, The," 166
Murphy, Thomas, 52
Murray Corporation, 81
Mussolini, Benito, 17, 21
Mustang, 205; greatness, 125, 142; paternity, 170; sales, 150-51; mentioned, 102, 125
My Life and Work, 200-01, 204
Myths, 84, 192

N
Nader, Ralph, 142
Nance, James J., 87
Nankin Mills (Mich.) mill, 108, 114
Nash, 125-26
Nashville, Ind., 160
Nashville, Tenn., 167
National Association for the Advancement of Colored People, 178
National Auto Racing History Society, 201
National Automotive History Collection, 80, 125, 128, 149, 191
National Farm Chemurgic Council, 28
National Motor Museum, Beaulieu, England, 150
National Museum of American History, 142
National Park Service, 88
National Register of Historic Places: "Honeymoon House" 27; Alexandria (Va.) Assembly Plant, 101; Atlanta Assembly Plant, 102
National Wax Museum, 45
National Woodie Club, 160
Naughton, John, 78
Navy buildings (Rouge), 101
Navy, U.S., 101, 104-05
Nazis, 17
Nebraska, 126, 138
Neiss, Roger, 198
Nelson, Brian, 139
Neskow, Cynthia (Mrs. Edsel Ford II), 7, 61
Nevada, 157, 179

Nevin, John J., 78
Nevins, Allan, 18
Newark, 144
Newark Ford District Dealers' Association, 156
Newark Meadows (Kearny) Assembly Plant, 103
New Baltimore, Mich., 201
New Deal, 21
New England, 111, 150
"New Ford Company," 68, 124
New Holland farm equipment, 171
New Jersey, 186, 200, 203
Newman Grove, Neb., 138
New Port Richey, Fla., 90
Newport, R.I., 203
News Department, Ford, iii, 60, 84, 101, 151
Newton, Wallace J., 13
New York City, 26, 91, 100, 144
New York Daily News, 73
New York State, 111
New York Sun, 136
New York Times, 124-25
New York-to-Seattle Race, 202-04
New York Tribune, 153
New York University, 73
New York World, 124, 153, 204
New York World's Fair, 91
New Yorker, 45, 131, 166
New Zealand, 42, 150, 157
Niarchos, Elena (daughter of Charlotte Ford), 2
Niarchos, Stavros, 2
Nicholas II, Czar, 141
Nigeria 142, 144-45
999 racing car, 70, 80, 190, 201, 205
Ninotchka, 55
Nissan U.S.A., 78, 200
Nixon, Richard, 20, 63
Nob Hill, 44
Norfolk Assembly Plant, 104
Normandy, 217
North America, 92
North Brooklin, Maine, 131
Northern Michigan, 74-75, 120, 130, 200-01, 210, 217
Northern States Power Co., 107
Northrup Corporation, 22, 174

Northrup, Tom, 143
Northville (Mich.) Plant, 107-08, 114
Norway, 74
Novak, Bill, 85
Novi racing car (1946-53), 201
Nuffield, Lord (William R. Morris), 22
N.W. Ayer & Son, 709, 154-55

O
Oakland Airport, 192
Oakland Avenue Baptist Church, Detroit, 30
Oakland Housing, Inc., 79
Oakville, Ont., 95
Ohio, mentioned 20, 146
Ohlemacher, Wilbert W., 98
Oklahoma, 134, 154, 176
Oklahoma Aeronautics Commission, 154
Oldfield, Barney, 12, 39, 70, 202-03, 205
Oldsmobile car/engine, 118, 125-26, 142, 163
Olney, Ill., 175
Omaha Assembly Plant, 106
Opel, 92
Orchard Lake (Mich.) Schools, 149
Orchestra Hall, 207
Original Glorious Church of God in Christ No. 1, Detroit, 96
Ormandy, Eugene, 208
Ormond Beach, Fla., 203
Osborne, Adam, and Osborne Computer Corp., 22
Oshawa, Ont., 95
O'Toole, John, 72
Ott, Carl E., 128
Overly, Lowell, 47
Owens, Jesse, 177
Owners, Ford, 134
Oxford, Pa., 167

P
Pace cars, Indianapolis "500," 206
Packard, 87, 125, 137, 142, 160, 190
Paint, 45
Palm Beach, Fla., 55
Panama Canal, 69
Panama-Pacific Exposition (San Francisco), 19

FORD COUNTRY **225**

Pantera, 170-71
Pantheon of Americana, 143
Papen, Franz von, 17
Parkersburg, W. Va., 75
Park Motor Co., 75
Parts & Service Division, 2, 66
Passaic River, 103
Paton, William, 195
Patterson, Frederick D., Dr., 179
Patterson, Pat, 56
PC (magazine), 22
Peace ship, 26, 184, 208
Pelzer, Alfonso, 148
Pennsylvanians, 206-07
Penny, Ford (coin), 40-41
Pepino's restaurant, 210
Pequaming, Mich., 34, 130, 200, 204
Perry, Sir Percival, 12
Pershing, Gen. John, 213
Petersen, Donald E., 68, 101
Petrik, Jim, 75
Peugeot, 92-93; Peugeot L76 racing car (1912), 201
Pharon, Ghaith, 34
Philadelphia, 154
Philadelphia Assembly Plant, 106
Philadelphia Bulletin, 165
Philadelphia Mint, 40
Philadelphia Orchestra, 208
Philadelphia Storage Battery Co., 130
Philco Transitone, 130
Philippines, 93
Phoenix (Mich.) Plant, 108
Pico Rivera (Calif.) Assembly Plant, 106
Pickford, Mary, 28
Pierce-Arrow, 126, 135, 137, 140
Pikeville, Ky., 74
Pinto, 125, 141
Piper Cub, 22
Piper, D.A., 175
Piper, Perry, 166, 175
Piper, William T., 22
Piquette Plant, 88, 98, 195; mentioned, 30, 92
Pitcairn Mailwing, 174
Pittsburgh, 32
Planning Division, FMC, 59
Plant, Louis V., 90

Plants: Size of, 122; Alexandria, 101; Atlanta, 102, Boston, 106, Buffalo, 196, Chicago, 106; Cleveland, 102; Columbus, 106; Cork, 94; Dagenham, 94; Dallas, 106; Dearborn (assembly), 153, (foundry), 90, 177-78, glass, 88; Denver, 106; Hapeville, Ga., 159; Highland Park, 88, 96-99; Houston, 106; Iron Mountain, 162, 217; Kansas City, 103, 106; Kearny, 103; Long Island City, 106; Los Angeles, 106; Louisville, 103-04; Mack Avenue, 69, 96; Memphis, 106, 196; Milwaukee, 105; Minneapolis, 104-05; Norfolk, 104; Omaha, 106; Pequaming, 204; Philadelphia, 106; Pico Rivera, 106; Piquette, 88, 90, 98, 195; Port Elizabeth, South Africa, 93; Portland, 106; Rouge, 88, 90, 99-101; St. Louis, 105-06; San Francisco, 106; San Jose, 106; Seattle, 106; Tire, 88, 99; Twin Cities, 104-06; Willow Run, 214-16; Wixom, 149; Woodhaven, 130; Yokohama, 139
Plantiff, Gaston, 12
Plastic car/parts, 47, 62, 74, 112, 123
Plymouth car, 155, 160
Plymouth, Mich., 118-19
Plymouth (Mich.) Plant, 108
Poland, 74
Poling, Harold "Red," 68
Pollard, Barney, 179-80
Pontiac car, 160
Pope John Paul II, 149-50
"Popemobile," 149-50
Porsche 356 (1950-64), 141
Port Clinton, Ohio, 174-75
Port Elizabeth, South Africa, 93
Port Huron, Mich., 180
Portland Assembly Plant, 106
Possellius, Barbara (Mrs. Walter Buhl Ford III), 7
Post Office, 42-43
Post, Wiley, 154
Potomac River, 101
Potter, Charles E., 38
Potter, Frank N., 213
Powerhouse, Highland Park Plant, 98

Preminger, Otto, 203
Presidents' cars, 161, 190-91
Presser, Theodore, 22
Pretoria, South Africa, 93
Prevention (magazine), 19
Prices, 139-40
Prince Charles, 53
Princeton University, 59, 64
Provencal Road, 5
Prudden Co., 123
Pryor, Richard, 21
Public Image of Henry Ford, The: An American Folk Hero and His Company, iii, 18, 41-42
Public Relations Staff, FMC, 91-92
Putnam's, G.P. Sons, 132

Q
Quadricycle, 29-30, 42-43, 70, 89, 125, 182, 190, 198
Queensland, Australia, 138-39
Quest/80 (magazine), 21

R
Rabbit car, 126, 144
Race riots, Detroit, 178
Racing, 190, 201-06
Rackham, Horace H., 89, 119
Radcliffe, Cary, 8
Radio broadcasts/programs, 69, 206-208
Radio Shack, 22
Radios, car, 130, 133
Rail Passenger Service, 23
Railcar, 146
Raines, Ella, 162
Raisin River (actually River Raisin), 110, 113
Rambler, Nash, 125, 135, 142
Ramblin' Wreck, 158-59
Rankin, Robert, 41, 47
Rawsonville (Mich.) Plant, 108, 114-115
RCA, 133
Reader's Digest, 12
Reagan, Ronald, 10-11, 168
Real Cigarettes, 165
Recreation, Highland Park Plant, 98
Recreational vehicle, 146

Red Cross, Pa., 136
Redenbacher, Orville, 67
Reed, Jim, 143
Reedsburg, Wis., 75
Reeves, Frances R., 37
Reich, Charles W., 139
Reith, Francis C., 78
Reliability runs, 141
Remick, Lee, 203
Renaissance Center, 89, 122, 142, 185, 208-209
Renault, Louis, and car, 22, 92
Republic National Life Insurance Company, 156
Republicans, 73, 210
Restaurants, Ford-related, 209-10
Restored Cars, 138-39
Restorer, 198
Retirees, 90, 201
Reuther, Elizabeth (daughter of Walter Reuther), 66
Reuther, Walter, 66
Revere, Paul, 22, 187
Revolution, American, 20
Reynolds Building, 104
Reynolds, Burt, 21
Reynolds Metals Co., 78, 104
Rhinebeck, N.Y., 193
Rhodes, Anthony, 17
Richards, William C., 18
Richmond (Calif.) Assembly Plant, 91
Richmond Hill, Ga., 33-34
Ritter, John, 21
River Lee, 94
River Rouge, Mich., 122
Rivera, Diego, 48
Robbins, Harold, 49
Robson, Aubrey Hastings, 96
Rochester, N.Y., 67, 141
Rockefeller family, 1
Rockefeller, John D. Jr., 52
Rockefeller, Nelson, 52
Rockwell International, 78
Rockwell, Robert R., 117
Rockwood, Mich., 91
Rocky Mountain News, 136
Rodgers, M.L. "Pete," 204
Roe, Frederick D., 145
Rogers, Will, 8, 29, 154

Rolls-Royce Silver Ghost, 126
Romantic cars, 126
Romney, George, 37-38, 142
Rooney, Jimmy, 91-92
Rooney, Mickey, 28
Roosevelt, Eleanor, 11, 21
Roosevelt Field, N.Y., 192
Roosevelt, Franklin D., 11, 22, 44, 91, 143, 190-91; V-8 car, 161
Roosevelt, James, 161
Roosevelt, Theodore, 191
Roper, Elmo, 71-72
Roper steam carriage, 190
Rosary High School, Detroit, 24
"Rosie the Riveter," 214
Ross, Roy, 142
Rotary engine, 93
Rothschild, Evelyn de, 18
Rotterdam, 95
Rotunda, Ford, 91-92, 151, 164
Rouge News, 116
Rouge Plant, 99, artwork, 100; commissaries, 74-75; Dearborn Assembly Plant, 102; Gate 4, Miller Road, 15; foundry, 90; historic site, 89; size, 68, 74, 99, 100-01; tours, 88, 100; visitors, 100; mentioned, 28, 50, 82, 91, 99-100, 120-22, 177-78, 197, 214
Rouge River (actually River Rouge), 73, 109
Rouge Steel Co., 100-01
Rubber 26, 99
Ruddiman, Catherine, 39
Rumors, 87
Runyon, Marvin T., 78
Russia, 41
Russell, George, 90

S
Saal, Tom, 201
Sable, 62, 125
Safety glass, 74
Saginaw, Mich., 90
St. Clair River, 79
St. Clair Shores, Mich., 51
St. Cloud, Minn., 75
St. Louis Assembly Plant/Branch, 105-06, 135
St. Louis Cardinals, 211

St. Louis Lincoln-Mercury Assembly Plant, iii
St. Louis Southwestern Railway, 23
St. Martha's Episcopal Church, Detroit, 24
St. Paul, Minn., 106
St. Petersburg (Fla.) *Times*, 213
St. Vartan Armenian Roman Catholic Church, 24
Sales/Marketing, 55-56, 124, 141
Salina, Kan., 76
Saline (Mich.) Plant, 109
SAMCOR (South African Motor Corp.), 93
Sames Motor Co., 75
San Francisco, 91
San Francisco Assembly Plant, 106
San Jose, Calif., 143
Saudi Arabia, Kingdom of, 16, 34
Sault Ste. Marie, Mich., 121
Savannah, 34
Sawmills, 112
Saxon, 135
Scarborough, Chuck (husband of Anne Ford), 64
Schauer, Harold, 41
Schmeling, Max, 17
Schools, 112, 210-12
Scioto River, 146
Scoon, Robert, 139
Scotch Settlement School, 187
Scott, George A., 145
Script, Ford, 24, 117
Schumann, Roy, 39
Schwimmer, Rosika, 12
Sears, Roebuck, 132, 143, 156
Seattle Assembly Plant, 106
Second Communist International, 70
Secret Life of Henry Ford, The, 180
Secret Service, 191
Sedan, Kan., 75
Segregation, 21
Sesser, Ill., v
Seventy-One Society, 162
Shambaugh's Garage, 76
Shareholders, 117-20, 185-87
Sharjah, 42
Sharland, John, 75
Sharon Hollow (Mich.) Plant, 109, 115
Sheeler, Charles, 100
Sheely, Edward V., 195-96
Sheffield, Inc., 103
Shelby Hotel, Detroit, 157
Shields, Brooke, 21
Shipbuilding, 21-22
Ships, 120-22
Shirley Temple doll, 35
Short Book of Detroit Lists, 122
Sicily, 217
Sierra Railroad, 146
Sikorsky, Igor I., and Sikorsky Aircraft Division, 187-88
Simms Edsel, Inc., Detroit, 164
Simpkins, Glenn L., 27
Simplot, Jack, 22
Singer, Marvin L., 102
Skala, David J., 113
Skinner, Lyle, 152
Skinner, Michael, 31, 95, 121, 168, 176, 203
Skramstad, Harold K., 186-87
Slankard, George, v
Sloan, Alfred P. Jr., 14, 41
Sloane, John Edison, 186
Slogans, advertising, 70-73
Smirnes, Carmelita, 96
Smith, Bob, 26-27, 35, 49, 180-81
Smith, Eunice Boon, 19
Smith, Jack, 146
Smithsonian Book of Invention, The, 69
Smithsonian Institution, 173, 187, 213
Smoking, 70, 81, 196, 214
Smyrna, Tenn., 200
Snow White, 215
Sociability runs, 134-35
Sonora, Calif., 146
Sorensen, Charles E., 9, 11-12, 78; Mrs. Sorensen, 80
Sorensen, Lorin, 42, 198-99
Sotheby's, 60, 100
South Africa, 93, 145, 160
South African Motor Corp. (SAMCOR), 93
South America, 16, 133
South Carolina, 74
South Gate, Calif., 106
South Middlesex News, 211
South Sudbury, Mass., 15, 19
Southampton, N.Y., 64
Southeastern Michigan, 210
Southern Michigan News Company, 86
Southfield Road, Dearborn, 27
Soybeans, 16, 46, 112; research, 27, 46
Spaulding Automobile Company, 75
Speakes, Larry, 10
Special Products Operations, 60
Spenser, Jay P., 213
Sperry Corp., 171
Sperry, Elmer, 213
Spirit of St. Louis, The, 26, 172-73
Sportsman, 162
Springfield, Mo., 84
Springwells, 37
Springwells Park, 181-82
Stafford car, 134
Stalin, Joseph, 80
Stamps, 42-43
Stanford University, 78, 83
Stark, Mrs. Harold Sr., and Harold Jr., 82
Station wagon, 45, 159-60, 162
Statues, 43-44, 148
Stearns Manufacturing Co., 110
Steichen, Joanna T., 54
Stewart, Jackie, 206
Stewart, James, 203
Stock, Ford, 117-19, 186-87
Stock market crash, 1929, 20, 199
Stockholders, Ford, 185
Stortz, C.B., 203
Stoughton (Mass.) *Enterprise*, 75
Stout Air Services, 192
Stout, Bob, 23
Stout, William B., 173, 192
Stratford, Conn., 187-88
Strebel, Rev. Milton, 144
Streeter, Larry, 206
Strelow, Albert, 89
Strikes, 196
Studebaker, 14, 126
Stutz Bearcat, 37, 190
Styling, 71
Succession, Ford Motor Company, 61, 63-64
Sudbury Pond, 15
Sullivan, Jim, 197
Sunal, George, 214-15
Sunbury (Pa.) *Daily Item*, 136
Sundance Kid, 133
Supplemental Unemployment Benefit package, 74
Suppliers, 122-23
Supreme Court, U.S., 21, 199
Sutton Place, Manhattan, 63
Swanson Ford, 75
Syria, 168
Sytkowski, G.D., 152

T

Taft, William Howard, 10, 191
Tahlequah, Okla. 23
Talbert, Bob, 85
Tanks, 145
Tarbell, Ida, 136
Taubman, A. Alfred, 6, 184
Taurus, 125
Taylor, Frederick W., 81
Taylor, Mich., 184
Taxis, 139
Teague, Dick, 142
Technion, 17-18
Tecumseh (Mich.) Plant, 109
Television, 21, 69-70
Ten-dollar bill (cars depicted on), 151
Teng, Hsiao-ping, 55
Tennessee, 200
Tenvoorde Motor Co., 75
Texas, 135-36
Texas Instruments, 134
Thatcher, Bob, 77
Theft, car, 150, 164
"There's a Ford in Your Future," 71-73
Thomas, Gordon, 151
Thornley, George H., 155
Thornton, Charles B. "Tex," 78, 83-84
Three Mile Island nuclear reactor, 142
Thunderbird, 62, 125-26, 141, 163-64
Tiegs, Cheryl, 64
Tiffany Motor Co., 75
Time, 40, 107
"Tin Goose" (see Trimotor)
Tippecanoe County, Ind., 131
Tippett, W. Paul, 78
Tip Top Division, Faberge's, 106
Tire Plant, Dearborn, 88
Tires, 25, 99
Today and Tomorrow, 200
Tofu, 46
Tokyo, 139
Toledo, 120-21
Toledo Mudhens, 91
Tours, 100, 136
Tow, longest ski, 145-47
Town Car (Lincoln), 125, 149
Town & Country, 203
Townsend, Lynn A., 139
Toyo Kogyo, 93
Toyota, 17, 93
Tractors, 99, 112, 171
Tracy, Spencer, 28
Transcontinental railroad, first, 199
Transportation [stamp] series, 131
Trans World Airlines, 78, 84
Travolta, John, 53
Trenton, Mich. 112
Treon, Samuel, 136
Tribune bicycle, 140
Trimotor airplane, 26, 70, 172-76
Triple E Building (aka Engine and Electrical Engineering), 89
"Trivial Trap," 131
Trotsky, Leon, 17
Troy, Mich., 171
Trucks, 69, 125, 138, 147, 160-61; mentioned, 76, 104
Trudeau, Pierre, 53
True House of God of the State of Michigan, Detroit, 96
Truman, Harry S., 21, 134
Tucson, Ariz., 23
Tunnels, 33
Tuolumne County, Calif., 146
Turnpike Cruiser, Mercury, 126
Tuskegee Institute, 28
Tutankhamen, King, 129
TV Magazine, 143

FORD COUNTRY **227**

Twain, Mark, 22
Twin Cities Assembly Plant, 104-07

U
Umm al Quwain, 42-43
Union, W. Va., 19
United Airlines, 175
United Automobile Workers (UAW), 74, 86, 101, 109, 111, 178, 189, 197
United Jewish Appeal, 54
United Negro College Fund, 179
United Press International, 142
United States Steel Corporation, 69
United Technologies Corp., 187-88
Universal Oil Products Co., 133
University Club, Detroit, 120
University of Illinois, iii
University of Louisville, 103-04
University of Michigan, iii, 81, 119, 195, 212
University of Michigan-Dearborn, 15, 41
University of Pennsylvania, 55-56
University of Wisconsin, 137
University of Wisconsin-Milwaukee, 105
Uruguay, 138
U.S.: Board of Tax Appeals, 127; Post Office, 42, 131, 165; Secret Service, 191; Treasury, 151; War Department, 180
USAir (magazine), 147
USSR, 74, 99, 140, 166-67
Utah, 133

V
V-8, 74, 124, 126, 160-63, 161-62; Deuce, 125; engine, 74, 95, 162-63; "gitaway" car, 160; greatness, 125-26, 142; unusual uses, 160; mentioned, 62, 102, 104, 139, 196
V-8 Times, 197-98
Vagabonds, 19
Van Nuys, Calif., 106
Van Tine, W.H., 32
Vanadium steel, 127
Vanderbilt, Gloria, 63
Vandersee, Lisa (Mrs. William Clay Ford Jr.), 7

Vargas, Alberto, 215
Varricchione, Louis, 211
Vauxhall, 92
Vega, 125-26
Vertical integration, 74
Vienna, Austria, 216
Vietnam, 21
Village Industries, 107-15, 191
Vintage Ford, 136, 139, 141, 146, 197-98
Vis, Yugoslavia, 216
Visnupada, Swami, 66
Volkswagen, 84, 126, 133, 142-45, 156
Volstead Act, 147
Volvo PV444, 126
Von Holst & Fyfe, 32

W
Waddell, Rex, 8
Wagon, station, 159-60, 162
Wall Motor Co., 75
Wall Street Journal, 85
Wallace, Henry A., 133
Walled Lake, Mich., 210
Walters, Barbara, 67, 85
Walters, John C., 130
Walworth County Fair, Wis., 152
War Between the States (Civil War), 20
Ward, Willis, 177
Waring, Fred, 206-07
Warm Springs, Ga., 161
Warp, Harold, 126
Waseca, Minn., 75
Washington, Lawrence, 177-78
Washington, George, 21, 73
Washington, state, 160
"Watch the Fords Go By," 73
Waterbury (Conn.) *American*, 140
Waterford (Mich.) Plant, 108
Watergate, 20
Waterworks, Dearborn, 26
Watters, M.R. "Dutch," 141
Way of the Zephyr, 149, 198
Wayne (Mich.) Assembly Plant, 64
Wayne County (Mich.), 114; Wayne County Building, 38; Wayne County Community College, 24;

Wayne County General Hospital, 147
Wayside Inn, 15, 19, 193-94, 211
Welch, William, 44
Wells, Mary (Wells, Rich and Greene), 71-72
We Never Called Him Henry, 18
West, Mae, 21
Westman, Mr. and Mrs., Pequaming, Mich., 200
West Bloomfield Township, Mich., 79
West Orange, N.J., 186
West Virginia, 74-75, 120
Westacres, 79
Western Electric, 103, 106
Western Electric News, 103
Western Front, 213-14
Westin Hotel, Detroit, 209
Wexford, Pa., 75
Wheaties, 72
Whipple, Jack J., 165
Whistle, 158-59
White, Albert C., 147
White, E.B. (pseudonym Lee Strout White), 131-33, 150
White House, 9, 191
White Motors, 78
White, Roger, 142
Whiting Corporation, 200
Whitney, Eli, 22
Whiz Kids, 78, 83-84
"Who Wouldn't Love You," 181
Wickline, Herbert, 19
Wigton, Eldon D., 151-52
Wilhelm II, Kaiser, 27
Wilson, Harold H., 141
William Clay Ford (lakeboat), 121-22
William Fisk Harrah: The Life and Times of a Gambling Magnate, 179
Williams, Roland "Bud," 117
Willoughby bodies, 149
Wills, C. Harold, 12, 50, 79-80, 98, 117, 179, 213; C.H. Wills & Company, 79-80; Wills-Sainte Clair car, 79-80, 179
Willow Run (Mich.) Bomber Plant, 214-16; mentioned, 11, 26, 38, 122, 191

Willys-Overland, 136
Wilson, C.R., Carriage Co., 123
Wilson, Woodrow, 10, 26-27
Windsor, Ont., 95
Winnemucca, Nev., 209
Winton, Alexander, 202
Winton car, 120
Wisconsin, 120, 157
Wisconsin State Historical Society, 14
Wismer, Harry, 38
Wixom (Mich.) Plant, 149-51
Woman's Home Companion, 21
Women, 21, 128
Wood parts, 130, 159-60, 217
Woodcock, Leonard, 178
Woodall, Charles J., 89
Woodhaven Stamping Plant, 130
Woodies, 159-60
Woodie Times, 159-60
Woodlawn Cemetery, 50, 82
Woodstock, Vt., 146
Wooloff, Warren J., 214
Workers, 97-99
World Almanac & Book of Facts, 21, 69-70
World Bank, 78, 84
World Headquarters, 50, 60, 74, 123, 210
World Series, 70-71, 211
World War I, 138-39, 145, 213-14; mentioned, 134, 148, 208
World War II, 92-93, 99, 101, 104-05, 179-80, 214-17; mentioned, 23, 68, 139, 161, 213-17
Worst cars, 125-26
"Wouldn't You Really Rather Have a Buick?" 72
Wright, Frank Lloyd, 32, 44
Wright, James O., 78
Wright, Orville and Wilbur, 69, 187, 213
Wyandotte, Mich., 3

Y
Yale University, 16
Yankee, 146
Yankee Air Force, 215-16
Yankee Air Force News, 215
Yeman, 42-43

Yen, Tjing-ling, 22
Yokich, Steve, 189
Yokohama Assembly Plant, 139
York, Alvin T., 21
Yorke, Don, 150
Young, Coleman, 52, 176, 178
Young, Fred C., 90
Yugoslavia, 216
Ypsilanti, Mich., 115, 214
Ypsilanti Plant, 108, 151

Z
Zahedi, Ardeshir, 53
Zephyr, Lincoln, 149; Mercury, 70
Zumstein, Frederick, Dr., 118